Gilgit Rebellion

To the memory of the Gilgit Scouts

Gilgit Rebellion

The Major who Mutinied over Partition of India

William A. Brown

Pen & Sword
MILITARY

First published in Great Britain in 2014 by
Pen & Sword Military
an imprint of
Pen & Sword Books Ltd
47 Church Street
Barnsley
South Yorkshire
S70 2AS

Copyright © William A. Brown 2014

ISBN 978 1 47382 187 3

The right of William A. Brown to be identified as the Author of this Work has been asserted by him in accordance with the Copyright, Designs and Patents Act 1988.

A CIP catalogue record for this book is available from the British Library

All rights reserved. No part of this book may be reproduced or transmitted in any form or by any means, electronic or mechanical including photocopying, recording or by any information storage and retrieval system, without permission from the Publisher in writing.

Typeset in Ehrhardt by
Mac Style Ltd, Bridlington, East Yorkshire
Printed and bound in the UK by CPI Group (UK) Ltd, Croydon, CRO 4YY

Pen & Sword Books Ltd incorporates the imprints of Pen & Sword Archaeology, Atlas, Aviation, Battleground, Discovery, Family History, History, Maritime, Military, Naval, Politics, Railways, Select, Transport, True Crime, and Fiction, Frontline Books, Leo Cooper, Praetorian Press, Seaforth Publishing and Wharncliffe.

For a complete list of Pen & Sword titles please contact
PEN & SWORD BOOKS LIMITED
47 Church Street, Barnsley, South Yorkshire, S70 2AS, England
E-mail: enquiries@pen-and-sword.co.uk
Website: www.pen-and-sword.co.uk

Contents

List of Illustrations		vii
Preface		ix
Chapter 1	My First Tour in Gilgit (August 1943 to July 1946)	1
	1. The Role of the Scouts	1
	2. The Gilgit Agency	4
	3. The People of Gilgit	7
	4. Sports and Pastimes	11
	5. Chilas	15
	6. The Gilgit Agency: Strategy	18
	7. The Gilgit Scouts	23
	8. My Life in Gilgit in the British Period	27
Chapter 2	Return to Gilgit (June to September 1947)	48
	1. Appointed Commandant of the Gilgit Scouts	48
	2. Flight into Gilgit	51
	3. The New Kashmiri Order	62
	4. Gilgit Politics and Oaths of Loyalty	72
Chapter 3	The Gathering Storm (September to October 1947)	92
	1. Plans	92
	2. October 1947 and the Crisis Begins	113
Chapter 4	The Coup d'État (October to November 1947)	136
	1. The Gilgit Agency Joins Pakistan	136
	2. The Defeat of the 6th Jammu & Kashmir Infantry	168
Chapter 5	The End Game (November 1947 to January 1948)	197
	1. Consolidation	197
	2. The Arrival of Sardar Mohammed Alam	205
	3. Peshawar	214
	4. The Sack of the Gilgit bazaar	220
	5. The Rawalpindi Conference	222
	6. The Last Phase	230

Appendix I	Precis of Recent Events in the Gilgit Agency (1 August to 16 November 1947)	252
Appendix II	A Short Note on Current Events in Gilgit	261
Appendix III	Precis of Events in Gilgit Since the Arrival of Sardar Mohammed Alam, Political Agent (16 November 1947 to 14 January 1948)	263
Appendix IV	Glossary	272

List of Illustrations

1. Company of Gilgit Scouts, 1947. William Brown is fifth from the left in the top row.
2. British and Indian Officers of the Gilgit Scouts prior to the British withdrawal from the Gilgit Agency on 1 August 1947. Front row, from left: Lt. Davies, Subedar Major Jamsud Khan, Major R.J.F. Milnes, Captain Brown, Subedar Azam Khan. Rear row, from left: Subedar Baber Khan, Jamedar Sida Ali.
3. William Brown with Jock Mathieson, 1943.
4. William Brown out fishing with Shah Khan, Gilgit 1945.
5. British Officers' polo team in Gilgit, about to play against Local Chiefs' team. From left: Captain Grierson, Brown, Captain Inchbold, Colonel Cobb, Dr. Marsh, Anwar Khan (Raja of Punial).
6. A fishing trip in Gupis, 1943. From left: Khurshid Mir (Indian Assistant to Political Agent Gilgit), Brown, Colonel Cobb, Hussain Ali (Raja of Gupis).
7. Polo in Gilgit. The Scouts v. the Local Team No. 1, 1943.
8. Major-General Scott (Chief of Staff of Jammu & Kashmir State Forces) with Brigadier Ghansara Singh (1st Kashmiri Governor of Gilgit), 31 July 1947.
9. The last British Political Agent Gilgit, Lt. Colonel R. Bacon, bidding farewell to the Mirs and Rajas at the Gilgit landing ground. From left: Captain Baber Khan, Jafar Khan (Raja of Gilgit), Sultan Ghazi (Raja of Ishkoman), Brown, Hussain Ali (Raja of Gupis), Anwar Khan (Raja of Punial), Raja of Yasin, Lt. Colonel Bacon, F. Mainprice, Jamal Khan (Mir of Hunza).
10. Lieutenant-Colonel Bacon saying goodbye to Major-General Scott, Gilgit 1 August 1947. Brigadier Ghansara Singh is in the foreground.
11. Subedar Major Baber Khan with Brigadier Ghansara Singh.
12. Arrival of Avro Anson transport plane from Peshawar at the 600 yard long Gilgit landing strip. 1947.
13. Major Brown leaves Gilgit for Peshawar to report on recent events, November 1947. From left: Squadron-Leader Ahmed, Captain Mathieson, Brown.
14. Pipes and Drums band of the Gilgit Scouts, 1947.
15. Start of operations by the Gilgit Scouts in typical Karakoram terrain, November 1947.
16. Platoon of Gilgit Scouts, 1947.
17. No. 2 Platoon (Nagir) Gilgit Scouts on the Babusar Pass, 1947.
18. Arrival of Sardar M. Alam, 1st Pakistan Political Agent Gilgit, 14 November 1947. The Pakistan flag is being carried in procession to the Gilgit Agency House.
19. Guard of Honour of the Gilgit Scouts presents arms while Sardar M. Alam salutes the raising of the Pakistan flag at the Gilgit Agency House, November 1947.

viii Gilgit Rebellion

20. The Pakistan flag flies over the Gilgit school, November 1947.
21. November 1947. Gilgit Scouts dancing after flag raising ceremony.
22. Qaid-i-Azam's birthday parade in Gilgit, 1947. Sardar M. Alam inspects the parade accompanied by Major Brown. 2nd Lt. Baber Khan is nearest to the camera.
23. Sardar M. Alam, 1st Pakistan Political Agent Gilgit.
24. Subedar Major Baber Khan is promoted 2nd Lieutenant under powers given to Major Brown by the Government of Pakistan. The insignia is presented on parade by Sardar M. Alam.
25. 2nd Lieutanant Baber Khan, Gilgit January 1948.
26. From left: Jamal Kan (Mir of Hunza), Shaukat Ali (Mir of Nagir). A Gilgit durbar in late 1947.
27. Portrait of William Brown as a young officer, 1942.

(All photographs © William A. Brown Estate)

Preface

William Alexander Brown, 1922–1984

William Alexander Brown, Willie to his friends, was born in Melrose in the Scottish Borders on 22 December 1922. His father, William Neilson Brown, had served with distinction in the Gordon Highlanders during the First World War, and had been awarded the Military Cross. His grandfather, Alexander Laing Brown, had been Liberal MP for the Border Burghs from 1886 to 1892. The Brown family had played a prominent part in the development of the woollen trade in the Borders: they were responsible for building some of the first mills in Selkirk, Galashiels and Hawick.

William Brown was educated at St. Mary's Preparatory School, Melrose, and George Watson's College, Edinburgh. In April 1941, on leaving school, he enlisted in the Argyll and Sutherland Highlanders.

In December 1941 he sailed for India. Here, he attended the Officer Cadet Training Unit at Bangalore and was then commissioned as a 2nd Lieutenant into the 10/12th Frontier Force Regiment. He transferred almost at once to the Frontier Corps of Scouts and Militias, serving initially in the South Waziristan Scouts on the Afghan border of the North West Frontier Province. He soon became proficient in Pushto, the language of the Pathans.

In early 1943 William Brown was posted to the Gilgit Agency where he spent the next three years, for a time serving as Assistant Political Agent in Chilas (when he was responsible for the construction of the Chilas Polo Ground, still in use today). He travelled widely throughout the Gilgit Agency, in Hunza, Nagir, Yasin, Ishkoman, Punial and Kuh Ghizr, gaining experience which was to stand him in good stead when he had to face the Gilgit crisis of 1947 which is described in detail in this book. While in the Gilgit Agency during this time he learnt Shina, the lingua franca of the region, as well as some Burushaski, the language of Hunza. Some impression of his first time in the Gilgit Agency is conveyed in Chapter 1 of this book.

In 1946, after Gilgit, William Brown served briefly in the Tochi Scouts, based in North Waziristan, and then in June 1947 he was posted to Chitral as Acting Commandant Scouts there.

In Peshawar, en route for Chitral, he was told by Lt. Colonel Roger Bacon, then Political Agent in Gilgit, that the Viceroy, Lord Mountbatten, had decided (for reasons which were not clear to Bacon and which are still not clear) that the 1935 British lease of the Gilgit Agency from the Maharaja of Jammu & Kashmir (a lease which still had 49 years to run) was going to be terminated and that the Agency, with a 99 per cent Muslim population, was going to be returned to the Hindu rule of the Dogra Maharaja, Sir Hari Singh. The actual transfer would take place, Colonel Bacon told him, on 1 August 1947, two weeks before the recently announced end of the British Indian Empire on 15 August. It was put to him that he would be a suitable candidate for the position of Commandant of the Gilgit Scouts during and after this period of transition. William Brown, while fully appreciating the difficulties and dangers involved, and angry that the British could so callously return without any preparation or warning the Muslim people of the Gilgit Agency to by no means congenial Hindu rule, volunteered for the task even though it meant leaving the British service and become in effect a mercenary employed by the Maharaja of Jammu & Kashmir.

After a very brief period in Chitral the position of Commandant of the Gilgit Scouts was indeed offered to him. He accepted at once. He was given the acting rank of Major. On 29 July 1947 he arrived in Gilgit, just in time to witness the formal handover on 1 August, when the British flag was lowered and that of Jammu & Kashmir raised in its place. Colonel Bacon, the last British Political Agent, departed: his place was taken by Brigadier Ghansara Singh, the representative of the Maharaja of Jammu & Kashmir.

What followed between August 1947 and January 1948, when William Brown was finally withdrawn from Gilgit (now part of Pakistan), is described in considerable detail in Chapters II to V of this book. One must always remember that when these events took place William Brown was only 24 or 25 years old (he celebrated his 25th birthday in Gilgit). One must also remember that once William Brown had embarked upon the process which resulted in the Gilgit Agency declaring for Pakistan he was technically in a state of mutiny against the Government of the State of Jammu & Kashmir. Had he been captured by the Maharaja's forces he would almost certainly have been put to death, as he well knew.

After his return from Gilgit in January 1948 William Brown transferred to the Frontier Constabulary, the Police Force of the North West Frontier Province (by now, of course, of Pakistan), in which he served in various capacities for the next two years.

In July 1948 William Brown was awarded the MBE (Military) with a citation so unspecific that it was not clear what lay behind this acknowledgement of his merits. He assumed that somewhere within the British military establishment there were those who approved of what he had done in Gilgit to ensure that this region went to Pakistan rather than to India. He was only too aware that there were other leading British figures, not least Lord Mountbatten, who were far from pleased by his intervention in the affairs of the post-British Subcontinent.

William Brown felt deeply attached to Pakistan and did not wish to leave the country. He sought, therefore, some position there in commerce after leaving the Frontier Constabulary. Sir George Cunningham, formerly Governor of the North West Frontier Province (and who figures in this book, as the reader will see), obtained for him a position in Imperial Chemical Industries (ICI) as a Sales Executive. Unfortunately, in this capacity his first posting was for Calcutta in India. During his time in Gilgit William Brown had evidently made a number of determined enemies among the Sikhs, perhaps because of his involvement (described in the book) in the destruction of the Sikh component of the 6th Kashmir Infantry in Bunji. In Calcutta he was set upon by Sikhs and left for dead in the street. Miraculously, he was found by a doctor and he recovered. He was then posted to Karachi in Pakistan.

In early 1957 William Brown met Margaret Rosemary Cooksley, who was serving with the UK High Commission in Karachi. They married. In 1958 a son, William, was born.

William Brown was a keen sportsman. While at school he had become a good marksman, having shot at Bisley where he captained the school team. When, with the war, cartridges became scarce, he became interested in falconry. While in Gilgit, the local national game of polo captured his enthusiasm and he became very skilled at it: he had already become a superb horseman. In later years in Karachi he played polo using at times Gilgit tactics, which did not always win universal approval. Also in Karachi William Brown took up racing as an amateur jockey and as a trainer, in both capacities with some success.

During these Karachi years he did not lose touch with the mountains of the old Gilgit Agency. He became the local secretary for Pakistan of the Himalayan Society and helped many expeditions coming to Pakistan to climb in the Karakoram, Hindu Kush, Pamirs and Himalaya.

In 1959 William Brown and his family returned to the United Kingdom. He felt that the day of the expatriate in the commerce of the Subcontinent was passing and that it was time to head for home. As by this time he could not imagine a life without horses, in 1960 he established a livery yard and riding school, Glenside Stables, in the village of St. Boswells in the Duke of Buccleuch's Hunt country. Here he remained, respected as teacher and judge of horses, for the next twenty-four years. During this time there were four more children, Frances, Timothy, Katy and Helen.

On 5 December 1984, a week before his 62nd birthday, William Brown died after a sudden heart attack. Few of his wide circle of friends had appreciated quite what an impact on the history of South Asia he had had during his time in Gilgit in 1947 and early 1948 since he never spoke of his adventures in those days: they were surprised when accounts of the Gilgit Rebellion, the subject of this book, appeared in obituaries in *The Times*, the *Daily Telegraph* and various local Border newspapers. Indeed, it was only after his death that the full truth about what he had achieved in Gilgit, and his enormous contribution to the future success of Pakistan, began to come to light. Hitherto, for a variety of reasons which need not concern us here, there had been a tendency to minimize, if not ignore entirely, his part in the great events of 1947 which are the subject of this book. In the end, justice to his memory was to some measure done with the awarding, on Independence Day 1993, of the medal Sitara-I-Pakistan as a posthumous recognition by Pakistan of his great contribution. His widow, Margaret, received the medal in Islamabad from the hands of President Leghari on Pakistan Day, 23 March 1994.

William Brown is buried in Benrig churchyard, in the heart of the Border country which he had loved so much. On his gravestone is engraved the ibex head badge of the Gilgit Scouts and the legend, DATTA KHEL 31.10.47 (the significance of which will become apparent to readers of this book).

A word about this book. William Brown kept a diary at least until his return from Gilgit in January 1948. The actual diary has been lost (apparently it was stolen), but at some point before 1950, probably as early as 1948, William Brown wrote it up in narrative form, perhaps intending to publish it. In the end it was not published and the top copy was lost. A carbon copy, however, survived. This is what is reproduced below. There has been the absolute minimum of editorial interference. A few pages have been omitted, mainly because they digress from the main thrust of the narrative. Spelling has, we hope, been standardized and there have been minor alterations in schemes of punctuation. Otherwise, this is what William Brown wrote when the events described were still fresh in his mind after the passage of no more than a year or so and with his diary before him. In many ways it is a unique document, the story of an adventure of a kind which William Brown may well have been the last Briton to experience in the Indian Subcontinent with the passing of the British Raj. It was an adventure, moreover, which changed the course of history to an extent that few other individuals can have achieved. Without William Brown it is more than likely that in the end the Gilgit region would have passed into the hands of India. Pakistan would have been cut off for ever from Central Asia. India would have been in direct contact with Afghanistan, in many respects at least as hostile to Pakistan as ever India has been. What would the fate of Pakistan have been in these circumstances?

Many people helped in the preparation of this memoir for the press. We would particularly like to thank Shah Khan for his assistance in the verification of material relating to the Gilgit region in the years 1947-48. Crown copyright material from the British Library (India Office Records) is reproduced with the permission of the Controller of Her Majesty's Stationery Office.

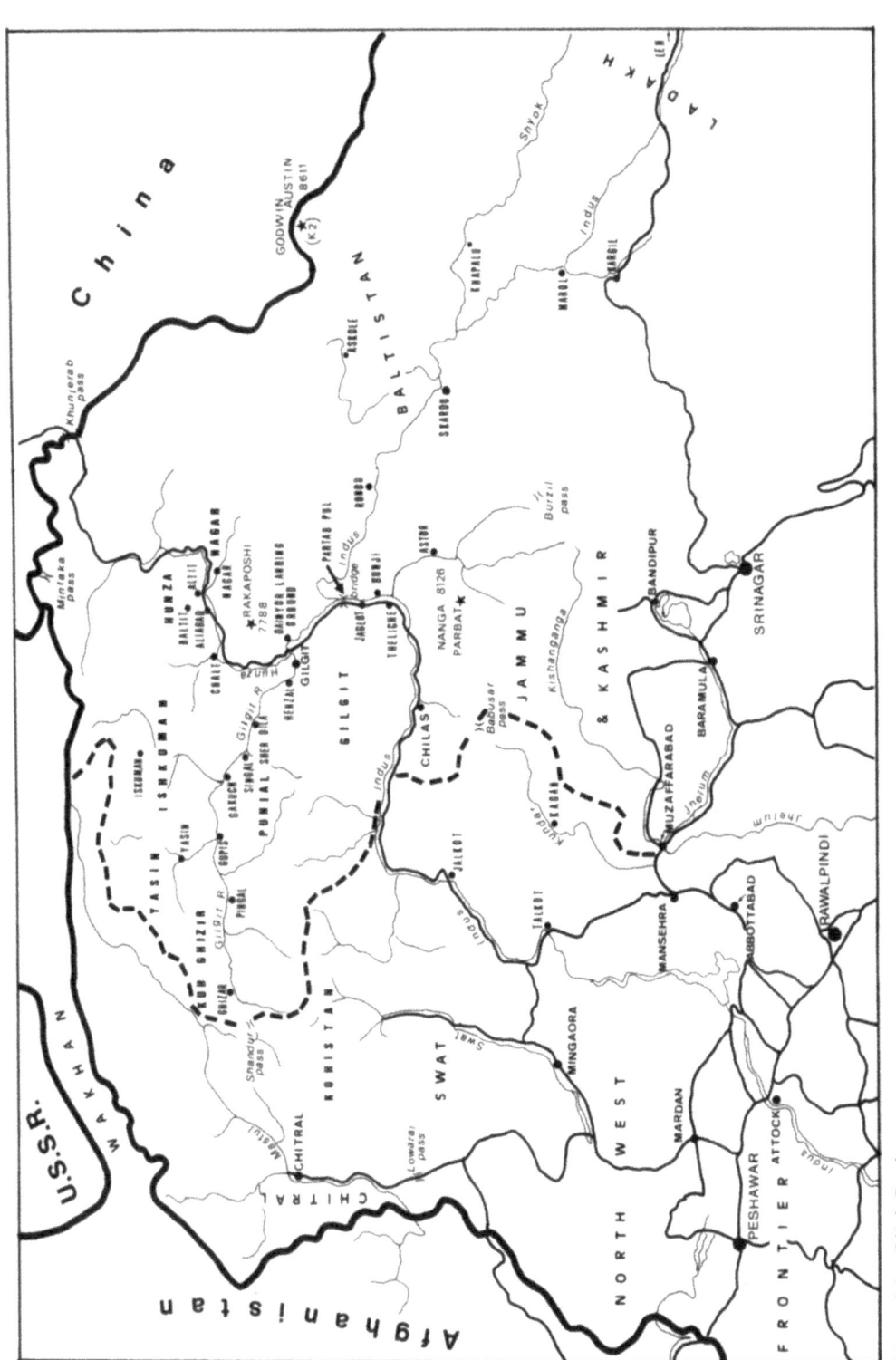

Map of the Gilgit Region.

Chapter 1

My First Tour in Gilgit (August 1943 to July 1946)

1. The Role of the Scouts

The marches of the North West Frontier of India (now of Pakistan), consist of two Borders. There is an administrative border where the settled districts of what was known as British Territory ends; and there is a second border known as the Durand Line which actually marches with Afghanistan. Between the two is that wild strip of rugged country known as "tribal territory". And here the trans-frontier Pathan lives; the Afridi, the Orakzai, the Turi, the Wazir and the Mahsoud live in conditions similar to that in which we Scottish Borderers lived in the good old days.

The British Government adopted a forward policy (wrongly in my opinion) with regard to this area and drove roads through it and garrisoned troops in large camps at strategical points.

Tribal territory is split up into a number of Agencies, each in charge of a Political Agent, who usually has an Assistant Political Agent to help him. The Political Agent was king in his agency and was responsible for safeguarding the interests of the British Empire and British subjects, though now of course he is answerable to the Pakistan Government. Tribesmen misbehave in two ways.

A sometimes reasonable and sometimes unreasonable grievance may provoke them to such an extent that internal feuds are forgotten and they unite as one and declare a "small war". Or, before independence, the "small war" might be a *jehad* when some fanatical mullah would appeal to them on religious grounds to rise up and drive the infidel from their country. Under these circumstances the army is called out from their camps, possibly reinforcements brought from down-country, the war prosecuted according to the rules until law and order have been restored.

The second type of misbehaviour is more of a nuisance variety. The hot-headed youngsters of the tribe in an exuberance of letting off steam will snipe at army posts and picquets, carry out daring raids on camps, blow up bridges and culverts, raid the settled districts and carry off cattle and Hindus, the latter for ransom in the case of males, for a worse fate in the case of young females or boys. Surprise ambushes or laying of mines on the road also add to the many annoying activities.

The suppression of such crime can not be carried out by the army. By the time the unwieldy army column with its retinue of mules, mess kit, and camp followers has reached the scene of the outrage the miscreants are miles away.

So a civil armed force called the Frontier Corps of Scouts and Militias was raised for this purpose. It was split into smaller Corps varying in strength from six thousand odd to six hundred according to the commitments in the particular area or Agency. Only Pathans were recruited with the exception of two Corps. Thus the entire force consisted of the Gilgit and Chitral State Scouts in the North, the Kurram Militia, the Tochi Scouts, and the South Waziristan Scouts in the centre, and the Zhob Militia in Baluchistan.

Since I joined Scouts in 1943 there have been other additions such as the reraised Khyber Rifles to guard the Khyber Pass and the Pishin Scouts in South Baluchistan.

The headquarters of the South Waziristan Scouts is at Jandola – a large stone fort at the strategic point where the roads from the military camps of Wana and Razmak meet above the narrow defile called the Hinis Tangi where South Waziristan debouches on the arid plain of Tank. The Scouts hold forts at irregular intervals along these two roads, the strengths of the garrisons varying from two to six or more platoons depending on the size and importance of the post.

The chief characteristic of the Scouts is their mobility. They are lightly equipped and armed only with rifles and can move incredible distances at an incredible speed over the hills. The uniform consists of leather *chaplis*, grey *partugs*, a grey shirt, and khaki *puggri* wound round a khaki *khula*. The equipment consists of a rifle, 70 rounds of ammunition in a leather bandolier, a water bottle and a haversack containing a needle and thread, *chapli* nails, a first field dressing, and an emergency ration of a handful of parched millet and some unrefined sugar sewn up in a piece of khaki drill cloth. Patrols which usually consist of some one hundred and fifty rifles under one British Officer are self-contained and carry a portable wireless set, stretchers, first aid haversack, and a basket of four carrier pigeons.

British Officers wear the same uniform as the men on patrol. There is usually one British Officer in each fort. Pushto is the only language spoken and an officer is no use until he can speak it fluently. Routine patrols are carried out at irregular intervals on an average of about two a week from each outpost but close touch is kept with the political and intelligence authorities so that special operations may be carried out when necessary on information received to assist in counter raiding.

The peace and tranquillity of an Agency entirely depends on the good relations between the Political Agent and the Commandant Scouts. When this breaks down the results are disastrous, as I have seen myself many times. A Commandant has therefore to be more than a parade ground soldier. He must be politically minded as well, and a diplomat who can pass on his own ideas without appearing to be usurping the Political Agent's position.

The Scouts, including their British Officer, are a happy-go-lucky band of irregulars. On parade they are as smart as guardsmen, on patrol as hard as nails, and as adept at their job as Roger's Rangers; brave yet wily in battle, they possess a fatalistic outlook on sudden death, which is by no means uncommon.

After parades, uniform is discarded and the leisure hours spent in football, tent pegging and other sports.

And so when I used to sit on the roof of Sora Rogha Fort in the evening, smoking my pipe in a pleasant tiredness after a hard day's work, with the sun sinking behind the grim hills, which took a purpled softness in the shadows, I knew I had reached a place where I was going to be happy. Under the circumstances how could I be otherwise?

I soon realized that my probationary period would end successfully so when one day a wireless message arrived to say that I was to come to Jandola for the week-end, I imagined the reason was to confirm me as a Scouts Officer.

It was, but little did I realize in what capacity.

I arrived at Jandola in due course and lunched in the Mess. It was hardly the type of dining room one would expect in a fort. There was tasteful panelling round a distempered wall on which hung Lionel Edwards prints. At one end of the room was a large sideboard covered with the mess silver. At the other end a large bow window looked out onto a beautiful lawn surrounded by rambler roses. Soft carpets covered the floor in the centre of which was a long highly polished table set correctly with crested crockery and cutlery, for lunch. The napery was snow white.

Just as I was leaving the table the Commandant, Lt. Colonel D.L.O. Woods OBE, said, "Oh, by the way, Brown, the Inspecting Officer of the Frontier Corps is anxious you should join the Gilgit Scouts. Think it over till tomorrow and let me know whether it appeals to you. If you do decide to go, we shall be very sorry to lose you from here."

I had never heard of Gilgit before. I questioned some of the more senior Scout Officers during the afternoon – men who had spent years on the Frontier. They were all vague. They thought that Gilgit was "somewhere up in Kashmir" but that was the extent of their knowledge. I determined then that I should go to this mysterious place, this unknown place, a place off the beaten track. Who knew what adventures it might hold. I felt like one of the merchants setting off on the Golden Road to Samarkand.

In the morning I went and saw the Colonel and told him that I had made up my mind and wanted to go to Gilgit.

"All right, I'll tell the inspecting Officer. Better be ready to move at a moment's notice."

That morning I helped out a friend who had gone on patrol by clearing his office work for him. One of the jobs was to settle the final accounts of a man who had completed eighteen years' service and was due to go on pension. I told the subedar to call the man in so that I could hand him his earnings. He entered and saluted smartly.

"What are you going to do now?" I asked.

"Go home, I suppose" he replied "but I'm still as fit as a fiddle and feel like a three year old."

He grinned in a most engaging way, flashing a set of beautiful white teeth. He was a small stocky man, tough as leather and his service did not appear to have aged him overmuch. He was a Khattack of the Bhangi Khel tribe – a tribe famous for their hardiness, prowess in the hills, and above all loyalty.

"You wouldn't care to become my retainer?" I said. "It will mean a hard life and you will have to go to all sorts of far places, but I need a man such as you."

"I'll follow you anywhere, Sahib," was the reply.

And thus Shawar Din was enlisted and I never regretted it. He accompanied me everywhere henceforth, has always been a tower of strength in awkward situations and has never failed to satisfy my comforts and requirements under the most trying circumstances from Waziristan to Central Asia.

4   Gilgit Rebellion

I left in the train in the following morning – not without a twinge of sadness as I had been very happy. But the thought of heading for the "unknown" speeded me on my way as the train pulled out with the escort who had accompanied me to the station shouting *puh makha de khuh*.

Life seems to be all goodbyes.

2. The Gilgit Agency

In the North West of Kashmir and on the southern slopes of the Roof of the World at the point where the three Empires of Russia, China and Britain meet, lies the Gilgit Agency. The capital of the Agency is the township of Gilgit, which lies in the Gilgit Valley some 24 miles above the point where it joins the Indus.

Some miles below the settlement the Hunza River meets the Gilgit River and in the valley of the former lie the two semi-independent feudatory States of Hunza and Nagir; through Hunza run the trade routes from Turkestan to Srinagar, the capital of Kashmir, and to Abbottabad in the north of the North West Frontier Province. All caravans from Central Asia using the Hunza route must pass through Gilgit on their way South.

Continuing up the Gilgit Valley, the Agency is divided into four States known as Political Districts administered by Governors, locally known as Ras, now developed into Rajas. The first is Punial; bordering Punial is Kuh Ghizr; to the East is Yasin bordered by the smallest, namely Ishkoman. Kuh Ghizr and Yasin march with the State of Chitral which is not in the Gilgit Agency.

The Political Districts are administered by four Governors under the control and supervision of the Political Agent, who also controls the Mirs of Hunza and Nagir.

Gilgit proper with its immediate surrounding district is known as the Gilgit Sub-division and up till 1935 the Sub-division was administered by Kashmir. The Gilgit Sub-division should not be confused with the Gilgit Agency. The former is about one tenth the area of the latter. In 1935 the British Government appreciated the necessity for the Sub-division being included in the Agency and coming under the direct control of the Political Agent owing to the increasing infiltration into Chinese Sinkiang of Russians. The Sub-division was therefore leased from the Maharaja of Kashmir for a period of sixty years and the entire area was taken under the absolute control of the Political Agent.

Gilgit is reached from Srinagar, the roadhead being the picturesque village of Bandipur on the shore of the Woolar lake. Thereafter a mule track climbs stiffly through pine and deodar forests to Traqbal which is the first stage on the two hundred mile or fourteen day trek. The track then winds up to the bare plateau which marks the summit of the Traqbal Pass, 11,800 feet above sea level. This plateau is frequently swept by frightful storms and it was in 1890 that 300 mules and their drivers of the Expeditionary Force perished in a blizzard. A wonderful view is obtained at this point of the whole of the Kashmir Vale spread out below like a map. The north bound traveller should note it well since it is his last look at civilization and his last sight of wide open spaces before entering the narrow valleys and gorges which are ahead of him.

The ascent is easy to the beautiful Gurez Valley which resembles some English country park. The Kishenganga River flows through it, full of brown trout running to a considerable size.

From Gurez the track climbs to the Burzil Pass, 13,773 feet, which is the gap in the Western Himalayan Range which divides Kashmir proper from the outlying districts of Astore and the Indus Valley. In summer the ascent is easy over sloping meadows covered with alpine flowers. In spring and autumn the going is treacherous owing to frequent avalanches and blizzards; between 15 October and 15 June the pass is virtually closed by snow except for the most intrepid traveller who takes his life into his hands and must travel at night when the snow is hardened by frost. The summit is a long exposed plain for many miles, the only interesting feature being a mail runner's refuge, built on stilts about one hundred feet high.

A distinct change in scenery takes place on the far side of the pass. The Astore Valley is a barren arid waste of stone and dust. In summer the heat of the day is unbearable and the traveller is well advised to travel by night. Mosquitoes and sandflies are frightful. The contrast to the delightful Gurez Vale is striking and the only comfort in this "Death Valley" is the little oasis of Astore with its poplar avenue.

At the mouth of the Astore Valley the track descends an alarming cliff face called the Hattu Pir to Ramghat and the Shaitan Nala (Devil Valley). In summer Ramghat is like a furnace but as you cross the suspension bridge over the Astore River a chilly breeze rises from the river and you feel as if you had just opened the door of a cold-storage compartment.

The road now debouches on the Bunji Plain, a long dreary waste of sand, boulders, and heat running along the left hand bank of the majestic Indus and ending at the somewhat miserable oasis and military outpost of Bunji. A company of the Jammu & Kashmir Forces is garrisoned here.

On the far side of the Indus – a patch of green in the middle of the desert – is the stage of Theliche. The only consolation in this depressing area is a wonderful view of snow-clad Nanga Parbat, raising her 26,660 foot crest into a dazzling blue sky. It is a breathtaking sight – sinister and mysterious for she is a killer mountain.

A few miles past Bunji the track crosses the Indus by the suspension bridge called the Partab Pul, just below the point where the Gilgit River adds her waters to the mighty flow. Above Partab Pul is the cultivation of the Government grass farm of Jaglote with its police post of Jaglote Chowki. The farm is irrigated by the water of the beautiful Sai Valley, famous for its brown trout and chikor (red-legged partridge).

The Partab Pul marks the Kashmir boundary and having crossed it the traveller is in the Gilgit Agency. The road now passes up the Gilgit Valley – desert between high bare mountains – but this monotony is relieved by the pleasant little villages of Parri, Minawar, Sakwar, and Jutial before the willow avenue is reached which leads into Gilgit from the south.

The first main feature on entering Gilgit is the Scout Lines where the headquarters of the Corps are located. The Lines are situated on the original site of the old Gilgit fort, the only portion left being the stout centre tower which is preserved as an ancient monument and as a signal station. The lines are neatly laid out – barracks accommodating some 250 men, magazine and guard room, Indian (local) officers' quarters and a well stocked vegetable garden. Around the tower is a good parade ground and next to it a full-sized football ground. Inside a walled enclosure is the Subedar Major's bungalow, well befitting his rank. The Gilgit river flanks the lines.

From the Scout Lines you pass the school and law courts, and enter the bazaar. It is a good bazaar, well stocked with the necessities of life. The streets are flanked with trees and a good cement drain runs the length and breadth which means that it is a lot cleaner than most bazaars in India. The shops are built of wood and look ramshackle but are in fact most substantial and the wares are well laid out: grain, rice, sugar, salt, cloth, saddles, bridles, blankets, saddle bags, silks, carpets, and skins are some of the many things available. Fruit of all sorts is for sale during the summer: apricots, peaches, apples, melons, pomegranates, and plums. Here is the blacksmith shoeing a pony; there a hillman from the back of beyond with a skin bag full of ghee (clarified butter) which he will barter for cloth and salt. The mingling crowd is cosmopolitan; locals, Hindus, Sikhs, Kashmiri Pundits, Turkis from Turkestan, Chinese, Tajik horse dealers from the Pamirs.

In the middle of the bazaar is the Police Station and opposite is the suspension bridge which links Gilgit with the routes through Hunza to Central Asia. Under the bridge on the maidan beside the river is the caravanserai where the merchants pitch camp on their way through. A romantic spot this, where many a horse and other transaction takes place.

In the centre of the bazaar is the mosque called the Juma Masjid – a large picturesque building where the Faithful say their prayers. Adjacent to it is the Shahi (Royal) Polo Ground, the scene of many a battle between giants in a country where polo is the national game.

Turning left at the end of the bazaar a road runs past the Christian cemetery or Hayward's Garden as it is known, for here the explorer Hayward was buried after he was cruelly murdered in Yasin on 18 July 1870.

The residential quarter has now been reached, situated on the foothills above the settlement.

Gilgit is famous for its trees and gardens. Every road, street and alley is lined with willow trees as are the two main kuls or water channels which bring the lifeblood to the oasis from the mountain torrent called the Kargah which enters the main river some three miles up the valley. Dotted about the gardens and cultivation are many stately chinar trees, giving ample shade in summer and turning the most glorious flaming brown in the autumn. Each garden is full of fruit trees; cherries, almonds, walnuts, apricots, apples, oranges, plums, peaches, pears, they are all there and in the spring when the blossom is in full bloom the township is a mass of white when seen from the far side of the river.

The dominating feature of the residential quarter, and the hub of the universe, as it were, is Agency House, the residence of the Political Agent.

A large gabled bungalow with an elevated two-way front porch approached by steps, it is situated well back off the road. A beautiful lawn, shaded by a mighty chinar tree, slopes down to a stone wall which surrounds the garden. At the southern corner is a cypress bush beside which is the flagstaff. To the north is another lawn covering some two hundred yards to the northern gate where a small fish pond lies surrounded by a horseshoe rockery which in spring is a mass of purple violets. At the gate a massive sentinel chinar tree stands on guard and between the lawn and the house is a bed of brightly coloured dahlias.

Behind the house is the all important stable of six roomy loose boxes and day standings; and adjacent to the stable is the vegetable garden and orchard. Every kind of vegetable grows in it; cabbages, cauliflowers, sprouts, tomatoes, carrots, lettuces, turnips, asparagus, luscious strawberries; in fact everything except potatoes which will not flourish owing to the heat of the summer. Potatoes are grown at the hill station of Naltar, some ten thousand feet above sea level, and brought to Gilgit on pack ponies.

On entering the main hall of the Agency House you might be in a baronial mansion in England. Round the walls are fine specimens of the heads of the big game found in the Agency; *Ovis Poli* (Marco Polo's sheep) with their corkscrew twists, the spiralling markhor, the curving ibex, the circling oorial, all tastefully hung to balance them and show them off to the best advantage. Comfortable unholstered furniture covers a large Khotan carpet and the windows are shaded by pretty chintz curtains. On the far wall hangs a picture of the King Emperor. To the left is a drawing room equally well furnished and to the right a dining room with a large polished table round which as many as thirty guests have been accommodated. To the rear are the bedrooms and adjacent to the dining room an office.

In the old days in Gilgit, that is prior to Partition, the complement of British Officers, in addition to the Political Agent, consisted of a Commandant of the Scouts, his Adjutant and Quarter Master, an Agency Surgeon and his assistant, an Assistant Political Agent, a Resident Engineer and sometimes a Nursing Sister. Each was lodged in a comfortably furnished bungalow with a garden and each lived a life of normal standards on good English food cooked by well trained cooks.

3. The People of Gilgit

To attempt to trace the origin of the numerous tribes of the Gilgit Agency is a difficult task as no records are available. I have never studied their history in detail; I prefer to believe in the old traditional stories handed down from generation to generation as I consider they are much more in keeping with this romantic land.

Experts such as Drew, Biddulph and Schomberg who have really studied the history of the Agency have all disagreed on the origin of the various tribes; far be it from me to argue with my elders and betters, so any factual statement I make in this chapter is merely my own idea and not the result of any careful study.

The two senior States are of course Hunza and Nagir. The men of Hunza are fine upstanding specimens of manhood. They are fair skinned, well built and of a generally pleasing countenance. They are cheery, friendly and humorous. Active and strong, they can turn their hand to anything whether it be agriculture, arts and crafts, road and water channel engineering, bridge building, cottage industries, or service with officers in Gilgit either in the house or in the stable. They are pleasant companions on trek and wily *shikaris*. They are first rate on the hillside and their powers of endurance are remarkable. Before the Agency was occupied the hotter blood was accustomed to raiding but years of Pax Britannica have reduced the tribe to a peace loving but in no way indolent race.

Across the river lies the neighbouring state of Nagir. The appearance and characteristics of the men of Nagir are vastly different from those of Hunza. They are smaller and darker; their standard of living is lower and they are less enterprising.

This is a hard description and is based on the average Nagiri. There are, however, folk in Nagir who are as fine men as you could wish to meet and I have many good friends there.

The question therefore arises whether the Hunza folk and Nagiris are of the same origin. I personally think they are. But in the old days before the ever moving glaciers closed it, there was a route from Nagir to Baltistan, and the Baltis were allowed to intermarry with the Nagiris. Later there was intermarriage with Kashmiris and with the, by then, heterogeneous Gilgitis. Such intermarriage was never allowed in Hunza; and this, I think, accounts for the fundamental difference between the two tribes.

The Hunza people disclaim a common origin with the Nagiris. They claim that they are descended from some of Alexander the Great's soldiers who settled in Hunza during the campaigns of the famous conqueror.

The story also goes that in olden days two princes of Persia named Abul Faiz and Abul Ghani came to Baltistan. There was a queen reigning there then whose custom was to live with any man she liked and when tired of him she would have him put to death. A similar fate awaited all sons born from such illicit love affairs. However, she fell in love with Abul Faiz but he only consented to return the love on the condition that he became her husband. As the queen was considered divine, a divine sign was required before marriage was possible. So one day Abul Faiz concealed himself on the top of a high rock. The queen fired an arrow in the direction of the rock and announced to the ignorant bystanders that in the area where the arrow fell her future husband would be found. Abul Faiz then appeared and was duly married to the queen. A son was born by the name of Jamshed. One day Jamshed set off on a shooting trip and passed down the Indus through Haramosh to Dhanyor which is on the left bank of the Gilgit river some three miles below the settlement. There he entered into conversation with the locals who informed him that there was a frightful tyrant ruling in Gilgit called Sri Badat. On one occasion Sri Badat went to a woman's house and demanded food and she fed him with the meat of a kid that had been raised on her own milk. The king enjoyed it so much that ever after he ate nothing but the flesh of young children. Jamshed crossed to Gilgit and by chance met Sri Badat's daughter. They fell in love with each other at first sight and they conspired to kill the king so that Jamshed could usurp the throne. Only fire could harm Sri Badat so they dug a pit near the castle gate and covered it with leaves. During the night the alarm was raised and the cannibal king rushed out of the gate to investigate. He fell into the pit and was killed by the villagers throwing burning torches on him. Sri Badat was the last Hindu king of Gilgit.

For many years after that an effigy of Sri Badat was publicly burned at the annual festival of Nauroze. The custom however died out but was revived again in 1944 by that great lover of legend and folk lore, Lt. Colonel E.H. Cobb, OBE, who was Political Agent, and an effigy of the tyrant ruler was burned at Sonekote amidst great excitement.

Jamshed ruled Hunza and Nagir and later his descendants, and from him the origin of the ruling families is claimed. But this genealogy is more legend than fact and little trust can be placed in it, although there was in actual fact a Hindu ruler called Sri Badat in Gilgit.

I believe myself that the tribes of Hunza and Nagir came from some faraway place in Central Asia in the olden days and settled in the valleys they inhabit today.

Now let us look at the people of Gilgit Sub-division, Punial, Ishkoman, Kuh Ghizr, and Yasin. I am of the opinion that they are all of one stock and probably came from that strip of country called Indus Kohistan which borders the great river before it debouches on the Peshawar plain. The people of Gilgit Sub-division show traces of intermarriage with Kashmiris, Balds, and nomadic tribes which earn their living by gold washing. Ishkoman used to be a penal settlement. In the Puniali, the Yasini, and the man of Kuh Ghizr you find a specimen of manhood which can almost vie with the Hunza folk. They are less active as their economic situation is not so serious; but they are tough, good *shikaris* in the mountains and capable of tremendous endurance.

The Yasini and Kuh Ghizri seem at first sight to be very dull in the head – they blame the intense cold of their country for this – but when shown what to do and how to do it, will persevere until the task is completed. The Punialis are famous as polo players – they have a team of giants.

The two main characteristics of the dress of the folk of the Gilgit Agency are the *koi* and the *choga*.

The *koi*, which is the headgear, consists of a bag of homespun woollen cloth some two feet in length with a round circular bottom. The bag is rolled up tightly round the edges until the padded circle so formed reaches the circular bottom or top as it now is. This cap is the traditional headwear. For festive occasions and for off duty hours a white *koi* is used in the rim of which is usually stuck a heron's crest or the head feathers of the beautiful Minal pheasant. This looks very attractive indeed and suitable for these hardy mountaineers. For work, the colour of the *koi* is brown or grey.

The *choga* is a long homespun cloak reaching to the ankles with long sleeves. It is usually coloured grey or brown through the ruling classes and richer people possess white ones with beautiful designs embroidered on them by the women folk. The *choga* is worn over the shoulders and the sleeves hang loose. They are chiefly worn in winter as protection from the bitter winds. Everyone possesses a *choga* including the children.

The remainder of the dress consists of baggy trousers drawn in round the ankles and a shirt worn outside, both of whatever cloth is available in the bazaar. Striped cloth is a favourite among the Hunzawals and the more enlightened, but the average peasant wears something more sombre. There is no rule, however, and it depends on what is available.

In the Gilgit Sub-division the Pathan *chapli* is mostly worn on the feet. In the States and Districts, however, long soft boots of home cured ibex hide are used; they are called *paboos*. But for the mountains and rough work and by the poorer people, the *taoti* is worn.

A *taoti* is a strip of roughly cured goat skin wound round the leg and foot and held in place by a leather lace. It gives a grand grip on the hillside either on rock, shale, or grass.

European dress is much liked by the ruling classes and Officers of the Scouts and they take every opportunity of wearing it. A portly gentleman, with fair skin and possibly red hair, wearing a well cut plus-four suit, correct to a detail, might well be the village squire in England. Or the long lanky sportsman with sharp features, dressed in corduroys and long riding jacket nicely waisted, could take his place without comment among the horse copers at the Dublin Horse Show.

The houses of the peasants and *zemindars* are low squat buildings of stone and mud. The living quarters are entered through the byre as this keeps out the winter wind and the warmth exuding from the goats, sheep and cows acts as central heating. The living room is usually sunk below the ground level and is lit by a smoke hole in the roof. The open fire is in the middle of the floor and the smoke escapes through the roof. The floor is of dried mud and along one side of the room is a raised dais where the family sits during the day and lie crosswise at night. Adjacent to the living room is the storeroom where grain, dried apricots, and the necessities of life are kept. In Hunza the houses are spotlessly clean – elsewhere they are not so. The Mirs and Rajas have built themselves bungalows in European style with all modern comforts.

Two main meals are eaten in the day. The peasant will normally rise at sunrise and work in the fields till 9 am when he will return for breakfast. This will consist of a vegetable stew cooked in *ghi* (clarified butter) and chupattis – flat pancakes of bread made from wheat, barley, or maize flour depending on stocks. At midday he will take a light snack of fresh or dried apricots or mulberries, depending on the season, washed down by buttermilk. The evening meal at about 6 pm will be the same as the breakfast. On occasions a sheep or goat will be slaughtered and meat added to the diet though this is not regular. The ruling classes like European food too, and when entertained by British Officers in Gilgit they consume it with relish.

The entire population of the Gilgit Agency is Mohammedan apart from some hundred Sikhs and Hindus who are traders, merchants, and clerks. Three separate sects of Mohammedanism exist in the Agency.

Hunza, Punial, and most of Yasin and Kuh Ghizr are Maulai. The Maulais are followers of H.H. The Agha Khan who claims direct descent from Ali who married Fatima, daughter of the Prophet. They care little for Muslim prejudices and are fond of locally produced wine. They unquestionably believe in God but do not indulge in praying, fasting, making pilgrimages, veiling women folk and the other religious observances of Islam. There is no religious fanaticism to contend with and an event of really great significance would be required to occasion a *jehad* or Holy War. They have as practical an outlook on religion as they have on life.

Nagir is entirely Shiah. The Shiass believe that the first three Khalifas or disciples of the Prophet, Abu Bakr, Osman, and Omar, were bogus and recognize only Ali whom the Sunnis believe was the fourth. The best description of the difference between the Shiahs and the Sunnis is that the former might be regarded as High Church Mohammedans and the latter as Low Church. The Shiahs are fanatically religious in Gilgit and obey the lessons of the Holy Quran to the letter.

The Sunnis are tolerant and liberal minded though devout. There are a few Sunnis in Yasin, and Kuh Ghizr; Ishkoman is mixed Sunni and Maulai; Chilas is wholly Sunni; there is one Shiah family in Hunza; the Gilgit Sub-division is mixed Shiah and Sunni and this is the only real danger spot on account of religion in an otherwise contented Agency. The rivalry between the Sunnis and Shiahs (or Shi'ites) is extremely serious, especially in the Sub-division and unless the situation is handled very carefully there is always the likelihood of a regrettable breach of the peace. Only under exceptionally significant circumstances would the Sunnis and Shiahs unite in one movement. In the Sub-division a balance of power must always be maintained and the usual modus operandi of trouble makers is to aggravate this rivalry. Such methods never fail and such persons must be crushed with a strong hand.

The languages of the Agency are interesting.

Shina is the lingua franca of this area and generally talked. Shina belongs to the Indo-Iranian branch of languages and is akin to Pushto, Hindustani, and Persian. For a scholar with a knowledge of these three languages Shina is easy to master, especially since the vocabulary is necessarily limited.

Khowar, the language of Chitral, is of the same stock and is talked in Yasin and Kuh Ghizr owing to the Chitrali influence in these two districts.

The language of Hunza, Nagir proper, and the upper portion of the Nagir valley, and certain villages in Yasin is Burushaski, which is really akin to no known language in the world. Its vocabulary is entirely its own and it is a very difficult language to attempt to learn. There is simply no information to give on the origin of this language so it must just remain one of the mysteries of Central Asia.

Shina is talked in Punial, Gilgit Sub-division, the lower portion of Nagir, and a dialect of Shina is found in Chilas, varying very little but pronounced more broadly.

Hindustani or Punjabi, as it is called, is understood everywhere and is a sufficient go-between for the unenterprising foreigner.

4. Sports and Pastimes

When talking of sport the first game which comes to mind is polo. Polo is the national game; polo is the life of the country; in fact polo is Gilgit. During the season, which lasts from September to early April, polo is talked, thought, and dreamt by most of the population.

In Gilgit proper the game is played twice a week on Mondays and Thursdays and it might be of interest to give the routine and description of a normal playing day in the capital.

The previous evening the local band, which normally consist of two pipes rather like clarinets, a bass drum, and a brace of kettledrums, will turn out and play the *ghulawar* which is the old traditional warning for polo, which has been handed down from time immemorial. It is a wild tune, well suited to this rugged mountain country and never fails to quicken the heart and elate the spirit. Thus the people know that on the morrow there will be polo – even the ponies recognize the *ghulawar* and prick their ears and restlessly paw the ground with their forefeet on hearing it. On the following morning the *ghulawar* will be played again and by 2 pm all roads lead to the polo ground.

There are two grounds in Gilgit, the Shahi or Royal Ground in the bazaar which is new, and the Old Ground surrounded by shady chinar trees where polo has been played since living memory. The polo ground is about three hundred yards long and thirty feet broad and surrounded by a stone wall about four feet high. There are goals at either end – previously heaps of stones but nowadays high pillars bedecked in red and white cloth. In the centre of the wall on one side of the ground is a raised platform made of stone with dried mud for flooring. On polo days carpets are laid out on this and rows of chairs.

This dais is reserved for the privileged classes who have come to spectate. On the wall opposite, there is a smaller dais and here sit the band who play continuously while the game is in progress. You cannot play polo without a band – the horses won't gallop and the players are listless. On big occasions an awning is erected over the larger dais and wire netting is fitted round it for the very necessary protection of the spectators. The crowd squat along the walls on either side.

A team consists of six players. The ponies are all stallions from Badakshan or the Pamirs and they are tastefully equipped with silver inlaid on the leather of the bridles and beautiful embroidered saddle covers under high pommelled wooden saddles which are cushioned for comfort. The ponies' tails are knotted up to prevent fairies catching hold of them and impeding their speed.

In the good old days a game would continue until one side had scored nine goals. This sometimes took two or three hours, with consequent suffering to the ponies, tough as they are. This later changed to the first to get nine goals with a limit of an hour to get them in, otherwise the side leading at the end of the hour was the winner. During the war when ponies and fodder were scarce the Political Agent wisely ruled that there would be two *chukkas* of twenty minutes each with a rest between. Two half hour *chukkas* were allowed in competitions.

All being ready the players mount and as they reach the saddle they touch the ponies' withers, their own lips, and their foreheads in that order with the fingers of their right hands as the symbol of silent prayer to Allah for protection in the coming battle. And well they need it too – the occasional violent death is not unknown, broken bones and heads frequent, and to be clashed on the ground or against the walls with a struggling mass of ponies and humanity on the top of you is quite the order of the day.

The opposing teams now line up on opposite sides of the centre line. The polo stick is held in the right hand – the shafts of wild almond, the heads of willow or mulberry. On the left wrist dangles a *chabuk* or whip by an ornamental tassel. The reins are knotted to facilitate the intricate movement of passing them to the right hand in order to whip up a lagging pony. The band strikes up, the ball is thrown in and the battle is on.

There are no rules apart from really outrageous crimes, and by the latter I mean deliberately striking an opponent with your stick, whip, or clenched fist, or placing your stick between the forelegs of your opponent's pony so that the pony goes for a series of somersaults and the rider to hospital or the cemetery. Crossing, knocking a stick from an opponent's hand with your own, dangerous riding, pinning a man's arm down by putting yours round his waist, riding off and so on are all in the game, the object of which is to get the ball through the opposing goal.

In this feudal country the polo ground is the only place where real democracy is found. Polo the leveller – no respect is shown on the polo ground for Political Agent, Mir, Raja, or British Officer. They are merely players and take their chance with the peasant and shopkeeper.

In representative and inter-district polo free fights are frequent, disputes are common, and if the police arrangements are not good the crowd will sometimes invade the pitch and mob the players.

The spectators sit along the walls and shrewdly observe the play. Good play is applauded, bungling treated to whistling and cat-calls. But an exciting match will raise a fervour quite equal to a cup final and the cheering following a goal, echoed through the silent mountains, is a worthy peer to the "Hampden Roar".

If the player catches the ball he may score by galloping through the goal with it. But woe betide him if he is caught in possession as his opponents are free to tear him to bits if they want. Many a ball catcher has emerged from the ensuing scrum with barely a stitch of clothing left. After a goal the scorer gallops down the centre of the field with the ball and stick in his right hand. As he reaches the centre the music rises to a crescendo, he throws the ball in the air and hits it with his stick. This is called the *tambuk*. A good eye may result in another goal but a good *tambuk* hitter is judged on the height he hits it in the air regardless of direction.

Full time is signalled by a blast on a bugle. Then follows a "second division" match between the more humble villagers on their minute shaggy ponies – both enjoying themselves just as much as their elite seniors. Events of the game, and form of ponies and players, and speculation on future results make the main topic of conversation till next polo day.

British Officers have never attempted to introduce Hurlingham rules to Gilgit polo. The policy has always been to preserve the ancient traditions of this king of games where the mightiest and lowliest are united in the common bond of love of the greatest game in the world, Gilgit polo, and I am sure that any other British Officer who has played it and who reads this will agree with me.

I have dwelt a long time on polo, but purposely, because polo is the spirit of the Agency, it is a deep-rooted symbol of an ancient civilization which will endure till all time and he who does not appreciate this cannot understand these simple mountain folk.

As for the other sports and pastimes, there is *boz kashi* which is gradually dying out. Those participating mount their ponies, with a prayer to Allah, and line up in the middle of the polo ground. The throat of a goat is slit, the band strikes up, and the carcass is thrown in among the competitors. The object is that he who can secure the carcass and ride off with it is the owner and will have meat for dinner that night. The inevitable result, however, usually is that the carcass is torn to bits in the ensuing melee and the game ends in a welter of blood, flesh, and entrails mixed up in a rugger scrum of men and ponies. The cloth shortage of the war years curtailed this game somewhat.

Tent pegging on horseback is popular, especially in Hunza and Nagir but the customary peg is usually replaced by a beaten out rupee bit of about three inches in diameter. It calls for a good eye to strike, draw and carry this small target at full gallop. [Major Brown was a champion at tent pegging. His widow, Margaret, still has the beaten rupee piece with which he won at the 1943 Nagir *jalsa*.]

Another favourite in Hunza and Nagir is *tarandazi* or archery; but this does not consist of shooting at a stationary target with a bow and arrow. A small white disc slightly bigger than a match box is placed on the side of a mound of earth in the centre of the polo ground. The marksman mounts his pony, places the arrow in the bow which he grasps in the left hand with the string half taut. He then urges his pony to full gallop down the polo ground, guiding it with his right hand so that it will pass on the right of the target at some five to ten yards distance. As he approaches the mound holding the disc he must drop his reins, guide the pony with his legs, grasp the bow and arrow in both hands, take aim and fire without slowing up. This sounds incredibly difficult – it is, and requires a high standard of skill and horsemanship. Admittedly a bull's eye is a rare thing but it is gained especially by the Hunza folk. I have seen Prince Shah Khan of Hunza, about whom we shall hear much later, pierce the disc on three consecutive runs.

Lastly there is *tambukbazi* or shooting the popinjay – a sport which was stopped during the war owing to the lack of cartridges.

A long pole, or two poles joined together, about fifty to sixty feet high is erected in the middle of the polo ground. At the summit a target such as a bunch of balloons, or a gourd filled with sand is suspended. At the coronation of the present Mir of Hunza, Mir Mohammed Jamal Khan, a silver model of an ibex was the target; the winner was presented with the ibex as a prize and he in turn presented it to Frances Bacon, daughter of Lt. Colonel R.N. Bacon, OBE, who was Political Agent and presiding over the ceremonies.

The competitor then mounts his pony and takes a loaded shot-gun – an old fashioned matchlock in village competitions usually. The band strikes up and he gallops down the polo ground at full speed. As he approaches the popinjay he drops his reins, turns in his saddle, takes aim, and fires at the high target. It is considered cheating to fire both barrels of a double-barrelled gun. Again this is a very difficult task but somebody always hits it. The winner is the first to do so. The element of danger in this sport is when the general difficulty of handling a horse and a gun at the same time causes the trigger to be pressed before the enthusiast has taken aim. A load of shot is then directed into the spectators lining the walls. To the amusement of those who escape injury, some poor wretch will be winged. Such incidents do not mar the day's sport, which continues, and the casualty is usually left to nurse his wounds till the competition is over.

It is even more exciting with matchlocks owing to their occasional delayed action which the marksman thinks is a misfire. When turning his pony at the end of the run with the muzzle nicely lowered, there will be a flash of flame and a noise like a shell exploding and two or three spectators will bite the dust with a load of garnets, tin tacks, and boot nails in them. This is considered a highlight of the day's sport.

Mention might be made of the local dancing, as it is performed at every festivity and joyful occasion; after polo the winning team has the honour of dancing first, followed by the losers. The players dance with their sticks in the right hand and whips in the left. The band strikes up and the dancers enter the circle in great leaps. They then circle in measured tread in time to the drums with long and short steps alternately. As they warm to the job the tempo becomes quicker; they twist, turn, stamp, leap, rotate on one foot whilst tapping the ground with the other; the arms are thrown about, and waved with attractive movements of the fingers. The dance ends in a long drawn out whirl and the dancers withdraw exhausted. The band plays to the dancers who do not improvise independently but attempt to co-ordinate their movements.

5. Chilas

The Chilas Sub-agency is, roughly, the country which drains into the Indus between Ramghat and Thor, the latter being about twenty miles downstream from the town of Chilas which is 84 miles or four stages from Gilgit. The journey from Jaglote to Chilas is one of the dreariest imaginable and I always think God must have had an ironical smile on his face when he created this bit of country. The valley is shut in by barren lofty mountains which give a dismal impression of utter desolation. The country is treeless and the only sound to be heard is the sullen booming of the Indus. The villages and cultivation are in the upper reaches of the side valleys.

The heat in the Indus basin is intolerable in summer and all travelling is done by night or in the early morning. Frequent graves by the roadside are reminders to the unwary that it is better to lie up in the heat of the day.

The settlement of Chilas proper consists of a Beau Geste fort on the top of a cliff. Round the fort nestles a well stocked bazaar. The valley broadens out here but there is little cultivation and nothing to see but everlasting sand stretching down to the mighty Indus. In the valley below is a most attractive small oasis.

Here is situated the Assistant Political Agent's bungalow with the appropriate name of "Journey's End". The bungalow is low and rambling with somewhat dark rooms. Surrounding the front and sides there is a verandah around which wild roses ramble. A horseshoe rockery, which in spring is one purple mass of the most glorious violets, leads down to a small lawn which in turn leads to a park some two hundred yards in length ending at the stables. This park is full of fruit trees planted by some enterprising A.P.A. But the main feature of the garden is some beautiful lofty blue gum trees surrounding the bungalow. The clear waters of the mountain burn of Batogah flow through the garden and the pleasant trickle of water over stones gives the little estate an atmosphere of peace and tranquillity. There is a well stocked vegetable garden on the far side of the stream. At the main gate a sentinel chinar tree stands with the flagpole beside it and on the far side of the road lies the well populated jail. Above the jail there is a newly constructed polo ground carved out of the hillside. [The polo ground was, in fact, constructed by Major Brown.]

It is difficult to trace the history of the Chilasi race as there are no records or even folklore. The Chilasi takes little interest in the past or future but concentrates on his immediate life and the easiest way to live it with the minimum amount of exertion and effort.

I spent a year in Chilas as A.P.A. and took a great deal of interest in what information I could glean from the village elders and mullahs regarding the history of Chilas; so any facts or presumptions I give are the result of my personal investigations.

The whole area of the Sub-agency is now called Chilas although this is the name of the headquarters of the A.P.A. only and the rest of the country is known as Shinaka. The country is geographically split up into six main communities which are loosely administered by a usually indolent and corrupt board of village elders under the supervision of the A.P.A.

The most northern and best behaved community is Gor and the most southern and worst behaved is Thor. Both these communities have always remained loyal to Government and did not resist but rather helped the expeditionary force when Chilas was taken over by Algernon Durand in 1893 after some fighting.

Below Thor are the independent Shinaka states of Darel and Tangir which are akin to Chilas in language and customs. I always maintain we should have taken over these two communities as well: they are richly wooded and the income obtained from tree felling would easily have covered any other outlay. Instead the forests have been ravaged through indiscriminate cutting by contractors and the states have always remained a thorn in our flesh on account of their cattle-rustling raids on the Agency. They are also an ideal refuge for outlaws and absconders.

The older headsmen generally agree that all the Shinaki people are descended from a Hindu chief who came from Lahore by way of the Kaghan Valley and the Babusar Pass. It is not known when this occurred but it is said that nine generations ago the people were converted to Islam by Sayeds, or descendants of the Prophet, from the Kaghan.

The people of the community, however, claim a different origin. They say that they are descended from the Qureshi family of which the Prophet himself was a member. During the Prophet's final struggle to establish Islam at Mecca a brother named Gauri Thum refused to embrace the new religion. When the Prophet was eventually successful, Gauri Thum fled the country and came to Thak where he originated the people who live there today. The people of Thak, therefore, consider themselves superior to the rest of the Chilasi who are merely descended from a petty Hindu princeling.

The people of Gor claim an attractive descent. The story goes that a female fairy called Rattas descended from heaven one day accompanied by her brother. She drank some divine water from a spring at Am Ges, which is about eleven miles up stream from Chilas, and this water made her pregnant. She bore a son and later a daughter was born to her by her brother. The two children married and their three sons founded the three main villages of Gor.

I would repeat that these descriptions of the origin of the Chilasis are legion. These are merely the gleanings I managed to extract from some of the greybeards round campfires and whether they are true or not will never to be known. I personally cannot believe that the Chilasis are of the same stock as the tribes of the political district. I think the Shinaki tribes are a degraded northern Pathan tribe which migrated here or were, more likely, driven here by their finer brethren. In features they resemble the Pathan, and the only similarity with the men of the Gilgit districts is in language and dress.

The Chilasis are mainly flock owners and their only contact with civilization is annual sheep and goat selling expeditions in Kashmir or the North West Frontier Province. They are very rich but they seem to excel in nothing except in flock coping.

The Chilasi will not do manual labour. He prefers to hire vagrants or lease the land to tenants to do the work for him. His normal existence consists of wandering about with his goats or squatting on a convenient rock sunk in gloomy abstraction, a black sheet wound round him and looking for all the world like a vulture. Chilasis quarrel much amongst themselves but usually it is only disputes over women and water that lead to bloodshed. The rows about loans, sheep dealing, and other such grievances usually culminate in a slanging match or by opposing parties throwing stones at one another.

Quarrels over women inevitably lead to a brutal murder in which the victim will probably be ambushed and have his head chopped off with a none too sharp axe. Local custom with regard to women is interesting and worth recording. If a husband finds his wife "in flagrante delicto" with another man he is at liberty to kill them both, but on the spot. If he delays or kills the paramour only, forgiving his wife, he is liable to the limit of the law which is fourteen years in jail from the hand of the A.P.A. If however he does dispatch both of them without premeditation, he will receive a nominal sentence of one day's imprisonment. In cases of rape the injured wife's husband, or nearest male relative in the case of the unmarried, may kill the ravager provided it can be proved that he lost no time in doing so. If he delays he is a murderer. The result is that there is very little *actual* adultery. Over the last period of years the annual murder rate averaged about twenty – more than any other district in British India in proportion to the population – and most of these were due to women or to ancient blood feuds originated by women.

Murder and other serious criminal cases are tried in the court of the A.P.A. who has the power of a first-class magistrate. A council of village elders attend all trials in much the same capacity as a jury. The maximum sentence is fourteen years' imprisonment and the death sentence is never given. Local custom is always respected. Minor crimes are tried by councils of elders. The A.P.A. has an assistant called a Raja Orderly or R.O. who is a nobleman of Hunza, Nagir, or the Political Districts and whose tenure is normally three years.

The Shinaki tribesmen are without exception Sunnis by religion. They seem to profess great devotion to Islam and obey the ordinances and laws of the Holy Quran. They do not drink wine. Despite this devotion, neither the people nor the priests use religion to create trouble. Religion may be used as a means to an end but it is never the sole cause of a disturbance; despite these conditions which appear ideal breeding ground for fanaticism there is no religious prejudice and the mullahs do not preach bigotry though it is most unlikely that the people would respond if they did. It would therefore require momentous circumstances to foster *jehad* in Shinaka.

The Sonewals are a strange race; they are settlers and were obviously nomadic. Some have now settled in Chilas proper and live by leasing land from the indolent Chilasis at enormous rent. Others wander up and down the banks of the Indus and wash gold dust from the silt and sand. Occasionally a lucky strike may bring in a small fortune; normally existence is pretty precarious. They are a happy little inoffensive community, fond of singing and dancing, and personally I think they are of Romany stock and akin to gypsies.

The Assistant Political Agent under the supervision of the Political Agent is entirely responsible for the Sub-agency of Chilas. His word is law and he is the little king in his own right of the twenty thousand population. To consult the records and discover how much Chilas has developed since the advent of the British says much for the enterprise of the officers who have held this post. The murder rate has been lowered, education has been started, tree felling has been controlled, reforestation started, a thriving bazaar encouraged, agriculture assisted, fruit trees planted, roads and bridges constructed, law and order maintained, export of antimony, gold, wool and goat's hair started, the possession of rifles controlled, and the sons of some of the leading headmen have even been given scholarships to the Church Mission School in Srinagar.

A.P.A.S have sometimes felt they were battering their heads against stone walls but they persevered under trying circumstances with remarkable results.

A.P.A.S have been much too liberal in the issue of rifle licenses and today fifty per cent of the population possess one. Another twenty five per cent, fully, possess unlicensed rifles so the country is full of arms. The rifles are mostly Sniders and Martini Henrys but there are a number of modern sporting rifles nowadays. There are, I believe, about two thousand modern rifles in Darel and Tangir.

6. The Gilgit Agency: Strategy

In 1842 the Ra of Gilgit was Karim Khan and he invited the Sikhs of the Punjab to occupy Gilgit. They did so but throughout their stay (1842–48) their commander, Nathu Shah, received much trouble from Gohar Aman of Yasin. An attempt was made to subdue Gohar Aman by a Hindu, Mathra Das, but the former thoroughly trounced the Hindu in battle and drove him back to Kashmir. In 1847 Nathu Shah and his ally Karim Khan attacked Hunza, as a reprisal for raids on Gilgit Territory. In the ensuing battle the Hunza men were triumphant and both Nathu Shah and Karim Khan were killed. Karim Khan's grandson now became Ra with the official recognition of the Dogras, who are the ruling class in Kashmir. They are Hindus and come from the hills to the north of the Punjab.

Gohar Aman decided to drive the Dogra troops of the Maharaja of Kashmir out of Gilgit. He attacked them, and they sent a message for help to Bhup Singh who was the Dogra commander of Bunji. Bhup Singh on his march to Gilgit made the fatal frontier mistake of failing to picquet the high ground bordering the road. At the famous Bhup Singh Parri (of which we shall hear much, later), where the road is bordered on one side by steep heights and on the other by the river, Gohar Aman assisted by a Hunza detachment fell on the Dogras who were annihilated to a man – in all about a thousand.

The Gilgit fort was then reduced and the Dogra garrison massacred; and another Dogra force of some five hundred men was attacked and destroyed. Thus the brave Gohar Aman completely wiped out the army of the Maharaja of Kashmir and Dogra occupation was at an end.

In 1860 Ranbir Singh became Maharaja of Kashmir, and he decided to reconquer Gilgit. This proved an easy task as the great warrior Gohar Aman had died and there was no one to take his place capable of uniting Gilgit in concerted action. In 1866 the Dogras invaded Hunza as a reprisal for raids and enlisted the help of Nagir. These new allies, however, deserted in large number, with the result that the Dogras ran for their lives in panic.

In 1851 a Kashmiri force of Dogra troops invaded Chilas proper where they were exterminated in battle. Two years later the forces of the Maharaja again attacked Chilas and having reduced the country retired to Kashmir. An annual tribute of sixty goats was levied by the Kashmir Durbar on the country and this was the position when the Imperial Government took it over in 1892.

It will be noticed, however, that on the whole the people of Gilgit gained a larger share of success in these campaigns – especially the Hunza men who were never beaten in battle, and this to some extent accounts for the supreme contempt in which Kashmir has always been held.

The value of Gilgit to Kashmir State is obvious, as it is a key point for keeping in check raiders from Hunza, Nagir, and the Indus basin. But it was not till the 1880s that the Government of India fully appreciated the strategic importance of Gilgit to the defence of the Empire. Russian expeditions had already explored the Hindu Khush and had also infiltrated into the north of Chitral, a state under British protection. Thus the Czar had violated treaty obligations and apparently with impunity. Captain Gromchevtsky crossed the Pamirs and entered Hunza. He made attractive overtures to the Mir and did his best to antagonize the people against the British. Frequent reports were being received of further Russian troop movements and infiltration.

From the *Statesman*, dated Calcutta, 3 August 1887 (Extract from Editorial)

Derided though it may be, in political optimism, as the bug-bear of Anglo-Indian alarmists, like other creatures of the imagination, the phantom of approaching Russia still diffuses its atmosphere of dread about the Central Asian question.

There certainly appears to be no doubt that Russia's advance in Central Asia since 1847 has been like an increasing tide, noiseless, ceaseless, but effective. Within a quarter of a century Russia has moved down from the north of the Caspian Sea 500 miles south and 1,400 miles east, until she is now within 250 miles of Peshawar, with her influence extending, where her arms have not reached. The railway system, rapidly developed in European Russia, is now stretching its arms into Asia. Her possession of the valley of the Oxus, like her conquest of the Caucasus, cannot be considered as an ultimate point, but only as a resting place or stage in advance.

Turkestan with its simple nomad population, can scarcely be the goal of her wishes, and it might altogether seem as improbable that Russia should remain content with the comparatively barren districts of Central Asia, while India, the gem of the East, lay beyond.

So Whitehall sat up and took notice. It was obvious that if this sort of thing continued without reprisals, the small states on the southern side of the Hindu Khush would naturally throw in their lot with Russia as the likely winner in this race for domination of the natural barrier between the three Empires of Britain, China and Russia. What Russia did on the northern slopes of the Hindu Khush was interesting yet not vitally important. But it was essential that her influence should not extend to the southern slopes of the Gateway to India as this would mean a constant potential threat to the defence of the Empire. The threat was not so much the danger of a full scale invasion from this quarter, as the possibility of the arrival of skilled infiltrators backed by small bodies of troops to poison the minds of the tribes against the British by pointing out the strength and far reaching sway of Czarist Russia. A well planned insurrection, so caused, might have had far reaching effects in the plains of India, especially as an ill-spared expeditionary force of troops would have been required on the frontiers. And the Russians love fishing in troubled waters.

From *The Times*, dated London, 9 December 1892 (Summary of an article from the Russian paper *Svet*)

Adverting to the Pamir question, the *Svet* strongly condemns Russian policy for the Convention concluded with Lord Granville in 1872, whereby the Russian frontier in that region was formed by a line from Lake Sarikol to Panja, crossing the Pamirs in such a way as to cut off Russia from access to the Hindu Khush. The newspaper describes this range as the key to Great Britain's Asiatic possessions, and points out if Russia commands the passes leading to Chitral, her troops would only have to march some 250 miles along a good route to enter Kashmir, their entry into which country would be the signal for a formidable insurrection against the British throughout India. This, pursues the *Svet*, is the Hindu Khush, which she intends to render impregnable and this is why Russia should take advantage of the short time left for her to preserve this key to her power, and, since it is impossible for her to act against India by way of Afghanistan, to do so through Chitral. After declaring that the Convention of 1872 was not a formal treaty, and owing to the change in the situation since it was concluded, it has practically lapsed, the newspaper urges the Government to show no delay in securing the Khanate of Wakhan, extending Russian influence to the Hindu Khush, placing Chitral under Russian protection and hoisting the Russian flag on the passes before Great Britain hoists the English colours. At the same time a military road should immediately be constructed from Marghelan across the Pamirs, so as to permit at any moment of a Russian descent into the Chitral valley.

It was imperative for the Imperial Government to take over the whole area and to instil in the tribesmen a confidence in the might of the Empire and the Pax Britannica.

Another important point was the fact that a route crosses over the Shandur Pass from Gilgit to the State of Chitral, thus linking this State with Kashmir and India as an alternative to the route over the Lowari Pass to Peshawar.

Through the Lockhart Mission in 1886, the Imperial Government was treaty bound to protect Chitral from aggression. But the routes over the Hindu Khush from

Bokhara and Badakshan into Chitral are infinitely lower and easier than those entering Gilgit. Russian military experts are generally agreed that they would use the former in the event of a large scale invasion of India and there is a comparatively easy road from the State to the North West Frontier Province. An outflanking movement from Gilgit would have been of paramount importance in stemming such an invasion.

The vital importance of the political and strategical considerations are thus apparent, especially in the light of the present international situation. Never, under any circumstances should the Agency be treated as a backwater.

Soviet Russia did in fact start troop movements and infiltration in the Hindu Khush, but the British Government appreciated the situation and in 1935 leased the Gilgit Sub-division from Kashmir, thus uniting the entire Agency under the (British) paramount power.

With the previous considerations in view a British Agency was established in Gilgit in 1889 by Colonel Algernon Durand, with a handful of British Officers to help him. The work of these pioneers in extending influence, subduing and pacifying the country, and building the foundations of an Agency which endured till thrown away on 1 August 1947, cannot be praised too much. These great men, three of whom won the Victoria Cross for outstanding acts of bravery in the establishment of the Agency, must have turned in their graves when Gilgit was flung into the melting pot in that memorable autumn of 1947.

When Durand and his assistants arrived in Gilgit they found the settlement garrisoned by a contingent of Kashmir State troops. They were a useless rabble of dirty, slovenly, ill equipped, ill disciplined humanity; their lack of success in previous operations was not surprising. But the fault lay not in the sepoy but in the corrupt and dishonest officials of the Kashmir State who were responsible for the maintenance of the force. The money sanctioned for rations, equipment, training, and uniform found its way into the pockets of these rascals. I might add here that in 1947 the integrity of the officials of Kashmir State had improved little from those days, and with very few exceptions it would be difficult to find anywhere a more unsavoury gang, preying on the poor sepoy and peasant. The leasing by the British of the Sub-division in 1935 was therefore acclaimed with great enthusiasm by its inhabitants.

Durand immediately set things right. He replaced the State troops by Imperial Service troops under British Officers. He came down on corrupt officials with a firm hand, and personally supervised expenditure. He raised a Pioneer Corps of five thousand Pathans for road and bridge building.

He raised a corps of 160 irregular militiamen from Punial as skirmishers and guides. He armed them with Snider rifles but they wore their local dress and also carried swords and shields. They were given a little instruction in the use of the rifle which was sufficient military training to serve the purpose, as they were natural mountaineers and well trained in stalking and camouflage from hunting expeditions after markhor and ibex. They were led by the Raja of Punial in person, Akbar Khan, who received a subsidy from the Maharaja of Kashmir in return for guarding the frontiers of his state and rendering service in time of war. This force was named the Punial Levies and was the direct forebear of the Gilgit Scouts.

In 1889 Durand concluded a treaty with the Mirs of Hunza and Nagir whereby they agreed to stop raiding and to allow British Officers to pass through their territory unmolested. On the other hand Government agreed to pay the Mirs annual subsidies.

The Mirs however soon broke their obligations and the old lawlessness started again. Safdar Ali, Mir of Hunza, started parleying with Russia and China and Uzr Khan, son of the Mir of Nagir, murdered his two brothers on account of their friendship with the British. They then joined forces and declared open hostilities by marching on the garrison at Chalt.

Durand with 150 men and a British Officer made a forced march to Chalt and reinforced the small garrison. The tribesmen, taken aback at the speed of this movement, retired immediately to their countries. Such defiance could not be tolerated so Government ordered Durand to occupy the country and to build military roads through Hunza and Nagir and beyond if need be, in short to take whatever steps be considered necessary to safeguard the passes of the Hindu Khush despite opposition.

Colonel Durand did so. I do not propose giving details of the campaign, which is a story in itself, and well described in the commander's own book, *The Making of a Frontier*. It is sufficient to say that this was one of the heroic unsung small wars which helped to make Britain the greatest power on earth at the turn of the century, and which was executed by men who possessed all that is best in British manhood. The climax came at Nilt when Durand's force after a protracted hold up at an impregnable narrow gorge, scaled the towering heights and turned the flank of the Hunza-Nagir army. The Punial Levies played their part well and fully justified the trust Durand had placed in them.

To me the Battle of Nilt in its own way was as memorable and great a feat as the evacuation from Dunkirk or the victory at Alamein. Nilt was virtually the end of the campaign. Nagir was occupied first. The Mir, Zaffir Zahid, surrendered unconditionally and laid the blame for the opposition on his son, the fratricide Uzr Khan. Letters in the meantime arrived from Hunza stating the people were ready to submit. The Mir, Safdar Ali, and his advisor come commander-in-chief Dado, had fled the country and had taken refuge in Chinese Sinkiang.

Both tribes were treated extremely leniently in the terms of surrender which did much to woo them away from Russia and China, and to enhance British prestige. Nazim Khan, half-brother of Safdar Ali, was put on the throne of Hunza and a good choice it was too. Nazim Khan developed into the greatest, wisest, and shrewdest ruler of all time in Central Asia and his loyalty never wavered. He is now a legendary figure and his grandson, Mohammed Jamal Khan, the present Mir, emulates him in many respects. Zaffar Zahid continued as nominal ruler of Nagir till his death in 1904. He was succeeded by his son Sikander Khan, younger brother of the villain Uzr Khan, who failed in an attempt to flee the country and was clapped in Hari Parbat prison in Srinagar.

A treaty was now prepared and signed by the new Mirs. A significant fact which should be remembered in future events is that the treaty was between the Crown Representative *and* the Maharaja of Kashmir on the one part, and the Rulers of Hunza and Nagir on the other. The articles briefly were that both States recognized the suzerainty of the Queen Empress. The countries would be kept open and roads maintained up to the Pamirs in the case of Hunza. British Officers would be free to tour in both States. Slave dealing and raiding would cease. Both Rulers would be permitted to manage their own affairs but under the general supervision of the Political Agent. In return for this Government agreed to pay both Mirs annual subsidies.

This was a triumph for Colonel Durand and for his officers, sepoys, and all those who participated in the expedition. Captain Aylmer, Lieutenant Boisragon, and Lieutenant Manners Smith were decorated with the Victoria Cross for outstanding bravery at Nilt and their names immortalized in Gilgit history. I, for my part, always felt proud to have the privilege of serving in an Agency which had been founded by such really great men.

The strategic importance of Chilas is that a route runs from it over the Babusar Pass, some 13,000 feet high, and hence down the Kaghan Valley to Abbottabad and the North West Frontier Province, providing an alternative to the Kashmir journey.

In 1892 the Shinaki tribesmen adopted a truculent attitude by refusing to pay their tribute, expelling the news writer, and increasing the raiding. Colonel Durand therefore decided to take over the country. Accordingly an expeditionary force under Surgeon Major Robertson moved down the Indus in 1893 and after some fighting occupied the Chilas fort and established the Sub-agency. The Punial Levies under their newly appointed leader, Sifat Bahadur, again distinguished themselves. Chilas has given no trouble since and this says much for the manner in which the operation was conducted.

7. The Gilgit Scouts

As has been described in the previous chapter the direct forebears of the Gilgit Scouts were the Punial Levies, raised by Colonel Durand in 1889 and who took part in the Hunza and Nagir War in 1891 and in Surgeon-Major Robertson's expedition to Chilas in 1893. They again saw service and lived up to their fine reputation when they accompanied Colonel Kelly on his famous march from Gilgit to Chitral in 1895 to relieve the garrison besieged in the fort there.

In 1913 the Punial Levies were disbanded and the Gilgit Scouts formed with the nucleus coming from the levies. The Corps consisted of eight companies, Hunza and Nagir supplying two each, and Punial, Yasin, Gilgit Sub-division, and Kuh Ghizr one each. The Corps was raised by Major J.C. Bridges, 5th Gurkha Rifles (Frontier Force) who was then Military Adviser to the Kashmir State Troops in Gilgit.

The new Corps was embodied for one month's training each year, living in their homes for the remaining period. They drew full pay of Rs 12 (or 18 shillings) per mensem when under training and a retaining fee of Rs 1 (or 1/6d) per mensem for the remaining period.

During the Great War the Scouts were partially embodied and safeguarded the Hunza-China border. A post at Beyik was instrumental in capturing two German Officers who were making their way from China to Afghanistan. In 1919 the Scouts were employed in guarding the passes into Chitral during the Third Afghan War.

In the summer of 1925 and 1926 the people of Darel and Tangir made many raids on the Agency and lifted flocks. In order to bring pressure on them to return these flocks a blockade was imposed to prevent them entering the Agency to buy stocks of salt and cloth in the bazaar. The Scouts were responsible for enforcing this blockade. It was during this operation that a post in Thor suffered very severely from what is supposed to have been dysentery. Nine men of the Nagir Company died. Until 1935 there were no changes in the composition but the training period was increased from one to two months.

In 1935 the Gilgit Sub-division was leased to the Imperial Government by the Kashmir Durbar and the Kashmir State Troops withdrew to Bunji. The Scouts, therefore, became solely responsible for the defence of the Agency.

In April of that year (1935) four companies were permanently embodied, one each from Hunza and Nagir and a half company each from Gilgit, Punial, Yasin, and Kuh Ghizr. Two reserve companies were also retained on the same basis as before.

In October 1935 Colonel C.E.T. Erskine CIE, DSO, MC, Inspecting Officer of the Frontier Corps, was deputed to report on the Gilgit Scouts with a view to reorganization. If I remember rightly, the description of the Corps in his report contained phrases like "harlequinade" and "comic opera," but he submitted a plan which was finally accepted and brought into effect in 1937.

The Corps was reorganized on a platoon basis, the old company organization was dropped, and the reserve companies were disbanded. Hunza and Nagir gave three platoons each; Punial, Yasin, Kuh Ghizr and Gilgit one each. Each platoon consisted of 50 rifles and one Indian Officer. The designation "Indian" is perhaps misleading for the local officers who hold a commission granted by the Resident in Kashmir, but as it is official, I must use it. There was also a Headquarter company consisting of the Subedar Major (the Commandant's right hand man and go-between with the men), a Jemedar Adjutant, a Quarter Master Jemedar, a drill staff, a signal detachment, wireless detachment, buglers and bandsmen, orderlies, followers and civilian office staff. Latterly an education staff was sanctioned. The only supporting weapons were a few medium machine-guns. This was the organization of the Scouts when I joined them in 1943 as Adjutant, and when I took over as Commandant in 1947.

In September 1938 the Scouts were in action for the first time since 1895 when a patrol at Ton was attacked by Jalkotis, an independent tribe from Indus Kohistan. The attack was driven off, the Scouts suffering no casualties, the Jalkotis losing four killed. Subsequently there were one or two more skirmishes with tribesmen but apart from vast quantities of ammunition being expended, neither side suffered much damage.

The Gilgit Scouts are not a military force, but rather a civil armed force and as such are intended to assist the Political Agent as he may desire. The Political Agent controls promotion to and of commissioned ranks as this has direct repercussions on the political situation.

The members of a ruling family in Gilgit are called Gushpurs. The country is still so intensely feudal that these Gushpurs have the advantage of being leaders of men by birth despite their possible lack of practical qualifications. It follows that an inefficient Gushpur Indian Officer can lead his platoon better in the long run than an efficient *zemindar* or peasant Indian Officer who cannot control men of his own status in life. So the bulk of the Indian Officers in the Scouts are Gushpurs who have been directly appointed to the job without going through the ranks.

Some *zemindars* have risen from the ranks to Indian Officer, few have managed to hold their jobs, and such appointments have invariably caused trouble from the political angle in the States and Districts.

All higher policy, movements, occupation and evacuation of posts, higher finance and ordering stores is controlled by the Political Agent.

The duties and responsibilities of the Gilgit Scouts are detailed as follows:

1. the protection of the Agency from minor acts of aggression on its Border;
2. the maintenance of law and order within the Agency;
3. the provision of guards and escorts;
4. systematic patrolling of the Agency within its sphere of influence.

It is a great pity that some of the previous Commandants of the Scouts did not read and digest these duties. I have copied them direct from Standing Orders. Some Commandants appeared to think that the Scouts were a unit of the regular army which should be trained up to regular army standards and then let loose to terrorize the countryside. The brunt of the repercussions which ensued, invariably fell on the Political Agent who was forced to waste valuable time in restoring normal conditions again. Such Commandants were merely a disturbing influence in an otherwise peaceful Agency, and should have remained in the regular army to work efficiently to their hearts' content. And the same applies to any Indian Officer or member of the rank and file who does not like irregular soldiering: nowadays he is at liberty to join the regular army. The Scouts, however, are just as they are an ideal force to fulfil the duties required of them. Efficiency drives have been the cause of many upheavals – even of major operations on the North West Frontier.

To ensure that the administration of the Agency runs smoothly, close co-operation is required between the Commandant of the Scouts and the Political Agent. A Commandant is really a military adviser to the Political Agent. Some Commandants failed to appreciate that the Scouts were a political force, and were inclined to look on them as their own private army, in the administration of which the Political Agent had no right to interfere. This, of course, created an intolerable situation which not only upset the social life of the small community at Gilgit but had an adverse effect on the Agency as a whole.

The disturbances and minor mutinies which have sometimes taken place in the Gilgit Scouts have all been occasioned by circumstances such as those I have just described.

I shall now describe my own impressions of the Gilgit Scouts when I first joined them in 1943.

On parade they were as smart as any unit of the 1939 Indian Army, which is saying a great deal, and they could turn out a Guard of Honour which it would have been difficult to better. The uniform consisted of brown leather *chaplis*, grey socks over khaki hosetops, khaki drill shorts, a leather belt, a grey shirt with breast pockets and rolled up sleeves, leather bandolier, and a brown homespun *koi* for headgear. In winter khaki serge plus-fours were worn in place of shorts and a khaki pullover above the shirt. On the front of the *koi* was the badge, a small silver ibex, under which was facing cloth, flush with the roll of the cap.

The colour of the facing cloth varied according to tribe. Headquarters was dark green, Hunza light green, Nagir red, Punial yellow, Yasin blue, Kuh Ghizr maroon, and Gilgit black. On ceremonial parades and guards a white *koi* was worn.

Discipline was fair and inclined to become very slack unless a firm grip was maintained. A few Indian Officers were excellent, the bulk indolent and idle, but could be good when forced to shoulder responsibilities and earn their pay. This slackness of course reflected in the rank and file. Morale was good and, except for a few trouble makers, all were happy and contented and held their British Officers in great esteem.

Musketry was average though a correct estimate was difficult to judge as one and all cheated to the best of their ability and there were not sufficient British Officers to supervise and ensure fair play. Specialists, that is wireless and signals, were weak which is not surprising when one considers the condition of the country where the ploughshare, sporting rifle and polo stick are mightier than the pen. Knowledge of guerrilla and irregular tactics in frontier and general warfare was pathetically low. There was a certain lack of responsibility and sentries on important posts such as the magazine and treasury would normally sleep from midnight till dawn.

But it was on patrol, or *gasht* as it is called, that the Gilgit Scouts came into their own and I defy any other troops in the world to compete with them in mountain craft, endurance, trail work and camp life. The kit for gashting would consist of *chaplis*, woollen socks (leather socks if snow was likely to be encountered), grey *partugs* or baggy trousers, a grey shirt worn outside, a brown *koi* without facing cloth, a rifle and bayonet, seventy rounds of ammunition in a bandolier, a greatcoat slung on the back, one blanket between three men, a water bottle, three day's rations in a haversack, first field dressing, and anti-glare glasses for snow and sun.

A patrol would consist of anything from ten to thirty men and would normally be led by a British Officer or Indian Officer. Patrols would average 20 to 25 miles a day over incredibly steep and mountainous country and in each day's march would cross one, if not two, passes of over 15,000 feet. A patrol was entirely independent and self contained for three days: on longer *gashts* coolies would be required to carry extra rations. On the mule tracks of the valleys even longer daily *gashts* would be carried out.

I am sorry I kept no records of some of the more incredible marches, the reason being that I gradually came to take them for granted, but if I remember rightly there was an occasion, when I was Commandant, when a Hunza platoon covered the fantastic distance of 120 miles in two and a half days from Kalamdarchi Post on the southern slopes of the Hindu Khush, through the State of Hunza, to Gilgit.

I might add here the dispositions of the Corps. In Gilgit there were Headquarters and four platoons. Four platoons were stationed in Chilas, one in Gupis the capital of Kuh Ghizr, and one at Kalamdarchi in the northernmost corner of Hunza under the jagged peaks of the Mintaka ("a thousand ibex") Pass leading into Sinkiang.

Games were played in the Scouts: football, hockey, basketball and athletics and the general standard was very good in friendly games. Any attempt to promote representative or inter-platoon games ended in an uproar. Tempers would be lost, kicking, tripping and striking indulged in, and the match would end in a free fight whilst two or three unfortunate creatures would be carted off to hospital on stretchers with broken limbs and heads.

I have given a very frank description of the Scouts as I found them. In all fairness, I have described their talents and their faults. Should they read this, and should my criticizm raise recriminations I can only pray forgiveness if I have erred. For I have eaten their bread and salt, lived as one with them, and since then have come through so many adventures with them that eventually I felt I too belonged to the race of those hardy mountaineers.

To conclude I would reiterate that the Scouts as they were, form an ideal force for the Agency, and one ideal for the duties and responsibilities required of them. [Major Brown always considered it the height of folly to use the Scouts, as in 1948 his immediate successor did, in direct confrontation with Indian regular troops and away from the Agency.]

8. My Life in Gilgit in the British Period

I spent two years in Gilgit as Adjutant of the Scouts, and one year in Chilas as Assistant Political Agent – three halcyon years of which I enjoyed, every minute, and which will ever remain in my memory as an undiluted series of red letter days.

It was a happy little European community when I arrived. There were sometimes differences of opinion and petty squalls but there was never anything spiteful about them. Such quarrels were bound to arise when a small community lives in a small place, cut off from the rest of the world. When you felt a growing annoyance at the behaviour or characteristics of your neighbours, you knew it was time to go on tour where mountain breezes and the wide spaces would clear your mind and refresh your spirit after the imprisoning effect of the narrow valley at Gilgit.

Lt. Colonel E.H. Cobb, OBE was Political Agent, an admirable representative of the Crown in these wild and feudal parts as he possessed those great characteristics and traditions which made the British rulers of more than half the world. He ably upheld the prestige of the paramount power and of her subjects. An extremely well read and knowledgeable man, he could discourse for hours on a variety of subjects and never failed to retain the interest of his listeners. He had a love of field sports and the countryside, and there was little he did not know about shikar and mountain craft which he turned to a more practical purpose in successful shooting and fishing expeditions in the Agency. He was of a very hospitable nature and you were always welcome at Agency House at any hour of the day or night.

Then there was Major Jackson, the Agency Surgeon, and his wife. Another open door and a cheery welcome were always found from that kind couple. We used to gather in their bungalow of an evening and play family bridge, and as often as not would be persuaded to stay on to dinner. We used to laugh a lot about the funny little happenings in the Agency. There was always a fresh and cheerful atmosphere in Pete and Doreen's bungalow and I spent many happy hours there.

Major Vaughan, Commandant of the Scouts, and his wife kept more to themselves with a family to interest them; but their house was open too and he had a store of amusing tales to recount about his experiences in Chitral and elsewhere.

Then there was Alec Grierson, the tall thin tea planter from Assam, who was Quarter Master of the Scouts, a fellow countryman of mine who went to the same school. It is interesting to note that in a period of five years, no less than four Gilgit Scout officers had been educated at George Watson's College, Edinburgh, and as Gilgit Scout officers were hand-picked, as it were, this is a great compliment to the school.

The Assistant Surgeon was Dr Allen Marsh, an expert at his job: he patched me up many times after polo accidents. He himself was a redoubtable polo player and always used a local stick, a feat I could never emulate: I much preferred the English make.

The hospital Sister was Sister Cottrell: a brave lady to risk the hazards of the journey to Gilgit to help Major Jackson in his small but well-equipped hospital.

And finally there was our link between Gilgit and the outside world, George Kenny, the wireless operator.

This, then, was the little European community which fate had thrown together in the vastness of Central Asia.

I worked hard at my job as Adjutant in the Scouts, and attempted to teach them the rudiments of frontier and mountain warfare and elementary guerrilla tactics such as I myself had just learnt in South Waziristan.

One had to guard against introducing anything revolutionary which might have led to repercussions, but I think in the light of later events my efforts were fully justified. I emphasized co-operation between signals, wireless, and the foot sloggers, as each seemed to function as an entirely separate unit which of course is useless. I tried hard to instil in everyone a sense of responsibility by encouraging esprit de corps. Those who, during this period, served me well and backed me up, I never forgot, and before leaving the Scouts as Commandant in 1948 I had seen to the best of my ability and in accordance with circumstances that each of them had received a just reward in the form of promotion.

Crimes committed in public had to be punished by imprisonment but sleeping sentries could be dealt with summarily which was much more effective. Any sentry I found asleep I would kick hard as I could or beat with a stick. It saved spoiling an otherwise good conduct sheet, yet gave the defaulter a lesson he would never forget. I never found men erring again after such treatment and I dealt with many too. There was no ill will either and they seemed to prefer it to a stretch in the guard room. Sentries improved generally a tremendous amount, but I couldn't help feeling a sense of frustration when a few days before I was finally transferred from Gilgit in 1948, when inspecting some very important night guards, I found the sentry asleep and the remainder of the guard absent. But this was exceptional at that stage and not the rule as it was previously. And yet it made one realize how careful one had to be.

I have no doubt that I became somewhat unpopular when I introduced the measures I have just described but I did notice a marked improvement; it did show one and all that I was not a man to be trifled with and this stood me in great stead later.

To be a successful leader of Scouts there are five points of paramount importance:

1. ensure the men get as much leave as is consistent with the exigencies of service and discipline;
2. take a sympathetic interest in the troubles of their home life and do your best to help them in every way;
3. ensure the men get their full pay and allowances and immediate payment of any arrears due to them;
4. ensure that the standard of rations is good and ample;
5. create a colourful atmosphere about yourself, yet refrain from showing off.

I spent a great deal of my time in the lines and conversed freely with the Indian Officers and men. One could do this in the Gilgit Scouts without the danger of familiarity breeding contempt, on account of the feudal nature of the country. I soon knew the name, family history, characteristics and capabilities of every single man in the Corps. If I met a man outside the lines I would stop and pass the time of day with him. I did not confine this personal acquaintance to the Scouts only but to as many people of the entire Agency as possible.

I played games regularly with the Scouts, football, hockey, basketball and athletics, as I was a good average at all of them. Sometimes I would promote popular representative matches such as headquarters against the platoons, or Indian Officers and NCOs against the sepoys, myself playing for the latter.

There was great enthusiasm and after the games I would sit under the big chinar tree with the Indian Officers and chat about horses, polo, and shooting while the men danced to the wild strains of the band. Or else the Scottish pipe and drum band, which Alex Grierson and myself had trained up from Scouts, would play a selection of the rousing war songs of my own native heath. Some of the Hunza and Nagir men learned the bagpipes very quickly and expertly and the pipe band was a great feature of the Scouts.

Gradually the sun would sink behind the mighty hills which silently watched over our lines. As the chill evening breezes blew down the valley a halt would be called to the festivities. I would mount my pony and ride home through the gathering twilight well contented.

I remember one day when I organized a polo match between headquarters, captained by Alec Grierson, and the platoons, captained by me. The players and their supporters all came up to our bungalow before the match. After some dancing in the garden we formed a procession and with the band playing for all it was worth in front and the supporters cheering their lungs out, we rode down to the polo ground. Needless to say the local population coming out of doors to see the fun, could not resist joining the throng. The game was one sided and the platoons won easily but it was the sort of day that the Scouts and locals thoroughly enjoyed. To me, as an individual, it was exhilarating; to me as an official it was useful as the festivity would form conversation and discussion among the Scouts and populace for days after the event, leaving little time for intrigue and devilment. The maxim of Satan finds mischief for idle hands holds very strong in the Scouts as I discovered later.

Id, the day of celebration in the Muslim calendar, marking the end of the annual fast during the month of *Ramazan*, was a gala day; though for sheer abandoned merrymaking the Gilgit Scouts could not be compared on this occasion to the Pathan Corps of the south. The Gilgit lads required encouragement to which they reacted; the Pathan celebration is a mild outburst of high spirits, pent up by a month of strict religious observances – spontaneous combustion which requires a steadying hand rather an encouragement.

For all that, Gilgit *Id* went with a swing. In the morning the Scouts would bedeck themselves in their best clothes and proceed to Agency House to receive congratulations from the Political Agent. He would treat them to tea after which there would be dancing on the lawn. In the afternoon there would be polo: usually *Id* coincided with the opening of the season so this was an added interest. More tea would be served on the polo ground after which the luckier amongst us would get a short rest before the evening's programme started. I never did: on such occasions I was never done with organizing, ordering, counter-ordering, encouraging, and scolding but it was well worth it.

In the evening, the Scout Indian Officers would usually give a dinner party to the British Officers and local notables, after which we would be entertained to firelight dancing. An enormous beacon of wood blazed in the centre of a large circle formed by spectators. Each tribe of Scouts in turn, according to seniority in the Agency, would perform and the normal straightforward dancing would be varied with novelty turns.

Some strapping lads from Hunza would perform a sword dance; and effective it was too, with the flames flashing on the pale skins of their races and on their brandished swords.

The Yasinis and men of Kuh Ghizr would join forces and sing ancient Chitrali love songs in plaintive soft voices; the lilting tune would end abruptly and the marked contrast of a raucous chorus would cheerfully chant the praises of some legendary warrior or polo player.

There would be no lack of comedy in the form of sketches in which they emulated officers and officials – this was always very popular – and short acts of clowning in which the humour would vary from sheer crudeness to the ridiculous.

One Scout, dressed up as a woman, would lie on the ground, supposedly in the pangs of childbirth. Another, as the doctor, accompanied by his assistant, would enter carrying the proverbial black bag. The doctor started operations and manipulations under the bed sheet, his assistant from time to time handing him the necessary instruments which consisted of a hammer, a chisel, a saw and a pair of pliers. Eventually the doctor and the assistant had a prolonged tug-of-war on pliers with the lady's anatomy. After a tremendous struggle the woman would give birth with a yell of triumph, and the doctor and his assistant would fall in a sprawling heap with a large black cat held in the pliers. This brought the house down and the players scampered off the stage to an accompaniment of cheers.

And then there would be the burlesque version of a day's big game shooting – a different kind of humour but nevertheless always popular. A pantomime ibex consisting of two men covered with blankets, and surmounted by real ibex horns, would enter and dance round the ring with ridiculous antics.

Two creatures now appeared crawling on their stomachs. One was evidently supposed to be a Sahib and the other his *shikari*. They would be accompanied by a boy dressed up as an uncontrollable dog of a very mixed breed. The shikari saw the ibex and pressed the Sahib down flat on the ground. He scanned it for some two or three minutes through his binoculars which evidently were not strong enough as he borrowed a clarinet from one of the band and gazing through it seemed more satisfied. He informed his Sahib by gestures of the presence of the ibex and a long altercation took place regarding its size and the easiest way of approach to the animal which was contentedly grazing three or four paces away.

The Sahib then wriggled over the ground till he was within range of the ibex – two inches at most – took a careful aim and fired his rifle. The ibex scampered off unhurt to watch further operations from a safe distance, and the Sahib vented his feelings at missing such an easy shot by kicking the dog.

Another stalk followed and this time the Sahib made no mistake with the rifle held hard against the ibex's heart. The ibex collapsed with a scream and was promptly torn to pieces by the comic dog; the Sahib was exultant, the shikari flattered and received his customary reward; and so ended the shooting expedition.

The dance finished, we would thank the Indian Officers and ride or walk home – a little procession of swinging hurricane lamps wending its way up the hill.

And as I smoked a last pipe before turning in, a great satisfaction at life came over me and I thought how kind Fate had been to me in shaping my destiny in this remote part of the world.

I remember the long hard patrols I did with the Scouts when the spirit of the hills and established unwritten laws of mountaincraft welded a common bond between me and the men which brought me very near to them.

My first patrol still sticks in my memory.

We left Gilgit at the crack of dawn and marched all day some twenty-five miles up the Kargah Valley to a pleasant little camp in the pine trees where two clear mountain torrents met and mingled. The next day we were on the move early and followed a steep path bordered by wild roses. The pine belt ended and was replaced by silver birch and mountain ash. Up and up to rolling alpine meadows, covered with gentians, edelweiss and other mountain flowers. Shepherd lads could be heard singing as they grazed their flocks on the luscious pastures, the sky was clear blue, larks whistled in the virgin air. It was most exhilarating.

But at about 14,000 feet the effects of the altitude and the thinness of the air caught me. Breathing became difficult, my heart thumped like a hammer, and every step was an effort. An old shepherd gave me a gourd of milk which was like nectar but made me feel sick afterwards.

We had now left the meadows and were crossing huge boulders which covered the last few miles to the top of the Dugo Harai Pass. It was as if some giant had picked up a handful of boulders and rocks and hurled them together as a barrier against would-be crossers of the divide. We jumped from rock to rock, on and on, it seemed interminable. I really felt I wanted to lie down and die but it was the knowledge that this was a test in the eyes of the Scouts which kept me going.

"I would not take off my equipment, I would not rest, I would not drink water, I would reach the top of the Pass," those were the thoughts flashing through my brain. Gone was the scenery, gone the romance and glamour; only the knife-shaped ridge which marked the summit and goal was left. With a last final effort I reached it and sank down on a rock. But all at once the majestic awe inspiring panorama of country flung out before me made me jump up, and just gaze and gaze.

Our height was over 16,000 feet, and the purple hills in the foreground merged into the snow-covered mountains of the Greater Himalayas crowned in the background by the jagged peaks of the Karakorams: Nanga Parbat 26,600 feet, Haramosh 24,270 feet, Rakaposhi 25,550 feet and, hundreds of miles away, an immense peak which seemed to be floating in air and which I think was K2. I no longer felt tired; I felt uplifted and I gave a silent prayer to the Great Architect from whose hand these mighty works had sprung.

As a tribute to Him, I scribbled a few lines of my favourite psalm on a message form.

"I, to the hills will lift mine eyes,"

"From whence doth come mine aid." This I tied up in a piece of silver birch bark, and added my name, the date, time, and names of the men in the patrol on it. We buried it under some stones and threw a cairn up on the top.

I wonder if any traveller will ever find it reposing there.

I then ate a hearty lunch of chupatti, a cold chicken leg, and some dried apricots and walnuts before we went on our way down treacherous rock and shale slopes to the Singal Nullah leading to Punial.

I never again felt lassitude or sickness at altitudes – even at twenty thousand feet I felt perfectly all right except for a little loss of breath. From that day on Dugo Harai onwards, I knew that I had gained the real respect and admiration of the Scouts and they accepted me as one who was capable of mountaincraft equal to their own.

I did many patrols covering every corner of the Sub-division, Chilas, and the north of Hunza, and I could write pages about the adventures and experiences found on them; but here I must confine myself to the more memorable ones.

I remember the day we were marching from Haramosh to Gilgit. It's a very hot road through barren desert all the way so we set off early in the morning to escape the midday heat. But at the junction of the Indus and Gilgit River we spotted a herd of oorial and spent an unsuccessful three hours stalking it. In was noon by the time we were on our way again and the heat was like a blast furnace. There was not a spot of shade anywhere and by the time we reached Chamogarh we were at our last gasp. We tore off our equipment and plunged into the mountain torrent which tumbles down from the hills there, drinking sparingly, however, as the water was icy cold. There was no necessity to warn these lads about drinking large quantities of cold water, as one has to do with other troops. It was second nature to them. Clean and refreshed we continued the journey in the cool of the evening.

And I remember the day we crossed over the Jutial Pass back to Gilgit from Pahote. It started raining buckets in the middle of the morning when we had reached about twelve thousand feet. It was blinding rain, blowing straight into our faces, but I decided not to turn back. Our speed was naturally slowed down and we crossed the summit in a fury of sleet and snow in the late afternoon – much too late to be out in the mountains in wild weather. It was dark by the time we had completed the steep descent to the valley. The journey down the valley to where it debouches at Gilgit proper was a nightmare. The men did not want to attempt it but we were all soaked to the skin and I knew that if we camped down for the night the less hardy would catch pneumonia; so we pushed on. The rain had loosened the hillsides with the result that frequent avalanches of rock and heavy stones came crashing down on the path with a noise like thunder. It was pitch black and we could not see the falling rocks to avoid them. We just had to trust in Allah. The track crossed the stream about six times – normally an easy task over stepping stones or shallow fords. But the little mountain burn was a raging torrent now, sweeping boulders and uprooted trees down to the main river. At each ford I made the stronger lads take off all their equipment and form a human chain across the torrent. The others then took off their heavy equipment and this was passed across in relays. Inevitably one or two men and their loads would be swept away but they would be caught up and rescued by the human chain. Not one rifle or bandolier fell in the water.

Eventually our somewhat weary band reached Gilgit, soaked to the skin, but in high spirits at a task well accomplished without the loss of a single life or article of equipment. I inspected the patrol, saw them into their lines, and wended my weary way home. It was 2 am. All day I had been looking forward to a good supper washed down by a frothy tankard of beer when I reached home. It was ready. Scotch broth, roast chicken, fried potato chips, toast and butter and beer; but on sitting down I sudden realized I was too tired to eat: I hadn't realized this whilst on the move. So I had a good hot bath and went to bed. I was up at 6 am and on parade at 7 o'clock feeling wonderfully refreshed. I gave the men who had been with me a holiday to dry their clothes and clean their uniform and equipment: they had no Shawar Din to do it for them.

It is a very pleasant sensation to get back from a long patrol, discard your filthy, sweaty, clothes, steam in a hot bath, shave, put on clean clothes, and relax in an armchair to ponder over the completed task.

Periodical tours were carried out by Officers to the various outposts. These were performed on horseback with baggage ponies for the kit: much more civilized than patrolling. I did my share of touring, to the very ends of the Agency in every direction, for the sheer love of breaking new country and meeting new people.

I remember visiting Kalamdarchi in December. It was so cold that after fording the Hunza River the ponies' tails froze as stiff as iron spikes. Some eggs we had brought from lower down froze, everything liquid was frozen as hard as iron. The Hunza platoon stationed there gave me a right royal welcome and the post was in first class order.

I took a patrol out and we explored the Mintaka and Killik Passes which lead from Hunza into Chinese Turkestan (Sinkiang). I saw a herd of ibex and I stalked one old patriarch with a big head. Just as I was taking aim an avalanche came down between me and him and when it had cleared the herd had disappeared. Jemedar Shah Khan shot this head later and I think it measured about 46 inches. It was bitterly cold, well below freezing, but the rest of the patrol had lit a birch fire in the valley in which I thawed out after the descent. We spent the night at the sheep fold at Murkushi.

The next day I walked down to Misgar, probably the most remote Post and Telegraph Office in the world, to meet Colonel Cobb, the Political Agent, accompanied by Prince Jamal Khan, heir apparent (now Mir) of Hunza who had pitched camp there. As I approached it was a moving sight to see a little Union Jack bravely flying in the middle of this camp in High Asia. I felt a strange emotion and pride at belonging to a race whose just arm of power reached the remotest places in the world. Colonel Cobb welcomed me in his customary hospitable way, and insisted that we should join forces and continue the tour together. We did, and I thoroughly enjoyed it.

One night a pack of marauding wolves broke into the camp and stampeded the ponies. Before we finally managed to drive the wolves away, one pony was killed outright and another died later after striking its head on a wooden beam in a frenzied effort to escape.

I toured to Gupis with its little "Foreign Legion" fort and inspected the garrison. On one occasion I marched from Gupis up to Yasin and on to the Darkot Pass where Hayward was murdered. On another occasion I traversed Kuh Ghizr to the Shandur Pass leading into Chitral, and caught my share of brown trout from the lochs, streams, and rivers of this District. The upper reaches of the Kuh Ghizr probably contain some of the best trout fishing in the world and Colonel Cobb actually landed a monster which turned the scale at 10 lbs.

Kuh Ghizr is beautiful country in the summer as the valley broadens out into rolling green pastures and the Gilgit river meanders along slowly like the Jhelum at Srinagar. But in winter it is fiendishly cold and snow-bound.

To the south I toured to the extremities of Chilas but of this I shall have more to say later.

I had a passion for leaving no place in the Agency unexplored and I had a map on which I marked out all my treks and patrols in red pencil as soon as completed. I used to pore over this map in the evening, planning new excursions, but it was not always easy to put them into practice, as I was a junior officer then and had to do what I was told, and not what I wished. However, in three years I think I covered more of the Agency than others had for a long time.

One notable exception to my record of treks was the northern route along the Hindu Kesh from Kalamdarchi via the Chapursan Valley and Chillinji Pass to Ishkoman. It is far from easy, but if ever I go back to Gilgit it will be the first trek I undertake.

Why did I interest myself so much in the Gilgit Scouts and the Gilgit Agency? Why did I use personal initiative in improving the Scouts and creating an impression and atmosphere about myself? Why did I explore the Agency to become acquainted with every district, every personality, every language and custom? Was it just to satisfy a personal whim or was there more to it than that?

I had a strange notion that I would some day become Commandant of the Scouts; and I saw then that the changing conditions of the outside world would for the first time be really felt in Gilgit; and I appreciated that victory over Germany and Japan would not result in the brave new world of peace between the nations, as we were being led to expect. A leader would be required in Gilgit who could cope with such eventualities and I argued to myself that, although there were others who were capable of being the leader, there was no reason at all why I should not be the one.

I had lost my heart to the country, I had found the place I had been searching for, and where I was really happy. I am not a hero worshipper but a man I have always admired as really great is T.E. Lawrence. If circumstances demanded it, I felt I could do in Gilgit what that famous leader had done in Arabia. As will be seen later, I very nearly succeeded but at the critical moment, at the approach of the climax when years of endeavour and preparation were about to be put to the test, which I was supremely confident would be successful, I was checked; but I was so sure of ultimate victory that I did not feel frustrated but merely rather sorry for those who would have benefited from it.

Some men have a weakness for women, some have a weakness for drink and other so-called vices. In Gilgit I became a confirmed polo addict. The game held an attraction for me which would not be denied and at every opportunity and on every occasion I played polo. To quote Kipling:
"Four things greater than all things are"
"Women, and horses, and power, and war." Counting out women who, anyway, only lead a man to endless complications and burnt fingers, the other three symbolize Gilgit polo.

There is the interest of buying, selling and training horses; the respect in which a polo player is held in the Agency gives the power; and inter-tribal polo in the knock-out competition at the annual Gathering of the Clans is only tribal war without lethal weapons.

I always had a good stable of ponies, thoroughbred stallions from Badakshan; the great horse breeding province of northern Afghanistan.

There was the handsome gentlemanly Rufus, well mannered, handy, who could turn on the proverbial plate.

Wicked little Nonsense with the white blaze, who kicked and bit strangers, and knocked his loose box to bits in fits of temper. A good polo pony he was for all that, but rather on the slow side. I liked Nonsense, as he was very coy and showy and attracted much attention.

The slow steady Quicksilver, perfect for touring and capable of great endurance but much too sober for my temperament and little use for polo.

And Sultan, the dangerous black devil on whom nobody else would ride owing to his reputation for falling and being uncontrollable, but the fastest pony in the Agency at that time. I had only one accident on Sultan, which I created on purpose to make him more careful. I rode him straight at the wall of the polo ground. If he had been sensible he would have swerved away at the last moment as all good ponies do, but Sultan continued on his way and hit the wall head-on with the most terrific wallop.

I jumped clear but was not quick enough and the next thing I knew was the semiconscious Sultan being levered off the top of me with polo sticks. From then on the pony was perfectly under control, having paid the price of such rashness.

Latterly Samarkand, Tadjik, and Roshan joined the stable but we shall hear more of them later.

I found I got a supreme emotional satisfaction from polo, and that it was the only way to prevent the mind from becoming warped and unnatural after a prolonged stay in Gilgit without a break among the fleshpots of Srinagar. Before polo, when the bands were playing the warning tunes, I always felt excited and tense – even before ordinary games. But after polo an intense sense of satisfaction came over me and I felt refreshed both physically and mentally.

Colonel Cobb was a very keen player and taught me the rudiments of the game when I started. He was a hard taskmaster and on occasions annoyed me much, but in the long run I appreciated his methods and shall ever be grateful to him.

I remember when Chilas beat Hunza in the first round of the polo tournament at the Gathering of the Clans at Gilgit. When I took over as Assistant Political Agent Chilas, I found little interest in the game as they had never survived the first round of the tournament and had always been hopelessly beaten. I therefore collected the best players of the Sub-agency – all Sonewals needless to say – and with the help of the Raja Orderly, Gushpur Muzaffar-ud-Din Shah of Nagir, himself a good average player, we trained up the Chilas team. We encouraged them in every way, gave them extra rations for their ponies, lent them ponies, cursed and abused them, praised them occasionally. The result was that we had a very fair team ready for the tournament.

In the first round we were drawn against Hunza. The game started at a great pace with the better mounted Hunzawals out to force a quick decision. They had mostly partaken of copious draughts of *arak* before the game, which added extra dash and zeal to their play. I decided to play a waiting game and allow the Hunza ponies to tire and the drink to dry out of the players. I therefore concentrated on keeping the Chilas team from becoming disconcerted at this onslaught and on merely stemming the attack. Time and time again our back playing on Nonsense made some wonderful clears. At the end of the first chukka we were losing by two goals. But my plan proved correct and in the second chukka we gradually drew equal; then a goal to Hunza and a goal to us and it was 7 all. The excitement had reached fever pitch. The Hunza supporters, with visions of being beaten by the much despised Chilasis, were almost frantic at the prospect of disgrace.

The rest of the Agency were backing Chilas, with the human characteristic of sympathy for the under-dog and in the hope of seeing proud Hunza humbled. The excitement spread to the players and play become very rough and disputes were many. I followed up a hit ahead, the Hunza back missed his clear, and I made no mistake with a long straight shot from about 150 yards. I knew we had won then. I hit a short *tambuk*, our number 3 was up, and went straight through the defence at full speed on the fast Sultan to score a perfect goal just as the bugle went for time. We were almost mobbed as we left the field. The Chilas polo team had risen from a nonentity to a serious competitor. We were well beaten by Yasin in the semi-final but I was contented with what we had achieved and the happiness and pride it gave the Sub-agency did my heart good.

I had, later on in my career, further successes at polo. For example: in 1947 I captained a Scout team in the tournament and in the first round we came up against the unpopular but formidable Gilgit Sub-division side.

It was a hard fought game, rough and exciting with every dirty tactic and foul being used by both sides. In the second chukka I ordered the Scouts to play a clean game for fifteen minutes and we soon drew into the lead. With ten minutes to go, I caught the ball in my hand some twenty-five yards in our own half. I was playing on the Mir of Nagir's speedy Punjabi stallion called Gulmarg. Two Gilgitis attempted to pull me from the saddle and it gave me great delight to hand them off in the face in true rugger fashion. I then urged Gulmarg to full speed, outstripped the remaining opponents and galloped through the goal posts to complete the necessary quota of nine goals before full time. I have never heard such continuous cheering as the Scout supporters put up. Hats and coats were thrown in the air, they invaded the pitch and almost tore us apart with hand shaking and back slapping.

In the semi-final we beat Kuh Ghizr in a hard but colourless game, and in the final we went down fighting to the invincible Punialis. It was quite an achievement to reach the final as we were an unco-ordinated team; yet for me it was not to be compared with the day when Chilas beat Hunza!

I had my full share of shooting in the Agency. I shall never forget the first *markhor* I shot. It was on my birthday in December. I had camped in the snow at about 8,000 feet in the Dhanyor Nullah. It snowed all night, which was good as it drove the herd we were stalking down low. I rose at dawn from my sleeping bag, collected my rifle and binoculars and climbed onto a small ridge with the *shikari*. It was bitterly cold. Just as first light was streaking the hillside, I heard some stones clatter down over the cliff on the far side of the valley. We both froze to the ground. The herd of *markhor* was there. When it was light enough to see, I picked the herd up in the binoculars. I took the telescope and searched the animals for the old patriarch with the big head of spiralling horns which I had determined to get. He was there all right, standing in the middle of a group of females looking straight at me.

"*Maro, Maro,* Shoot, Shoot!" whispered the *shikari*.

The target seemed very far away and difficult to see in the half light. I set the sights at 350 yards, loaded, half knelt behind a big rock and took aim. My head and left eye were bandaged owing to a recent polo accident, and I had great difficulty in getting the sights aligned on the vulnerable shoulder. I pressed the trigger. The muzzle flashed and a whiff of cordite blew back into my nostrils.

"*Laggaya, laggaya,* he's hit, he's hit!" shouted the *shikari,* jumping up in great excitement.

I did not think so. I saw the herd moving slowly up the hillside, with bewildered looks in our direction. My victim moved with them. I reloaded, aimed, and fired again.

"*Matkaro, matkaro,* don't, don't," shouted the *shikari*.

The old *markhor* continued walking. I fired again. The herd went off like a flash over the brow of the hill. The old *markhor* halted in his tracks.

"Come on!"

We scrambled down to the valley, dived into the icy cold stream, and as we reached the bottom of the cliff on the far side there was a minor avalanche of stones on our heads and a huge black shape shot over the edge and landed with a sickening thump five yards from where we were standing. It was the big head! The *shikari* and my orderly, who had arrived on the scene by then, rushed up to it, and cut its throat with a murmur of "*Bismillah Rahman ur Rahim,* in the name of God, the all Compassionate, the all Merciful," as is enjoined in the Holy Quran for making meat lawful to eat. I gazed at the old warrior; I felt no pity for him; rather I felt supremely delighted and thought to myself, "You are the wiliest and most cunning animal in the world. Your instincts of self-preservation are greater than any other of the mountain fauna. I challenged you, the mere human against the cleverest animal of the Himalayas; the odds were all on you, it was a fair duel, but I have won."

I examined the carcass. It was hit twice in the shoulder and once through the back. It was as big as a small pony and covered with shaggy hair. The orderly made a fire, the *shikari* cut out the liver and heart which we grilled on a stick whilst our clothes, frozen stiff from the water, gradually thawed out. We cut off the head and measured it. It measured 49 inches along the curve. We cut haunches of meat and tied them up in the skin. We carefully removed the little bag of snake bite antidote from the belly and placed it in a cigarette tin. *Markhor* eat snakes, hence the name. *Maris* the Persian for snake and *khor* means eater. From the masticated snake a secretion accumulates in a small bag in the intestines of the animal. This secretion, taken after a snake bite will render the victim immune from ill effects.

We then struck camp and trudged homeward. It was impossible to reach Gilgit that night so in the evening I pitched camp in the rocky bed of the valley. Just after tea the *shikari* spotted another herd. After an hour's stalk I dropped another fine specimen, though slightly smaller than the bag of the morning. We sat round the camp fire late that night, I smoking my pipe under the clear starry sky feeling well contented, the *shikari* telling stories of the feats of the Sahibs on shikar in the good old days and how degenerate the present generation was in comparison. At last I turned in and slept soundly. It has been a red-letter birthday.

I have had many a good day's shooting since; after ibex when they leave their glacier homes in the spring to eat the shoots of young grass on the lower slopes; frantic chases after oorial in the low hills in the vicinity of Gilgit proper; dangerous stalks after man-killing red bear near Chalt in Nagir; days on the Pamirs after *Ovis Poli* (Marco Polo's sheep); long waits in hides for snow and spotted leopard. I could write pages on my big game experiences in Gilgit.

I remember the small game shooting. Glorious frosty mornings with that first class shot and sportsman, Colonel Bacon, when the sporting little *chikor* shot over the butts like bullets from rifles; the swing, the crack of the gun, and the thrill of satisfaction as a little ball of feathers dropped from the sky and landed with a tell-tale plump on the ground. I revived the old custom in Chilas of arranging a two-day *chikor* shoot at Gor to which all the Gilgit folk were invited. We shot all day for two days and bagged about 140 *chikor,* we revelled all night in an outburst of spirit and thoroughly enjoyed ourselves.

I remember soft autumn afternoons in the gardens below Gilgit, when Colonel Cobb and I would walk up woodcock. The trees were a russet brown and the country a glorious mass of colour. The smoke from bonfires would fill the mellow air and the farmers were busy tilling their fields before the hard winter set in. It always brought to mind Shelley's *Ode to Autumn* which seemed written for Gilgit alone.

And the evenings out on the duck *jheel* at Sonekote, sitting in the little stone butt with my Spaniel at my feet and my pipe smoking well. As the sun sank behind the purple hills, a flight would come winging in to their fate. Bang, bang! Usually one and sometimes two mallard or teal would splash on the water to be retrieved to hand by Sammy. He would shake himself all over me and wait for the next flight. If I missed, he would give me a reproachful look with his sad Spaniel eyes. Presently it would be too dark to see, so I would mount my pony and jog back home through the gathering twilight. Fires twinkled at each little homestead on the way and the savour of evening meals cooking would fill the air; a short cut through the Scout Lines and the friendly shout from a sepoy, "What luck, Sahib?" and then, "*Shabash* (well done)!" or, "Never mind, Sahib, it's not a good evening for duck flighting."

During the war years lack of cartridges made shooting impossible, so Colonel Cobb started falconry. It was thrilling sport. On a crisp winter morning, we would gather with our goshawks and take up positions on some high promontory. The *chikor* could be driven below us. As they approached a hawk would be cast from the gauntleted right hand. It would streak downwards like a thunderbolt through the air, the stoop, the puff of feathers, and the hawk and its victim would drop to the ground. A good hawk would kill five or six *chikor* in a drive and would be rewarded by being allowed to eat the heads. I once saw a goshawk kill a heron at Yasin. As the hawk stopped, the heron turned on its back and attempted to impale its assailant on its long beak. But the hawk with a clever twist avoided the danger and struck the heron a killing blow on the neck. I wore the head crest of that heron for a long time in my *koi*.

Many a pleasant evening I had in the Kargah Valley after the brown trout. The setting was peaceful, the mountain stream of clear water bubbling down over the rocks and eddying back into large pools. High mountains towered on either side but they did not give the impression of confinement, but rather of friendly guardians. The trout were not big but fought well. It was thrilling when the trout took the fly, the strike, the scream of the reel, the skilful pressure and manoeuvring to keep the fish out of the fast water; then the flick of the landing net and a nice trout of just over a pound would be on the bank. Tea from a thermos and scones with butter and honey, a little more fishing and then the ride home with a heavy creel on the shoulder.

As the road swings into the Gilgit Valley there is spread before you a view which I think is one of the most impressive in the Agency. To the left the pyramid peak of Dubani rises from Bagrote like a cold silent sentinel clad in white robes. From her slopes a black ridge leads off and descends gradually to the river. Beyond this, and level as far as the eye can reach, stretches the mighty Haramosh Range, pale white in divorce from the evening sun. And in the centre is Haramosh Peak, rising into the fading sky like a saffron beacon, aloof and proud in her privilege of alone holding the last rays of the setting sun.

Gradually the sun fades, even from her, and one by one the stars appear in the sky. Slowly the moon rises over Minawar and bathes the country in a ghostly light. Many times I have seen this transformation, and each time it was more beautiful.

"If there be a paradise on earth, this is it," as Firdos, the Persian Poet, wrote.

In September 1945 I loaded up my caravan and took the four days' march to Chilas where I was to take over from Peter Inchbald as Assistant Political Agent.

Peter met me at the gate of "Journey's End" to the strains of the local band which played the customary welcome tune. The Indian Officers of the Scouts, the local levy corps, the Chilas headmen, the shopkeepers, and other notables were lined up to meet me. I knew most of them already so there was no necessity for introductions. I passed along the line, shook hands and spoke a few words with each. The shopkeepers offered tribute of sums of silver rupees tied up in silk handkerchiefs which it is custom to touch and remit. They all seemed genuinely pleased to see me, though the blinding heat was not conducive to outbursts of enthusiasm.

Formalities completed, we entered the shade of the bungalow and refreshed ourselves with long cold drinks. We decided that it was impossible to undertake the change over under such conditions – a temperature of 100 in the shade was being radiated off the barren countryside like furnace heat, beastly little flies which left a festering sore bit one at frequent intervals, and the nights were full of malaria-carrying mosquitoes; so the following morning we rode out of Chilas before dawn and travelled up the long steep ascent to the hill station of Babusar, some twenty-one miles from Chilas at a height of about 10,000 feet and lying about seven miles below the summit of the Babusar Pass.

Each village we passed through turned out in force to meet me with presents of fruit and eggs. The last half mile to Babusar village is up a very steep hill, and as we approached I could see a large crowd of people assembled on the top of this promontory and hear the strains of at least two bands playing the welcome tune. It turned out that nearly all the headmen of the Sub-agency had left their grazing grounds and had come to Babusar to meet me. As we approached the tempo of the bands increased, modern rifles, shot-guns and matchlocks were fired in the air, and a wild cheer rose from the huge crowd. I shook hands with the two Indian Officers of the Scout Detachment, and was then presented to the headmen by Muzaffar, the Raja Orderly. I knew only a few as most of them came from the more remote reaches of the side nullahs. There was nothing I did not know about them after two or three months however.

We then walked the last half mile to the bungalow. The Scouts in their Sunday best lined the route and saluted as I passed them; we were preceded by the bands and a troupe of dancing boys who twisted and whirled in long black embroidered skirts and bodices with wide sleeves; behind us came the vast crowd, still yelling and cheering and making free with rifles.

Babusar bungalow is an artistic little wooden chalet set in the middle of a grass meadow. It is surrounded by a low stone wall. It has a small sitting room, a dining room, and two bedrooms – all very snug and compact. It was very cold and a bitter wind was blowing down from the pass so we were glad to dismiss the multitudes and settle down before a roaring log fire to tea, of toast and marmalade, and home made cakes. It had been a moving welcome – a primitive spontaneous welcome which touched my heart and I knew that I would be happy in Chilas.

The handing and taking over completed, Peter left for Kashmir and I was King of Chilas.

The first few weeks were quite a revelation. The interim period had been marked by an unprecedented crime wave which seemed likely to continue. Every day, at least one if not two murders were reported. The reason was obvious. The Chilasis considered this an appropriate moment to settle old scores when a venal Council of Elders could easily be paid to persuade the green and inexperienced new Assistant Political Agent that the accused was not guilty.

Many of these murders were committed by hired gunmen, fugitives from the law who had made their headquarters in the tribal territories but kept close contact with the Sub-agency and were always prepared to do "jobs of work" for a consideration.

However, many murders were also committed by bona fide Chilasis, most of whom were arrested by the levies and flung into jail. The jail was full to overflowing with pending cases.

The next difficulty was the hundreds of civil suits lodged with me after taking over. All were old cases and had been settled by previous A.P.A.s, but the losers had opened them again in the hope that I, in my ignorance, might overlook former decisions and award a completely new judgement.

Finally, I discovered the bazaar to be completely empty. The shopkeepers had failed to import stocks of cloth, kerosene oil, and salt owing to difficulty over licences. The Chilasis were not bringing in their newly harvested supplies of wheat, maize, and *ghi* (clarified butter) as there was nothing to barter them for or more likely because they would have to sell them in the bazaar at the controlled rates which had been introduced to keep prices down. On the other hand if they kept their stocks till the following spring they would be able to smuggle them out into Kashmir and the North West Frontier Province where owing to short supplies there was a thriving black market, which could be purchased at fantastically high prices and sold at even higher.

The immediate outlook was therefore pretty grim and to crown all, two self confessed murderers in an important case cut their way out of the Babusar lock-up one night when the Scout sentry was asleep or absent, and absconded to tribal territory.

This, then, was the rather alarming position when I received news that Lieutenant Colonel Roger N. Bacon, OBE, and his wife, and two daughters had left Abbottabad for Gilgit to take over as Political Agent and were due to arrive at Babusar in a few days.

On a bleak September morning I gathered my entourage and rode up to the top of the Babusar Pass. The weather was foul on the top. A howling gale of wind blew alternate gusts of sleet and snow. About the appointed time the Colonel rode into sight through the blinding gale, with the easy seat and light hands of a born horseman.

He dismounted and I walked forward and shook hands with him. He was a short, stocky, cheerful man, who obviously took life as it came as he remained quite unconcerned in that howling blizzard. I introduced him to the Raja Orderly and to the other notables of my retinue and he chatted to them easily and naturally. I knew then that the Gilgit Agency would be happy and contented under him.

Presently Mrs Bacon and the two little girls, Frances and Laura, arrived accompanied by a cavalcade of orderlies and servants. The girls were slightly bewildered, Mrs Bacon friendly, cheerful, and confident. Cups of hot coffee behind a large boulder broke the ice of formal introductions and by the time we started the descent it seemed as though it was a reunion rather than a first meeting. The weather cleared, the sun came out and we were a happy party as we walked down over the springy turf. The girls' spirits brightened after the nightmare morning and soon they were chasing each other through the pine woods and rolling and falling down the slopes with cries of pleasure. The Colonel, to the delight of the Chilasis, took his .22 rifle and stalked marmots which screamed abuse at us from the rocks.

I accompanied the Bacons as far as Jaglote. The Colonel, I discovered, was a remarkable man. With only my sketchy outline of conditions in the Sub-agency where he had never previously served, he appreciated the situation immediately and gave shrewd and astute observations and suggestions on how to get the situation under control. His success in getting the utmost out of his juniors lay in his ability to pass on instructions in the form of suggestions and not as dictatorial orders; and yet they were always carried out. He would enter into the spirit of any scheme with great enthusiasm and discuss it in a matter of fact manner for hours until it was reduced to the simplicity of routine action rather than a major problem. He had great zest for a party, when work was over, and he joined in with a carefree abandon and yet maintained dignity. By the time I left him at Jaglote, I knew I was under a superior officer who could extract the last ounce of work from me, a man to whom it would afford me the greatest satisfaction to give of my very best, and a man to whom I would remain loyal, no matter what the circumstances.

Colonel Bacon often said that if he could live his life over again he would live it as he had lived it. And this, I think, is the true key to his character. Their house was always open to one and all and has an infectiously happy and homely atmosphere. I could never wish to meet a more friendly and happy couple, with such incomparable sympathy and understanding.

I now settled down to the problems of Chilas, and started by selecting my team and creating an atmosphere. Muzaffar, I discovered was an excellent assistant and levy leader. He commanded respect, he was honest, hard working and a shrewd and disinterested advisor.

The Agency Munshi or clerical Superintendent was an encyclopaedia of knowledge on the Sub-agency where he had worked for over twenty years, I believe. There was no case, the history of which he did not know. We formed a good trio and worked as a team all the time.

The first job was to dispose of the criminal cases and determine the destiny of the overcrowded jail. Day after day I held open court under the chinar tree in the garden, and recorded sordid accounts of abduction, rape, sodomy, adultery, seduction, kidnapping and brutal murders. At first I was thoroughly deceived by venerable Councils of Elders who through ill-gotten remuneration invariably returned a verdict of not guilty which I, in my ignorance, accepted. The result was that murders increased. I soon fell wise to their ways, however, and if after careful investigation, I was sure in my own mind that the accused was guilty, I would take steps to see that a verdict to this effect was returned.

The results were amazing. From 1 January 1946, until I handed over charge temporarily at the end of May there had only been one murder which was committed in accordance with local custom, and one attempted murder. I put all parties engaged in blood feuds on heavy security to keep the peace; I called in all unsavoury characters to Chilas and either put them on security backed by sureties of influential headmen; or banished them from the Sub-agency.

I then managed to get a large caravan of salt and kerosene oil up the Kaghan Valley for the Chilas bazaar, and the Assistant Political Agent of Gilgit kindly sent me a consignment of cloth from his quota. I started a grain distribution store in Chilas. Peter Inchbald had already surveyed the crops and flocks of each community and had worked out how much spare there would be after the amounts required for a liberal existence had been deducted. I gave each community a final date by which their spare wheat, maize, and *ghi* must reach the distribution store where full controlled prices would be paid, or else a heavy communal fine would be levied on the offenders. With a few exceptions, there were no defaulters. From the depot, I then issued out allotments to those departments which were dependent on buying in the bazaar for their livelihood, such as the Scouts, Levies, Public Works, Posts and Telegraph and so on. The shopkeepers in Chilas were quite good on the whole but most dishonest. For black marketeering I used to put them in jail by an executive order, and left them there at my pleasure.

Anyone reopening an old civil suit which had been previously decided was heavily fined. New suits, injustices, and grievances I settled as quickly and as fairly as possible, and on the spot when on tour. I had a letter box erected at the front gate, the key of which I kept myself, so that I knew that all petitions would reach me personally. This kept my junior officials up to the mark. About six hundred small civil suits used to be disposed of in the year: the Chilasi loves litigation.

Pending criminal cases completed, the bazaar in order, polo in full swing, there remained now only one problem. There were about thirty Chilasi outlaws and absconders who were wanted for murder. These individuals had their headquarters in tribal territory but frequently returned to the Sub-agency, with the connivance of the headmen, to settle some score on their own account or for others. There could obviously be no law and order so long as these creatures were around so I resolved that they must be brought to justice.

First of all, I issued an edict that anyone found harbouring an outlaw or anyone knowing the whereabouts of an outlaw and failing to report would be heavily punished, and if a headman, would be removed from his appointment. Thereafter Muzaffar and I got down to work, sometimes separately, sometimes with joined forces, and by fair means and foul, raids, forays, bribes, rewards, spies, informers, sometimes brain work, sometimes force of arms, we managed between us to round up about twenty of these customers before the end of May 1946, and we were well on the way towards bringing in the remainder. The trial of such offenders was very summary as nearly all of them confessed and it was merely a matter of establishing their guilt on paper.

I remember how we captured X, wanted for two murders as well as for burglary and housebreaking.

He had slit the throat of a woman one night, from ear to ear, because she had refused to elope with him, and he had shot a rival for the same woman in the back as the latter was prostrate in prayer in a crowded mosque.

I was in my bath one evening when my informer arrived. I threw on a shirt and a pair of slacks. I allowed him to come in. Many people used to come to the bungalow at all hours of the day and night so his arrival caused no comments.

"I have come to report the theft of some sheep from my village," he said, and proceeded to give details.

As soon as my orderly left the room Z whispered, "X is spending the night in A," and then continued his normal conversation. After about an hour, during which I had more visitors, I sent for Muzaffar and the two Indian Officers of the Scouts. I explained the position, gave them my cut and dried plan, listened to suggestions, changed my plan slightly, impressed on them the necessity of secrecy as to our destination, and in half an hour's time a strong fighting patrol of two platoons was ready. There were two sworn enemies of X in jail who had been arrested on a petty crime. I took them with me as guides, with a promise of release if the enterprise was successful.

We left Chilas at 9 pm and marched through a pitch black night; a steep descent of about two thousand feet over an almost sheer cliff face; comparatively easy marching up a main valley with a short halt after two hours for a gulp of water from the icy stream and adjustment of equipment; then on and on. Past a village where the watchdogs barked; a stiff climb over a promontory, a drop back to the valley, methodical walking stride after stride. I thought about many things – poetry, music, future plans for Chilas, my ponies, polo, shooting. Eventually we reached the junction where our route forked left up a narrow side alley. I halted the patrol by sending runners out with whispered words of command. I then made platoon commanders call the roll and check their platoons to ensure that no person or equipment had been lost. When *"sab achcha"* (all's well) had been reported, I moved on again as we were all perspiring hot from the march, and a bitter wind was blowing down from the snow-bound passes. It was midnight. The next part of the march was as difficult as there was no proper track. Accompanied by the guides, I moved up to lead the advance guard. We tripped over boulder-strewn ground, we sank up to the knees in marshes, we forded the ice-cold stream several times, we ascended alarming precipices, we struggled down the far side, climbing, climbing the whole time till we reached the rendezvous about two miles from the village of A.

It was 4 am. The height was about 10,000 feet. We halted in a hollow which gave a little shelter from the piercing wind. I called in the platoon commanders and ran over the final orders. One and a half platoons were to move forward immediately and quietly occupy the high features and exits surrounding the village. A half platoon, a dozen levies and the guides were to remain with me as the force which would enter the village at dawn and carry out a systematic search. I purposely kept fairly strong rifle power with me as it was possible that X might have a gang of desperate outlaws with him, who would prefer to contest the issue rather than being ignominiously led off to jail. The orders completed, I turned to the platoon commanders,

"Any questions? Right, move."

They disappeared in the darkness.

Presently I saw ghostly shapes silently moving away through the night and I knew the plan was under way. First light was about 6.15 am and I had purposely left them a margin of an hour and three quarters to reach their positions. This time margin is the secret of success on such round-ups. As a junior officer, I had been present on many such operations on the frontier and on nearly every occasion a good plan had miscarried through insufficient time being given to platoons to occupy their positions. The result was that some vital link in the chain surrounding the village was not joined before first light, and Fate would always have it that the quarry would choose that particular place to make good his escape. I think the dangerous life led by outlaws breeds in them a sixth sense which unwittingly protects them from danger. Outlaws usually move out from the village, in which they have been spending the night, just before the mullah cries the early morning call to prayer at first light.

I then moved my striking force up quietly to a position about half a mile from the village. The weather now cleared, the stars came out and a hard frost set in. It was indescribably cold as we waited. Sentries posted, the rest of us huddled together, pressed up against one another to catch the heat of each others' bodies, our hands pressed tight between our thighs. Our clothes, which an hour back had been soaked with perspiration, were now frozen stiff against our skin. I dozed off once or twice. At last the rosy fingers of a glorious dawn streaked the eastern sky and as soon as it was light enough to see, I signalled my contingent forward with a wave of the hand. It was all very automatic, despite the fact that any moment we might be fired on from the village. We moved forward in extended line and one section of the Scouts immediately occupied the roof of the highest house in the village to give us covering fire if necessary.

The remainder of us took up tactical positions. I then told the levies to order every man, woman, and child to quit their houses and collect in the square in the middle of the village. By using local levies for this task, rather than Scouts, I prevented panic and the danger of a regrettable incident. I then fired a green Very Light which was the signal to the troops on the surrounding hills that the search had commenced, and that all was going according to plan. Muzaffar then took one half of the village and I the other and with drawn pistols we carried out a systematic search of every building. The filth, dirt, and smell in the hovels were frightful.

Suddenly there was a "tak – doom" – the sound a rifle makes when fired in the mountains – from the hills to the north of the village. Then a Snider squibbed twice from the same direction. Then a Lee-Enfield again and silence. I handed over my share of the searching to Jemedar Shah Khan and moved out into the open. I called a signaller.

"Flash a lamp up there and ask what's going on."

The reply flickered back,

"Have captured X."

"Bring him in."

"OK."

He presently arrived escorted by a NCO and a couple of sepoys. He was a typical Chilasi – medium stature, thin, sharp faced with a straggling beard. I must say he didn't look an almost legendary outlaw but he was our man all right. He was quite undaunted, gave me a cheerful salute, and offered me his hand which I shook as I couldn't help admiring him in a way.

"Well, you've got me at last, Sahib," he said, "but it wasn't a fair fight."

"Why?" I asked.

"In my haste to escape from the village, when I saw you approaching, I forgot to take my reserve bandolier of ammunition. I then discovered that you had surrounded the village with Scouts but I decided to shoot my way out. I made a dash for the hills but the Scouts opened fire on me. I took up a position and replied but it was then that I realized I had left the bandolier behind. I knew it was hopeless to continue the fight with short supplies of ammunition so I surrendered."

I then began questioning regarding the whereabouts of his confederates but I knew it was hopeless. Even third degree would not have broken the honour among thieves so I gave it up.

"All right, you're for it now, laddie. You'd better get some food inside you, as you've got a twenty-four mile march in front of you and a nice hard bed on the cement floor of the Chilas jail at the end."

He grinned.

I snapped a pair of handcuffs on him, attached the chain to a Scout's belt, and he was led off.

The search was now complete with no more to show than X's forgotten bandolier. He later told me to keep it as a souvenir. I did. I then fired two green Very Lights in succession as the signal to the platoons on the surrounding hills to close on the village and carefully search the intervening ground on the way. They eventually arrived with the information that X had been spending the night in this village for at least a week. I allowed the men half an hour to rest and eat their haversack rations. I ate a hard-boiled egg, some dried fruit and walnuts, and smoked a cigarette. It was a bracing morning with the bright sunshine from a blue sky gradually thawing the hard frost of the night.

Before leaving I called the village headman and summarily dismissed him from his appointment for harbouring an outlaw and failing to report the presence of an outlaw in his village.

We marched at 10 am and completed the twenty-four mile journey to Chilas by 5 pm. The men were tired but not excessively. On the last big pull up the cliff face, to the plateau above the settlement, a few of the weaker ones began to straggle and both Muzaffar and I finished the journey with rifles and extra equipment. Looking back on it, it was a good day's work. The plan had worked like precision clockwork and it had been a perfect example of a minor round up or *barampta* as it is called in Waziristan. In twenty hours we had marched about fifty miles over difficult country, climbing from 4,000 feet to 10,000 feet and down again, and had captured a dangerous outlaw who was a menace to law and order.

That night as I sat by the fire smoking my pipe and sipping a well-earned whisky, I knew that I had conquered Chilas. Given the time and facilities I could develop plans projected by previous Assistant Political agents for education, agriculture, forestry, irrigation, social uplift, rural reconstruction and home industries, and so make this backward district into a model Sub-agency. I would add, however, that I could never have done what I did without the assistance of Muzaffar and the wholehearted backing of the Indian Officers and men of the Scouts. Muzaffar was always a tower of strength and a grand companion.

But it was not to be. Through circumstances beyond my control I was transferred in July 1946. I was given a heartfelt farewell by the Chilasis and the Scouts – so moving it was that I had a horrible lump in my throat and almost wept. But as I turned in the saddle on the heights of the Babusar Pass and saluted the Gilgit Agency spread out before me like a map, I knew that I was destined to return some day to this captivating country which would always hold a corner of my heart.

Chapter 2

Return to Gilgit (June to September 1947)

1. Appointed Commandant of the Gilgit Scouts

[In November 1946 Brown was transferred to Waziristan on the North West Frontier, as an officer in the Tochi Scouts. Here he met Jock Mathieson, who was later to serve in Gilgit as his Assistant. In July 1947 Brown found his way back to the Gilgit Scouts, this time as Commandant and in the service of the Maharaja of Jammu & Kashmir, as is related below.]

I reached Peshawar in the early afternoon and after beer and lunch I went to bed. I woke about 6 pm and after a bath and change I felt much refreshed. I decided to have a night out so made my way to the Club and went into the bar. I couldn't believe my eyes when the first person I saw was Colonel Bacon. I thought he was 300 miles away in Gilgit.

"Hullo William, come and have a drink and let's hear your news."

I took a refreshing whisky and soda and sat myself down on a bar stool beside the Colonel.

"Not much news, Sir," I replied, "except that I am on my way to Chitral."

We then chatted about things in general for a bit and as the bar emptied he suddenly turned to me and said,

"Listen to this one, William, but keep it under your hat," and this is the information the Colonel gave me.

"On 1 August this year the entire Gilgit Agency will be handed over to the Maharaja of Kashmir and we shall withdraw entirely. I have just flown from Gilgit to Srinagar to discuss this matter with the Resident and with the Maharaja. As yet I have not approached the matter with the Mirs, Governors, and people, so I cannot give you their reactions but they will all naturally be very sad to see us go. It is unlikely that the Maharaja will employ a British Officer as Political Agent and he will in all probability send up one of his own staff as Governor of the country. The Maharaja, however, is aware of the difficulties which will arise from officering the Scouts with Hindu, or Muslim Officers for that matter as they have never before served under anyone but British Officers. It is therefore probable that he will employ a British Officer as Commandant and possibly one both as second in command and Assistant Political Agent, Chilas. These officers would serve on a private contract until the transition from British to Kashmiri had been effected gradually. The officers would, of course, have to relinquish their commissions and be taken on in an entirely private capacity. They will always be in a very awkward position; they will have no redress for grievances, and at all times they will have to use the utmost diplomacy in dealing with Kashmiri officials.

It will be nothing like the old days and I know that none of the officers at present in the Scouts would ever dream of staying on. In fact I think the Maharaja will have great difficulty in getting British Officers who are prepared to accept this mercenary appointment. I don't suppose you would think of going back as Commandant under these conditions, would you?"

While the Colonel was speaking I was making a rapid mental appreciation of the situation. This news was an incredible revelation. It was monstrous to think that the Gilgit Agency, whose loyalty to the British had never swerved over half a century, should now be flung into the melting pot by handing it over to Kashmir. And the melting pot it would assuredly be, if the Agency was placed at the mercy of the bribery, corruption, malpractices, and inefficiency of Kashmir officialdom, at a time when the State's own position would be extremely doubtful. I wondered at first whether it was possible that a mistake had been made and the Gilgit Agency confused with the Gilgit Sub-division. Or was it sheer ignorance of the strategic position of the Agency which had prompted this step which might quite well lead to a Soviet wedge being driven into the two new imminent Dominions of the British Empire? But this folly was the politicians' concern and not mine. I appreciated that the repercussions would probably involve the Agency in a cataclysm of considerable importance in which a leader would be required if the happy land of Gilgit and its simple folk were to be spared from the horrors of being a pawn between warring nations. All that Gilgit wanted was the peace and security afforded under the Pax Britannica, and the method by which this could have been continued, despite partition, would have been to have made the Gilgit Agency an Agency of the North-West Frontier Province, directly under H.E. the Governor. This would have ensured a continuity in administration, peace, security and unity: unfertile ground for Soviet seed. My duty was obvious. I must return to Gilgit and lead, advise and help the people over the transition period.

So when Colonel Bacon put the question to me I replied, "Yes, I would like to go back, very much, Sir."

"Right William," he said. "When I get back to Srinagar tomorrow I shall put forward a strong recommendation on your behalf as I consider you are the right man for the job and you are fully aware of what you are in for and the difficulties and obstructions you will meet. I think the chances are that H.H. the Maharaja will probably agree, but anyway let's wait and see."

The bar was beginning to fill up again, and many friends had come in, so we switched the conversation to more topical events and had a most convivial night which ended in the "wee small hours".

In the morning I left for Chitral; in less than a month I was back in Peshawar. Whilst busy in this little Northern State forming personal friendship with the Ruler, His Highness the Mehtar, his many relations and other useful personalities, and making a rapid survey of the political situation, I received an urgent wireless message from the Inspector General of the Frontier Corps to reach Peshawar with all possible speed.

I immediately realized that Colonel Bacon had kept his promise and that I was going back to Gilgit. So I packed up all my kit in my yakdans, arranged a caravan with Shawar Din in command, and ordered him to march to Gilgit via the Northern Route over the Shandur Pass. He took the dogs with him, Sammy the Spaniel and Dinah the Yellow Labrador, and he rode the new Badakshani stallion I had just bought, as yet as thin as a rake and with a long tangled coat, but with the makings of a good 'un. I had named him Tadjik. I then bundled a dinner jacket, riding breeches, and a spare shirt into a light canvas bag, made my farewells, and set off south.

I left at 8 pm with Melville Towers, the Sapper, in his four-wheeled-drive station wagon, and used it as far as the foot of the Lowari Pass. It was an exciting journey along a narrow road with hairpin bends and twists overlooking high precipices, dangerous enough by day, doubly so at night.

From roadhead at Ziarat Post, I walked over the Lowari by bright moonlight and reached the Mahsoud Battalion camp at Goojer Post at first light. Here I was welcomed by Colonel North and his cheery Mahsouds from South Waziristan who were building a motor road over the Lowari. I sat down to a welcome breakfast of sweet tea, hard-boiled eggs and chapattis which the officers and men lavished on me in typical Mahsoud fashion.

The Colonel very kindly lent me a lorry and after farewells I was soon speeding through Dir, Malakand, Mardan and Nowshera until at about 3 pm the high rooftops and minarets of the wicked old city of Peshawar came into sight. A normal three-day journey had thus been completed in about nineteen hours.

Beer, lunch, bath and shave, two hours' sleep, a change of clothes (I always have several sets of clothes in Peshawar for such emergencies), and I felt a new man.

I then borrowed a car and reported my presence. I was told to come to office in the morning; so I decided to have a quiet night and read my favourite passages from the *Seven Pillars of Wisdom* till turning in about midnight.

The next morning I duly presented myself at office. The interview was quick.

"Well, Brown, you are flying to Gilgit tomorrow morning to take over the Scouts. I suppose you know that the Gilgit Agency, including the Scouts, is being handed over to His Highness the Maharaja of Kashmir. Here's the terms of service. I suppose you know what you are doing; but rather you than me. Anyway good luck to you, you'll need it. Oh, by the way we're trying to get you a British second in command but I doubt if we'll succeed."

"I'll fix the second in command, Sir," I replied.

I glanced at the terms of service disinterestedly, shook hands and left.

I immediately drove to the telegraph office and dispatched a wire to Jock Mathieson.

"Have appointed you second in command Gilgit Scouts stop presume no objection stop Willie."

I then settled some affairs with the bank, bought some books, and made my way to the Club about lunchtime. There were several parties sitting around the swimming pool. As I approached noses were withdrawn from tankards of beer, words passed, and I knew I was being discussed. I distinctly heard the words "mercenary, madman, bloody adventurer" being flung about and these evidently applied to me. Little did I care, however, still adamant in my resolve to fulfil the mission I had set myself.

I was greeted civilly and was asked to join a party of senior officers. They seemed to regard me with mixed respect and admiration which they glossed over in embarrassment by making futile jokes about my future. When the rounds had completed their course I departed and idled away the rest of the day with books and letter writing.

2. Flight into Gilgit

On Sunday 27 July 1947, I emplaned in the single passenger's cockpit of a small yellow Harvard aircraft at Peshawar landing ground at 6 am. By 6.15 am we were airborne and heading towards the River Indus where we banked left and followed the easy landmark upstream.

It was a glorious morning with a clear blue sky and the barrier mountains of Indus Kohistan on the horizon were tinged with the pink of sunrise. The effect of hurtling through the sky made me feel exultant, excited and supremely satisfied in the knowledge that I was returning to the happy land of Gilgit. But as we reached the foothills, the weather changed and storm clouds could be seen ahead. The plane began to pitch about but the pilot skilfully kept his course. In the Black Mountain area, where the foothills merge into the mountains of Indus Kohistan, there was a dark impenetrable barrier of an electric storm blocking our way. Spurts of lightning zigzagged across the sky in fantastic lines and rain beat against the wind shield of the cockpit. The pilot's voice sounded in my earphones.

"Can't go on, must turn back, can't go on, must turn back, over."

"OK, over."

"Out."

So we returned to Peshawar in rather an anti-climax.

The next day meteorological reports were bad and we did not even attempt the flight. I felt I was being thwarted at the last moment and I had an alarming notion that possibly fate had decreed I should not go.

On Tuesday 29 July, I emplaned again, and as I was strapping myself in and adjusting my parachute, I said to the pilot, "I hope to God we get through today."

"Don't you worry," he replied, "we will," and by the look of determination in his face I knew we would.

At exactly the same place as before, the black barrier loomed up again, but even more fearful this time. The pilot went up close to it, examined it carefully then turned sharply and continued parallel to it, looking for an opening. On seeing a likely one he would attempt to weave the plane through it. Several times he failed and had to turn back sharply with the starboard wing almost clipping the mountains bordering the valley. The plane was pitching about like a leaf in a storm. At last he entered a small gap in the impenetrable barrier and by coaxing, easing, a little to the right, a little to the left, now up slightly, now down, we gradually advanced.

I was thrilled with admiration at this man, pitting his skill against the elements and winning. As I gazed at the back of his head I thought of the intense concentration condensed inside and focussed on the immediate object of getting through. As we debouched into bright sunshine above Jalkote, I realized I had witnessed a supreme piece of artistry by a fine craftsman.

The journey was now uneventful.

The side valleys of Darel and Tangir passed on our port, looking for all the world like Kubla Khan's Xanadu, with luscious pastures, and mighty forests stretching as far as the eye could see.

The Hurban, a few hot looking mud huts clustered round a fort on the banks of the Indus, Thor of many memories, and from there on I knew every twist and turn on the white ribbon road stretching below like a snake.

Chilas, the bazaar, fort "Journey's End", and the new polo ground I had carved out of the hillside in the front of the garden, came and went; the chinar trees bordering the old polo ground flashed by to torrid yet magnificent desert.

Presently we swung past the white mass of Nanga Parbat, her face coyly veiled with wispy-clinging cloud, as though offering a seductive greeting to an old lover. The pilot made no mistake at the confluence of the Indus and Gilgit rivers, as a friend of mine did later with disastrous consequences, but banked left and soon the hills surrounding the Gilgit settlement came in sight. Minawar, Jutial, Dhanyor, and we flashed over the landing ground at about 4,000 feet. Built on a spit of land where the Gilgit and Hunza Rivers meet, and surrounded by cliffs on two sides and mountains on the third, the little six hundred yards runway looked minute from the air.

We coasted up to the Scout lines, gradually descending the while, and then banked very sharply in order to turn in the narrow valley. I thought we were going to turn upside down but the pilot flattened out again and losing height quickly approached the landing ground again. Just as we reached the southern extremity he side-slipped to the left and continued side-slipping until the plane was facing the direction from which it had made the "come in". The altimeter whizzed round madly, for an awful moment I thought we were going to hit the cliff, but the pilot's judgement was quite sound and we made a perfect landing with yards to spare. After covering two thirds of the strip we pulled up and taxied up to the rest house and store rooms which form Gilgit airport.

We unstrapped ourselves and climbed out. The pilot was cool and calm despite the fact that he had just completed one of the most difficult trips in the world under adverse weather conditions.

"By God, you're a wizard right enough," I said.

"I've done worse ones," he replied.

There was a Scout contingent waiting to guard the plane. They broke ranks, ran up to me, saluted, and shook me by the hand. They were genuinely pleased to see me. I conversed with them for a few minutes and by that time ponies had arrived from Gilgit.

I mounted Akbar, the magnificent beast lent by the Mir of Hunza to Colonel Bacon, and slowly cantered along the three mile track to Gilgit. Dismounting to cross the suspension bridge, I entered the bazaar to discover that almost the entire population had lined the streets to meet me. I saw many a familiar face among the crowds as with a wave to this one, a few words to that one, a thrown jest to another, it took a full half hour to reach Agency House.

I threw the reins to a *sais* and was about to climb the steps to the front porch when two little figures came hurtling across the garden towards me. They were Frances and Laura Bacon. They grabbed my arms and shouted in unison,

"We're playing pirates, do come and join us."

I took their hands and told them I must first of all see their Mummy and Daddy and after that I would accept the invitation to join them in the pirates' cave. Shouting with delight they scampered off and I ran up the steps to greet Mrs Bacon who was waiting to welcome me at the door in her usual hospitable fashion.

"Come on in, William, it's good to see you again. Roger is through in the office writing his handing-over notes. Isn't it a pity about the dear old Agency. To think of handing over this house too. Oh, it is too bad, but I am glad that you have decided to come back and keep the flag flying."

We chatted for a bit on general topics and I supplied Peshawar news.

Agency House was in a fever of excitement with everything being packed up. Servants, orderlies, and messengers were hurrying here and there, but the quiet control of Mrs Bacon prevented completed chaos.

Presently I went through to the study which had been stripped to bare essentials, and met the Colonel. The notes were almost completed so he stowed them away in the safe and we returned to the lounge for a drink before lunch. Paul Mainprice, the outgoing Assistant Political Agent Gilgit, and Charles Hamilton who was actually Assistant Political Agent Chilas, but was then officiating as Commandant of the Scouts since the Commandant had already left the Agency, joined us.

Not unnaturally, the main topic of conversation was the folly of handing the Agency over to Kashmir though it was mostly discussed in a jocular vein and no options were expressed then as to the shape of possible repercussions.

I gathered that the programme of events was that on the following day an Anson aircraft would fly from Srinagar to Gilgit via Peshawar, bringing Major-General Scott, CBE, DSO, MC, Chief of Staff of the Jammu & Kashmir State Forces, Brigadier Ghansara Singh, Governor Designate of the Gilgit Agency and Gilgit Wazarat (which is the country between Bunji and the Burzil Pass), and Captain Mohammed Said, of the Jammu & Kashmir States Forces who was to be one of my officers in the Gilgit Scouts. On the following day formal handing and taking over would take place, whilst Mrs Bacon and the children would set off by road for Srinagar. On the next day Colonel Bacon and General Scott would leave by air for Srinagar to report the handing over complete, and Paul Mainprice and Charles Hamilton would leave for down-country by road.

The Assistant Political Agent Gilgit elect or Wazir Wazarat as he was to be designated had already arrived from Astore, where he had been *Tehsildar* and was busy taking over from Mainprice, a tiresome task from Paul's account.

In the afternoon the Indian Officers of the Scouts present in Gilgit came up to Agency House to pay their respects to me.

Subedar Major Mohammed Baber Khan of Nagir: influential.

Subedar Mohammed Azam Khan of Kuh Ghizr: dashing, high spirited and one of the best officers the Scouts have ever produced, but always handicapped through having been born the wrong side of the blanket in a country where this is so significant. Poor Azam had now a permanent limp from a bad polo accident.

Jemedar Mohammed Shah Khan of the royal blood of Hunza: another high spirited individual, a great sportsman and a good friend of mine as we were alike in age and outlook and had more or less grown up together over the last three years.

Jemedar Safiullah Beg of Hunza: a tough steady type who could be relied on always.

Jemedar Fida Ali, the Quarter Master Jemedar: quiet, efficient and completely reliable.

Jemedar Sultan Feroze of Nagir: a direct descendant of the eldest son of Zaffar Zahid and a sophisticated man of the world who had already seen service in the Jammu & Kashmir State Forces.

They were genuinely glad that I was their new Commandant and expressed their loyalty to me in a straightforward manner. I tried as far as possible to evade any reference to the obvious question at that stage, but they indirectly made it clear how they despised and hated Kashmir and everything connected with it, how happy and contented they had been under the British Rule, and how they considered they had been betrayed by the British in the unconditional handing over of their country to Kashmir.

I kept Baber behind when the others left, and had a straight talk with him. He and I had never been the best of friends and had had many differences of opinion on Scout and political matters. I therefore told him straight that we had a difficult time ahead of us and the only way to succeed was for both of us to bury the hatchet and start afresh in friendship and co-operation. He agreed and we reached an understanding. He, as was his duty, informed me that the discipline of the Scouts had deteriorated to a dangerously low level while I had been away and he advised me to tackle this problem immediately otherwise there would be a regrettable incident; and after fifteen minutes in the Lines next day, I knew his information was not exaggerated.

Baber then put up a number of demands which the Scouts wished from the Kashmir Government; otherwise they would refuse to serve further. I told him that unless he withdrew the last part of his statement I would have nothing whatsoever to do with these demands, as I refused to have a pistol pointed at my head. He agreed.

I scanned through the list. The requests (as I called them) were with regard to the betterment of conditions of service. Some were reasonable and some were utter nonsense.

But the important thing was that it was obvious that the Scouts were endeavouring to get as much as they possibly could out of the Kashmir Government. Now, if at that period the Scouts had intended to revolt in three months time against the Kashmir regime, it is most unlikely that they would have submitted these requests, most of which were in connection with long term benefits such as pensions and gratuities. This, therefore, supports my theory that the revolt in Gilgit was entirely due to the Maharaja of Kashmir's accession to India, and if he had remained independent or had acceded to Pakistan the status quo would have been maintained.

I, therefore, told Baber that on the following day I would arrange an open Durbar for the Indian Officers, at which General Scott would be present, and the requests could be discussed, the more reasonable of which I would support and the foolish ones I would oppose. We parted on the best of terms.

Return to Gilgit (June to September 1947) 55

The next announcement was that the Rajas had arrived.

I decided a collective interview would be the best thing, as the conversation could be diverted into normal channels and kept off politics which I had no desire to hear at that stage; I was now well aware of how their set pieces would run.

They entered one by one.

First came Punial, tall, thin, sharp featured with long moustaches covering the upper lip, remarkably fit for his age, the only sign of which was a grizzling round the temples. He was a clever man, probably the cleverest in the Agency, and his advice, if given, was always sound. He gave me a wry smile, full of meaning, shook hands, and paid the usual greeting courtesies. I often wished I could have mind-read behind those moustaches as I am sure the result would have been quite interesting. He was playing on a good wicket now after the fealty his forefathers had always shown to Kashmir.

Next came Gupis, Governor of Kuh Ghizr, heavily built, strong as an ox, and with round placid features, not over blessed with brains, but of a kindly cheerful disposition and always an especial friend of mine. He showed great pleasure at seeing me and later that evening presented me with a pony, a little roan stallion with a cream coloured mane and tail. I named it Roshan in memory of many happy times the Raja and I had had together fishing in the Roshan Valley near Gupis.

Then came Ishkoman, a member of the Khushwaqt family, closely related to the ruling family in Chitral. Ishkoman found life was best taken easily and nothing could shake him out of his normal steady self. He was inactive, with the result that his District was happy and contented.

Lastly came the magnificent Mahboob, Raja of Yasin, Beau Brummell of Central Asia, the pleasantest man I have ever met. He came swaggering in with his usual devil-may-care attitude, greeted me warmly and sat down. Mahboob has had a colourful history. He was the second son of Mir Sikander Khan of Nagir. His elder brother, Mohammed Ali, predeceased his father, but unfortunately for Mahboob, Mohammed Ali's wife had just borne a son, Shaukat Ali, who was therefore the rightful heir to the Mirship when Sikander Khan died. So Mahboob just missed becoming Mir by the skin of his teeth, and one couldn't help feeling sorry for him at the cruel twist of fortune. Little daunted, however, he became Subedar Major of the Scouts and on retiral was made Governor of Yasin, to recompense him, some say, for his ill luck at not becoming Mir of Nagir; others, however, said that the appointment was to keep him away from Nagir and the temptation of liquidating the as yet childless Shaukat. The same argued that a more befitting place would have been Hari Parbat prison or exile in Madras; but whatever way of it Mahboob was a colourful, pleasant personality who enjoyed life to the full.

I chatted to the Rajas for about twenty minutes on polo, shooting, and hawking, and they were interested to hear my impressions of these three sports in Chitral. They eventually took leave and I accompanied them as far as the gate and renewed acquaintance with their followers.

On returning to the house, I found Colonel Bacon with a pile of cipher wires which had just arrived in connection with the handing over; so we settled down to them together and soon had them deciphered and the replies enciphered. One was regarding my terms of service. I replied that I accepted them with certain reservations which I would discuss with General Scott on his arrival.

I then approached the subject of a second in command with the Colonel. I pointed out to him that the future was most uncertain: in fact anything might happen – and it would be fatal if I had a second in command who did not see eye to eye with me implicitly.

"I must have a man who I know is suitable for Gilgit and who will co-operate and back me up to the end if need be."

I then gave a brief description of Captain Mathieson. The Colonel agreed with me entirely and promised he would do everything in his power on the morrow to persuade General Scott to appoint Mathieson as Assistant Commandant of the Gilgit Scouts and Assistant Political Agent in Chilas. It said much for Colonel Bacon's appreciation of my sense of judgement that he accepted this undertaking without having ever seen Mathieson.

I was up and about at the crack of dawn on the following day (30 July), and moved my belongings, such as they were, and my rapidly increasing staff, ponies, polo sticks, and saddlery into the bungalow adjoining Agency House which was then occupied by Paul Mainprice. I wanted to stake a claim before the Kashmir contingent arrived and this residence suited my every purpose best. It was large and roomy, it was well furnished; the office and sitting room had a beautiful view looking up the Gilgit Valley; it was sufficiently near Agency House to enable me to keep a finger in the pie there yet far enough away to be private; it had good stables; it was defensible and had excellent getaways.

I left my staff which now consisted of two orderlies, Shukar Ali of Nagir and Munajat Khan of Kuh Ghizr, Wilayat of Hunza the cook, Zaril of Nagir the head *sais* and his assistant, a gardener from Baltistan, a Gilgit lad for washing the dishes and doing odd jobs, and several boys and others who comprised my retinue wherever we went, to get on with the job of putting the place in order.

It should be noted that my staff was very cosmopolitan, an elementary precaution. The major domo, the redoubtable Shawar Din, was meanwhile somewhere in the Hindu Khush.

I then mounted Roshan and trotted over to Agency House where I was joined by the Political Agent and retinue and we set off for the landing ground to meet the distinguished arrivals who were due to touch down at 10.00 am.

Almost dead on due time an Anson aircraft came in sight, circled once and made a perfect landing. We were all lined up on the strip, senior on the right, junior on the left, as the plane taxied up to where we were standing. The door opened and there was a flash of red tabs as the group descended. Colonel Bacon was on the point of making a dignified advance to meet the party when a figure shot forward from near the bottom of the line and rushed towards the plane.

With a yellow coat and long spindly legs encased by tight jodhpurs of a red hue, the apparition looked exactly like a *chikor* running before the line of beaters. It was the new Wazir Wazarat, Kashmir's recently arrived representative from Astore. He flung himself upon a stout gentleman in olive green uniform, who had just descended from the plane, and passionately embraced him. The stout gentleman was visibly taken aback, but before he could say anything the Wazir almost choked him by thrusting a large garland of flowers round his neck which effectively silenced any protest.

The Raja of Gupis caught my eye, and we both almost burst out laughing. Colonel Bacon moved forward as soon as this pantomime was finished, shook hands with three military officers and escorted them towards us for introduction.

First came Major-General H.L. Scott, CBE, DSO, MC, Chief of Staff of Jammu & Kashmir State Forces. He was a real soldier; of medium stature. He was as straight as a ramrod despite his age which must be considerable; neat, tidy and well turned out; pleasant and friendly yet decisive in his speech and clear thinking. This was the man who had, devoted his life to the State Forces which he himself, through sheer personality and will power, had transformed from a rabble in arms into a first class fighting machine which had played a full share in the Second World War and had eventually returned with no mean record of achievement.

Behind the General came the stout gentleman with the garland round his neck, composed once again, except for his cap being slightly askew. There was Brigadier Ghansara Singh, a high ranking officer of the State Forces, chosen by H.H. the Maharaja as his first Military Governor of Gilgit. When I saw him I recognized his type immediately. He was a typical Dogra, that race of hillmen which produced first class soldiers for the Indian Army; quiet, steady, loyal and brave soldiery, but lacking brain, tact, imagination and personal initiative. Such was Ghansara Singh; and a worse choice could not have been made for the person who was to steer the ship of Gilgit over the stormy transition period. The qualities required for the job were exactly those he did not possess.

He was of medium stature, very strongly built but now running to fat, heavy faced, and inclined towards baldness. He wore olive green slacks and bush jacket with brigadier's badges of rank, and a cheese cutter cap. He looked slightly embarrassed.

At the rear came Captain Mohammed Said of the Jammu & Kashmir State Forces, my new Scout officer. I immediately summed Said up as potentially unreliable and a man who would have to be watched carefully. He was pleasant and plausible to meet and obviously an officer of average ability. He was tall and thin and, except for a rather prominent nose, handsome. He would have made a good aide-de-camp.

Introductions completed, we mounted and rode back to Gilgit with Colonel Bacon, General Scott and Brigadier Ghansara at the front of the procession. There was quite a large turnout at the bridge to meet us, a band, and a "Welcome" arch of juniper branches. Ghansara Singh was greeted effusively by the Sikhs and Hindus, and in a no way hostile manner, yet without enthusiasm, by the locals.

Actually the full import of the British leaving had not yet sunk into the populace: it was too incredible to be appreciated by these loyal people, who, as long as they could remember, had enjoyed peace, prosperity and justice under the paramount power which they took for granted and considered eternal.

We eventually reached Agency House and accompanied by the Rajas and notables we entered the lounge and slaked parched throats in mulberry juice. Presently the Rajas and others left, and General Scott, the Governor elect, and Colonel Bacon went through to the office and got down to serious business. There was some light excitement when the Brigadier discovered he had lost his briefcase, and after I had dispatched levies to scour the country, it was eventually found in the plane. He was quite irascible about it.

I left the "Big Three" to complete their onerous task and returned to my bungalow. I found the servants had done a good job of work and all was in order. I would do no more arranging until Paul Mainprice had actually left, as his rooms were in the usual chaos of preparation for a journey.

After lunch together, I went and said Goodbye to Mrs Bacon and Frances and Laura who were leaving on the two-hundred-mile trek to Srinagar. She was very cheerful and I could not help admiring the courage of this brave lady who undertook the formidable journey on her own with two children as if it were an everyday event. There were some touching scenes when the Agency House servants bade her farewell with tears in their eyes: some broke down completely and openly wept.

In the evening a Durbar was held on the lawn of Agency House. General Scott presided and the Indian Officers of the Scouts were present. The Subedar Major read out the list of requests and again foolishly concluded by saying that, if these requests were not granted, the Scouts would refuse further service. The General may not have been in a position to give a direct reply regarding the requests but he certainly had the answers to the conclusion. I think the Indian Officers associated everybody connected with Kashmir as despicable and cowardly but they now discovered they were up against a real man in General Scott.

"I shall not be forced into anything," the General said quietly and decisively, "and if you don't wish to serve on, we can quite easily bring a Battalion of the State Forces up here to keep law and order or raise another Corps of Scouts for which, I have no doubt, many recruits will come forward."

This rather took the wind out of the Indian Officers' sails. Discussions and clarifications now took place on the points included in the petition, and from the ignorance displayed by most of the Indian Officers I rapidly came to the conclusion that the whole matter had been concocted by Baber himself and a few chosen cronies without reference either to the other officers or to the rank and file. This lack of unity meant there was little danger of an issue being forced so I ceased to worry. After a lot of useless nonsense from the Indian Officers, the Durbar gradually developed into a coffee shop, so the General concluded it by turning to me and telling me to investigate each request and to submit my views and recommendations to him at the earliest opportunity. The Indian Officers departed, still arguing among themselves like a lot of fishwives.

As I was leaving, General Scott called me back, and we walked up and down the lawn talking on general subjects. He then asked me if I knew a Captain Mathieson who was a *khassadar* officer in Waziristan. I said I had met him in the course of my duties, but I kept my reply carefully guarded.

"Did I think he was a suitable officer for the Gilgit Scouts?"

"From what I've seen of him, I consider him ideal." I replied. "He is quiet, steady and reliable; he also appears to have a nice appreciation of political and military situations. He is popular and is a good mixer. I think he would do very well here, and would make a good second in command and Assistant Political Agent Chilas."

It was time to change for dinner now so we walked into the house. I had given the General the terms of service I was prepared to serve under; he considered them not unreasonable and promised to recommend to the Maharaja that they should be accepted. They were very reasonable. Before we parted the General remarked, "I suppose your terms, except for the basic rate of pay, apply to Mathieson as well."

"Yes," I said casting a quick glance at him. But he had entered his room and closed the door.

On the following morning (31 July) the official handing over ceremony took place.

At an early hour I called Baber and ran through the order of parade with him. There was to be a mixed Guard of Honour of Scouts and Kashmir Infantry, commanded by the Scout Subedar Major as the senior Indian Officer present. Baber soon had a grasp of what was required so I told him to be off and get on with it. I then raked out my old ceremonial uniform and put it in order; white *koi* with a silver badge and dark green facing cloth, a khaki drill patrol jacket buttoning to the neck with green piping round the cuffs and neck; the buttons, badges of rank, and collar dogs were silver; khaki drill trousers, white socks and brown *chaplis*, a Sam Browne belt and sword.

The ceremony was due to take place at 10.00 am. The troops were in position on the Agency House lawn at 9.30 am and I carried out a preliminary inspection and rehearsal. All went well. I chatted to the Kashmir lads and found them in good spirits. Just as we officers were about to leave the house and take up our positions at about 9.50 am, an excited little Captain of the Kashmir Infantry buzzed in like an angry hornet, rushed up to me and said,

"My men refuse to come under your Subedar Major in the Guard of Honour. They will not obey his orders. I shall command the Guard of Honour."

"Oh indeed," said I. "I don't give a **** what you do with your men; you can take them away to Bunji if you wish, but you will have nothing whatever to do with the Scouts who will be commanded by my Subedar Major only."

He then fussed away to Brigadier Ghansara Singh. There was much whispering and gesticulating. The Brigadier scratched the single hair on the top of his head, and looked worried. More whispering, and the little hornet disappeared. Unobtrusively I looked out of the window, and saw that the Captain had taken up a position in front of the Kashmir Infantry. A trusted servant of Colonel Bacon's was handing round cigarettes. I quietly told him in Shina to go and tell Baber to carry through the parade as previously ordered and to have nothing to do with the Kashmir Contingent. If I had allowed the Captain to command the Scouts they might quite well have refused to obey him, and my name would have been mud for handing them over to what they considered a despicable little Hindu babu.

We then moved out and took up our positions. The Guard of Honour was drawn up facing the flagstaff. We stood in line facing Agency House whilst opposite and facing us stood Colonel Bacon and Brigadier Ghansara Singh. Although the event had been much publicized there were very few spectators.

One of the most moving ceremonies I have ever witnessed now began. On the stroke of 10.00 am, Subedar Major Mohammed Baber Khan, in a stentorian voice, ordered the Scout Guard of Honour to present arms. The Kashmiri Captain attempted to emulate him but the outcome was a thin piping squeak. Half the Kashmir troops reacted, half continued to stand at attention. The Scouts, however, responded to Baber's command like a machine and carried out the movement with the precision of Guardsmen. The bagpipes and drums of the Scouts struck up the "Royal Salute" and the Union Jack was slowly lowered whilst the officers in uniform saluted and those in civilian clothes raised their hats in homage. For me it was a deeply emotional moment and I do not doubt that the other Britishers present were also profoundly moved. In that short period the glories and triumphs of Durand, Hayward, Younghusband, Manners Smith, flashed through my mind; and now the symbol of peace, prosperity, and security, which had so proudly flown over the Agency since first raised by Durand and his gallant band in 1889, was being lowered for the last time; a glorious epoch cut short through stupidity and ignorance. And then I remembered the happy times I had had in the Agency under Colonel Cobb and Colonel Bacon, the last of a line of famous predecessors: a thousand and one memorable incidents, passed through my thoughts in a few fleeting moments.

As the last strains of the "Salute" rang out I gazed at the majestic mountains which had stood sentinel over Gilgit from time immemorial, and had silently gazed down on the changes wrought by time. Once more the old inspiration came to me,

"I to the hills will lift mine eyes From whence doth come mine aid."

And I prayed to God for guidance and help in the difficult days which assuredly lay ahead.

"Guard of Honour, order arms."

I snapped back to reality again.

Colonel Bacon and Brigadier Ghansara Singh changed places and after a short pause the Guard of Honour presented arms again and, as the band played the Kashmir National Anthem, the red and yellow flag of the State replaced the Union Jack at the top of the pole.

I thought to myself, "I wonder how long that will stay there?"

Colonel Bacon shook hands with Brigadier Ghansara Singh, new Governor of Gilgit province, and the parade broke up.

Was it imagination I wonder; or did I really see tears in the eyes of some of the British and Gilgit folk who were present at the ceremony?

The Governor, angry that such a small crowd of spectators had witnessed the event, strode off to draft telegrams to His Highness the Maharaja, informing him of the acquisition of further lands to his empire.

After the parade was finished General Scott and the Governor came down to the Scout Lines, and I took them round on a quick tour of inspection. The former asked many questions and made some shrewd comments. The latter was pleasant and interested but his remarks were inane. It was very different from the normal inspection of a unit when the Commanding Officer is on tenterhooks all the time in anticipation of a question being asked, the answer to which he does not know. I felt supremely confident that no question could be asked regarding the Gilgit Scouts to which I could not give a genuine reply. In this connection, however, I always impressed upon my junior officers the necessity of making some reply to questions put by inspecting officers. If ignorant, it is fatal to appear so, and the issue must be either tactfully evaded or an answer concocted. Bluff goes a long way with most Generals. In the course of trailing round behind official parties as a junior officer, I have heard the most utter nonsense being talked, but I naturally remained as quiet as the proverbial mouse.

It was really too hot for polo at that time of the year but in the afternoon we enjoyed a scratch game on the Old Ground. The Rajas took part and we paired ourselves off into two teams by throwing our sticks together in a heap on the ground, and then allowing a stranger to draw them one by one and place them alternately on his right and left. We did not play hard as it was not long before both our ponies and ourselves were in a bath-of sweat, but it was good fun. Two *chukkas* of a quarter of an hour each was quite sufficient, with a welcome cup of tea under the awning between games. I remember Colonel Bacon took about six *tambuks* that afternoon on the mighty Akbar who thundered down the field in full confidence of his peerless strength and speed. I do not think I have ever seen such a striking pony.

At night Colonel Bacon gave a formal feast, on behalf of the paramount power, to the Rajas, their followers, and three hundred guests present. The lawns of Agency House were covered with large Kashgari carpets on the top of which long white tablecloths had been laid. We squatted cross-legged alongside these cloths and stuffed ourselves with mutton pilau, chicken curry of many different varieties, chutneys, vegetables, and the other delicacies which make up a frontier feast.

But it was a very different atmosphere from the parties which had graced Agency House in the past. Gone were the laughing and joking, gone were the inevitable pranks played on the simple Raja of Gilgit, gone was the easy flow of conversation emanating from the Political Agent. There was a tense embarrassing silence, and the expression on the faces of those loyal folk of the Agency was one of sadness mingled with hurt at their abandonment by the British on whom they had learned to rely and trust. The Kashmir contingent were obviously ill at ease. I tried to make some conversation to break the tension but soon gave it up and sank into my own thoughts.

This was no Central Agency diplomacy of faked sorrow at seeing the last of the imperialistic British Overlords. No, this was something genuine. The events of the morning had at last brought home to these people that British rule was finished, that the Briush were leaving for ever, a fact which they had not been able to appreciate as possible up till then. And now they felt like sheep gone astray, not knowing which way to turn, and filled with the awful feeling of entering the melting pot. And now that the full significance of the change of power had sunk in they were filled with grief.

After dinner some of the officers made futile attempts to encourage dancing and singing but we were all glad when the guests eventually left. When the others had gone to bed, Colonel Bacon and I sat down in the lounge for a last cigarette. We started talking and decided to have a last gin.

We discussed many things, mainly concerning the future of the Agency. The futility of the Kashmir administration was never far from our thoughts. At 4.30 am the kerosene in the pressure lamp became exhausted so we decided to take a short rest in bed before breakfast. We had talked a great deal, we had drunk a great deal, but as the Colonel rose and stretched himself he spoke these prophetic words,

"I give the Kashmir administration three months in Gilgit. Then something will happen." A truer prediction was never made.

Colonel Bacon and General Scott left for Srinagar, via Peshawar, that morning (1 August). Again there were touching scenes at Agency House when weeping servants and levies kissed the Colonel's hands and feet in a last farewell. The streets were lined with silent crowds out of which individuals frequently came forward to shake the last Political Agent's hand or touch his stirrup iron in salute.

The procession was headed by the pipes and drums which played the skirl of that famous old Pathan song *Zakhmi Dil* or "The Broken Heart", of apt significance under the circumstances.

Formalities at the landing ground were cut short purposely, for by this time we were all on the verge of a nervous breakdown of emotion; and after the Colonel had shaken hands with everybody, he entered the plane. As he said goodbye to me, he jokingly whispered,

"You'll probably be King of Gilgit next time I meet you."

I then said farewell to General Scott. We shook hands and looking me straight in the eyes he said,

"Good bye, Brown, and good luck to you."

The plane took off with yards to spare and I watched it till from a speck it dissolved into the blue sky above Minawar ridge. I then rode quietly back to Gilgit myself.

In the evening I completed the final farewells by riding out to Jutial with Hamilton and Mainprice and wishing them God speed on their journey to the Punjab. As they trotted from sight I turned round and looked over the Gilgit Valley laid out before me. The settlement lay tranquil in a soft evening haze and a great feeling of elation came over me as I realized that I was the only British Officer left to carry on the traditions of famous predecessors, but different from them in that I owed no allegiance except my personal dedication to the Agency.

3. The New Kashmiri Order

The following morning (2 August 1947) I put on uniform and went down to the Scout lines. I ordered a full drill parade for everyone and for two solid hours I put them through their paces personally, until they had reached the standard I desired. They responded favourably to rating mixed with encouragement and I could tell from their attitude that my influence and control over them was still secure.

After that I inspected the lines, accompanied by the Subedar Major and issued some extensive orders regarding a general tidy up and improvement. The garden was well stocked and I passed a few words of encouragement to the gardeners; I carefully checked the issue register to ensure that the men were getting their full daily quota of fresh vegetables. The Quarter Master's store was visited next and stocks of cloth were found deplorably low. I noted the immediate requirements.

The magazine was the next port of call. Ammunition was sufficient but not excessive, so I issued orders that until further stocks were received there would be no musketry – a safeguard against eventualities which later proved a wise precaution.

I then moved over to the office and carried out a quick check of all accounts and correspondence. I was glad to note that the office routine was in full swing under the capable direction of the head clerk, Vida Lal, a high caste (Pundit) Kashmiri Hindu. There was no love lost between us, but he respected me and worked his hardest for me. By plausible and cunning tactics he had previously made himself "indispensable" with certain British Officers with the result he had gained a great deal of influence in directing the policy of the Corps. He was an expert in causing faction feeling and had done much to cause discord between British and Indian Officers. He was therefore heartily detested by the latter. Conceited and pompous, he had annoyed me at sight when I was a junior officer. I had always treated him as a clerk, pure and simple, and had always steadfastly refused to be dragged into his machinations. He therefore disliked me intensely and he cannot have relished the thought of my being Commandant. But to give him his due he served me to the best of his ability, and it was chiefly due to him that the internal administration of the Corps continued without a hitch during the transition period. *De mortuis nihil nisi bonum*, poor Vida Lal was later killed by a bomb in an air raid on Gilgit by the Indian Air Force – an ironical twist of fortune.

Tired yet contented, in the evening I realized that I had completed a good day's work, and that all that was required now was the enforcement of strict discipline and the Scouts would be where I wanted them.

I called in at Agency House on the way home. The Governor was sitting in a large leather-covered chair on the verandah, puffing away at an immense hubble-bubble pipe. This was in a position I became very accustomed to seeing him in during his tenure. In fact I doubt if he moved out of his chair for more than four or five hours during his entire governorship, except to go to bed at night. He greeted me effusively with apparent sincerity. I asked him how things were going.

"Well," he said, "I have been discussing the situation with the Wazir Wazarat and we have both come to the conclusion that it is impossible to administer this province without a proper staff, which we have not at present. I have therefore decided that until a staff arrives from Srinagar, the Agency Office and Treasury will be sealed and all public institutions closed down. We shall do nothing till the staff arrives."

This struck me as very odd.

In the first place sufficient Hindu and Sikh clerks of the old Agency Office had elected for service under the Kashmir Government to form a skeleton staff which could have kept the boilers warm until reinforcements arrived. With a bit of effort, the entire administration could have been set in motion. It would take at least three weeks for the proposed staff to arrive from Srinagar and in the meantime everything would be at a standstill. It was ludicrous and I tactfully said as much. But he was adamant and refused to do anything whatsoever about it.

"All right," I said, "but one thing is necessary; staff or no staff, the Scouts must get their pay from the Treasury and their rations from the districts, otherwise there will be trouble. And what about my own pay?" I added jokingly to sweeten the pill of having to take a strong line so soon.

He scratched his head, screwed up his face, puffed at his hubble-bubble, and pondered deep in thought for a few minutes.

"I'll tell the Wazir Wazarat to arrange that," he said eventually. "But only for the Scouts. I shall make no further attempt at administration."

This suited me and he actually kept his word, but it was a revelation to me of the lack of initiative, lack of enterprise, and sheer idleness which typified Kashmir officialdom, about which I had heard so much but had not yet encountered directly.

"What a show!" I thought to myself.

As I was leaving I remarked that Captain Mohammed Said had not appeared in the Lines that day.

"Oh no," replied the Governor, "I've sent him to Chilas to raise the Kashmir flag there and to distribute money to the people as a present from His Highness."

I saluted and departed, imagining the Governor sinking back in his chair with a sign of relief and thanking God that the disturber of his peace had gone away.

Immediately on arrival home, I called a trustworthy informer of mine and ordered him to proceed to Chilas immediately over the hills and check up on Said's movements and actions. I also told him to ensure that Said received as uncomfortable a time as possible in Chilas, as I did not wish him to get ideas about becoming Assistant Political Agent, or Assistant Governor as the post was now called, with the possibility of Mathieson's appointment being cancelled.

My trusty servant did his job well.

In a few days Said returned in a disgusted frame of mind. He had been unable to get rations or transport. Only a handful of people had turned out to see the flag-raising ceremony. The Chilasis had refused to come in to receive their gracious presents, despite orders. The road had been beastly hot; he was covered with bites from the Chilas flies, and he had a sore bottom from an uncomfortable saddle. Captain Said would definitely not go back to Chilas, nor would any other Kashmiri Officer.

I continued my discipline drive with the Scouts and gradually morale and esprit de corps returned.

An example had to be made of one or two wretched individuals by sending them for a spell of imprisonment in the Quarter Guard, but it certainly clarified the position and showed one and all that whatever had been happening in the past, there would be no more nonsense now. After parade we lost no opportunity in playing games, dancing, and arranging for displays by the pipe band. It was gratifying for me to notice the general improvement which set in during the month of August.

Said now settled down to learning the work and I was pleased to find him keen, interested, and quick in the up-take. He asked questions, and took a lot of trouble in picking up the peculiarities of Scout service. If I had been able to overcome my personal distrust of him, I would have classed him as a very suitable officer.

The next event of importance was the arrival of two more officers for the Scouts, Lieutenant Ghulam Haider and Lieutenant Mohammed Khan of the Jammu and Kashmir State Forces.

I liked Haider on first sight. He was aged about nineteen or twenty, tall and thin, with handsome aristocratic features and of wheat coloured complexion. He was full of the irresponsible gaiety of youth and laughed much, showing a perfect set of white teeth. He was loosely built, lithe, energetic and obviously a good sportsman and athlete. I likened him in my mind to a young unbroken colt. If I could gain his confidence, gradually break him in to my methods, he would turn out to be a real asset, both to me and the Scouts. I started this task immediately by making him Adjutant and as later events will show he fully justified my impressions and the trouble I took.

Mohammed Khan was small, cheerful and bouncy. An ex-ranker, he was not over blessed with brains, but he looked on life with a carefree, happy attitude.

Accompanying these two officers on their trek up from Srinagar was a small, fat, slimy individual who might have been a night club steward or a white slave trader. He greeted me in a greasy obsequious manner, and his hand was hot and clammy. He informed me that he was the Personal Assistant to the Governor.

"God help the Governor and everybody else with whom this creature has contact," I thought to myself.

Haider had brought with him an immense horse, with a sword attached to the saddle. I have knocked about with horses all my life, but never have I seen such a big one as this, which must have stood well up to 18 hands. On enquiry, I discovered that the monster belonged to the Governor.

On the few occasions when he ventured forth from this during the tenure, the operation of mounting this horse was a pantomime for which gate money could have been charged. A chair would be placed in the front drive and with much difficulty the Governor would climb on it. The excited animal would then be led to the chair round which it would revolve like a top. The Governor, after frequent attempts, would at last get his foot into the stirrup iron and would then be suspended in mid-air until a bevy of servants had hoisted his huge bulk into the saddle, groans and grunts emanating from him the while. Dismounting also proved as difficult an operation.

Haider had about thirty pony loads of luggage with him. This seemed strange for a junior officer so I made enquiries. It turned out that this was the Governor's personal kit. I asked myself; "why on earth had the fool brought so much stuff to Gilgit?"

A Hindu doctor had also arrived, a pathetic creature who knew nothing about doctoring and who hated leaving the comforts of home life for the far outpost of Gilgit. He sometimes used to come along to my bungalow in the evening, and pour out his woes over liberal glasses of gin, which he liked very much.

Whatever the faults of Said, Haider, and Mohammed Khan, they were my first staff of officers on an independent command and I determined to treat them in exactly the same way as I would have treated British Officers. I took great pains to teach them their work. I encouraged them or cursed them as the situation demanded. Off parade I was friendly but not familiar and frequently invited them up to my bungalow for drinks or meals. I was approachable at all hours of the day and night for reports or questions. I assisted them in their private troubles and backed them up to the best of my ability in any request they made to the Governor, if it was a question beyond my control. On Sundays I used to take them out on fishing trips and picnics, and later when polo started I lent them ponies and gave them private instruction in the evening.

When Mathieson arrived, I showed him no favour in the company of the others or about which the others might hear. I also cultivated, as far as I could, the rather doubtful friendship of the Kashmiri officials and had them round to the bungalow on occasions for a meal. I encouraged them to talk, but they were always guarded and reticent on State affairs.

In due course the Mirs of Hunza and Nagir arrived back from Srinagar, where they had been holding discussions with H.H. the Maharaja of Kashmir.

It seemed impolitic under the circumstance to be seen in their private company too much. I knew that all previous differences of opinion between them had been temporarily buried and that they were united in policy with regard to the cession of the Gilgit Agency to Kashmir, so I merely asked them both to an informal lunch with no one else present. They arrived together, a sure sign of unity.

Mir Mohammed Jamal Khan of Hunza was a well built man of about thirty-five years of age, with round somewhat florid features. He was entirely self-educated and took full advantage of studying the methods of his famous grandfather, Nazim Khan, the "Great Mir". Jamal's manners were impeccable and he spoke English well. He was a thorough gentleman.

Mir Shaukat Ali Khan of Nagir was a much younger man, actually just my age, which was twenty-four in that year of grace 1947, and for that reason there had always been a bond between us. Small, sharp featured, and of very fair complexion, the effect of shouldering the burdens of State at a tender age, and much too seriously at that, coupled with the uncertainty of succession and life, had left their mark on him. Some considered him dour and morose. I did not agree. I always found him ready to laugh and joke when encouraged, and he possessed a keen sense of humour. He had been educated at the Church Mission School in Srinagar.

Both Mirs were dressed in well-cut lounge suits. Jamal wore a white *koi*, Shaukat carried a smart soft hat. We greeted one another as old friends and I led them through to the cool sitting-room. We sat down in the large comfortable easy chairs facing the broad window through which we gazed up the Gilgit Valley, within its confining mountains, until it swept out of sight round a narrow bend.

Cigarettes, soft drinks, and we started to talk. We went through the normal Oriental routine of discussing various topical events which had no bearing whatever on the matter dominating our thoughts. Then gradually the conversation veered to Kashmir and we were talking business.

Hunza tactfully, Nagir downrightly, reproached me for the British withdrawal from Gilgit. Not wishing to enter upon any argument on this point, I replied that it was the Will of Allah. They then said that they were both very pleased that I had elected to return as Commandant Scouts, and padded this with the usual flattery as demanded by good manners and custom. They warned me that I had a difficult time ahead, but loyally promised their wholehearted co-operation, assistance, and advice on any matters I cared to refer to them. This was no idle assurance as I discovered later.

Jamal, as spokesman, then gave me an account of the negotiations with the Maharaja.

"The Maharaja was extremely friendly," he began, "and treated us in Srinagar with due regard to our position. We were State guests and the best of everything was placed at our disposal. The Maharaja agreed that Durand's Treaty was now null and void as one of the joint contracting parties, namely the Crown Representative, had withdrawn. The Maharaja therefore desired that we should enter into a new treaty agreement direct with him. We pointed out that although our intention was to remain on the friendliest of terms with him, and to co-operate with him as far as circumstances allowed, we were not at present prepared to come under treaty obligations. We promised we would continue to supply recruits for the Scouts, but our States would be independent. The Maharaja brought much personal pressure to bear on us to conclude a treaty but we steadfastly maintained our resolution. There was a great deal more discussion but that is briefly the gist of the negotiations. We departed in a very cordial atmosphere. "So, Sahib, we are now completely independent."

"Why, Mir Sahib, did you refuse to enter into a treaty?" I asked offhandedly, lighting a cigarette.

"It will be very difficult for us if the State of Jammu and Kashmir accedes to Hindustan" (India) the Mir of Nagir replied quickly and promptly changed the subject.

This was the clue I wanted. This was the clue which must be investigated immediately, so I allowed the conversation to veer and after a suitable period I suggested we should have lunch.

Over lunch, the Mirs started ridiculing the Kashmir administration in Gilgit. They openly joked about every department, except the Scouts, being at a standstill; the old Governor sitting on his verandah smoking his hubble-bubble from morn till night; the Governor's immense charger; the Wazir Wazarat with the thin legs who had now changed his designation to Revenue Assistant as more understandable by the ignorant; the fat little Personal Assistant, a living symbol of bribery and corruption; the poor useless doctor who drank gin. They spared no one and had me in fits of laughter. They finished by saying words to this effect in Urdu, "How on earth can this comic opera rule Gilgit!"

"God knows," I said still shaking with laughter.

After lunch I accompanied them as far as the front gate according to custom, and wished them God speed on their journey back to their little mountain strongholds.

It had been a valuable lunch party and had given me much for meditation. As a sequel to this, a few days later I tactfully turned a conversation with the Governor on to the subject of treaty agreements between the Maharaja and the States of Hunza and Nagir. The Governor told me that he had written instructions from the Kashmir Government to the effect that Durand's Treaty still held good, despite the withdrawal of the Crown Representative, and that Hunza and Nagir were still under the same obligations as prior to 1 August 1947. But since there was no longer a Crown Representative, the Mirs acknowledged the absolute suzerainty of the Maharaja only. This was food for thought, but I played the idiot and appeared to have no interest in treaties and politics.

15 August was Independence Day, that memorable day in the Sub-continent when united India was partitioned into the two Dominions of Pakistan and Hindustan and the Paramount Power withdrew.

I rather imagined that the Governor would arrange some sort of celebration, a tea party or other such entertainment at State expense to mark the momentous occasion. However in the middle of the morning an orderly staggered into my office with a cardboard box full of candles and a directive from the Governor to the effect that all public places, including the bazaar and Scout Lines, would be illuminated that night to mark Independence Day. I was duly given twelve candles for the Lines and six for my bungalow and the orderly departed. It seemed that this was the extent of the celebrations. But a howling gale blew up in the evening which lasted well into the night; so the proposed illuminations were impossible. The candles came in useful later when my pressure lamp went wrong, which it frequently did.

One Monday morning the Subedar Major made an important report to me. He told me that on the previous day a group of Scouts had gathered in the sepoys' recreation room. They had held a meeting at which a resolution had been passed that the Gilgit Agency must accede to Pakistan and otherwise the whole Corps of Scouts must consider laying down arms, as it was contrary to their religion for them to serve under the Hindu Maharaja. Actually my own informers had told me about this and it was not as serious as Baber made out.

What had actually happened was that some argument had started with regard to Gilgit's position *vis à vis* Pakistan and India. But this sort of thing could not be tolerated and unless eradicated immediately would lead to endless trouble, especially if the Governor heard about it.

The first thing I did was to close down the recreation room once and for all. I had never agreed with it anyway. Recreation rooms in most units are the meeting places for gambling and intrigue. It is much more satisfactory, for all concerned, that the sepoys should spend their spare time in the barrack rooms under the watchful eye of reliable NCOs who can keep in touch with what is going on. I then ordered the entire Gilgit strength to assemble in the Subedar Major's garden where I gave them one of my frequent "pep talks" from a raised platform. I then told them quite straight I would tolerate no trouble, and no political intrigue of any sort in future. Any kind of subversive activity would be dealt with by me personally and offenders would be punished so drastically that they would never forget it. I pointed out to them that at present the Maharaja was feeding them, paying them, and clothing them adequately, and offering them the same terms as service as previously, with possible improvements. I then called upon any man who was not content to step forward and I would release him from service forthwith. One man came forward.

"All right, the rest of you," I said. "No more trouble or you'll be sorry."

A voice from the back suddenly sang out, "We're loyal to you, Sahib" with great emphasis on the "you". The parade then dismissed. From that day onwards there was no more trouble from the Scouts in headquarters.

One morning I was sitting on the verandah of my bungalow, smoking a cigarette over the last cup of breakfast coffee, when I heard commotion in the garden. Suddenly my two dogs, Sammy the Spaniel and Dinah the Labrador, came bouncing up the steps and flung themselves at me. Sammy leapt straight at my chest with the result that I caught him in my arms. Dinah kept jumping at me, and at the same time making passes at Sammy's ears. I knew that my caravan had arrived from Chitral. Presently Shawar Din appeared on the scene. He looked a bit weather-beaten, but quite undaunted and as cheerful as ever. He saluted in military style, as was his custom, and made his official report.

"*Sab achcha*" (all's well) "except for one yakdan lock broken, and Tadjik has cast a shoe from the near fore." He then came forward and shook hands.

"*Shabash*," I said. "Take an hour's rest and then get the boxes into the bungalow and unpacked. Watch the Hunza lads don't get their hands on the liquor. Put it straight into the cellar," I added jokingly, with a grin at the cook who was hovering about in the background.

I gave the dogs some milk to slake their thirst and then went out to the stables to look at Tadjik. Zaril was giving him the once-over. He turned, with sweat on his forehead, and gave the brush a few reflective rubs with the curry comb.

"You've picked another good 'un," he said, "but the animal looks too slow for your style of polo. He'll be grand on tour though."

Tadjik was certainly much changed from the last time I had seen him. The journey seemed to have done him good. Shawar Din was neither a horseman nor a horsemaster, in fact he never had anything to do with horses until he joined my service. He held these wild Badakshani stallions in great respect, and considered that the best way to keep on good terms with them was to supply them with ample rations. Shawar Din also believed in leisurely travel along the roads, to prevent any possibility of his mount getting out of control. He had obviously applied his principles to Tadjik, who was as fat as a barrel with a bay coat shining like the sheen of silk. Despite the length of the journey, he was not tired and with his head held high he was taking stock of his surroundings. I gave some orders to Zaril regarding shoeing and trimming and then passed down the line to Sultan and Roshan.

"Get Sultan tidied up," I said, "I am sending him to the Mehtar of Chitral as a present." I thought that this would be a useful and diplomatic move under the circumstances. "As for the others," I continued, "the polo season is approaching so you can bring them in from grass, and put them into hard feeding. See that they are taken out for long walks in the morning, and long slow trots in the evening – that is if I am not going out myself."

I then returned to the bungalow to find the mail had arrived. The one telegram I dealt with first. It was from "Dogra" (General Scott's code name) and read: "Mathieson's appointment confirmed – stop – his estimated date of arrival Gilgit 10 September."

This was the vital news I had been awaiting. There was also a letter from Jock in which he said that General Scott had written offering the appointment to him, and he had naturally accepted. So I sent for a stenographer and dictated a long letter to him, giving him full details of journey procedure, clothes and stores required, and all other details peculiar to a permanent move to Gilgit. I told him to come via the Kaghan Valley as he would see more of the Agency and also the experience in the heat of the Indus basin would serve to toughen him up for future eventualities.

That completed, I went along to report to the Governor. He was still sitting on the leather chair on the verandah, still smoking the hubble-bubble, and still wearing the olive green uniform in which he had arrived. His expression on my arrival as much as said, "Why do you have to come here on this beautiful day and disturb me from my reverie? Keep away and let me sleep." However he controlled his thoughts, and was as usual very friendly.

I told him about Mathieson's confirmation and estimated date of arrival. He seemed quite pleased. I told him that my plan was that Mathieson should come via Kaghan direct to Gilgit, where he would spend at least ten days with me under instruction. The Governor objected. He said there was no necessity for Mathieson to come to Gilgit at all but that he should take over as Assistant Governor as soon as he arrived in Chilas.

Now under normal circumstances I would have insisted that a new Scout Officer spent some time in headquarters learning the work, but it was even more important now. The future of the Province was so uncertain that it would have been criminal for me to have agreed to the inexperienced Mathieson taking over Ghilas direct, where he might suddenly be plunged into a situation with which he was unable to cope through sheer ignorance. My genuine intention was merely to give him a grounding in the peculiar conditions of this part of the world and the methods which I employed, and insisted on being employed, in the Scouts.

Why did Ghansara Singh do his utmost to prevent our meeting? Did he mistrust our motives then? That I cannot answer and though I later searched his confidential letters and files, I could not find a clue. We had an extremely heated argument but I eventually forced my point and the Governor agreed that Mathieson could come to Gilgit. A joke, a bit of flattery, and we were back on the best of terms again.

I now tackled a subject which had been attracting my attention. I knew that the Governor had been sending off countless telegrams and wireless messages to the Prime Minister and other officials in Srinagar with requests for the dispatch of staff, advice on important matters of policy, and the supply of certain commodities for the bazaar, such as salt and sugar which were almost exhausted. I asked the Governor whether he ever received any replies to these messages. He attempted to evade the question but, on pressure, eventually admitted that the only messages to which he ever received replies were those addressed to General Scott. Complete silence was being maintained by the Prime Minister and other officials. This was interesting. He also informed me that General Scott had dispatched a large consignment of grey muzri cloth for the Scouts and that it should arrive in Gilgit soon. This was very satisfactory.

I then departed, and considering I had completed a good day's work, I decided to go fishing. On reaching the Kargah I completely divorced myself from troubles of State and had a most enjoyable afternoon and evening. I rode home in the evening with a fine creel of trout. Some I ate for dinner – they are delicious freshly caught – and the remainder I sent down to Said & Co.

Ramzan had almost run its course. *Ramzan,* one of the five pillars of Islam, the holy month of the year when devout Followers of the Prophet keep a strict fast from sunrise to sunset: no food, drink, or tobacco smoke may pass their lips. At the end of the month comes the festival of *Id ul Fitr,* when, penance completed, a riotous celebration takes place. On *Id* in the old days, it was the custom for the Scouts to attire themselves in new mufti clothes and to march up to Agency House, where they would be welcomed by the Political Agent who would treat them to a lavish tea party followed by dancing and other festivities. In the afternoon there would be polo and in the evening a firelight dance in the Scout Lines.

I explained this to the Governor and he said he saw no reason why the old procedure should not be carried out as usual. He thought, however, that the dance at night might be omitted owing to lack of firewood, and I agreed.

The "night of nights" came at last and the thin silver sliver of crescent moon showed momentarily in the sky, signifying that the fast was over for another year. The Scouts duly arrived at Agency House in the morning, dressed in their Sunday best and intent on making merry. I entered and informed the Governor of their arrival. He went out onto the verandah. He extracted a one hundred rupee note from his pocket, and flourishing it in the air descended the steps, and presented it to the Subedar Major. His attitude was that of some grumpy old "Scrooge" who, annoyed by carol singers, gives them a few pence and tells them to be off. Baber, flabbergasted, accepted the note at a nod from me. The men, unaccustomed to such treatment, looked on in open-mouthed amazement.

"This is your *Id* present," said the Governor, "go and buy yourselves sweets or something in the bazaar." There was a stony silence.

"Go on, thank the Governor Sahib for it," I said in Shina.

There was a faint mutter round the ranks. The Governor entered the house again.

"Looks like we've had our *Id* celebration," said Baber.

"Yes," I said, "Never mind. You'd better get away back to the Lines and prepare for polo. There's no future here."

We had a good game of polo in the afternoon and it was pleasant to see everyone happy again after the anticlimax of the morning. The standard was not high as most of us were schooling new ponies for sterner stuff later. I was well contented though as it showed the populace that whoever was the ruler, the king of sports continued so far as I was concerned.

One morning I was dealing with routine correspondence in the office when I noticed the first official letter from the Governor. It was a copy of a telegram received from "Dogra", Srinagar, to the Governor and read: "At a time and occasion selected by you and the Commandant but personally" (I presume this meant "preferably") "soon all ranks Scouts should be enrolled in State Service and take usual oath of allegiance – stop – suggest quietly no ceremony – stop – fresh enrolment forms or countersign old suitably endorsed on Sheet Rolls."

The Governor's covering note read:

"Forwarded for early action. Please let me know the date and time when the oath is held."

It was marked SECRET.

I called the Subedar Major and we went out for a stroll together on the football ground, far from the ears of prying Kashmiri Pundits. I informed him about the necessity for all ranks taking an oath of allegiance to the Maharaja of Kashmir.

I must say I did not expect a direct reply but Baber said, "Why not, Sahib? We'll complete this any day convenient to you. There will be no trouble about it."

Later in the morning Baber asked if he could speak to me privately. We entered his garden.

Baber said, "I don't think it would be a good thing to order the Scouts to swear an oath of allegiance at present. They are still disturbed and upset from the changeover. It would be fatal, Sahib, to run the risk of a mass refusal to obey orders at this stage. Nobody has the power to force them, and if they get away with one refusal, this will lead to another such incident and the whole show will be completely out of control. Far better to wait until the Kashmir regime is functioning properly here, for the whole world to behold. By that time the Scouts will have appreciated the benefits of the Kashmir administration and will take the oath without the risk of refusal. Anyway we have all sworn an oath of allegiance to you, Sahib, and since you are under contract to the Maharaja of Kashmir, it follows that we too hold fealty to His Highness."

Quite apart from the question of the oath, I definitely could not run the risk of a mass refusal from the Scouts on any order. I had no power other than my own personality to enforce orders. One refusal, and the Scouts would be out of my control. And now Baber was warning me that there was a possibility of this with regard to the oath of allegiance. But I did not trust Baber.

"All right, Subedar Major Sahib," I said, "I'll think it over."

Later in the day I had occasion to talk to Subedar Mohammed Azam Khan privately with regard to the question of a disability pension on account of his damaged leg. I trusted Azam implicitly. I approached the question of the oath of allegiance.

"Bide your time, Sahib, till things have settled down and then make them swear their oath," he said. "I don't advise your trying it at the moment."

So that evening I dispatched a Secret letter to the Governor which read: "Owing to the fact that the Corps is widely distributed in outposts, camps, and on leave the completion of all ranks taking the oath of allegiance will probably take two to three months. As soon as this has been completed you will be informed."

4. Gilgit Politics and Oaths of Loyalty

The secret of success is looking and working ahead. I had now collected only two pieces of the jigsaw which, when merged, would give me the clue to the run of future events. The Mir of Nagir had said that it would be very difficult for Hunza and Nagir if Kashmir acceded to India as the Scouts were at present unwilling to swear allegiance to the Maharaja. If I was to steer Gilgit through a crisis – and a crisis of some sort there must be – then it was imperative that I should first solve the puzzle and plan my course of action from the finished picture.

And this could not be done by sitting in Gilgit. It was imperative that I visited the outlying districts and really felt the pulse of the province. I decided to visit my onetime home, Chilas, first.

I told the Governor of my intentions. He refused to let me go under any circumstances. I do not think that was due to mistrust so much as to his feeling of insecurity when I was absent from Gilgit. He was clever enough to see that the person who controlled the Scouts controlled the Province. And they might well get out of control whilst I was in Chilas to the detriment of his safety.

But I knew I must go, so I played a trump card.

"I know that the condition of the Scouts at Chilas is bad owing to a prolonged absence of an officer," I said. "There are also many important decisions pending with regard to promotions and punishments which can only be settled on the spot. But my real intention in going to Chilas is in order to supervise every man swearing an oath of allegiance to the Maharaja."

This was a dangerous statement to make. If I failed to make the men there swear the oath then everything, all I had worked for, would be lost; but it was the only way in which I could persuade the Governor to let me go. I watched his reaction. He was visibly surprised.

"Can you really give me an assurance that you will make every man in Chilas take the oath," he said.

"Yes," I replied decisively, and I knew from the tone of his voice that he had learnt that the Scouts in Gilgit had shown unwillingness to declare their loyalty to Kashmir at present.

"In that case you may most certainly go," he said eagerly.

I departed and made preparations for the journey. First of all I dictated a long and confidential letter to the Governor, regarding certain promotions in the Scouts. Although they were not really important, I stressed that they were, and pointed out that the dire consequences which would ensue, if he did not reach a satisfactory decision. I included many obscure references to old Agency Office files.

"This," I thought, "will keep him busy while I am away, and will keep him from interfering in any dangerous matters, should he suddenly snap out of his lethargy." Tracing the references alone would take at least a week.

I then decided that this would be no ordinary tour from daily stage to stage with a train of pack ponies and a retinue of servants. I would travel completely alone, as fast as I possibly could.

My reasons were as follows. I did not wish to be away from Gilgit proper longer than necessary as it was the nerve centre of the Province, the place where I could keep my finger on the pulse of events. Secondly I wished to make it clear to locals and Kashmiris alike that I had not returned to Gilgit for a holiday as a neutral observer of their political relations. I wanted to make it quite clear that I meant business and that I was prepared to go to any length of discomfort and trouble in the discharge of whatever duty I considered necessary. And lastly I wanted to show the Scouts and populace that my year's absence in Waziristan had in no way affected my powers of endurance or nerve.

It was a somewhat dangerous undertaking without a doubt. If the Governor had any doubts regarding my intentions he could easily signal the 6th Kashmir Infantry at Bunji to intercept me, and either liquidate or imprison me.

I had, moreover, many enemies in Chilas, relations of miscreants I had sent to jail for fourteen years on murder charges. With the spirit of freedom in the air they would not think twice about assassinating me in revenge.

But my fatalistic outlook accepted the decision without thought, on the grounds that if my destiny was a sticky end on the way to Chilas, this was God's unalterable will.

I departed on the following day, which was 27 August 1947, having given Said careful instructions regarding the running of the Scouts in my absence.

After lunch I put on my trail clothes; a grey bush shirt with large flap pockets, corduroy trousers, thick socks and *chaplis*, and an Australian bushman's hat which shaded me from the burning sun and also served for drawing water for my pony where the terrain prevented natural watering.

I ordered Zaril to saddle Tadjik, as he was best fitted for the long journey. I filled my saddlebags with chapattis, dried fruit, and shelled walnuts. I also packed my usual first aid kit which consisted of a first field dressing, sticking plaster, iodine, quinine, and a violent stimulant called Pervatin which was only used as a last resort. At the rear of the saddle I attached a full water bottle, balanced on the other side by a canvas bag containing four or five pound of grain for my pony. Buckling my pistol and dagger round my waist, I mounted up, and cantered out the Sonekote road at about 3.00 pm.

At Jutial I watered Tadjik and let him drink his fill. After much experience of trial and error, I have found that the best way to get the most out of a horse and to prevent lameness, is to water three miles out after departure and about three miles before arrival. Apart from that, I never allow watering on the march. I know this will shock the cavalrymen, who advocate watering on every possible occasion according to the rules of the text book. But it is results that count and I know that Badakshani stallions, watered on the principle I have described, on long marches have performed feats of endurance in Central Asia which it would be hard to equal.

After a walk down to Sakwar, I settled Tadjik to a steady pace of six miles an hour and soon the milestones were flying past. He was going very well. No urging or holding was required; without a stumble or peck he kept on at his comfortable gait, mile after mile. The hazard of the road at that pace were too great for detached thought and my concentration was fully occupied in preventing an accident.

It was hellishly hot and we were both bathed in sweat. The 30th mile was completed as I cantered across Jaglote grass farm at 6.30 pm.

I passed the time of day with the police piquet at Jaglote Chowki. The Head Constable begged me to stop and take refreshment. I refused but promised to halt an hour or two on the way back and hear their news. They waved a cheery farewell as I disappeared in a cloud of dust in the sandy desert; across the Sai River, and then a steep ascent to a perilous narrow path which lasted for some three miles along the sheer face of a precipice above the Indus. On the far side of the river lay Bunji – attractive in the peace of the evening – and as I carefully jogged along I could hear Retreat being blown on massed bugles, clear and distinct in the great stillness. Ahead, Nanga Parbat raised her lofty white peaks into the pale sky. For a moment the summit was saffron clad with the last rays of the setting sun; the colour faded as though washed out by the hand of an invisible artist and in mysterious, awe-inspiring aloofness the "Naked Mountain" gazed down on the vagaries of the world, as she had done from time immemorial, and would continue to do till the end of time.

Tadjik was getting a little tired now, so I was not sorry to see the welcoming camp fires of Theliche. I rode into the little settlement and approached the rest house. As soon as the *chowkidar*, or caretaker, recognized me he ran forward and with an exclamation of surprise kissed my hand. By that time some of the local levies had appeared, loyal men from Gor. They did likewise.

"What brings you here at this late hour, Sahib, and alone?"

"I'm going to Chilas," I replied simply.

"Is there trouble in Chilas?"

"No, I am merely paying a quick visit to settle some of the pending cases, and ensure that the Raja Orderly is looking after your interests in the absence of a "Mulki Sahib" (the local expression for A.P.A.)

"Truly," they said, "it is only a British Officer who would undertake such a journey, alone and unattended. What a pity the British have gone and left us thus. It is most unworthy of them, Sahib. Do you think there has been some mistake and they will return?"

I told them that I would see to my horse and after that we'd talk.

I led Tadjik round to the stables and saw to his comfort. I slackened his girths slightly but did not remove saddle or bridle. I looped a length of rope over a convenient branch of a tree and tied Tadjik's head up so that his nose was almost on a line with his withers. He would remain in this position with his head tied up until he had made water twice. This usually takes an hour. Then the girths would be slackened fully, the bridle removed, head freed, and the animal would be allowed to relax with a nosebag of maize and an armful of lucerne.

If I had allowed Tadjik to relax immediately on arrival, and to feed with saddle and bridle removed as the text books advocate, the horse would in all probability be lame within a couple of hours. On removing the saddle after a hard journey the blood rushes back into the body suddenly with ill effects. If a horse is allowed to relax immediately, the blood collects in any blows or knocks received on the road with the result that the legs stiffen up and the horse goes lame. A footballer may suffer the same experience. If, after a game, he sinks down into an armchair to rest, it is not long before his limbs stiffen up with aches and pains. On the other hand, if he keeps on the move and allows his accelerated flow of blood to return to normal gradually, there will be no after-effects whatsoever. Exactly the same it is with a horse. By tying his head up he remains restless and paws the ground so that his blood flow and pressure slowly become normal instead of instantaneously, with the result that the blood does not concentrate in bruises. This is a Central Asia custom called "yarricking" devised to prevent lameness after polo and long journeys. From records, I have discovered that it was introduced to this part of the world by Alexander the Great of Macedon, and I am positive that it is the reason why there is so little lameness in Gilgit in comparison to the rough tasks which ponies are called upon to undertake.

So having put Tadjik into a "yarrick" I detailed a small boy to attend him, and to rustle a handful of lucerne occasionally to encourage the passing of water.

I then walked round to the verandah of the bungalow and sat down on an armchair facing Nanga Parbat.

He who says that the Chilasis are not hospitable speaks false. If they know, and like you, they are as hospitable as the Pathans themselves, to the limited extent their rude existence allows. The Gor levies had prepared tea, boiled eggs and roast chicken which they lavished upon me whilst a young lad massaged my legs and shoulders. They talked openly as was their wont. They were very reproachful towards the British for having withdrawn and considered it gross injustice. They talked much and I made a mental note of all relevant statements, which would eventually help me in my appreciation of conditions.

After a couple of hours I felt much refreshed and decided to continue the journey. I told the levy havildar to phone up my old friend, Dost Mohammed, at Gooner Farm and to tell him to have a fresh pony waiting for me there. By the time I reached that stage, Tadjik would have had enough. Swinging into the saddle I gave the Muslims' hail or farewell, *Salaam Aleikum* and with the reply of *wa Aleikum Salaam* in my ears I rode into the darkness.

It was a bright moonlight night, but as I rode on disturbing clouds blew up from Nanga Parbat and presently it was pitch dark. This made it extremely difficult as the road was far from easy. Between Theliche and the Raikote Bridge over the Indus there is a dangerous *parri* to cross. *Aparriis* where a large abutment of land juts out into the river. As the road cannot follow the bank of the river as usual, it must climb dizzy spirals until it reaches a place where it can cross the summit of the *parri*. If the summit is too high a track will be carved across the sheer cliff-face some distance from the top. On the far side the road descends steeply again to the river bank. Tadjik slowly but steadily climbed up onto the *parri* till we were a good two thousand feet above the river which could be heard booming below. The road then level led out and for about half a mile crawled along the side of a precipice. It was a path of some three or four feet wide carved out of solid rock.

Looking back on it now, I suppose it was a foolhardy action to attempt to cross this portion. It was pitch black. Neither Tadjik nor I could see an inch except for the feeble light from my small torch. Thousands of feet below us the Indus thundered and roared. I could not see the river of course, but I knew full well what it looked like. Tawny water churned to foam by awful rapids, immense boulders which swung the water back into fearful whirlpools; one false step and Tadjik and I would be hurled into this cataclysm. I dismounted and led Tadjik forward. He never hesitated. We crawled along slowly and gradually reached halfway across.

I was just congratulating myself that all was well and that we would soon be on the far side, when there was a deafening roar above us. An immense avalanche of boulders and shale came hurtling over my head and went crashing back into the chasm below. Tadjik jumped back in fright and jerked the torch out of my hand. The little light, like a firefly, twisted and turned as it fell through space till lost to sight. There was another roar and another avalanche came crashing down.

Tadjik stood stock still, thank God, or the strength of my stable would have been reduced. I pressed myself flat against the cliff face. We remained in this position for about a quarter of an hour. When it became apparent that there would be no further stone chutes, I crawled forward on my hands and knees to discover whether the road had been damaged. I groped in front of me with my hands and suddenly felt space. I felt around in the pitch dark and realized that the road had been swept away.

This was a pretty pass. The path was too narrow to turn Tadjik, and we would have to spend the rest of the night on this precipice until the light of dawn allowed me to carry out a full reconnaissance. There was nothing else for it, so I sat down with my back against the rock wall and Tadjik's rein looped loosely round my wrist. I ensured that it would slip off easily if the horse moved as I had no wish to be jerked over the edge.

Eventually I dozed off to sleep. When I woke up it was about 2 am. Tadjik was asleep, firmly planted on his four legs. I looked at the sky and to my joy I noticed that the clouds were clearing. Presently it was bright moonlight again.

I walked forward to where the road was damaged. I discovered that although a large portion had been swept away it was not irreparable. I set to work and soon had constructed a ledge about two feet wide over the gap. My hands were cut to ribbons by the sharp rocks.

I led Tadjik forward. As he placed his forefeet on this temporary bridge, I thought for a sickening moment it would collapse under him, but with a rattle of loose stones he reached the far side safely.

I walked down the steep descent to the wide suspension bridge at Raikote which spans a deep gorge of the Indus. Tadjik's hoofs echoed loud on the wooden boards of the bridge. Cool air blew up from the river.

"Who passes?" shouted the levy sentry from within the guardhouse.

"'Tis I, Waliullah of Gor," I replied, imitating the broad accent of Chilasi Shina. "I am going to Chilas to barter a little grain for cloth and salt."

"Pass brother, and the Peace of God be upon you."

"Upon you Peace," I replied and vaulted into the saddle.

The moon had sunk by now but it was bright starlight. Tadjik pressed on and on, untiring and steady, and mile after mile was left far behind. The false dawn appeared, a sudden brightening in the sky for about fifteen minutes, and then darkness again. The real dawn started to streak the eastern sky with pink shafts of light as I approached Jallipur, the quaint little fortified post house, built on a natural pier jutting out into the Indus.

By the time I had completed the steep descent to the settlement it was full daylight. I did not stop here, but swallowed a cup of tea gratefully which the levies had prepared for me. I ordered them to send a road gang out immediately to mend the break on the *parri*. I then continued on my way, to complete the last eight or nine miles to Gooner Farm. Tadjik was beginning to feel the strain now so that I did not press him over hard.

The farmer, old Dost Mohammed, was waiting to welcome me, as I approached the little green oasis in the middle of arid desert. His eyes were flashing with delight at seeing me again, and his red beard bobbed up and down as he recounted the adventures which had befallen him since I left Chilas. He is a Pathan so we talked in Pushto. I like talking Pushto more than any other language, it is so expressive.

He had quite a feast waiting for me of tea, bread, fried eggs and delicious little bits of grilled mutton. We sat on string beds, well upholstered with a multitude of pillows. The talk naturally veered to the regime and the old man exclaimed in typical downright Pathan fashion.

"God uproot these Hindu pigs in Gilgit, and you British are not much better the way you have handed this country over to them. You had no right to go away and leave us. You mark my words. Sahib," he said with a final wag of his beard, "if that three times moulted Maharaja accedes to Hindustan there will be a fine to-do."

"It is in God's hands," I replied, "where's my horse?"

Dost Mohammed rushed away and presently appeared leading an ugly looking grey with a figure like a hatrack. He proudly offered it to me. I tightened up the girths of the local saddle.

"Now look after my Tadjik well," I adjured, "and fix up a new shoe on the off-hind. He's cast it."

"Very well, Sahib, *puh makha de khuh*."

"Amen," I replied conventionally, "and many thanks for your kind hospitality, which was in the true Pathan custom."

The grey, despite its appearance, went well and by 1 pm the squat grey fort of Chilas came in sight. As I descended the hill I noticed that a huge crowd of people had collected at the gate of "Journey's End" to welcome me. A band was playing the old familiar tune and strings of bunting had been erected. The scene took me back to the old happy days when, on a homecoming, I would have ridden down the hill on one of my own prancing stallions, followed by a retinue of half a hundred henchmen. There would be bands, flags, and all the splendour of a triumph in Ancient Rome. And now here I was completely alone, riding Dost Mohammed's old screw, a day's growth of beard on my face splattered with blood from the night's adventure. It seemed very strange. But to those who had turned out to welcome me I was still the "Mulki Sahib"; nothing could change that.

I dismounted and shook hands with one and all, Muslims, Sikhs, Hindus: they were all very pleased to see me and I spoke a few words with each. The crowd then dispersed and I entered my old garden accompanied by Muzaffar and the Indian Officers of the Scouts.

A curious incident then happened. I noticed Shaft, an old retainer, raising the Union Jack on the flag pole.

"Hey! What are you doing there?" I called.

"The British have come back, so I am raising the British flag," he said proudly.

"The British have not come back and you are not going to raise the British flag," I said firmly.

He knew I was not really angry. Tears came to my eyes at his loyalty.

We entered the now bare bungalow and I issued my programme. I would do political work all afternoon with Muzaffar and the Munshi. There would be a tea party in the evening in my bungalow for all the officials and notables. I would have dinner at night with the Indian Officers in the Fort. The following morning I would devote my whole time to the Scouts. In the afternoon I would rest. In the evening I would tour the bazaar and public places. There would be a dinner party at night in my bungalow. The following morning at the crack of dawn I would leave for Gilgit.

We set to work. I discovered that, in general, conditions in Chilas were satisfactory. Muzaffar had a good grip on the country. But the idea, which was then so prevalent down country, that independence from British rule meant that everyone could do exactly as they wished, regardless of law, order, and the common decencies of life, had also poisoned Chilas.

Muzaffar was much hampered by holding no executive powers. I therefore conferred on him sufficient powers to prevent a breakdown before Mathieson arrived, but I ordered him not to try murder cases. There had been instances of refusals to pay fines, and forfeited securities, and refusals to disgorge controlled ration quotas. I therefore issued an Edict to the people of Chilas, warning them that lawlessness would not be tolerated and that in the absence of a proper Assistant Governor, the Raja Orderly had full executive powers conferred by me. Any disobedience of orders would be dealt with by me personally, in the same strict way I had dealt out justice in the past. I signed it, sealed it, and dispatched copies to each community. Muzaffar was very pleased.

I then settled some fifty civil suits and passed orders on them. I issued orders that, whatever was happening in Gilgit, all Government servants and officials would be paid their salaries from the Chilas sub-treasury at the end of the month.

The Hindu Agent Munshi, my old friend Krishnan Gopal, requested that he might be given two weeks' leave to take his family down country. I knew he would never return, but I thought the least I could do for the old boy was to let him leave this place where anything might happen.

Muzaffar was a much happier man at the end of the afternoon and showed it.

The tea party was a great success and it was quite like the old days. However the usual table talk on sport and local affairs gradually veered to politics. One and all present advocated that it was imperative to peace and prosperity, that Kashmir should accede to Pakistan. Even the Sikhs and Hindus agreed on this point and I am sure they were sincere and not influenced by being a minority.

After tea I had a talk with my old servants; the redoubtable Daulat, the best Jack of All Trades I have ever known, small, squat and with a quiet sense of humour. I told Daulat to hit the trail in the morning and proceed to Abbottabad where he would meet Captain Mathieson. He was to escort this officer back to Gilgit and to attend to all his needs en route. I warned Daulat of the terrible things that would happen to him if Captain Mathieson was dissatisfied. Daulat chuckled.

Then there was Biko, the perfect Falstaff, always cheery and happy, even more so when in his cups, which was frequent, but most efficient at his job, and an expert at pitching and striking camps and arranging journeys. Drunk or sober, Biko never failed. The unintentional buffoon of the party was Shafi: he just looked comic. I never really found out what his job was.

I felt pleasantly tired when I turned in that night in my old bed on the mosquito-proof verandah. Before going to sleep I summed up the journey which was very satisfactory. A normal four-day journey of 86 miles had been completed in 22 hours on two ponies. But for the three hours delay on account of the avalanche, the time would have been considerably less. It was not outstanding but the satisfying part was that I had proved to myself that my physical condition was such that, but for eventualities, and my inability to have fresh ponies waiting every twenty miles or so, I could have ridden the 86 miles without food, rest, or halting, except to change ponies at each stage.

In the morning I rose early. Muzaffar was also up and about. It was a pleasant cool morning, the babble of the stream and the scent of wild roses filled the air. We wandered about the garden together under the blue gum trees, sunk in our own thoughts. Muzaffar broke the silence. He obviously had something to get off his chest so I let him talk without interruption.

"You know, Sahib" he said, "times have changed and we have a difficult period ahead of us. The whole of what was the Gilgit Agency is pro-Pakistan. There is no doubt about it. We are all Muslims: do you blame us? We could never swear allegiance to Hindustan. Apart from religion, the Gilgit Agency is really a part of the North West Frontier Province and is therefore a part of Pakistan. If Kashmir remains independent, well and good. We shall be independent here but we can also keep the friendliest relations with our brother Moslems in Pakistan. If Kashmir accedes to Pakistan even better. But if the Maharaja through pig-headedness, bad advice, political pressure, or attractive remuneration accedes to Hindustan, then there will be trouble here."

"What sort of trouble?" I asked. "What will the people do?"

"The people can do nothing. By themselves they are helpless and the 6th Battalion of the Kashmir Infantry at Bunji would soon put a stop to an insurrection of any sort. But the Scouts can do something, as the only local, armed force which has been disciplined and trained. If Kashmir accedes to Hindustan you will have to be very very careful how you handle the Scouts. I cannot emphasise this too much. I don't think there has ever been a Commandant who had so much influence over the Scouts as you, but this will test your powers to the utmost. You know what the Scouts are like. Faction feeling is rife. There are some good loyal platoons, and there are some platoons whose actions are unpredictable and who would turn their coats at a whim. I need not mention names. If you mismanage the Scouts in any way now or more especially if Kashmir accedes to Hindustan, then you'll fire a powder barrel which will cause a catastrophe such as there has never been in Central Asia. For God's sake, Sahib, watch what you are doing and keep your finger on the 6th Kashmir Infantry in Bunji. I am loyal to you, Sahib. My father on his death-bed called his sons and adjured them to remain ever faithful to the British and to ensure that not one single hair of the head of a Britisher in Gilgit should ever be hurt, even at the expense of their own lives." (I have made careful enquiries regarding this statement and believe it to be true.)

I thanked Muzaffar for the advice and deemed it wiser to ask no further questions. Actually there was no necessity. The ever faithful Muzaffar had voluntarily given me the most invaluable information and I was grateful.

Sitting on the verandah eating breakfast brought back many memories, but no longer was the table set with my Willow Pattern crockery, embroidered breakfast napery, and the Cona coffee percolator which produced a grand strong morning beverage.

After breakfast I walked briskly up to the fort and made my way to the parade ground. Ten minutes there was quite enough. It was not a parade: it was a slovenly mob of dirty ragamuffins. I knew I could do nothing about it in the short time at my disposal so I left in very apparent disgust before I lost my temper. This was a bad legacy which Jock would have to tackle.

I then made a quick inspection of the fort and found it filthy and quite out of order. Another job for Jock, I thought.

I then went to the office and called for the senior subedar. I proceeded to let him have it in no mean way. To my shame I lost my temper – I seldom do – and cursed him for about ten minutes without stopping. I think he got the fright of his life but the tirade was not without effect. When I later visited Chilas, along with Jock Mathieson, the garrison had improved out of all recognition.

As quickly as I had flared up, I cooled down and quietly yet deliberately said,

"I now want the whole shooting match on parade in front of the office. I shall first of all give them a pep talk and after that every man will swear an oath of allegiance to the Maharaja of Kashmir."

I knew how high the stakes were. If the men refused, I was ruined, both in the eyes of the Governor and in the eyes of the Scouts. But it was a good moment to choose. The senior subedar, having just had a taste of my tongue, had no wish to infuriate me further by having to report that the men refused to take the oath. He sprang to attention, saluted, said, "Very good, Sahib," and departed.

After about fifteen minutes during which, I have no doubt, there was a mighty lot of discussion and quick thinking, he returned to report that the men were ready for their pep talk and to take the oath. I felt a great surge of relief but took care not to show it.

I mounted the soap box and started off by telling them exactly what I thought of the parade I had seen, and the condition of the fort. They looked genuinely sorry. I then continued on the lines I had addressed the Gilgit garrison and headquarters.

Nobody threw the sponge in, but once again there were cries from the back,

"We're loyal to you, Sahib," with great emphasis on the "you".

I ignored it. What else could I do? The oath ceremony now took place.

The Quran Sharif is always kept wrapped up in cloth. The cloth bundle was duly produced and placed on the table. I do not suppose for one instant that the cloth contained a Quran Sharif, but probably some other book of similar size. I did not mind however. The Governor would not know, and I was not supposed to know so I could assure him, in all good faith, that the oath had been taken. All I wanted was for this wretched ceremony to be completed in a seemingly satisfactory way to all concerned without a showdown either on the part of the Governor or the Scouts. And of course this was the answer, for the oath to be taken on a copy of the *Oxford Dictionary*.

One by one the Scouts came up, placed their right hand on the cloth bundle and repeated the oath after the clerk who had read it out from the back of the cigarette packet on which Haider had hastily scribbled if for me as I was leaving Gilgit.

The ceremony over, I had a cup of tea with the Indian Officers in their mess to show there was no ill feeling. Then a quick run through the accounts, which were in order, and I returned to the bungalow for lunch and sleep.

In the evening I visited the bazaar.

Thanks to the foresight of Muzaffar, a large caravan of cloth and salt had jut arrived and I found the stock position very satisfactory. I recalled to the Hindu shopkeepers the occasions on which I had put them all in jail for black marketeering. This raised a roar of laughter; but I warned them again that if any further illicit transactions took place they would certainly return to the cells. They assured me they would behave themselves, with the usual vociferous gestures of Hindu Traders.

I noted with irritation that a number of new shops had been built. In fact the bazaar was quite cluttered up with new shops. Whoever granted permission to build these made a great mistake. What Chilas requires is a small thriving bazaar of good rich shopkeepers who can afford to import the requirements of the countryside. It is hopeless having a conglomeration of small shopkeepers, with no capital, who cannot possibly conduct the import business required in Chilas. Also the beauty of the once picturesque little market had been spoilt by these frightful mushrooms, and the safety of the fort imperilled.

I ordered all building to stop until the arrival of Captain Mathieson. I then visited the hospital where I found an overworked, unqualified compounder doing his best to cope with cases of malaria and dysentery. His stock of medicines was completely exhausted. A proper Doctor and medical supplies were needed immediately. The school was closed for the summer vacation, the Public Works Department non-existent, and the Post and Telegraph Department functioning normally.

On the way back to the bungalow I visited both polo grounds which were in good order. I issued orders regarding certain improvements and grass cutting, as the season was now fast approaching.

After a cheery dinner party I bade farewell to all the officers and officials, as I had no wish they should rouse themselves at an unearthly hour in the morning to see me on my way. They would all have come, without a doubt, if I had not issued a direct order to the contrary. Muzaffar and I sat up late, completing some civil cases, and we turned in about midnight.

I rose at 3 am and was mounted and away by four o'clock.

The faithful Biko accompanied me for the first three miles as a spate had come down a valley on the way and had washed the bridge away. I had no desire to attempt to ford the raging torrent in the darkness without assistance. Biko had a stocky little pony so he kept downstream in case the farmer's nag should be swept away. We urged our mounts into the wild roaring flow of water. Towards midstream, I felt the grey give a little lurch and I knew he was swimming. So I slipped out of the saddle on the upstream side and was pulled along, hanging onto the mane. Eventually we reached dry land – Biko as cheery and happy as ever though we were both soaked to the skin with icy cold water. I waited until he had re-crossed, and with shouts of "God protect you" we went our ways.

The journey was uneventful. I travelled fast to Jaglote, only stopping to change onto Tadjik at Gooner Farm. By 2.30 in the afternoon the trees and police post of Jaglote came in sight, 54 miles in just over ten hours and the hazard of fording a spate thrown in. It was satisfactory, but as Tadjik climbed the last steep dune leading to the Chowki, I realized he was almost at his last gasp. This journey on the top of the long trek from Chitral had been too much for him. I urged the gallant animal forward but I knew he would never make Gilgit that day. A good rest was essential. On arrival I tied him up in a "yarrick" and put a call through to Gilgit on the telephone. I contacted Haider, who assured me that all was well, and I believed him. So rather than leaving Tadjik behind, and proceeding on a borrowed pony, I decided to rest him till midnight, and then complete the last lap.

The head constable, a Hunza lad of the Wazir family, was an old friend of mine, and he soon had a good tea ready. One of his hobbies was baking cakes and he produced some, made in the morning, which were really delicious. We sat on string beds under a chinar tree which shaded an artificial pond built by the head constable and his merry men. In the evening a crowd of people from the Sai Valley came down to pay their respects.

Amongst them was my old friend Wazir Abdur Rahman, the leading headman of the valley, and a dashing polo player. We talked well into the night. After the usual discussions on polo and shooting the conversation swung to politics. Again the trend was the same as I had found in Chilas; bitter reproach toward the British for having forsaken them, contempt and ridicule for the Kashmir regime, and the now ever increasing cry of "Pakistan, Pakistan! We are Muslims, the Kashmiris are Muslims, Kashmir must accede to Pakistan."

After an excellent dinner, the Sai folk lit their lanterns, shouldered their rifles, and slouched off into the darkness. I rested for a couple of hours and saddled up at midnight.

Tadjik was much refreshed and pushed well ahead. I slept steadily for an hour in the saddle between Parri and Minawar and by 6 am I had reached Gilgit without mishap. I have trained myself to be able to sleep in the saddle on long marches and consider it quite safe if the horse is reliable and the road over open desert, and far from dangerous cliffs.

Shawar Din was glad to see me, but not surprised. He had by now learned to expect me at any hour of the day and night under any conditions. He soon produced a steaming mug of sweet black coffee well laced with whisky. I felt I could about turn and ride straight back to Chilas after I had drunk it. Then a bath, shave, change into uniform, a plate of scrambled eggs with scones and marmalade, and dead on the stroke of 7.30 am I walked on parade in the Lines.

If I expected to find the officers absent and the parade a shambles, I was wrong. Everything was in excellent order. Said, Mohammed Khan, and Ghulam Haider were genuinely pleased to see me back, especially the latter, and it was very gratifying to see they had been keeping up the standard of the Scouts in my absence. It was, however, amusing to note the expression of surprise on their faces when they saw me, and on the faces of the Indian Officers and every Scout on parade.

I intended forming my personal and final appreciation of the situation in the Province after I had visited Punial, Kuh Ghizr and Yasin, but in the afternoon I wrote a carefully worded report on Chilas for the Governor.

It has been said that I lulled the Governor into a false sense of security and then banished this at one fell stroke later when the situation was irretrievable. To give one instance of dispelling this idea I shall quote the first paragraph of the report I submitted on Chilas. Under the heading of "General condition of the Sub-province" I wrote: "It seems that the population is pro-Pakistan."

I dared not write then that the population insisted that Kashmir must accede to Pakistan. The Governor might have construed this as my personal sentiments or as personal pressure to bring about the accession of Kashmir and the Gilgit Province to Pakistan. This would have given him grounds to dismiss me or arrest me which would have undoubtedly precipitated a crisis, which had to be avoided at all costs at that particular time.

I presented the report personally. He read it, screwed up his face, and grunted. Before he had time to comment on it I told him that the Chilas garrison had sworn the oath of allegiance to the Maharaja. His manner changed. He beamed all over this face, rubbed his hands and offered me a cigarette.

"That's grand," he said.

Striking while the iron was hot, I replied, "Yes, it is Sir. Tomorrow the Scouts in Gilgit will follow suit, and in a few days I shall proceed to Gupis and carry out the ceremony there."

"Yes, of course," he babbled, "Good work Major Brown, good work!"

I then drank a cup of tea with him. He was in excellent spirits and I departed in a very cordial atmosphere.

In the evening I called the Subedar Major and told him that, on the morrow, all Scouts in Gilgit would take the oath of allegiance.

"Very good, Sahib, of course, why not?"

He had obviously heard what had happened in Chilas: the frontier telegraph is the fastest in the world.

In the morning the ceremony was carried through in the same manner as in Chilas (with the *Oxford Dictionary* or something similar wrapped in a cloth). All concerned were very pleased, especially the Governor who was very hale and hearty when I reported to him at lunchtime.

In the evening I went out fishing with Jemedar Shah Khan, feeling quite at peace with the world.

In fact affairs seemed so satisfactory, for the moment anyway, that I decided to make the Kuh Ghizr tour a holiday come work, and prepared a programme on easy stages ensuring that there was good fishing to each halting place. With the polo season approaching I bought a new pony which had come over in a draft from Chitral. He was a big, raking chestnut who seemed fast and handy. I thought he would fill Sultan's vacant box well. I intended taking the latter to Gupis with me and then sending him on into Chitral as a present for His Highness the Mehtar. I named the new acquisition Samarkand and decided to take him on this tour with me as I would have the opportunity to correct his head carriage between stages.

My caravan left Gilgit on 2 September 1947. It was a small compact one consisting of one personal servant, one cook, two orderlies, a *sais*, and three pack ponies with the kit. We were all mounted and departed at the crack of dawn as the weather was still very hot. We headed up the Gilgit Valley and by 10 am had entered the District of Punial. We halted at the rest house at the first big village of Gullapur which is 24 miles from Gilgit.

The only interesting part of the road is above Hinzal where an immense avalanche, about one thousand feet high, had blocked the valley. The river had carved a course through this avalanche, after remaining a lake for a long time.

This happened in olden times. The story goes that once upon a time there was a village here, situated on the bank of the river. One day a Pir or holy man approached this village, and, parched from the heat and dust of the journey, asked for a drink of water. The villagers informed him that no water was available as only wine was drunk in this village. The Pir told him that, as a holy man, he could not possibly drink wine, and he insisted on getting water. When he discovered it was hopeless, his thirst overcame his scruples and he drank a jar of wine. But as he left the village he invoked Almighty God to punish these wine tipplers, and suddenly an immense portion of the hillside broke away. The village and its inhabitants were completely buried and the avalanche, their tomb, remains to this day.

I lay up in Gullapur all day and allowed the baggage to go on ahead to Singal, 10 miles away, where I intended spending the night.

In the cool of the evening I saddled up and accompanied by my *sais* set off for Singal. We passed Sher Qila on the far bank of the river.

Sher, as it is called locally, is the capital of Punial and is the head-quarters of the Raja. It is joined to the main road by a rope bridge. Three stands of plaited twigs span the wide fast-flowing river. You place your feet on the lowermost strand and your hands on the other two which are level waist high. Crossing is easy provided you proceed in your stocking soles, and do not look down, as the fast current is inclined to make you dizzy.

The Raja was in the hills on a shooting trip so there was no point in my crossing on this occasion.

We jogged on steadily and reached camp about 7 pm. Everything was ready under the expert direction of Shawar Din; tea, hot buttered toast and scones, on the verandah of this picturesque little one-roomed rest house, surrounded by poplar trees. After a pipe, I soaked in a good hot bath and then put on fresh clothes. The local contractor had meanwhile sent round two bottles of wine, which I sampled and found to taste. Then came an excellent four-course dinner, washed down by more wine, and I was ready to sleep the sleep of the just.

I was up betimes in the morning, and was soon out on the Singal stream with rod and tackle. The famous mill pond lived up to its reputation and provided two nice trout turning the scale at 2.5 lbs each. I then fished steadily down to the mouth of the stream where it joins the Gilgit River. A minnow trolled along the distinct line where the clear mountain water meets the grey silty main river, soon caught another beauty over 3 lbs. Well content, I returned to a breakfast of freshly caught trout fried in butter and breadcrumb. A plateful of wild raspberries and cream was also delicious.

After breakfast we mounted up and in three hours had completed the day's march of 11 miles to the windswept flats of Gakuch. I rested all day and re-read *Kim*, my favourite novel.

In the evening I tried rod and line again and brought in half a dozen weighing about 10 lbs in all. A fish pie for dinner varied the monotony of diet, though it really is sacrilege to mess up the beautiful flesh of the brown trout like this.

The next day we journeyed slowly the 24 miles to Gupis, capital of Kuh Ghizr and headquarters of the Raja.

The Raja, accompanied by the Scout Post Commander, Jemedar Sardar Mohammed Ayub of Hunza, and the usual retinue of followers met me some three miles out of the town at the little village of Roshan where the mountain stream of that name meets the Gilgit River. The Raja had prepared an excellent tea under a shady walnut tree. After tea we both fitted up our fishing rods and went our ways. After an hour we joined each other again and compared our luck. I had caught three big ones of well over 3 lbs each, and he had three of like size and one slightly smaller.

We then mounted and rode into Gupis, chatting to each other in the easy conversation of real friendship. After bathing and changing, we had a quiet dinner together with delightfully refreshing conversation, completely free from politics.

The following morning I went on parade and watched the Hunza platoon at work. They were very satisfactory. Clean, tidy, and well turned out, they drilled like guardsmen. I was very pleased and showed it. The Jemedar had an unfortunate appearance. He seemed to have a very weak character and looked "wet", to use a vulgarism. The only admiration I had for him at that time was his prowess on the polo ground. The platoon I knew was a good one, with excellent havildars, so I did not lay its undoubted efficiency to the credit of Ayub. But this was one of the occasions on which I badly misjudged character. When the fun started later, Ayub turned out to be a pillar of strength and one of the best native Officers in the Corps.

After parade I inspected the fort and found interior economy of a high order. No pep talk was required here so instead I chatted to each man individually. It did my heart good to notice their simple friendliness and their genuine delight at seeing me again after an absence.

The swearing in ceremony was completed without incident in the same way as in Gilgit and Chilas. The Hunza lads then brought me tea and refreshments and hovered round to attend to all my wants. In the afternoon I checked the accounts, which were in order, and concluded a firewood contract for warming purposes during the bitterly cold winter which was now approaching.

The Raja came over to the rest house to have tea with me. We were sitting on the verandah talking, whilst the servants clattered the tea cups in the back premises. Suddenly there was a thunder of hoofs on the road, and a rider came galloping into the garden of the bungalow. He drew his horse up smartly on its haunches. The animal reared up on its hind legs, pawed the air with its forefeet, and then came to rest with nostrils distended, flashing eyes and mane and tail flowing in the breeze. The horse was a handsome grey Badakshani stallion, the silver mounted saddlery was brightly adorned with silken tassels, and the large saddle cloth was beautifully embroidered with scrolled design in a medley of colours.

The rider wore baggy white pyjamas and a long flowing shirt. On his head was a silken turban wound round a khula of golden thread in which a heron's crest was stuck. It was Mahboob the Magnificent, Governor of Yasin, looking for all the world like a figure from the Arabian Nights. He dismounted with a flourish, threw the reins to his solitary servant, who had meanwhile arrived, and with a gallant salute shook hands with us both.

"*Salaam Aleikum*, how's life treating you, Raja Sahib?"

"Well Sahib, I heard you had come to Gupis, so it was only befitting that I should present my humble self before you to pay my respects."

We had tea and talked on polo, horses, hawks, and shooting. When cigarettes had been lit, the real object of his visit came to light.

Before I recount the conversation which now took place it is necessary to give a brief history of Yasin and Kuh Ghizr.

At the end of the 16th century, a ruler named Kator held sway over all the country from Jalalabad in Afghanistan to Gilgit. From him are descended the Kator and Khushwaqt families. The former is the present ruling house in Chitral and the latter until recently, was the ruling family in Kuh Ghizr, Yasin, and Ishkoman. After an abominable series of patricides and fratricides by Kators and Khushwaqts in attempts to gain the throne of Yasin and Kuh Ghizr, which was one dynasty then, this shocking state of affairs culminated in the famous siege of Chitral in 1895.

When order had been restored, the Government of India installed Shuja ul Mulk, a Kator, as Mehtar of Chitral, and separated the Khushwaqt country from Chitral by including it in the newly formed Gilgit Agency. Yasin and Kuh were placed under one Governor, whilst Ghizr was separated. In 1896 Ishkoman was made a separate political district and in 1911 Kuh was given to Ghizr, which is the division which has remained to this day. Members of the Khushwaqt family were appointed as Governors of Yasin, Kuh and Ghizr, and Ishkoman, but it was made quite clear that their tenures were neither fixed nor were their positions hereditary.

The Khushwaqts were notorious for their greed, indolence, cruelty, and intrigue. Gradually their misconduct in Kuh Ghizr and Yasin became so flagrant that the Government decided to depose them from Governorships and appoint aliens instead. As has been already described, Mahboob Ali, uncle of the present Mir of Nagir, was appointed Governor of Yasin, and Hussain Ali, whose family originally came from Baltistan, as Governor of Kuh Ghizr. The sole remaining Khushwaqt ruler is the inoffensive Sultan Murad Khan of Ishkoman.

The Mehtar of Chitral has always claimed that he is the rightful owner of Kuh Ghizr, Yasin, and Ishkoman. It is, however, not in fact a question of right, but that Yasin and Kuh Ghizr are the two richest districts in the Gilgit Agency. If it was not for the surplus grain, butter, and flocks of these two districts, the Agency would be a great deal less self-sufficient than it is. In fact they are the granary of the Agency. And it is on these riches that the Mehtar has always had his eye.

So long as Chitral was a feudatory state to the Imperial Government, she could do nothing about this. But when the paramount power withdrew, a different light was shed on the situation, and Kator brains got to work. A direct *coup d'état* was obviously impossible. So Chitral adopted tactics which a certain great power is using with considerable success at the moment.

Despite the fact that the Khushwaqts misgoverned the country so badly, they still have a surprising amount of influence and are held in much respect by the people. This is remarkable but it is true. Through infiltration, promises, and other means, Chitral decided to instigate an internal insurrection in Kuh Ghizr and Yasin against the alien rulers. When the situation was completely out of hand and chaotic, Chitral would march in on the plea of restoring order, and once established would never be ejected again. It was hoped that Kuh Ghizr and Yasin platoons in the Scouts, under Khushwaqt platoon commanders, would join the rebellion and cause such disruption in the corps that it would be impossible for the loyal platoons to be dispatched north to deal with the situation. It was even rumoured that Punial and the Punial platoon would join the rising, and would be given Ishkoman as their share of the loot.

This was the interesting story which Mahboob told me and which was confirmed by Hussain Ali. They said that at that very moment instigators and infiltrators were hard at work in their respective districts, sowing the seeds of rebellion. With my knowledge of the country, I knew immediately that they were both speaking the truth. Another thought struck me then, but I made no mention of it to the Rajas. If Kashmir (which included the Gilgit Province) acceded to India, Chitral would in all probability fulfil her ambition of annexing Kuh Ghizr and Yasin by invading the Province on the grounds of freeing the people from Hindu rule. Then there would be a show-down of no mean dimensions.

On the following day, Yasin and I went out on a fishing picnic as guests of the Raja of Kuh Ghizr, and political troubles and personal worries were forgotten for the moments in pleasant company, good sport, and delightful surroundings. On the next day I returned to Gilgit by two stages, the 35 miles to Singal on the first day, 34 miles to Gilgit on the second, arriving at lunch time.

After lunch I went along to see the Governor. He was sitting on the verandah on the leather-covered armchair, he was still wearing the olive green uniform, he was still puffing away at his hubble-bubble and he did not have a care in the world. After the usual small talk, I explained very carefully, very deliberately, and perfectly truthfully the situation in Kuh Ghizr and Yasin. The only part I omitted was the reference to the Scouts, because I knew I had absolute control over the three platoons which might join the insurrection. I even went so far as to suggest that the Kashmir Government should be informed of the situation immediately with a view to opening negotiations with Chitral. For some reason he did not like my suggestion at all and showed it.

"What they (meaning Chitral) can do?" he asked. "We, (meaning himself) can deal with such situations ourselves."

"Of course, Sir," I said, and no more. I had no wish for a row with him and I could see he was becoming annoyed. "The garrison in Gupis have all taken the oath," I replied, changing the subject.

He beamed.

"Good work, Major Brown, that's the stuff."

In a minute he was happy again and offered me a cigarette. Once again we parted in a friendly atmosphere, he ushering me through the door with his arm round my shoulder, and walking with me as far as the gate.

In the evening Said and Haider came up to my bungalow. Mohammed Khan, I gathered, had gone to Sonekote to visit a fair and obliging young Gilgit lass with whom he had struck up an acquaintance. We sat on the lawn on deck chairs. We exchanged news – theirs was unimportant, mine was carefully guarded. I offered them gin – it's inclined to make tongues wag more quickly than whisky. Said, the perfect ADC poured the drinks out and I noticed that he gave himself and Haider very stiff ones from which I gathered that the solitary existence in Gilgit was beginning to have effect.

As the evening wore on, I carefully plied them with more gin. They both waxed eloquent and I turned the conversation to Kashmir politics. Said said he had no idea what the intentions of the Maharaja were but he thought the State would remain independent, having concluded a stand-still agreement with both dominions. He then leant forward and addressed me in a confidential whisper.

"If Kashmir accedes to India, then I, as a true Muslim, will have to resign my commission in the State Forces. So in the event of such an accession, Sir, you must be prepared to release me from the Scouts."

"And that goes for me too," said Haider in a slightly tipsy mumble.

With this statement coming from Said, I immediately thought it was a trap to draw out my sentiments, which would be communicated to the Governor in due course. So I made some non-committal reply about it being a democratic world and that everyone should act according to their own wishes.

The following morning I was lingering over breakfast coffee on the verandah, when Haider appeared with a bundle of files under his arm.

"I have some Scout work to discuss with you, Sir," he said whilst the servants were present.

I poured him out some coffee in the extra cup which always lay on my table for the unexpected guest. He looked a bit pale around the gills and his hand wavered slightly as he lit a cigarette. I could tell from his manner he had come to discuss something much more personal than Scout work. He eventually started: "Do you remember what Said said last night about our resigning our commissions, if Kashmir acceded to India. Well, it's perfectly correct, so far as I am concerned."

"What of Mohammed Khan?" I asked.

"God knows," Haider replied, "he's not interested in politics. His main object in life is sleeping with women, and the best way to give his undivided attention to this without distraction, it is to keep on the winning side."

This was very interesting as it confirmed my own opinion of the happy-go-lucky little fellow. We then walked down to the Lines together and carried through a normal day's work.

I noticed in my rack several futile routine letters from the Governor from which I gathered that his office had started functioning. On enquiry, I discovered this was the case. Evidently the Personal Assistant and the Revenue Assistant were finding that the inertia, though convenient, was extremely unprofitable. And the Kashmiri brain soon appreciated that there was good scope for reaping unlawful profits in Gilgit. So these two worthy gentlemen had gathered round them all the bad-hats of the countryside – all the rascals who had been dismissed from Government service during British rule for bribery, corruption, and other nefarious crimes. This happy little gang had now opened the Governor's office and law courts, and had settled down to relieve the local population of all spare cash.

The modus operandi was to get their henchmen to reopen old cases already decided by Assistant Political Agents. A reversed decision would always bring in a handsome present from the previously aggrieved but now favoured party. Heavy fines, in lieu of imprisonment, would swell the day's takings which would be split on a fifty-fifty basis each evening and placed to the private credit of the two gentlemen concerned.

Sahdev Singh had evidently seen my letter to the Governor regarding Indian Officer promotions. He approached the prospective candidates and suggested that for a small remuneration he might use his influence with the Governor to secure a favourable decision. Unfortunately for him, I heard about this. On a suitable occasion, I warned him that if I discovered any more interference whatsoever in Scout affairs I would have no hesitation in using physical violence. He evidently made a distorted report regarding my threat to the Governor, for I received a long lecture from the latter on the necessity for co-operation between departments. It appeared that the Governor had implicit faith in the integrity of his Personal Assistant so I deemed it wiser to refrain from enlightening him on the abuses in the law courts. With all respect to Ghansara Singh, however, I must say that he himself was perfectly honest and straight-forward, and under no circumstances would he have lowered himself to the level of his minions. It was merely a case of misplaced trust.

That evening I locked myself in my office with orders that I was not to be disturbed. I intended completing my final appreciation of the situation in the Province. I noted down on a sheet of paper the relevant facts I had gleaned on my two tours.

I then started piecing the jigsaw puzzle together.

The Governor's administration was hopeless, and tolerable only if Kashmir remained independent or acceded to Pakistan. The ninety-nine per cent Muslim population unconditionally supported Pakistan. But the only way that the passive support could be converted into direct action would be if the Scouts joined the movement.

I knew I had complete control over six platoons of the Scouts and could make them obey my will, whatever it might be.

These were the three Hunza platoons, the Punial platoon, the Kuh Ghizr platoon, and the Yasin platoon. I had no faith in the three Nagir platoons. They were in the power of the Subedar Major, who if led astray by others, through his gullible nature, might do any foolish act.

The Gilgit platoon was, I thought, unreliable and might do anything. Unity in the Scouts was essential. A hint of disruption would lead to chaos, as the Governor would immediately order disbandment and would enforce the order through calling on the help of the 6th Kashmir Infantry from Bunji. A clash of arms would then be inevitable. A Khushwaqt insurrection was boiling up in Kuh Ghizr and Yasin. The crushing of this would result in the loss of many lives as I would most definitely use the Scouts and use force for this purpose.

I could prevent this rebellion by making a personal appeal to the Mehtar of Chitral to withdraw his instigators, and use his influence over the Khushwaqts to stop them rebelling.

The Mehtar, who had now acceded to Pakistan, would certainly agree to my appeal provided I did not owe allegiance to India. But if Kashmir acceded to India then my fealty would be with that dominion. If Kashmir acceded to India then the Mehtar of Chitral would invade Kuh Ghizr and Yasin on the grounds of liberating them from Hindu rule; and the invasion might not limit itself to these two districts only. Such aggression would naturally be opposed by the Scouts and the 6th Kashmir Infantry with a resultant war.

Furthermore, I had received reports of infiltration by Swatis into Darel and Tangir. In the event of Kashmir acceding to India, the Wali (Ruler) of Swat might well order his armies to advance on Gilgit and Chilas to liberate them, not so much for material gain, as the spiritual satisfaction of striking a blow for Islam.

It was obvious that if the dogs of war and destruction were to be held in leash in Gilgit, then the Province must join Pakistan, even if the Maharaja decided that his State should accede to India.

As I recalled the halcyon years I had spent in this happy country, amongst the simple folk who had been so content under all that British rule meant, I shuddered at the thought of the havoc which would follow a decision by the Ruler of Kashmir to join India. The blame for the widespread destruction of life and property would lie directly on the British Government. I therefore felt it was my duty, as the only Britisher left, to follow a course which would prevent this. And further, as a liberal member of the world's paragon of democracy, I considered that the whole of Kashmir, including the Gilgit Province, belonged indubitably to Pakistan in view of the fact that the population was predominantly Muslim. Partisan, traitor, revolutionary, I may have been, but that evening my sentiments dictated that if the Maharaja acceded to India, then I would forego all allegiance to him and I would not rest content until I had done the utmost in my power to ensure that not only the Gilgit Province joined Pakistan, but the whole of Kashmir also.

The Rubicon was crossed, and in the future all my actions were governed by these ideas.

Chapter 3

The Gathering Storm (September to October 1947)

1. Plans

[In September 1947 Major Brown was joined by his friend Captain Jock Mathieson as Assistant Commandant of the Gilgit Scouts.]

Through intelligence reports, I carefully watched Mathieson's progress up the Kaghan Valley. He eventually reached Chilas and we had a short talk over the telephone. It was good to hear his voice again. I told him to come up to Gilgit as quickly as possible with light kit only. On the morning of the day on which he was due to arrive, I rode out to Jutial to meet him, accompanied by the Subedar Major, the usual crowd of retainers, the local band, and my dogs. We amused ourselves in a shady garden by listening to the band. Some of the followers danced. Eventually the lookout man signalled riders in sight. A small cavalcade came over the brow of the hill, with Jock at the head.

"Would you like to spend a penny?" I said significantly, after I had introduced him to the Subedar Major and other notables.

We went behind a wall.

"Don't appear too friendly with me and don't talk politics when others are present," I said.

We then mounted and rode towards Gilgit, preceded by the band. I let Jock do the talking and he told me about his journey which he seemed to have enjoyed very much. He was full of the beauty of the Kaghan Valley, the bare ruggedness of Ghilas, the fresh air, the camp life, and this majestic country of God's creation.

He told me about my friends in Waziristan and Peshawar; who had deserted on Partition, who had remained, weddings, births and all the other little bit of gossip which it is human to enjoy.

I had arranged a little surprise for Jock. He was not aware that there was a bagpipe and drum band in the Scouts, almost as good as that in any Highland Regiment. I had concealed the band in a spinney at the Sonekite road end, with orders to strike up as soon as we approached. On entering the long willow tree avenue, I ordered the local band, which was blowing its insides out, to take a rest. Far away in the distance came the skirl of Scottish pipes playing the old war song of my Border, The Blue Bonnets.

I watched Jock's reaction. I do not think he could believe his ears at first, when the sound became unmistakable, he turned in the saddle and said with a delighted smile, "My God, so you have a real band top, and as fine as any at home by the sound of it."

This was a compliment as Jock is no mean performer on the pipes himself.

"Well, The Blue Bonnets are over the Border today, all right, and though there are only two of them, folk will do well to heed as usual our old slogan of 'wha daur meddle wi' me'."

"Yes indeed," I replied.

As we approached the road end the band swung onto the main track with perfect precision and took its place at the front of the procession. They accompanied us as far as the Scout Lines and went through a specially selected repertory: The Cock o' the North, The Highland Laddie, The Barren Rocks of Aden, The Black Bear, and a contrast in the Zakhme Dil and Krishna, the latter a rousing Punjabi march. As we approached the Lines the band played The Green Hills, the customary tune of Highland Regiments on approaching camp after a long march.

We entered the Lines, and I introduced Jock to the Officers and Indian Officers.

Old Shawar Din was waiting on the doorstep, a broad grin from ear to ear, and grasping Jock by the hand he welcomed him in true Pathan fashion with the usual series of enquiries regarding his health.

"Kher raghle (welcome), Sahib," he said. "May you never be tired. Are you well? Are you strong? Are you happy? Are you quite well? Are you quite strong? Thanks be to God."

We were due to lunch with the Governor and his staff.

The Governor met us on the doorstep. I introduced Jock. The Governor was most effusive, put his arms round Jock's shoulders, and greeted him like a long lost son. They entered the lounge in this posture and introductions to the various official were carried out. We then sat down and were offered soft drinks and cigarettes.

We were grouped round the room in an orderly circle, Jock and I lounging in our chairs and making easy conversation. The others sat bolt upright in their chairs and gazed at Ghansara Singh in obsequious admiration. Jock later named them Guv and Gang which was most apt. There was a newcomer, a young Muslim engineer named Hamid. He was a timid, quiet creature. Muslim Government servants in Kashmir have to be if they want to hold their jobs. I felt very sorry for him: he looked like a lost sheep.

For about fifteen minutes Jock and I waffled away, as the others considered it irreverent to talk in the presence of the exalted one, who sat with his arms folded, benevolently beaming on one and all. When the Governor was not present, the gang would chatter away merrily enough.

We presently went into lunch, which, as I had prophesied, was excellent: tomato soup, pilau, two or three kinds of curry, and jelly to finish. The staff seemed fond of their food. In the course of the conversation Jock began explaining the reactions to partition in Pakistan. He told us about a hectic Independence Day party in the Razmak Club where great friendship and goodwill was shown between British and Pakistan Officers. He explained how many British Officers had elected to serve on in Pakistan whereas very few had decided to do likewise in India.

He was just beginning to explain how bright the future of Pakistan was as the leaders had sensibly decided to retain as many British Officers as possible in key positions until the Dominion was in her stride, when I glanced at the Governor. He looked extremely angry. He was breathing hard and perspiration glistened on his bald head, in the centre of which a single hair stood straight up on end. Evidently the name Pakistan was to Ghansara Singh as a red rag is to a bull. The officials looked on in shocked silence. Obviously the conversation had gone far enough: I had no wish for the Governor to have an apoplectic fit or for him to assume that Mathieson's sentiments lay with Pakistan. So I gently kicked Jock under the table and he changed the conversation.

When we were leaving after lunch we dallied at the gate for a chat with Said, Haider, and Mohammed Khan.

"You know," said Said with a hint of reprimand in his voice, "the mere mention of Pakistan is taboo in the State of Jammu & Kashmir. Any infringement of this unwritten law is followed by immediate dismissal from service and probably a stretch in Hari Parbat prison."

I thought a lot, but said nothing except a tactful joke to gloss the matter over. No harm had been done, as everyone realized that Mathieson's conversation had merely been the impressions of a neutral observer in inter-dominion politics. But the interlude had produced invaluable information as it was now clear where the Governor's sentiments lay and that freedom of speech was not encouraged in Kashmir – especially in connection with Pakistan.

On returning to the bungalow, we both went into the sun parlour, sat down in easy chairs, and lit pipes. I then talked to Jock for three uninterrupted hours on the political, strategical, and tribal structures of the old Gilgit Agency and the extent to which they affected the Scouts. I finished by saying,

"What I've just told you is with regard to conditions prior to 1 August 1947. I want you, during your stay in Gilgit, to study the present set-up in the light of the background I have just given you. Before you return to Chilas, I shall ask you to give me these impressions. We shall not discuss the matter further till then."

"Right oh!" said Jock, "but what you've just told me is amazingly interesting. I had no idea there were such complications."

"There are no complications," I replied, "provided you use common sense; and retain your sense of proportion whatever happens."

I then sent for tea, which Jock noted was well up to Khajuri standards; hot scones, fresh butter, strawberry jam, pancakes, and cakes, all found a ready home. We lingered over it and laughed much at the funny collection of people with whom we had lunched.

"How on earth," asked Jock, "does that comic opera govern the Province?"

"They don't," I replied.

After tea I whistled up the pack, now augmented by Jock's Alsatian Bruno and his small Dachshund named Oscar. We went for a walk through the settlement so that I could point out the places of interest.

We finally strolled through the bazaar so that Jock could meet the shopkeepers and traders. They were pleased to see us, no doubt noting with satisfaction that another "pale face" would help to consume the large stocks of articles used by Europeans, which they now regarded as almost a dead loss. However, motive or no motive, they were genuinely friendly and cheery.

On the way home I decided to pay a call on the civil wireless operator, Mr. Limbuwala.

The Gathering Storm (September to October 1947)

This would be a convenient stage to describe the wireless set up in Gilgit. The Scouts had five obsolete sets which some Commandant had been swindled into buying. No spare parts were therefore available, and by cannibalization over a period of years only two serviceable sets were left. They were both most unreliable, and maintained a spasmodic intercommunication between Gilgit and Chilas. The civil wireless operator in Gilgit had a powerful modern set, installed just before partition. Limbuwala was the only person in Gilgit who could operate this set, though on one occasion he had shown me the essentials of procedure and wavelengths for contacting Peshawar and Srinagar. I could have operated the set in an emergency but, so far as I knew, he had divulged the information to no one else.

Limbuwala was therefore an exceedingly valuable man: in fact indispensable. He was in the process of entering into a contract with the Kashmir Government, with a view to remaining in Gilgit, but as far as I could gather the Maharaja and he did not see eye to eye with regard to salary.

Prior to 1 August 1947, two daily contacts were made with Peshawar. Nowadays intercommunication was being attempted with State Force signals in Srinagar but with little success. Contact with Peshawar was forbidden but I have no doubt that Limbuwala slipped in the odd call from time to time to exchange news with his operator friend, Donaldson. It could be said, therefore, that the only reliable wireless contact was with Peshawar.

As we entered the compound of the station, Limbuwala came out of the wireless room. A Parsee from Karachi, he had married a Kashgari lass which accounted for his desire to stay in this part of the world. He had spent many years as operator in His Britannic Majesty's Consulate in Kashgar. Tall, thin, and of sallow complexion, he was always immaculately dressed, over-dressed in fact for Gilgit. He was of a highly excitable temperament, though when calm he was capable of shrewd observations. He was now dressed in a smart pinstripe, collar and tie, a red carnation buttonhole, a neat felt hat, and suede shoes, in marked contrast to our scruffy clothes.

He seemed extremely agitated and without apparently noticing Jock he started a wild tirade against the army signallers in Srinagar.

Jock was much surprised at this incredible behaviour.

"The man's as mad as a hatter," he said.

"Maybe," I replied, "but he can do his job all right and he's absolutely indispensable. If anything happens to Limbuwala, the consequences may be disastrous. It is essential that we keep on good terms with him and humour him. If he is mad, then we must ensure that the madness does not take a turn which will put him *hors de combat.*"

It was ironical that such an insignificant creature could hold such important cards.

The next ten days were uneventful. I put Jock through the mill the hard way in learning the Scout work. As with Said, Haider, and Mohammed Khan there was to be no trailing round with the Commandant, watching theory. Practical experience was required, so Jock spent five days in the Adjutant's department studying and practising every branch of the work from drilling recruits to balancing monthly accounts. A further five full days he spent in the Quarter Master's Branch, checking and issuing stores and ammunition, ledger keeping, learning indent procedure and so on. Higher policy he picked up from me during conversation at home. I made no discrimination between Jock and the other officers except due regard to his being second in command, and I soon discovered we had a very happy cadre which pulled together as a team. Said and Haider came up to the bungalow often, as also did Mohammed Khan when more important matters allowed, and they invited us down to their bungalow to drinks and dinner.

In his cups Said still seemed pro-Pakistan, yet I could not make up my mind whether this was genuine or an attempt to probe my sentiments for the benefit of the Governor.

Sometimes in the evening the five of us would ride out to Sonekote and I would give the learners instruction in polo. These were happy outings; we laughed and joked a lot especially at Jock's new pony which Subedar Jamshed of Hunza had lent him. It was minute, standing about eleven hands high and had a fluffy mane and tail. We named it Bimbo. Jock used to fall off frequently but the distance was short and no damage was done. On one memorable occasion he was shot over Bimbo's head and landed on his feet, to the delight of Said and Haider who roared with laughter. Yes we were a happy team. If only clouds had not been on the horizon, if only it had been the old days, it would have been perfect.

One evening Jock and I were sitting on the lawns before dinner. We had had a hard day with the Scouts and now, having bathed and changed, we had the delightful feeling of being pleasantly tired. It was a beautiful night: the sky was bright with stars and Konidass, the mountain on the far side of the river, was clad in a yellow mantle of moonlight. It was very still, except for the incessant buzz of crickets and the occasional high-pitched scream from a stallion in the stable. As we sipped our sundowners and smoked our pipes a great feeling of peace came over us. A shooting star blazed over our heads and disappeared over the chinar tree.

"This is a heavenly paradise," said Jock, "if it wasn't for …"

"I know," I said, interrupting him, "but the pill is more bitter for me, who knew the old days. By the way, Jock, let's have it out now. What is your frank opinion of the situation in the Province?"

"Well, Willie," Jock replied, "the politics up here are so intricate that I could never hope to understand them in such a short time. I leave that to you, who understand them better than anyone else. We have both lived amongst Muslims and sometimes lived as Muslims for a long time now. All our friends in Waziristan are Muslims and we both supported partition when it became obvious that independence was inevitable; we supported partition because our liberal-minded sense of fair play saw that the Muslims would never get a fair deal in a united India under a Congress Government."

"The big question of the moment is which side of the fence is the Maharaja of Kashmir going to jump? If he has the sense to jump toward Pakistan good and well. But if he accedes to India, the people here will not stand for it. There will be an upheaval of some sort. The question is what are we going to do? Are we going to support the Kashmir regime as we are duty bound to do? If we do, surely we shall be acting against our own democratic sentiments, which could never agree with the hundred thousand Muslim inhabitants of the Gilgit province being forced against their wills to become members of the Indian Union. Or shall we actively join and naturally lead the revolution in favour of Pakistan which will undoubtedly take place?"

"Or shall we take the coward's way out by sitting back and watching the entertainment from a neutral point of view? I know neither of us would dream of adopting the latter attitude, so let's discard it. As for the other two courses, whichever we take with a unity of purpose, that one will end in eventual success. My opinion is that our combination is so strong that we can undertake any task here and emerge triumphant. Further, my sentiments dictate that I am bound to support any movement, the object of which is to make the Gilgit Province, and Kashmir for that matter, an integral part of Pakistan. It would be downright tyranny, it would be against the ideals of the Atlantic Charter, and all we fought for in two World Wars, if the predominately Muslim Kashmir, including Gilgit, should be forced against the will of the people to join India. That is my own idea, and I know, Willie, that it is yours too."

"Yes, Jock, you are quite correct," I said, "and now we must make a plan which can be put into operation in the event of Kashmir acceding to India. Guv is pressing that you should return to Chilas so I shall persuade him to allow me to accompany you. That will give us plenty of time to think, which is most necessary as nothing can be left to chance."

I charged up our glasses.

"Here's to the two revolutionaries!" I whispered jokingly, "and now, Jockie boy, we are going to get blind drunk for the last time until the Gilgit Province has become a part of Pakistan."

"To hell with Guv, to hell with politics, to hell with everything: here's to us, wha's like us, nane, they're a' deid," we chanted simultaneously and emptied our glasses down our gullet.

Neither of us have a very clear recollection of what happened after that. But, as far as I can gather, we became uncontrollably hilarious, created a terrific disturbance by singing every song we could think of at the pitch of our voices, which certainly must have wakened the Governor over the way. With three bottles of gin inside us, and Konidass heaving as though in the throes of an earthquake, we weaved an unsteady way to bed as dawn broke. As a grand finale, we stood on the verandah with our arm round each other's necks and bellowed Land of Hope and Glory.

"I hope Guv heard it," muttered Jock as we fell into our beds.

That was the last time we touched more than a minimum amount of alcohol until our mission had been fulfilled.

We were awakened about 10 am by Shawar Din with the usual hangover paraphernalia on a tray: aspirins, Alka Seltzer, Eno's Fruit Salts, and Worcester sauce. After liberal doses, I felt capable of reading a chit which had just arrived from the Governor. He requested our presence.

"Now we're for it," I said, recalling the disturbance of the night.

"Better play the 'mad white man' Englishmen at play and all that sort of thing. He'll fall for it," said Jock with a laugh.

However it was on an entirely different matter that the Governor wanted to see us. He made no mention of the nocturnal revels but as usual welcomed us cordially. He explained that close relationship was required between the Scouts and the 6th Kashmir Infantry at Bunji. He had therefore arranged that the Battalion should come to Gilgit for a few days so that friendly contact could be established.

I wrongly thought that the motive was something much more ulterior so I tactfully evaded the request to billet the Kashmiri sepoys in the Scout Lines. I suggested they might go under canvas at Sonekote, on the plea of limited accommodation in the Lines. Actually this was correct, but on no account did I want the 6th Kashmir Infantry housed where they had access to all the important magazine and rifle *kotes*, once they were in their possession, the Scouts would be no more use than a polo pony with a broken leg.

"Now I want you two to make out a programme of entertainment for the sepoys," the Governor continued.

"Oh yes, Sir," we chanted. "Football, polo, athletics, physical training displays, oh yes, we'll fix that, Sir."

Ghansara Singh beamed.

I considered this a good opportunity to request permission to go to Chilas with Jock. The Governor readily agreed. He was in excellent spirits, which made me extremely suspicious.

In the evening we returned with the draft programme. The Governor was still seated on the verandah on the leather-covered chair, smoking his hubble-bubble. He was surrounded by his staff who greeted us with smarmy salaams and leers.

The Governor read the draft.

"Very good, very good," he said, "but we must have Japanese stunts."

A vision of Guv and gang performing weird gymnastics in the middle of the football ground flashed across my mind. I looked at Jock. He winked. Our thoughts were evidently running on similar lines. We both bit our lips hard to prevent laughing.

"Yes, we must have Japanese stunts," the Governor continued.

There was silence.

"Please, Sir, what are Japanese stunts, Sir?" asked the Personal Assistant.

"You fool, don't you know Japanese stunts? We'll hide half the 6th Kashmir Infantry in the hills near Jutial. Then I shall ride out with the Mirs of Hunza and Nagir who will be unaware of the troops along the rocks. As we approach the sepoys will fire live rounds at us, but slightly above our heads of course. The Mirs will be very surprised and thrilled. The other half of the Battalion will then attack and chase away the raiders. The Mirs will be very pleased and will realize the might of the Kashmir Army. These are Japanese stunts, as happened in the Burma jungles during the war."

I realized then that there were no grounds for suspicion. There was no ulterior motive in this. In fact I was witnessing a comic opera such as one would pay money to see in a Variety Palace in London. I looked at Jock. He was gazing at the floor with a large lump of his lip held tightly between his teeth. The others looked extremely worried.

"Had their Lord God Omnipotent gone mad?"

As for me, I found it very difficult to keep a straight face.

"The Mirs surprised, thrilled, perhaps pleased," I thought to myself. Surprised they would be all right, but they would also be mad with rage if such a prank was played on them. They would immediately summon their respective platoons from the Scouts, and annihilate the Governor on the spot, irrespective of repercussions.

The Personal Assistant was clever enough to see this too. He glanced at the programme and turned up what he thought was a trump card.

"There is no available time for Japanese stunts in the programme, Sir."

"Of course there is, you fool," Ghansara Singh replied, "we'll have Japanese stunts before polo on Thursday morning."

"But polo starts at 9 am. We'll all be still in bed when the Japanese stunts are taking place," countered Sahdev Singh.

"Shut up, you blithering idiot," bellowed the Governor, "whatever happens we shall have Japanese stunts."

Ghansara Singh was now livid with anger. His bald head glistened with sweat and the single hair in the centre stood on end. And this is where Jock came to the rescue; thank goodness, too, as I feared physical violence would be done shortly. It was not long before he had persuaded Ghansara Singh that a much better way of displaying the might of the Kashmir Army would be to have a drill exhibition, followed by a demonstration of Bren guns and three-inch mortars, but without live rounds of course. Something nice and quiet on the Parade Ground, where spectators could be accommodated at ease in deck chairs.

The matter settled, we excused ourselves. We hastened back to my bungalow and loosed our pent-up mirth in roars of laughter.

"That old fool along there, babbling about Japanese stunts, and quite oblivious to the fact that he was sitting on a powder barrel!"

It was quite ludicrous; but presently an informer arrived with news which brought us back to all seriousness again. The police picquets had been withdrawn from Jaglote Chowki and Partab Pul bridge and the posts had been occupied by detachments from the 6th Kashmir Infantry by order of the Governor. On considering this move in the light of future events, I do not think it was made through a full appreciation of the seriousness of the situation in the Province, but rather through a personal desire on the part of the Governor to have Kashmiris holding what would be key point if he had to make a sudden dash back to Srinagar; a sense of self-preservation, in fact, rather than a master stroke of strategy. But it made us both think.

In the morning about 5 am Jock and I left Gilgit with a Scout patrol of about fifty men, including the Subedar Major and Jemedar Shah Khan. Our intention was to proceed to Chilas over the hill route. We marched out to Basin and bearing left entered the mouth of the Kargah Valley where an immense figure of Buddha is carved in the cliff face.

The locals, ashamed of their Buddhist ancestry, claim that the figure is not Buddha. Their story goes that in ancient times an ogress inhabited Basin who lived on human beings. One day a Pir arrived. He offered to use his divine powers to turn the ogress into stone and cast her on the cliff face, provided that the people promised to ensure that his bones were buried in Basin when he died. If his remains should be buried elsewhere, then the ogress would come to life again and continue her cannibalistic propensities. The people promised, and the ogress was duly transformed. But to ensure that the Pir's bones were eventually buried in Basin, they slew him and laid him to rest under the stone figure cast on the cliff. His grave, which has now become a shrine, may be seen to this day.

Having marched about three miles up the Kargah we reached the mouth of the Shinghai (Wild Rose) Valley which branches off to the left. Our route lay up this valley, but the entrance is so narrow and the flow of water so great that we could not proceed direct through the mouth. Instead we had to climb up the sheer cliff face on the true right-hand side of the mouth, to a height of about three thousand feet above the Kargah and then drop down an equally steep precipice into the Shinghai. The valley up which our route lay that day is the very devil to negotiate. There is no track, one has to march up the bed of the stream which is covered with immense boulders; the valley is very narrow and bordered on either side by sheer precipices; one has to ford the stream continually, backward and forwards; if the water is in spate it is impossible to penetrate this nullah, and there is always the danger of a sudden flood coming down from the mountains with fatal results. Our progress was therefore slow, but not unsatisfactory considering that most of our strength was recruits on their first patrol.

I had set a definite schedule and ensured that it was adhered to by moving with the advance guard myself. We reached the midday halting place at the correct time, and a good many people were extremely glad of the breather. It was a pretty glade of mountain ash trees where a tumbling burn joined the Shinghai. Jock and I found a secluded spot and sat down together. Our clothes were soaked through from the constant crossing of the stream but they soon dried in the hot mountain sun. We ate our lunch of bread, dried fruit, and walnuts washed down by delicious water from an ice-cold spring. We then lay back and rested in the heavenly atmosphere.

It was a great temptation to lie there forever, but dead at the end of one hour I blew my whistle as the signal for "prepare to march". Whilst the men were fixing their equipment I focussed my binoculars on the green slopes below the glacier summit of Kurkun, 15,520 feet high. I saw Shah Khan doing the same. We must have spotted a herd of ibex at the same time, as he gave me the knowing wave of one keen sportsman to another. We watched them until they had disappeared from sight round the shoulder of the mountain.

"Going up?" I shouted to Shah Khan.

"I'll go if you will," he replied.

"Too high, for the time at our disposal," I said.

The afternoon was hard work with some very steep ascents over marble-covered slopes. About 4 pm we reached the deodar belt at 10,000 feet and the valley started broadening out. It was very pleasant walking up through the woods on pine needle carpets after the rock and conglomerate. But the route was still very steep and I noticed that several of the recruits were beginning to feel the strain. So I called a half hour halt. Shah Khan and I took a section and decided to push on ahead to find a suitable campsite for the night. Up and up we went. The deodar gave way to silver birches. At about 12,000 feet the birches receded and the valley widened out into a broad grassy plain about four miles in breadth, bordered on either side by bare mountains of rock, utterly devoid of any vegetation whatsoever.

We reached a large shallow dip in the ground which we considered would be suitable for a camp. It was sheltered from the bitter winds which would blow down from the passes at night; there were a few stunted juniper bushes, which seemed to be

The Gathering Storm (September to October 1947) 101

growing there by mistake, but they would serve as firewood; there was a convenient spring nearby; and the location was sufficiently near tomorrow's trial of endurance, the Kinejut Pass 16,000 feet high, so that the ascent would be made in the energy regained by the night's rest.

As the rest of the patrol was not in sight, Shah Khan and I climbed a nearby peak to see if there was any shikar in sight. We spotted a herd of markhor and stalked them. They escaped us, however, and we returned to camp as the others arrived.

Some welcome sweet tea was ready, so after posting guards and picquets, Jock and I settled down beside the campfire. The men proceeded to make themselves comfortable for the night, as only these hardy mountaineers of Central Asia could do in such a bleak place.

After tea, I took a walk round and chatted with the recruits. I was well pleased with them and told them so. We had covered 21 miles that day over incredibly difficult country and in good time. Jock and I then cooked ourselves some chicken and potato stew, which tasted delicious. We yarned for a bit round the fire, but the long day in the invigorating mountain air had made us sleepy. Gradually the camp fires went out, one by one, and silence fell. We climbed into our sleeping-bags and fell into the sleep of the just under the bright starlit sky.

We both slept well, on our grassy couch, and woke at dawn feeling much refreshed. A wash in the icy stream cleared the cobwebs away, and whilst I sat on a hillock studying the route, Jock prepared an excellent breakfast of sweet tea, boiled eggs and bread. By 6.30 am we were on our way again, swinging over the springy turf with renewed vigour and gulping down great breaths of the intoxicating mountain air.

We continued over this plain for about seven miles. The ascent was steady and not objectionable. In fact it was difficult to believe we had climbed 2,000 feet from the camp site. We had now reached the foot of the watershed dividing the Gilgit Sub-division from Chilas. We halted for a quarter of an hour whilst I checked the route. We were in a large amphitheatre round the top of which were about six passes. Some led back to Gilgit, some led into the tribal territory of Darel, but only one, the Kinejut Pass, led into Chilas.

Although I had crossed this pass before, I had no wish to make a mistake. It is the most galling experience imaginable to make a difficult ascent to a pass and then find it is the wrong one. I had previously erected a cairn on the Kinejut Pass, but I now noticed that cairns had been erected on all six. A watershed is most confusing and looks different every time you approach it. So I took no chances and confirmed our direction by a quick compass bearing. We then proceeded and had a most trying two miles over a depression between the plain and the foot of the pass. This depression was filled with immense boulders and we had to hop from one to another. A false step meant a broken leg. Eventually we were all safely across. Now for the final effort. The ascent, though normally fairly easy, looked difficult today as the rock face was covered with fresh powdery snow which made the going very slippery.

Shah Khan and I led the way, leading alternately as we helped each other over the more difficult hazards. We soon reached the summit along with one or two of the more stalwart Hunza lads. As we climbed the last lap Muzaffar and his henchmen appeared from the Chilas side. We greeted each other warmly. We then turned and shouted encouragement to the others labouring up below us on respective sides, and chucked snowballs at them. Eventually we were all on the summit and the usual exchange of news took place.

It was disappointing weather. Dull and cloudy, there was little view to be seen. There was a howling gale blowing which cut through our lightly-clad bodies to the very marrow of our bones. I was sorry that this should be Jock's initiation to the normally uplifting effect of the higher altitudes. He was undaunted, however, and was speechless with emotion at having reached such a height for the first time in his life.

It was no time for lingering so the Gilgit patrol withdrew on the Gilgit side under the Subedar Major, and we joined Muzaffar, Subedar Sher Ali and the Chilas patrol.

The descent into Kinejut was awkward, over sliding shale slopes, but we eventually reached the bottom without mishap. Muzaffar had pitched camp at the little village of Dangdalosh, some fourteen miles down the valley, a long way after the recent endurance test but it was all down hill, and I thought it was much better to push on to the comparative comfort of the village rather than spend another night in the mountains. The scenery was much the same as on the Gilgit side. First of all a long grassy plain, now deserted by shepherds and their flocks as winter was drawing close; through the silver birches and into the deodar and pine forests.

We reached camp late, about 8 pm, and the last few miles were completed in the dark.

A good night's sleep revived us but I decided to do a short march the next day. So we struck camp at 7 am, and moved easily down into the Khiner Gah Valley. The only excitement en route was the discovery of a large black snake among the rocks. We soon disposed of it with sticks and stones. After about ten miles we reached a pleasant camp site in a garden of shady walnut trees beside the clear Khiner Stream and I gave the order to halt and pitch camp.

We spent the rest of the day in well-earned idleness and guddling for fish in the burn. Both Jock and I were quite successful with the result that we had some excellent grilled fish for supper that evening. They were not trout, but an indigenous variety called *Choosh* which are capable of surviving the heavy mud slides which occur from time to time in the streams of Chilas. Trout have been tried, but have always been washed out in these floods. The flesh of *Choosh* is rather cotton-woolly and full of small bones; but one becomes much too particular when accustomed to the delicious flesh of the incomparable brown trout.

In the evening the local headmen came to pay their respects and I introduced them to Jock. Many of the local folk arrived in camp with petitions so I set up open court and gave the new Assistant Governor a demonstration of the effectiveness of summary judgement on the spot. I must have decided about twenty disputes in a manner agreeable to all concerned before it was too dark to continue.

One interesting case was a dispute between two men over the ownership of an extremely weedy goat. After extensive enquiries I found it quite impossible to establish ownership as there was absolutely no proof one way or the other. I noticed one young boy, sitting in the audience, whom I knew to be an orphan and in very poor circumstances. So to the delight and wholehearted agreement of all present, I awarded the goat to him. Even the contestants applauded the decision as fair. Faces were wreathed in smiles and beards wagged as the Elders muttered,

"Verily, the Sahib has not lost his touch."

One man accused another of raping his wife. Now I knew that these two men were deadly enemies and lost no opportunity of bringing false accusations against each other.

"Produce the wife," I ordered.

Presently a woman arrived whose face was covered with a cloth.

"Take her aside."

I then told a venerable and respected elder to examine the beauties concealed under the head cloth and report the result to me. He returned with a smile on his face.

"She is an aged woman of well over eighty who is long past the stage of inviting rape or sexual passion of any sort."

It is not etiquette for a young man like myself to gaze on the fair countenance of a young Chilasi lass, but no objection can be raised to looking on those who are no longer eligible. So on the strength of the elder's report, I decided that no harm could be done if I examined this creature whose attractions were alleged to have raised the passions of another man. She was the most frightful old withered hag I have ever seen. I would have said she was getting on for at least a century. She screamed abuse at me in a cracked voice. I turned to the village elders.

"Do you believe this woman was raped?"

"Never, Sahib," they replied.

So the accuser accompanied us to Chilas on the following day to cool his heels in the jail for a period. This little session was a very good object lesson for Jock and gave him an insight into the wiles of the Chilasis and the countermeasures required in dealing with them.

On the following morning we set off on the last lap of the journey to Chilas, some 22 miles. By noon we had debouched on to the sandy plain bordering the grey Indus at Thalpin, and the Chilas settlement lay before us on the far bank. Owing to dangerous currents at this time of year the ferryboat was plying about three miles downstream. So it was necessary to cover this tiresome distance over furnace-hot desert. But the thought of ice-cold beer waiting for us at "Journey's End" spurred us on. The boat was waiting at the appointed place with the skilful old bearded skipper at the helm, and his sturdy sons on the oars. We piled in well nigh exhausted. The Chilas band was in attendance and it struck up a lively tune which revived us somewhat. As the boat reached the centre of the river, it circled three times in our honour whilst the music reached a crescendo.

Our ponies, which had come down the main road from Cilgit, were waiting for us on the far bank, which was fortunate as the ascent from the Indus to the settlement is far from easy. With the band in front, we gradually climbed the hill and approached the bazaar. The bazaar was *en fête* such as I have never seen it before. The streets were lined with cheering crowds, waving strips of cloth and bunting, among which were many Union Jacks. Every forty yards or so triumphal arches had been erected, gaily decorated in red, white and blue. The shops were also decorated and long strings of bunting traversed the street. We could hardly force our way through the dense crowds which had now swarmed onto the road to kiss or shake our hands.

"The British have come back," was the cry on every lip.

It was really most embarrassing but we had to carry the ceremony through with acknowledgements, waves, salutes, a word here, a word there, a handshake and so on. Jock leant over in his saddle and whispered in my ear.

"They really think the British have made a triumphal comeback. Go and raise the Union Jack on the fort. We can then dispatch a cable to Mr Churchill to the effect that we are both fed up with the way the British Empire is being frittered away, so we have decided to regain as much as possible, and have started by taking over Chilas again."

The excitement eventually calmed down in bewildered astonishment that the red and yellow of Kashmir was still flying.

It was well past 2 pm when we reached "Journey's End". We decided to call the rest of the day a holiday, so we dismissed the staff. We lingered long over an excellent al fresco lunch of Spam, cheese, pickles, and beer and conversed idly. In fact we lingered so long that lunch ran into dinner, after which we retired to get as much sleep as possible, as there was much important work ahead.

There was quite a big Hindu population – probably about a hundred head – which kept shops and traded in the Chilas bazaar. They were a clever gang, and worked in close co-operation. They had definitely done well for themselves as there is excellent scope for trading in Chilas as already described. They had transformed some of their gains into a palatial Hindu Quarter, consisting of large bungalows built of dressed stone, which stood out in marked contrast to the rude little Chilasi dwellings.

Unfortunately for the Hindus their quarter had been built some distance from the fort, so in times of stress they became extremely concerned about the safety of their persons and their property. They considered this such a time.

My policy had always been to have mobile patrols of Scouts moving about the entire bazaar area, including the Hindu Quarter, at irregular intervals throughout the night. This had seemed to me sufficient and had proved very effective. There had been no thefts at all in my time and the culprits had been captured by these patrols in three attempted raids. The entire area was surrounded by a heavy barbed-wire entanglement.

The Hindus, however, had always wanted a strong standing patrol posted in the middle of their area at night. I was much against this, especially at this time of the year when Chilas strength was low owing to our temporary two-platoon post at Babusar and constant patrols to the passes. With my knowledge of the country and conditions, I knew there was no immediate danger. I offered any Hindu who considered himself in danger, complete protection if he moved his household into the fort area, where I was prepared to let him have, if necessary, tents. However the Hindus appealed to the Governor for this standing patrol and backed their appeal with reports of recent thefts from their houses at night.

I investigated these alleged reports carefully and found them completely false. I told the Governor so, but nevertheless he insisted that a standing patrol of half a platoon should be posted in the Hindu Quarter at night. This meant that the Chilas garrison was constantly on duty and never had a night's rest in bed. Now the night before we arrived in Chilas this standing patrol had been fired on ineffectively from the direction from the cemetery. I think about six shots had been fired and the Scouts had replied.

I therefore asked the senior Subedar, Subedar Jamshed of Hunza, to make an immediate report on this incident, unprecedented since Chilas had been taken over at the end of the last century. He reported that it was the work of some wild Chilasis imbued with the spirit of freedom and independence. I doubted it as I knew the Chilasis would never fire on the Scouts under any circumstances for fear of the consequences – so long as I was Commandant.

I therefore consulted my own trusted informers who supplied a much more likely story which I later confirmed as true. Evidently during the night two Scouts had moved from the picquet to the cemetery. They had then fired six shots over the heads of the rest of the patrol, which returned a similar fire. The two Scouts had then rejoined their comrades. The object of this was to frighten the Hindus so much that they would decamp to the fort area on the following day. This would save the Scouts the extra trouble of manning the picquet nightly and what they considered the ignominious task of guarding Hindus.

I decided that any direct action on my part would only lead to dangerous religious hatred, which was the very thing I wanted to avoid. So I told Jock to maintain the standing patrol for about a week and then withdraw it and revert to irregular mobile patrols again. I also told him to offer all Hindus who considered themselves in danger, complete safety for their persons and property in the fort area. Retaining the standing patrol for a week would show the Scouts that they could not force my hand by such methods, and yet a week was not sufficient time to cause a religious flare-up. All concerned would attribute this decision to Jock, which would raise him in their esteem.

I then dispatched a wire to the Governor to the effect that the Scout standing patrol had been ineffectively sniped by Chilasis. This would give him something to think about and keep him from the possibility of interfering in other more important matters. The telegram had the desired effect, incidentally, for on my return to Gilgit he babbled for days about building concrete block-houses in the Chilas bazaar, owing to the disturbed nature of the country. He even went so far as having blueprints prepared.

After disposing of this affair, I decided that the rest of the day could be well spent in giving Jock an insight into the judicial work. So I told Muzaffar that Court would be held that morning, and that the case which had been pending longest should be brought up for trial.

At 10 am we took our places under the big chinar tree in the garden and I declared Court duly open. The prisoner was summoned. He was a very typical Chilasi; thin, sharp featured, with a scraggy beard and a long drooping moustache; he was dressed in a dirty grey shirt and pyjamas and he wore a black *koi* on his head; I shall call him X.

The Council of Elders convened for the case appeared, venerable old greybeards with black sheets round their shoulders, and after salaaming, they squatted down on their haunches in front of my table. The accused was asked whether he objected to any member of the Council. He replied in the negative so the case proceeded.

The main prosecution witness, the levy who had investigated the crime, came forward and, after taking the oath, gave his evidence. It appeared that X had murdered his wife, his sister-in-law, and another man named Y. For a long time X had been suspicious that his wife was carrying on an illicit love affair with Y, a handsome young Chilasi lad, barely out of his teens.

So one day X announced his intentions of going to Gor to collect a debt. He set off at dawn, but as soon as he had reached the hills above his house, he hid himself in the rocks. He lay there all day. It became terrifically hot as the sun reached high heaven but he endured it with infinite patience. As the evening shadows afforded him a little respite, his long wait was rewarded. His eye, as sharp as a hawk, saw Y approach and enter his house. His sister-in-law took up guard at the door by busying herself in a noncommittal way with wool winding.

X drew his axe from the girdle round his waist and slowly whetted it on a convenient stone. He then stealthily slipped down the hillside, using the cover of rocks and bushes as only a born shikari can. The last hundred yards to the house he covered at the double. His sister-in-law, on seeing him, let out a wild scream. He grabbed her by the hair and dragging her with him, flung open the door, and went inside. He found his wife and Y locked in the embrace of the supreme act of love on a string bed. With the animal rage of primitive civilization increased by the long day among the hot rocks, he swung his axe at the nape of Y's neck, and with one blow half severed the head from the body. Another wild swing completed the ghastly work and the grinning head fell to the floor like a football. He kicked the twitching body off the bed as a fountain of blood spouted out from the neck.

The sight of blood maddened X even further. He yanked his wife to her feet and with three sharp strokes of the axe slit off her nose and ears. Holding her head back by the hair he cut her throat and as the body fell to the ground, he abandonedly hacked at her breasts in a final gesture of rage. X now turned his attention to his sister-in-law who was cringing in a corner, hypnotized with horror. He caught her by the hair and stretching her head back until the throat was taut, slit it from ear to ear. Tearing a strip from the dress of the body, now kicking its last drop of lifeblood out on the floor, he calmly cleaned his axe and wiped his hands. Without so much as a glance at the dreadful carnage, he turned on his heel and left the house. He walked straight to Chilas and reported the incident to the Raja Orderly in a typically fatalistic way.

In Court, X confessed to the crime as just described, so there remained only the question of judgement and punishment. His fatal mistake had been the murder of his sister-in-law. The double liquidation of wife and paramour in flagrante delicto had been committed in accordance with local custom which was recognized by law in Chilas and which was punishable with imprisonment till the rising of the Court at the most. But local custom definitely did not cover the killing of the sister-in-law.

I asked the Council of Elders for an opinion. They agreed that the murder of the sister-in-law was unlawful but they pleaded for leniency on the grounds that the accused had been acting under grave provocation.

The Gathering Storm (September to October 1947)

I agreed to the extent of not imposing the limit of the law which was fourteen years' imprisonment. But on the other hand local custom must be adhered to strictly otherwise it would be abused with disastrous results.

So I sentenced X to five years' rigorous imprisonment. He smiled, thanked me, and walked away with the levy escort.

I rapped on the table to denote that Court was closed.

That night was the memorable occasion when we formed the plan which was the swan song of Kashmir rule in the Gilgit Province.

As was our custom before all-night sessions of difficult work, we ate a light early dinner, a plate of tomato soup followed by some macaroni and cheese. We then proceeded to the operations room, which was the mosquito-proof verandah, and laid out the tools of our trade: maps, paper, pencils and a large pot of strong black coffee.

"Now for it," we said as we settled in our chairs in the flickering light of a hurricane lamp.

To ensure continuity and lack of vital omissions we adopted the army procedure but not method. A military plan is usually straightforward and few factors have to be taken into consideration except those directly related to the object. The textbooks teach that a cut and dried plan should be made which, when once set in motion, should be carried through without change of purpose, whether the original decision was right or wrong. Quick decisive decisions are advocated which it is considered fatal to alter when once accepted. But for any scheme in Gilgit, of the magnitude and importance of the one we were planning, Hamlet decisions are required, decision sicklied o'er with the pale cast of thought, of political considerations, tribal structures, religious jealousies, mistrust, in addition to strategy and tactics. A fluid plan is very necessary which can be moulded to fit the most incredible situations which may easily arise. Any officer with a reasonable amount of common sense can form a plan. But the brilliant tactician is the one who can foresee every way in which his plan may miscarry through force of circumstances, and have a ready remedy at his finger tips to meet every eventuality which may arise.

Assuming that the Maharaja of Kashmir would accede to the Indian Union, our object was to perform a *coup d'état* in Gilgit with as little bloodshed and disturbance as possible, and then accede to Pakistan of our own accord. We now reasoned the factors affecting the object.

Would Pakistan accept the accession of the Gilgit Province? From the spiritual point of view, Islam preaches democracy and freedom of the will of the people. She would therefore undoubtedly accept a country, the population of which was ninety-nine per cent Muslim, and a population which unanimously desired to join Pakistan. From a practical angle, Pakistan would surely be as anxious as the British were to guard the northern frontiers against aggression and infiltration from Central Asia.

Did the people of the Province genuinely desire to join Pakistan? Or were they prepared to accept the accession of Kashmir to India with their usual fatalistic outlook on life?

Most Muslims assume that the British prefer them to Hindus owing to the close similarity between Islam and Christianity as opposed to the ramifications of Hinduism.

Had the people, therefore, given me a false impression that they were pro-Pakistan on the understanding that this was the impression I would like to gather? The people of this part of the world, incidentally, are experts at giving the answer or impression which they know will please, rather than a straightforward opinion.

Everything pointed to active Pakistan proclivities but there was just that shadow of doubt. Nothing could be left to chance and this doubt had to be eliminated before we fixed on a day to launch the revolution.

Success, or otherwise, of our cause hinged entirely on the two armed forces in the Province, the Scouts and the 6th Kashmir Infantry.

What of the Scouts?

Hunza, Punial, Yasin and Kuh Ghizr were completely under my control. This represented six platoons, and most of headquarters, giving a total strength of about three hundred and fifty rifles.

We were at that time not so sure about Nagir and Gilgit Sub-division, with four platoons numbering about two hundred men. Dispositions would therefore have to be arranged so that there was a majority of platoons of unquestioned loyalty in Gilgit headquarters and Chilas.

The 6th Kashmir Infantry was the greatest factor in the whole enterprise.

The battalion consisted of about five hundred men. One third were Sikhs, one third were Dogras, and one third were Muslims. The battalion was well trained, with an excellent war record, and was equipped with all modern weapons such as Bren guns, Sten guns, 3 inch mortars, and grenades: a great contrast to the Scouts. There was no doubt that the Sikhs and Dogras were implicitly loyal to the Maharaja and they would fight to the last man and the last round in opposing a revolt in the Gilgit Province.

The Muslims were a doubtful quantity. They might remain loyal to Kashmir, they might forego their allegiance and join their co-religionists. It was impossible to say at that stage.

Individuals?

Captain Mohammed Said, as I have already said, I did not trust. He would have to be removed from Gilgit.

Lieutenant Mohammed Khan would, I suspected, wait until he saw which side was winning before he cast in his lot. He was therefore useless to us and must also go.

Subedar Major Mohammed Baber Khan I also did not trust, but nothing could be done about it. Any attempt to get rid of him would give grounds for grave suspicion, and might have regrettable consequences. He would have to stay.

Our brains were now working at full speed and with these factors in mind we proceeded to form the method of achieving our object. As the first grey streaks of dawn were filtering through the gauze netting, we finally competed our task. This was our plan:

1. The operation was to be called DATTA KHEL and would be put into immediate effect as soon as I signalled this code word to Jock in Chilas.
2. It was impossible as yet to fix a day for the *coup d'état*. I would watch developments carefully in Gilgit and the burden of choosing the correct day would lie on me, as

The Gathering Storm (September to October 1947) 109

soon as I had decided that the time had come. The day would be called D day and subsequent days D+ 1, etc.

3. On D day in Gilgit I would act as follows:
   (1) put the Governor and his staff under protective custody;
   (2) put all Hindus and Sikhs in a refugee camp under guard;
   (3) cut all telephone links;
   (4) take over the civil wireless station;
   (5) set up my own administration of the entire Province;
   (6) signal the Prime Minister of the North West Frontier Province in Peshawar, to the effect that there had been a revolt in Gilgit in favour of Pakistan, and with the request that he should inform the Pakistan Government;
   (7) take whatever steps I considered necessary to uphold the new regime.
4. In the meantime Jock would take similar action in Chilas as relevant, but the responsibility of dealing with the 6th Kashmir Infantry also lay on him. If the Muslims of the battalion turned out to be loyal to the Maharaja, the action would be as follows: A fighting patrol of three platoons of Scouts would move out from Chilas and move with all haste to the Raikote bridge. From here the patrol would continue on the left hand bank of the Indus and move secretly to Bunji via the Hattu Pir and Ramghat bridge. Their arrival at Bunji would coincide with the start of the operation in Gilgit and Chilas which would be at night. They would then make a lightning surprise attack on the quarter-guard, rifle *kotes*, and magazine of the 6th Kashmir Infantry. These were all in the same area so the task would not be difficult. They would liquidate the sepoys on duty on the quarter-guard, and secure the rifle *kotes* and magazine. It had already been ascertained that except for those on quarter-guard duty, all rifles were placed in the *kotes* at night. The battalion would therefore be *hors de combat* now, and could easily be made prisoners *in toto*. At the same time as this attack was being carried out, a fighting patrol from Gilgit would liquidate the 6th Kashmir Infantry picquets at Jaglote and Partab Pul Bridge. Scout picquets would then be posted on the bridges at Chamogarh, Partab Pul, Ramghat, and Raikote and our tactical position would be secure for the meantime. If on the other hand, the Muslims of the 6th Kashmir Infantry were prepared to forego their allegiance to the Maharaja and join us, then we would leave the task of crippling the rest of the Battalion to them. This would be very simple if done with surprise. A patrol from Chilas would merely wipe out the Battalion picquets at Jaglote and Partab Pul Bridge; the Scout patrol would secure the latter to ensure that in the event of the Muslims in Bunji failing to carry out their task, the Sikhs and Dogras would be unable to cross the river and play havoc in the Sub-division.
5. Prior to D day I would get rid of Said and Mohammed Khan by some means or other. I would also send the Nagir platoon in Gilgit to Gupis and withdraw the Hunza platoon from Kalamdarchi. The Governor had already agreed to the evacuation of this post. The Mir of Hunza had agreed to garrison it with his own levies. I hoped to have my dispositions on D day as follows: one Nagir platoon, one Punial platoon, and one Kuh Ghizr platoon in Gilgit headquarters; one Hunza platoon en route to Gilgit (or actually arrived) from Kalamdarchi; one Nagir platoon and one Hunza

platoon in Gupis; one Nagir platoon, one Gilgit platoon, one Hunza platoon, one Yasin platoon, plus about fifty armed levies in Chilas.

As an old rooster hailed dawn in the compound, and the sparrows in the roof eaves started twittering noisily, we completed the last formalities by memorizing key words for our private code.

Shawar Din and Daulat presently appeared with a plate of fried eggs, toast, and piping hot coffee. We ate ravenously, laughing and joking the while, almost hysterically, after the long and intense concentration of the night. Breakfast over, I told my followers to saddle up.

The summer had now given way to the early autumn so, without the burning heat, I looked forward to a comfortable journey by day. We rode leisurely. There was much to think about and there were many opportunities on the way to usher in the *chikor* shooting season. It was grand to shoot the sporting little birds out of the sky again. What could be more delicious than a roast *chikor* for the evening meal in camp and a cold bird for the picnic lunches. I never shot more than were actually required for the pot en route: that would be a waste of useful time and senseless slaughter.

As I jogged along over the soft sandy desert, I reflected on the legacy I had left Jock in Chilas. I was not at all happy about the Scouts. Lack of supervision and idle Indian Officers throughout the summer had lowered their discipline and morale.

The present Subedar, Jamshed of Hunza, though pleasant and jovial, was not popular. He had a knack of raising the hackles of everyone serving under him. He ruled through fear, and on the Frontier this inevitably ends in one sticky way. The men of his platoon however were faithful to him under every circumstance: they had to be because a brother of the Mir wielded considerable influence in Hunza, and all sorts of nasty things could happen, such as the confiscation of their land, should they incur his wrath.

The Hunza and Yasin platoons were loyal and would unquestionably obey Jock's every order. But the two platoons were at daggers drawn with one another owing to the Yasinis' hatred for Jamshed. In Chilas I sensed that it would not be long before they caused a show-down of some sort: mutiny, instigation of mutiny, desertion with arms, general trouble-making would break out soon.

The resignation of the Nagir platoon commander, Subedar Jan Alum, was significant in itself. He refused to give any reasons for his resignation except for the lame excuse of a bad leg. But he obviously foresaw trouble in which he had no wish to take part. With the short time at my disposal in Chilas, I had no time to probe further into the condition of the Nagir and Gilgit platoons. And furthermore the complaint required the delicate operation of a skilful surgeon, who had taken time and trouble in studying X-ray plates of the affected area. Any attempt to remove the cancerous growth with a sudden hack of the scalpel would undoubtedly cause the flare-up which I was trying so hard to avoid. I therefore deemed it better to refrain from interfering.

At even-fall we had completed the 26 miles to the stage of Jalipur. Comfortably tired, we spent the night there. We were on the trail again at the crack of dawn. The air filled with the tinkle of pony bells as we jogged past the baggage caravan.

I treasure a pony bell. It was given to me by an old Turki caravan leader on the top of the Mintaka Pass as he bade me farewell and headed away into the unknown of mysterious Central Asia with his loads of merchandise. Wherever I am, be it the big cities with their dirt and din, or my beautiful Borderland, the sound of this little bell transports me immediately to the mighty peaks of the roof of the world, to the good companionship of the mountain trails unspoiled by noisy motors, and to nights under the clear starry sky in the dancing shadows of the twinkling camp fires. The bell, and the call of a stallion at dawn! [Margaret Brown still has the bell: it adorns her sitting room in the Borders.]

At about noon we reached Jaglote Chowki, 28 miles from Jalipur. I had been looking forward with interest to our arrival as the post was now manned by the 6th Kashmiri Infantry, and we were halted by a smart Sikh sentry. When he realized who I was, he called out the guard. They presented arms and paid me full honours.

We dismounted and the ponies were led off to the standings. I met the Post Commander, a stout Dogra Subedar, a typical old time Viceroys' Commissioned Officer, brave, tough, and loyal to the hilt. He was very friendly and invited me to take tea with him. I accepted. He yarned about his service, his war experiences, and his home along the Kangra Hills. The next time I saw the Subedar he was a naked corpse, being torn to bits by dogs and vultures, his body riddled with bullets by my order, after he had gallantly fought on single-handed against the Scouts when his sepoys had been wiped out to a man. How few of the unsung acts of the bravery of the small wars are remembered? To what dire limits one reaches, what a futile loss of life takes place on account of the stupidity of rulers and politicians.

I kept my eyes and ears open, and gathered that the strength here consisted of one Subedar and twenty sepoys. Twelve sepoys were posted to the Partab Pul Bridge. At Jaglote two thirds of the strength were Sikhs and Dogras, one third was Muslim. At Partab Pul all were Sikhs and Dogras. Discipline was obviously good as the post was neat and tidy. The sepoys were all clean and turned out smartly. They seemed well trained and handy with their weapons. I noted carefully the day dispositions of the sentries.

After announcing my intention of spending the night in Jaglote, I phoned up the Adjutant in Bunji and told him I was coming across that afternoon on a goodwill visit. He extended a warm invitation. Escorted by a handful of armed followers, I descended the steep sandy slope to the right hand bank of the Indus.

The big flat-bottomed ferryboat was waiting for us, as the river had now fallen sufficiently to allow it to ply. In summer it is necessary to make the tiresome journey round by the Partab Pul bridge. We cast off and soon reached the other side. The summer floods of silt and mud had now run themselves out and the water was crystal clear. The Adjutant of the 6th Kashmir Infantry, a big well built Sikh named Captain Baldev Singh, was waiting on the far bank to meet me. He was effusive in welcome and we were soon on friendly terms as we climbed the steep slope to the Battalion Lines. We proceeded to the mess. It was a ramshackle building with a few sticks of old furniture. Its only redeeming feature was a fine view looking over what had been a pretty garden to Nanga Parbat, the inscrutable, seeing all, knowing all, yet saying nothing.

I was introduced to the other officers.

The Commanding Officer was Lieutenant Colonel Abdul Majid, a Muslim from Jammu. In his early fifties, he seemed ponderous and heavy, rather like an elephant, but kindly, likeable and possessed of a clever sense of humour. I gained the impression that he would be a skilful, if slow, commander in the field, and I later discovered that he was very popular with his men of all castes and creeds. He appeared to have his battalion well under control. But he was tired and disinterested. His main topic of conversation was the pension he was about to receive from the Maharaja for some thirty years loyal and uneventful service. He would then retire to the peace and comfort of Jammu, far from such Godforsaken outposts as Bunji. He was very friendly and seemed very glad to see me as a break from the monotony.

Next came Lieutenant Raganath Singh, a fresh looking Dogra boy, still in his teens. He lacked personality and seemed very nervous.

Lastly came Captain Mirza Hussan, anglicized, dashing, and quite the man of the world. He was tall, thin yet well built, he had a fair complexion with handsome features, a neatly clipped moustache, and dark wavy hair. He wore a well cut uniform of the cavalry style which showed off his figure to perfection. He carried the purple and white ribbon of the Military Cross. His family were ordinary peasants in Gilgit proper. They had managed to educate their son, who had repaid their trouble by doing well for himself in the Jammu & Kashmir State Forces. Whatever Hussan's failings were, one could not help admiring his original initiative.

The Colonel suggested I might like to see the Infantry Lines to which I readily agreed.

Again I kept my eyes and ears open. As I thought, the quarter-guard, rifle *kote*, and magazine were all in one building. I carelessly enquired and noted the dispositions of the day and night sentries. I confirmed my previous idea that the Battalion was well disciplined and under control.

Good Sikh soldiery is very good, bad Sikhs are worse than useless. These men were good Sikhs, of pure Jat stock, soldiers by trade and tradition.

The Dogras were also good materials, loyal little men from the Kangra Hills and good fighters. It was obvious that both the Sikhs and the Dogras were a foe to be reckoned with.

The Muslims were a poor crowd. Some of the older NCOs seemed better but the rank and file was chiefly made up of inexperienced recruits. It was of course impossible to tell where their sentiments lay and I deemed it wiser to stay very clear of this subject.

By way of conversation Majid mentioned he was finding it very difficult to run the battalion with so few officers. A brainwave struck me. Why not get rid of Mohammed Khan by having him posted to Bunji? So I suggested to the Colonel that he ought to inform the Governor regarding his officer position and the latter might be able to have another one sent up from Srinagar. I would ensure that the other one would be Mohammed Khan from Gilgit by hook or by crook.

We returned to the mess for a rather inferior tea but obviously the best that could be produced. The officers seemed to be living under very poor conditions. As it was getting late, I bade farewell after tea and left requests to pay another visit soon.

Mirza Hussan volunteered to accompany me as far as the ferry. He seemed genuinely keen to cultivate my friendship and I responded as I thought it might lead to something interesting and useful. Little did I know then that there would be times later when we would gladly have buried a knife in each other's bellies.

When I returned to Jaglote, I found my camp had been pitched some little distance from the post. This was wise. The ponies had their nosebags on, the followers were cooking their evening meal, a good tea and hot bath were waiting for me; in fact everything was as it should be in an orderly camp. Before turning in for the night I made a more careful check than usual that my protection arrangements were satisfactory and I also quietly noticed the dispositions of the battalion night sentries. I then coded all the information I had received that day in a wireless message, which would be dispatched to Jock in Chilas as soon as I reached Gilgit on the morrow. I relaxed on my camp bed and fell asleep.

We struck camp at 4.00 am and reached Gilgit at 10.00 am. I carefully noted the strength and dispositions of the picquet at Partab Pul en route and included this in my code message to Chilas. All seemed well in Gilgit; Sammy and Dinah gave me a great welcome, sniffing the game bags significantly in the knowledge that the season had started and that the idle summer was over. After the usual routine of bath, shave, and change, I ate an excellent breakfast of *chikor* covered by poached eggs, washed down by a frothy pint of beer. I then felt fit to face the world.

I paid a customary call on the Governor. He was still sitting on the verandah in the leather-covered chair, puffing at his hubble-bubble, and still wearing the olive green uniform.

He looked worried, but brightened up slightly on seeing me.

"You know, Major Brown," he said, "I never receive any replies to the messages and letters I send to the Kashmir Government. It's most disturbing. I really feel quite helpless."

I told him about my tour and reiterated the fact that the people of Chilas were still pro-Pakistan. He winced: the very mention of the word Pakistan made him jump as though a pin had been stuck in his vitals. He changed the subject abruptly and I saw there was little point in trying to tell him more.

In the afternoon I checked up on the Scouts. All was well, which was very satisfactory.

On my way home I called in on Said, Haider, and Mohammed Khan. The latter had gone to Sonekote, but the others were in good spirits. We talked on topical subjects and they pressed me to stay to dinner. I declined, however, on the plea of being tired, which was true.

2. October 1947 and the Crisis Begins

Despite the great changes which the summer had seen in Gilgit, and despite the storm clouds now ominous on the horizon, another glorious autumn began to spread her gorgeous mantle over the countryside. As I sat in the butts at Sonekote in the evening, waiting for the mallard to swing in over my ready gun and dogs, as I walked up the gardens on a quiet afternoon to drop the odd woodcock, as I wandered round the foothills behind my bungalow to keep the larder stocked with *chikor*, as we played polo on Mondays and Thursdays with the same old fire, it was difficult to realize that a crisis was approaching. The season was now mid-October.

A particular stroke of luck fell my way one day in connection with DATTA KHEL. The Governor summoned me. He was holding two papers and seemed agitated.

"Look here, Major Brown," he said, "Colonel Majid has just written to me from Bunji. He tells me that he is finding it extremely difficult to run his battalion with such a small cadre of officers. Do you think you could possibly spare one from the Scouts?"

This was a Heaven-sent opportunity to get rid of Mohammed Khan, but it was necessary to show no eagerness which might arouse suspicion.

"Well, Sir, it will be difficult," I replied. "We are right in the middle of our autumn training and I am finding all three officers satisfactory and essential. But, at a pinch, I might spare one."

"Yes, yes," he said, "who do you suggest should go?"

"I think Mohammed Khan," I replied. "He is an ex-ranker and therefore much more suited to regular soldiering than Scout work."

The Governor was aware of Mohammed Khan's inclinations *vers les femmes* and he also had a shrewd suspicion of the alliance with the wee lassie at Sonekote from hints dropped by me. He knew that this might lead to alarming repercussions with consequent trouble to himself in settling the affair.

So with visions of getting rid of this troublesome creature, the Governor readily agreed to Mohammed Khan going to Bunji. This was a load off my mind. I was sorry, in a way, to see him go, but it was vital in the interests of DATTA KHEL. He left the following morning.

The Governor's other paper contained more luck for me. It was a report from the Governor of Yasin that he was fully expecting a Khushwaqt revolt any moment now. He pointed out that he had no means whatsoever of protecting himself or putting down the rising. The one Scout platoon in the neighbourhood would naturally be required to protect Gupis where a similar conflagration would be taking place. The Raja therefore requested that a Scout platoon should be sent from Gilgit to Yasin immediately.

The report was exaggerated. I knew that the time was not yet ripe for the Khushwaqt revolt. Mahboob was obviously becoming nervous.

"That rather tallies with my report," I said. "It seems to be quite a serious situation. There is no doubt, though, that the presence of a Hunza or Nagir platoon up in Yasin would definitely nip trouble in the bud. A platoon can easily be spared from Gilgit since reinforcements are always handy, if required, from the battalion in Bunji."

The Governor pondered long and scratched his head.

"You are right," he said eventually, "send a platoon to Yasin as quickly as possible."

So on the following morning one of the two Nagir platoons in Gilgit set off up the valley to guard the man who they considered ought to be Mir of Nagir.

It had been an incredibly satisfactory interview with the Governor, little did he know just how satisfactory. I had always thought the completion of these two necessary precautions for DATTA KHEL might prove extremely difficult if suspicion was to be

1. Company of Gilgit Scouts, 1947. William Brown is fifth from the left in the top row.

2. British and Indian Officers of the Gilgit Scouts prior to the British withdrawal from the Gilgit Agency on 1 August 1947. Front row, from left: Lt. Davies, Subedar Major Jamsud Khan, Major R.J.F. Milnes, Captain Brown, Subedar Azam Khan. Rear row, from left: Subedar Baber Khan, Jamedar Sida Ali.

3. William Brown with Jock Mathieson, 1943.

4. William Brown out fishing with Shah Khan, Gilgit 1945.

5. British Officers' polo team in Gilgit, about to play against Local Chiefs' team. From left: Captain Grierson, Brown, Captain Inchbold, Colonel Cobb, Dr. Marsh, Anwar Khan (Raja of Punial).

6. A fishing trip in Gupis, 1943. From left: Khurshid Mir (Indian Assistant to Political Agent Gilgit), Brown, Colonel Cobb, Hussain Ali (Raja of Gupis).

7. Polo in Gilgit. The Scouts v. the Local Team No. 1, 1943.

8. Major-General Scott (Chief of Staff of Jammu & Kashmir State Forces) with Brigadier Ghansara Singh (1st Kashmiri Governor of Gilgit), 31 July 1947.

9. The last British Political Agent Gilgit, Lt. Colonel R. Bacon, bidding farewell to the Mirs and Rajas at the Gilgit landing ground. From left: Captain Baber Khan, Jafar Khan (Raja of Gilgit), Sultan Ghazi (Raja of Ishkoman), Brown, Hussain Ali (Raja of Gupis), Anwar Khan (Raja of Punial), Raja of Yasin, Lt. Colonel Bacon, F. Mainprice, Jamal Khan (Mir of Hunza).

10. Lieutenant-Colonel Bacon saying goodbye to Major-General Scott, Gilgit 1 August 1947. Brigadier Ghansara Singh is in the foreground.

11. Subedar Major Baber Khan with Brigadier Ghansara Singh.

12. Arrival of Avro Anson transport plane from Peshawar at the 600 yard long Gilgit landing strip. 1947.

13. Major Brown leaves Gilgit for Peshawar to report on recent events, November 1947. From left: Squadron-Leader Ahmed, Captain Mathieson, Brown.

14. Pipes and Drums band of the Gilgit Scouts, 1947.

15. Start of operations by the Gilgit Scouts in typical Karakoram terrain, November 1947.

16. Platoon of Gilgit Scouts, 1947.

17. No. 2 Platoon (Nagir) Gilgit Scouts on the Babusar Pass, 1947.

18. Arrival of Sardar M. Alam, 1st Pakistan Political Agent Gilgit, 14 November 1947. The Pakistan flag is being carried in procession to the Gilgit Agency House.

19. Guard of Honour of the Gilgit Scouts presents arms while Sardar M. Alam salutes the raising of the Pakistan flag at the Gilgit Agency House, November 1947.

20. The Pakistan flag flies over the Gilgit school, November 1947.

21. November 1947. Gilgit Scouts dancing after flag raising ceremony.

22. Qaid-i-Azam's birthday parade in Gilgit, 1947. Sardar M. Alam inspects the parade accompanied by Major Brown. 2nd Lt. Baber Khan is nearest to the camera.

23. Sardar M. Alam, 1st Pakistan Political Agent Gilgit.

24. Subedar Major Baber Khan is promoted 2nd Lieutenant under powers given to Major Brown by the Government of Pakistan. The insignia is presented on parade by Sardar M. Alam.

25. 2nd Lieutanant Baber Khan, Gilgit January 1948.

26. From left: Jamal Kan (Mir of Hunza), Shaukat Ali (Mir of Nagir). A Gilgit durbar in late 1947.

27. Portrait of William Brown as a young officer, 1942.

avoided. And now the whole affair had been passed to me on a plate. I felt very elated and prayed that this luck would last us to the end of the operation.

My radio was out of order which was a great inconvenience. An essential part and a high tension battery were being brought up from down-country by a Chilas trader but he had not yet arrived.

The Governor had a radio but allowed no one to listen to it. Each evening and morning, he and his Personal Assistant would closet themselves in what had been the gunroom and listen to the news. No outsiders were allowed at these sessions and the door and windows were kept locked. At that time there was no radio set in the bazaar either, though later a trader brought one up from Abbottabad. The passes were now officially closed, and could only be crossed by small parties at considerable peril. So we were virtually cut off from the rest of the world, and for our news of outside we had to rely on those rumours which filtered through as they do to remote places on the Frontier.

This is known as the Frontier Telegraph, and the strange thing is that it is almost always correct. And now the Frontier Telegraph signalled that the Maharaja of Kashmir intended acceding to India. General Scott (Chief of Staff) and Mr Powell (Chief of Police in the State of Jammu & Kashmir), had been sacked; they were British and therefore their sentiments lay with Pakistan.

The Prime Minister, Pandit Kak, had also been sacked [on 11 August 1947]. He had subsequently attempted to escape from Srinagar with the connivance of General Scott. He had been captured as he was boarding the plane and had now been thrown into prison. I might add here that Pandit Kak was one of the shrewdest men I have ever met. A Hindu himself, he saw that the future peace and prosperity of Kashmir lay in her joining Pakistan. And he and his brother Pandits could only continue their trade of amassing legal and illegal wealth in a peaceful and prosperous country. There would be no place for the cowardly Pandits in a clash of arms. This forced resignation and subsequent imprisonment was therefore significant.

The Government of New India had offered the Maharaja a vast sum of money if he would accede to this Dominion. Pandit Nehru, Prime Minister of India, himself a Kashmiri, would never allow Kashmir to join Pakistan. A mountain track from Pathankot in India to Srinagar the capital of Kashmir, had recently been developed into a first class military road at great expense.

"Kashmir will accede to Hindustan, Kashmir will accede to Hindustan!" rang the cry over the passes to the mountain fastness of Gilgit.

I would like to make it clear, however, that the reasons I have just given for the assumption that the Maharaja would accede to India, are merely rumours which the Frontier Telegraph gave us in Gilgit. Their reliability or otherwise is another story, irrelevant to the history of events on this site of the snowbound passes.

Gilgit proper remained remarkably calm. Admittedly there was a whispering campaign of Pakistan propaganda. The pulse of the bazaar, which I had learnt to feel instinctively, was now beating faster. There were rumours flying about that the Scouts would revolt any minute now and liquidate all the Sikhs and Hindus.

Mr Sahdev Singh, the Personal Assistant, was particularly nervous. He seldom ventured forth from his house and quaked like a big fat jellyfish when spoken to. He had told the Governor that he expected to be murdered in his bed by the Scouts. The Governor, being in a jovial mood that day, had thumped him on the back and told him there was nothing to worry about. So caught between the two fires of possible murder and thumping on the back, poor Mr Moto, as we had nicknamed him, was in quite a dilemma.

Some bright individual conceived the idea of writing Pakistan slogans on all the public buildings in the bazaar. So we woke up one morning to find "Pakistan *Zindabad*" (long live Pakistan), "Hindustan *Murdabad*, Kashmir *ka Maharaja Murdabad*" (to hell with India, to hell with the Maharaja of Kashmir) chalked everywhere. It was even chalked on the Governor's gate.

On the way to office I heard the Governor issuing orders to Mansur to have the slogan removed immediately. When I returned at lunch time it was still there. In the evening, whilst sitting on the verandah I saw the Governor come out of his front door. He was clutching a duster in one hand. He glanced surreptitiously to right and left. He then lumbered down to the gate, as fast as he could, and wiped off the offending notice. Glancing to right and left again, he hurried back to the house.

In the morning "Pakistan *Zindabad*" was again adorning the gate, this time in even larger letters. The procedure of the previous day was repeated exactly. And this little pantomime was re-enacted daily for weeks on end – in fact until the Kashmir regime concluded. People used to climb trees and hide in the ditches in the evening to see the unsuspecting Governor cleaning his gate.

My gate was also graced with the slogan. I did not erase it, but underneath in very large Urdu characters, I wrote, "Major Brown Sahib Bahadur *Zindabad*," (long live Major Brown the Brave).

I was not in the least worried about the situation in Gilgit for the moment. The all-important factor, the Scouts, was well under control and showed no signs of being affected by these manifestations.

But my time was fully occupied in studying the situation in Kuh Ghizr and Yasin, Darel and Tangir, Bunji, and Chilas, as some alarming reports were coming from these regions.

One evening Haider dropped in for a drink. He told me that Sahdev Singh had just paid him an unexpected visit. The worthy Personal Assistant had been in an extreme state of nervousness and had gone down on his knees and had begged Haider to save his life when the Scouts revolted. In a fit of confidence, he then proceeded to reveal the contents of a TOP SECRET dispatch which the Governor had received from Bunji.

Evidently a few days ago, there had been a disturbance in the lines of the 6th Kashmir Infantry. The Sikhs and Dogras on the one hand and the Muslims on the other had banded together and attacked one another, each shouting their respective war cries of "Hindustan *Zindabad*" and "Pakistan *Zindabad*." Fortunately the outburst was so sudden that there was no time to resort to arms, before the Officers got the situation under control. But a fair amount of damage was done with sticks and stones to both sides.

The Gathering Storm (September to October 1947)

By the remarkable Frontier Telegraph, which I have already described, the news of this incident reached Srinagar before it reached Gilgit.

An express telegram was sent to the Governor of Gilgit Province by the Kashmir Government (I think this was the first communication the Government had sent since Kashmir took over the Province) ordering him to place Captain Mirza Hussan of the 6th Kashmir Infantry under close arrest forthwith, and to send him under escort to Srinagar. The Governor, after consultation with Colonel Majid, decided to take no action on this order which if obeyed would most certainly have lit the fuse of the powder barrel. This was one of the few wise acts the Governor did in his brief term of office, though he must have been considerably influenced by the more astute brain of Colonel Majid.

This was very interesting news as it clearly showed the sentiments of the Muslim sepoys in the Battalion and the way they would jump in the event of a showdown. Secondly it showed that Colonel Majid must have considerable control over his men of all sects, if he was in a position to bring such an awkward situation under control so quickly. And finally it showed that the Kashmir Government's methods of dealing with such incidents were to arrest the Muslim company commanders, quite without regard to hearing the facts of the case and deciding who was really to blame.

That evening Haider attempted to pump my sentiments from me but I played the neutral observer and showed him the political situation in the light of a comic opera. He laughed much, and drank more than was good for him. I had grown to like him very much but the time was far from ripe when I could lay my cards on the table. I knew he would be a good friend when the time came.

I was giving Chilas my full attention but without worry as Jock was there and I was confident of his ability to cope with it.

The next incident which occurred with regard to Chilas came about the middle of October. Just as I was getting into my evening bath a chit arrived from the Governor demanding my immediate presence. URGENT was plastered all over it in red pencil.

"Now what?" I thought to myself.

I carefully loaded my small automatic pistol, fixed it up in my shoulder holster, and went along to Government House as it was called now.

Ghansara Singh was striding up and down in the lounge, muttering to himself and occasionally studying a telegram which he grasped firmly in his massive hand. When he saw me he waved the telegram in the air and blurted out:

"What is the meaning of this? Who sent this? Why was this sent? What are you going to do about it?"

The telegram was now being waved in my eyes so I gently removed it from his hand. It was addressed to the Governor, and the office of origin was Chilas. It read:

Unless Subedar Jan Alum reinstated as our platoon commander immediately, accept resignation of whole platoon – stop; (signed) No 10 platoon (Nagir).

It was reply paid.

I was almost speechless with anger but did not show it. I calmed and soothed the Governor but firmly placed the telegram in my inside pocket where he would have no further access to it. I asked him if he liked *chikor* to eat. He softened, and with a smile, admitted he did. Mansur had just entered so I whispered to him in Shina to bring a brace of birds from my larder. He arrived back quickly with the two *chikor*, which I presented to the Governor. He fondled them, beamed, and removed the barred breast feathers for his hat. He clapped me on the back, offered me a cigarette, and we were soon on the best of terms again, the telegram incident forgotten.

As soon as I returned to my bungalow I sent a code message to Jock asking whether all was well in Chilas.

A reply came to the effect that all was well.

I therefore dispatched a letter post haste pointing out that all could not be well if No 10 platoon (Nagir) was sending telegrams to the Governor announcing their resignation. Within a day a mounted levy arrived with a sealed letter from Jock (dated 17 October). [This showed that there was nothing to worry about. Troubles with Nagir and Yasin men were being handled adequately by Captain Mathieson; but, lacking a firm hand, they could have proved serious.]

Now apropos of recent incidents in Chilas, my own informers brought me information that the now notorious Nagir Havildar, whose name incidentally was Nadilo, was in the habit of holding daily conversation on the telephone with Captain Mirza Hussan in Bunji. They were unable to give me details of the theme of these talks however. So I summed up the situation as follows. There would shortly be a revolt in the Gilgit Province in favour of Pakistan. The revolt would be led by the Scouts backed by the Muslim element of the 6th Kashmir Infantry. The decision of the Hunza, Punial, Yasin, and Kuh Ghizr platoons as to whether to join this revolt or not would depend on me. The Gilgit and Nagir platoons would revolt anyway, regardless of the way I decided to cast my lot. In Gilgit headquarters there was only one Nagir platoon now, No 2, led by Long John's younger brother Shah Sultan, since No 8 platoon had reluctantly hit the Gupis trail.

So with Nagir in the minority and no Gilgitis I was spared from the troubles Jock was having in Chilas where Nagir and Gilgit made up half the garrison. I shudder to think what would have happened had Jock and I not been present in the Province and Ghansara Singh had been a more powerful personality. At the first hint of these troubles in Chilas he would have sent a strong unit of Sikhs and Dogras down from Bunji which with superior weapons and training would have either liquidated or disarmed the garrison. As later events will show, my summing up of the situation was not entirely correct: in rifle shooting language I scored a good inner but not a bull. Fortunately the mistake I made was not irretrievable, but it showed that my intelligence system was not as good as I thought it was. I take full blame for my inability to have made a correct forecast of the trend of future events, and I thank God that He inspired me in such a way that I was able to avoid serious consequences on account of my error.

One final matter remained before I was satisfied that the decks were cleared for action, and this was the removal of Captain Mohammed Said from the scene of operations. It was also time now that Kalamdarchi Fort should be evacuated and No 1 platoon (Hunza) withdrawn to Gilgit. The latter could be used as a means towards the former.

I told the Governor that I wished to evacuate Kalamdarchi. He agreed, as its upkeep was causing significant expenditure, and also the Mir of Hunza, at my instigation, had been bringing considerable pressure to bear on him to remove the Scouts from Hunza territory. I pointed out to the Governor that the evacuation would be no easy job. Immovable property would have to be left behind, listed, and handed over to the charge of the Mir's representative. About forty or fifty baggage ponies would have to be raised from the surrounding country. In fact, if the move was to be completed without treading on the Mir's toes and annoying him, it was essential that I personally proceeded to Kalamdarchi and supervised the operation in close contact with the Mir. It would result in my being away from Gilgit for about three weeks.

"Quite impossible, quite impossible," boomed the Governor. "To tell you the truth, Major Brown," he continued confidentially, "there have been some rather alarming reports of trouble in Kashmir in wireless broadcasts, and it is imperative you remain in Gilgit for the meantime."

"Well, Sir, the alternative is causing trouble in Hunza," I replied, "which will give you much more cause for direct alarm than disorder down-country."

"Well, somebody else will have to go, Said or Haider will have to go," he replied.

I still emphasized that I ought to go myself but eventually agreed to allowing Said to supervise the operation, on the grounds that he was more experienced than Haider. My luck was still holding and – everything was falling into place according to plan. A feeling of elation, power, and confidence of success gripped me.

I then gave the Governor the gist of what had been happening in Chilas, according to what Jock had told me in his letters. I explained that there was nothing to worry about as Captain Mathieson had the situation well under control.

If I expected the Governor to be alarmed or worried I was very much mistaken. He leant back in his chair, took a long puff at his hubble-bubble, and guffawed.

"What can they do against the might of His Highness the Maharaja?"

"Bloody old fool," I thought to myself, "one of these days the might of the Maharaja is going to come crashing down about your ears, shattered for good and all."

One might as well have been talking to a stone wall for all the reaction there was.

I informed Said that evening that he would have to leave for Kalamdarchi within the next two days at the latest, and supervise the evacuation of the Post. I saw he was about to demur so I repeated what I had couched as a request in the clipped decisive manner of a military order which I could always rap out on occasions such as this.

He clucked, stuttered, and eventually said, "Very well, Sir."

Sleeping on it evidently increased his distaste for the long journey, for the next morning he produced every imaginable reason why he should not go to Kalamdarchi. His pony was lame, his servant was sick, he had no warm clothes, he was suffering from diarrhoea, and many more futile reasons.

"You *are* going to Kalamdarchi, and you will leave tomorrow morning without fail," I ordered calmly, though possessed with a great desire to punch him on the end of his long nose.

Said saluted and scuttled away. He did depart for Kalamdarchi next morning.

A radio was most necessary. So the wireless havildar and I pooled our limited mechanical knowledge and attempted to put my radio on the air. After much footling we failed, and in despair I sent for Limbuwala.

He got to work and with the help of a screw-driver, signalling lamp batteries, and abuse, had a concert from the BBC in London booming in about ten minutes. He stayed for tea and wolfed down scones and honey.

I listened to the news that evening, which was 25 October, and heard that the Government of India had decided to send troops of the Indian Army to Kashmir. This made it obvious that accession to India would be announced shortly. D day was fast approaching.

On the morning of 26 October I switched on the wireless and listened to the news in English from All India Radio. The first announcement was that large numbers of Pathan tribesmen had entered Kashmir State at various places between Mirpur in Poonch and Muzaffarabad in the North and were advancing across country, leaving a trail of pillage, loot, arson, and rape behind them. All India Radio made it clear that these tribesmen were acting at the instigation of the Pakistan Government, who, it was alleged, was arming them, rationing them, and giving them free access across Pakistan territory in transport especially arranged for the purpose. It was also reported that the men in Poonch, a district of the State, who were ex-servicemen, had risen in revolt and had organized themselves into regular units which were advancing with the tribesmen.

I gave a long low whistle to myself and turned the dial of the set to Radio Pakistan from where I was just in time to hear the news in Urdu.

"The State of Jammu & Kashmir has acceded to the Indian Union. Sardar Mohammed Ibrahim has set up a Free Kashmir Government in Poonch in opposition to that of the Maharaja. The people of Poonch are unanimously supporting this Government, which represents the will of the Muslim population of the State, and have risen in revolt against the Dogra regime. The North West Frontier tribesmen, incensed at the thought of their brother Muslims in Kashmir being brought under the Hindu yoke, have declared *jehad* (holy war), and are entering the State in large numbers to support the Poonchis and free the country."

Details of some ghastly atrocities perpetrated by the Sikh and Dogra elements of the State Forces against Muslim civilians were then given.

I switched off the wireless. I had heard sufficient.

"Cry 'havoc!' and let slip the dogs of war." Through the senseless stupidity of the Maharaja in acceding to India, a welter of barbaric blood lust and communal strife had been loosed in the fair Vale of Kashmir. This was no minor revolt, which would fade or be crushed as soon as it had sprung up. It was civil war of no mean magnitude, fraught with the most dangerous possibilities, including the dreadful possibility of open war between the two new dominions of Pakistan and India.

The Pakistan broadcast had concluded by saying that the dominion was doing everything in her power to prevent the tribesmen proceeding to Kashmir. A lot of use this would be. The mightiest power on earth with tanks, automatic weapons, and aircraft could not stop the Pathans of the tribal territory of the North West Frontier when *jehad* had been declared against Hindu domination anywhere.

But whatever was happening down-country, my job was quite clear. At all costs Gilgit must be spared from the havoc referred to on the radio. So my first act was to proceed to the Scout Lines via the bazaar, where there was now a private radio, so the important information would be known to all.

The bazaar was buzzing. Little groups of people hung about the street corners, discussing the news and amongst them were Hindu and Sikh traders. All were, as usual, very friendly towards me. They invited me to express my opinion; I excused myself, however, on the plea of urgent work in the Scout Lines, but not before I had gathered that one and all agreed that the Maharaja had committed a faux pas of the gravest potentialities, no less so than that of the British, who had dishonourably deserted the sub-continent without ensuring that a firm decision had been reached on Kashmir and Hyderabad – decisions which should have been implemented by the Pax Britannica, rather than by force of communal arms which appeared to be the *modus operandi* now.

Everything seemed normal in the Scout Lines. Parade was in progress, the Quarter Guard smart and well turned out, the Quarter Master Jemedar was busy checking stores, the armourer was repairing rifles, the clerks were coming into the office. To the outsider it must have seemed just the usual daily routine such as had taken place since the turn of the century.

But during my tenure in the Scouts I had learnt that the Lines possessed a highly emotional spirit. Some days they were moody, some days they were happy, some days sad, some days tense. And today it did not take me long to discover they were in a high state of excitement: their pulse was throbbing at an alarming rate. I ran through my normal routine work, which I had now reduced to a minimum through force of habit and a well trained staff. This was an absolute necessity nowadays when there was so much else to think about and do.

At lunch time I looked in on the Governor on my way home.

Yes, he had heard the news.

"Our glorious Maharaja alone knows what is best for his State. Trouble? That will soon be crushed and those Pathan dogs and Poonchis will be hung by the neck over the walls of Hari Parbat Prison. Trouble in Gilgit? Never! The might of the Maharaja represented by the 6th Kashmir Infantry will keep the situation under control here. Now don't you keep worrying me, Major Brown," he concluded. "You get away and run the Scouts. I'll attend to all matters of higher policy."

He sat back in the leather-covered chair and folded his hands over his fat paunch. The interview was obviously finished. I departed. I was now beginning to get extremely fed up at battering my head against a stone wall, day after day.

We had an excellent game of football that afternoon in the Scout Lines. It was imperative now that the Scouts were kept busy at something, every minute of the day. There was far too much mischief floating round for Satan to gather up and dole out to idle hands. Those not engaged at football were put on strenuous athletics. The open ground in the Lines was one mass of sportsmen running, jumping, putting the weight, playing football, pulling in tugs of war, and racing round the obstacle course, whilst the pipe band played for all it was worth in one corner and the local band in the other.

Haider and I took a walk round together and ensured that such a pace was maintained, that there would be no energy left in the evening for hatching up trouble. This is always a sure way of keeping the peace in the Gilgit Scouts. When we had seen that the programme was running at full speed we settled down to football ourselves. Haider to the Indian and non-commissioned officers on his side and the other ranks joined me. Soon such a ding-dong battle was raging that the news spread to the bazaar.

Presently about two or three thousand spectators had gathered who crowded along the wall and shouted encouragement. We were leading one-nil most of the way, but just on time Haider headed a beauty into our net to finish the match in a draw. On the conclusion of play we gathered for a little dancing before breaking off for the night. It was just like the old days and I think this entertainment did much to settle the Scouts and local populace, and to postpone D day unul I was absolutely ready for it. Eventually Retreat rang out through the gathering dusk and I called a halt. The crowds dispersed, gathering their choghas around them for the evenings were chilly now.

I asked Haider to come up to my bungalow for a drink and dinner. He said he had some business to attend to in the Lines, but would come up later. This struck me as strange as I knew he had nothing of importance to deal with at that hour of the evening. I noted it momentarily, forgot it, until a few days later when I minded it again as a piece in the jigsaw puzzle.

Haider arrived at about 7.30 pm. He looked worried and he obviously had something on his mind. Conversation was rather strained at first; I noted with interest that he was downing whisky much more freely than usual. The liquor gradually took effect. His handsome features became flushed and he waxed loquacious.

"I have noticed, Sir," he said, "that you have been visiting the Governor a great deal lately. I know very well that you have been impressing upon him the seriousness of the situation, and that you have been urging him to take some action which will prevent a disaster here. I have known the Governor a good deal longer than you, and I know very well that you have received no change from him except to be told to mind your own business. Now I can tell you that the stubborn old fool is merely fiddling, in a sense of false confidence, whilst Kashmir burns. He is quite obviously incapable of rising to the occasion should trouble break out in Gilgit."

"Supposing, Sir, that trouble broke out here, such as that which is raging down-country, what would you do? I suppose you would just sit back and watch the fun as a neutral observer."

Now this was no drunken blether. It was a very obvious attempt to ascertain exactly what my views were on the political situation. Haider knew me well enough by now to appreciate that I would never remain a spectator but would always be in on whatever was brewing, on one side or the other.

But which side was Haider on? I knew that his family and his property were in Srinagar. If he joined the rebels he would lose everything: his family would be imprisoned, probably quietly liquidated, and all his possessions would be forfeited. Was it not possible, therefore, that he supported the Maharaja and was now acting for the Governor in attempting to ascertain my sentiments? On the other hand he was a Muslim, and as such, should naturally side with Pakistan. I therefore gave a guarded reply.

"I agree, Haider, that the Governor is not capable of dealing with a situation of any sort which may arise as the result of the present political position. In the event of any trouble here, I shall take over complete control myself and act according to the way in which I see that law and order can best be maintained and a disaster avoided. I shall then consult with Colonel Majid, for whom I hold great respect, as to the future policy."

"You are right," said Haider, "take over control; but I warn you, you will run up against the most awkward unforeseen difficulties, which will test your capabilities to the limit. Don't have anything to do with Majid. He'll not help you. He'll do everything he can to prevent being compromised. All he wants is his pension. But you can't set yourself up here as an independent Ruler. If you take over control then you will either have to uphold the Maharaja's regime or else throw in your lot with Pakistan."

"My God, it's nine o'clock," I interrupted, grasping the welcome opportunity to evade this very leading question. "We must hear the news."

"You bet," replied Haider enthusiastically.

I switched on the set. We first of all listened to All India Radio in English. India admitted that the raiders, as they called the tribesmen, had made fair progress in Kashmir. They also claimed that the invasion of Kashmir had been organized by Pakistan, and that this dominion was supplying the raiders with transport, arms, rations, and support of every kind – in fact Pakistan was conducting the campaign.

At 9.15 pm, I switched over to Radio Pakistan. Pakistan admitted that she pledged full moral support to the tribesmen who were risking their lives to free their brother Muslims in Kashmir from Hindu bondage. She claimed, however, that she was doing all within her power to prevent the tribesmen from going to Kashmir. It was also announced that the tribesmen had advanced with lightning speed from Domel to Baramula, a large and prosperous town some 20 miles from Srinagar. It was interesting news that the tribesmen were now so near the Capital.

I was glad that Haider decided to return home as soon as the news was finished, as it gave me an opportunity to cogitate on what I had heard. I stoked up the fire, lit a pipe, and meditated.

"Was Pakistan correct in her announcement that she was merely offering moral support to the tribesmen? Certainly she might well be doing all within her power to prevent the Pathans crossing her territory to Kashmir, but, as already pointed out, no power on earth, let alone Pakistan, could stop them if they decided to go. Or was India correct in her assertion that Pakistan was offering the raiders full material aid? I could well picture the scene in Baramula."

"If Pakistan had made up her mind to take Kashmir by force of arms of the tribesmen of the North West Frontier, then never, in all her senses, would she have instigated these irresponsible, uncontrollable hotheads to invade the country, unless she had made adequate arrangements to back the invasion with disciplined troops led by experienced Frontier Officers."

"I could well visualize, that if among these hordes of Mahsouds, Waziris, and Afridis, which had now entered Baramula, there were units of the Frontier Corps and Frontier Constabulary led by their own British (almost every British Officer in the Frontier Corps was fanatically keen to take his men to Kashmir and to assist in securing the country for Pakistan) and Pakistani Officers, then by the morrow Srinagar and the airfield would be in their hands."

"But if, on the other hand, the invasion was merely a disorganized rabble of tribesmen, who had voluntarily and without instigation taken advantage of the situation in the State as scope for loot and excitement, then the advance would most certainly peter out at Baramula, until the wealthy town had been stripped of its firearms, money and jewellery, women and boys. Only when this plunder had been collected, fairly divided, and safely dispatched to tribal territory, would the advance continue. There would also undoubtedly be endless arguments and discussions in Baramula as to the division of the anticipated spoil in Srinagar. And while all this delay was taking place, the Capital would have an excellent opportunity of arranging her defences and that of the airfield."

It was eventually proved that the latter supposition of mine was almost entirely correct; so I concluded that Pakistan was in no way responsible for organizing the invasion through direct action. Her support might amount to approval at the most, but even this seems unlikely, as she would almost certainly lose any chance of winning a referendum in a country which had been terrorized and pillaged by tribesmen who were virtually her own people.

The ghastly story of the sack of Baramula is too well known to be repeated. I would however like to say that an excess of blame for the dreadful atrocities must not be laid on the tribesmen. They committed atrocities no doubt, but they committed them while under the influence of blood lust. Blood lust is the most powerful human desire, even more so than the sex lust. When a man is under its spell he cannot be held responsible for his actions. As those with experience of warfare between so-called civilized nations will testify, the blood lust is not merely confined to barbaric races such as the trans-frontier Pathans. I am not attempting to condone the massacre of the Europeans in Baramula or the dreadful things which happened to the nuns of St Joseph's Hospital; but they were not treated thus because they were Europeans, rather they were victims in the general welter of blind fury and unbridled passion which raged in the township.

As the news on the morrow proved, this delay by the tribesmen was fatal, if the object of the campaign was to capture Srinagar. While they were arguing over the share of loot and future leadership, units of the Indian Army were landed on the Srinagar airfield without opposition on 27 October. When the tribesmen eventually advanced they found the defences of the Capital and the landing ground manned by crack units of regular Indian troops. In bitter fighting, in which the tribesmen gave a lot more than they received, they gradually fell back. Without rations, without lines of communication, without transport, without air support, without first aid arrangements, and with swiftly diminishing stocks of ammunition they contested every inch of the ground. But under such conditions resistance was hopeless. Full withdrawal set in down the Punjab road until they made a final stand on the high positions round Uri. And here a disorganized rabble of tribesmen held up the famous Indian Army. Despite the fact that the latter rushed up an overwhelming strength of reinforcements equipped with every weapon of modern warfare, the Pathans not only held their ground at Uri but also made several remarkable advances in some of the sectors in this area before a truce was called at the beginning of 1949. But they never reached the sight of the Takht-i-Suliman (the conical shaped hill in the middle of Srinagar which stands out prominently in the surrounding countryside).

My own views were that Pakistan had committed a fatal blunder. When, at the very beginning, she saw that the trans-frontier Pathans could not be stopped from entering Kashmir, she should have immediately supported their invasion in secret by reinforcing the tribal *lashkars* with units from the Frontier Corps and Frontier Constabulary, troops whose uniform was little different from the clothing of the ordinary tribesmen. All British Officers of the Political Department, Frontier Corps, and Police, who volunteered (and they were many) should have had their active services accepted for the prosecution of the campaign. If Pakistan had acted thus, there is not a shadow of doubt that Srinagar (which is as good as saying the whole of Kashmir) would have been in her hands before 27 October 1947.

India would never have disputed such a complete *fait accompli* by force of arms. If the latter had raised any objections she could have been given Jammu. India would also have received Hyderabad as part of the share-out, and both dominions would have settled down to development and progress in close harmony with one another.

But it was not to be, and Kashmir still remains a thorn in the flesh of amicable Indo-Pakistani relations.

My views may be influenced by my Scottish Border blood. In the good old days of receiving and robbing in the "debatable land" it was a case of every man for himself and the survival of the fittest. We had a slogan which went:

"Let him take who has the power,"

"And let him hold who can." And this, I thought, was what Pakistan should have done in Kashmir.

Yet, apart from that, Pakistan would have been justified in the eye of equity if she had actively supported the original invasion of Kashmir. Kashmir, with her predominantly Muslim population was Pakistan's right, if the question of acceding to either Dominion arose, and no democratic person can surely dispute this. India aggressively took over the administration of Junagadh State because she considered that the Muslim ruler was incapable of governing a Hindu population. It therefore seems to me to follow that Pakistan should have taken over the State of Jammu & Kashmir, with its Muslim population, when it was obvious that the Hindu ruler was incapable of administration.

My thoughts gradually faded into a delicious drowsiness and I fell asleep in front of the glowing fire. I woke up in the wee small hours of the morning feeling frightful. The fire was out, the kerosene was finished in the lamp, the room was bitterly cold, and my head was choked with excessive pipe smoking. I literally fell into bed in my under-clothes and pulled up my quilted sleeping-bag round my ears.

The morning of 28 October broke clear and bright. There was a bracing nip in the air as I threw open the windows of my bedroom and gazed out on the fresh snow on

Kurkun. It was exhilarating to gulp down the gusts of fresh air which blew off the mountain tops. As I shaved in front of the window I had an inward feeling that it would be an interesting day. It certainly was.

I had barely finished breakfast when Shawar Din announced that a strange looking creature clad in the most filthy rags had arrived for an interview. Shawar Din was, by this time, well used to ushering in the most remarkable individuals for interviews so he showed no surprise.

It turned out to be my informer, one X, who covered the Chitral side for me. The brief report, which he made in Khawar, was most interesting and significant. He reported that the Mehtar of Chitral was massing troops and tribal *lashkars* in Mastuj, which is the northernmost settlement in that State and the one nearest the Shandur Pass which leads into Kuh Ghizr. In X's opinion there was no doubt that a Chitrali invasion of Yasin and Kuh Ghizr was very imminent.

I never like to prolong interviews with informers. It is dangerous for them. I was certain that X's information was reliable, and sufficient for my purposes. So I paid him well, and bade him be back over the border to watch future movements.

He had barely been gone half an hour, during which time I had been cogitating, when another visitor was announced. A big strapping Chilasi boy swaggered in, with a Snider rifle swung over his shoulder. He propped the rifle up beside the fireplace, loosed the waist belt of his bandolier, and squatted down on the floor.

It was Y, my informer who covered the independent territory of Darel and Tangir. His news, also, was extremely interesting, especially coming on the top of that from Chitral. He reported that several companies of the army of the Wali of Swat had entered Tangir and were now massing at points on the border of the Gilgit Province and in Indus Kohistan. Their next move would obviously be an invasion of the Province and Chilas.

To crown this interesting accumulation of vital news, a wireless message in code now arrived from Jani (Jock's code name) in Chilas. I grasped immediately that this was an important signal, so set about decoding it without delay.

To: KUKI
From: JANI   271000

Datta Khel not far off – stop – increasing pro-Pakistan feeling among Scouts and population – stop – all insist on removing Kashmir flag from Fort and hoisting Pakistan flag – stop – dangerous tension in communities and tribal territories – stop – signal advice.

About lunch I went along to see the Governor.

"Now, what is it?" he said testily from the depths of his leather-covered chair, as he inhaled a mouthful of foul smoke from his hubble-bubble.

"I've merely come to tell you that a Chitrali army has collected in Mastuj which will probably invade the Province shortly. Also the Wali of Swat's forces have invaded Tangir and are now on the Gilgit border. And lastly I have just received a wireless message from Captain Mathieson to say that Pakistan feeling is rising dangerously in Chilas and tribal territory. I would suggest. . ."

But I did not suggest as my speech was interrupted by a sudden booming outburst from Ghansara Singh.

"This is sheer impertinence. I shall wire His Highness immediately and he will order those insolent chieftains to remove their *goondas* (gangsters) from the border forthwith. The cheek of it. As for Chilas, what can they do? And now, Major Brown, I hear you're playing polo this afternoon, so you had better go now and get changed. Otherwise you will be late, as you usually are."

I very nearly lost my temper. I was on the point of pulling out my automatic pistol from the shoulder holster and arresting him then and there. Fortunately I was able to appreciate that this was no time for hasty action: every move had to be thought out carefully, and I was in no condition to do this at the moment. So I departed and swallowed my rage.

We had a good game of polo that afternoon. The Scouts took on the Sub-division, a contest guaranteed to produce thrills. And a ding dong battle it was, raging from one end to the other of the long Shahi Ground. I am afraid I let off pent up steam in a most wanton manner, with complete disregard for my own safety and that of anyone else. Gilgit were leading 6-5, Five minutes from time. The Subedar Major, who was playing back, instead of clearing with a backhander, expertly turned on the ball. He then went straight through the Gilgit defence and hit a beautiful straight goal from about 150 yards out. The bugle blew for time. The Nagir contingent invaded the pitch and carried Baber away shoulder high. The remainder of the crowd roared with pleasure at the entertainment they had witnessed.

I threw myself from Samarkand, quite exhausted. He was in a shocking state as a result of my abandoned riding. He stood limply in one position, with his head hung low, nostrils distended, and bathed in sweat from head to foot. Zaril looked at me reproachfully; I felt immoral, but much calmer and more capable of level-headed thought than after my interview with the Governor earlier in the day.

"That game ought to delay D day till everything is ready, by giving the Scouts and Gilgit folk something to occupy their minds for a few days," I thought to myself grimly.

After a delicious soak in a hot bath, I took a hurricane lantern and went round to the stable to see Samarkand. He was as chirpy as a lark and quite recovered under the expert attention of Zaril.

I then returned to the office and studied Jock's message of the morning. It would be fatal if the situation got out of control in Chilas and they kicked off before the teams were lined up. I must ensure that this did not happen at all costs. But what to do? I could call the Subedar Major, explain the position and ask his advice. I would then be subjected to a futile hour of "whatever you think best Sahib, of course Sahib, very difficult Sahib, God knows Sahib," and so on, concluding with a long-winded account of the loyal services of his grandfather, father, and he himself had rendered to the British.

No, there would be no constructive advice from that quarter. A bit of bluff was necessary so I eventually composed the following message:

To: JANI
From: KUKI   282200

Mirs advise all ranks to keep calm and refrain from pro Pakistan activities meantime – stop – please pass on this message to all concerned – stop – message ends.

"That ought to do the trick for the moment," I thought to myself as I encoded the message and sent it to the wireless staff. It did. I must admit I felt rather nervous next day. A mercenary may have an alien cause at heart, but the sense of self-preservation is always present also, though not necessarily of uppermost importance. It only required that I should do nothing now, and the next thing I would know would be that I was in the middle of an internal upheaval while at the same time the armies of Swat and Chitral advanced to join the fray. It was hardly a pleasant prospect, and the odds were certainly against either Jock or I getting out of it with entire skins. This coupled with my pledge to see Gilgit through the transition until she was an integral part of Pakistan, helped me to size up the seriousness of the position.

I resolved that on the following day I would give the Governor a last chance to retain his position honourably but I would make it quite clear that he must dance to my tune, which would be the only tune which could avert a disaster, as long as the Governor was still at the helm of the Province. This seemed only fair to him. If he accepted my advice, then good and well. It would not then be necessary to put DATTA KHEL into operation. If he refused, then he would have to take what was coming to him.

As I fell asleep that night I felt as though I was sitting on top of a volcano which was likely to erupt at any moment.

At about 10.00 am, on the morning of 30 October, I rode along to Government House. The Scout guard presented arms smartly and levies rushed forward to hold my pony as I dismounted. Mansur ushered me into the presence of the Governor, with a knowing smile playing round his lips. It was not difficult to see I was bent on a purpose.

The Governor was sitting in the drawing room in front of a roaring log fire. It was much too cold on the verandah nowadays. As I sat down I conjured up visions of the past for a brief moment in the acrid haze of the smoke from the hubble-bubble – the days when this now bare room had been tastefully decorated with pictures, lace curtains, Khotan carpets, exquisite china of old Russia; sparkling State banquets with the gorgeous dress of the Mirs and Rajas contrasted against the sombre dinner jackets of the British Officers; fair ladies, wine, music, shaded lights, and lively conversation. What wonderful tales the old Agency House could tell.

With an effort I forced myself back to the present.

Ghansara Singh was in a jovial mood which made my task more difficult.

"Well, Major Brown, what can I do for you? Have a cigarette. I shall tell Mansur to bring some tea."

This counter-approach was rather disarming.

"I don't know whether you are aware of the gravity of the situation in the Province," I said, coming to the point without further ado.

"I think you are an alarmist, I think you are making a mountain out of a molehill," the Governor countered.

"Whether I am or not, and whether you like it or not, I am now going to give you an appreciation of the situation, followed by recommendations as to the course you must now take," I replied.

The Governor almost exploded; the veins stood out on his neck and forehead, and his dark face flushed with a sudden rush of blood. Without giving him a chance to interrupt I started:

"The population of the Gilgit Province is predominantly Muslim and it objects strongly to the fact that the Maharaja of Jammu & Kashmir has acceded to India."

"Swat and Chitral are slowly surrounding the Province. Both States have already acceded to Pakistan and they will presently invade Gilgit on the plea of liberating the Province from the Hindu yoke. There are not sufficient troops this side of the Burzil Pass to stem such an invasion as the Scouts will most certainly not take up arms against brother Muslims fighting in the cause of Pakistan."

"Khan Abdul Qayum Khan, Premier of the North West Frontier Province, gave a radio broadcast last night which was heard in the Gilgit bazaar. He pledged the support of all Pathans in liberating the people of Kashmir from Dogra domination. This rousing speech has had a profound effect on the people of Gilgit."

"The use of the Indian Army to suppress the will of the Kashmir people has shocked the entire Muslim world and no less so in Gilgit."

"World opinion on broadcast of the previous evening hinted at the exploitation of tyranny in Kashmir by India."

"Unless either you or I take some decisive action now, Gilgit too will be plunged into a bloodbath similar to that raging down-country. If a referendum had been held in Kashmir on the transfer of power and the State had joined the Dominion which the majority had wished, the present chaos would never have existed. Since the Maharaja's Government appears to have abandoned all interest in the Gilgit Province, it is now most necessary that you operate on your own initiative. I suggest you hold an immediate referendum in the Province. It goes without saying that the result will be in favour of accession to Pakistan but that is beside the point. You can then announce that the will of the people has been ascertained, though confirmation must be kept pending until a plebiscite is completed in the rest of Kashmir. The Governor General of India has made it clear that such a plebiscite will be held as soon as order is restored. With the will of the people here a *fait accompli*, you can continue to govern the Province in a temporary capacity, though I would suggest that you feign a nervous breakdown and hand over charge to Colonel Majid who is a Muslim. I assure you that such action will be very acceptable and will be disputed by none. Swat and Chitral will never invade a country which has decided by its own free will to accede to Pakistan, even although the decision requires confirmation later. Anyway, it is a foregone conclusion that the rest of Kashmir, with the possible exception of Jammu, will accede to Pakistan if a fair referendum is held."

"The second course open to you is that you, your staff, and the 6th Kashmir Infantry pack your bags, and clear off to Srinagar. Leave the Province to decide its own destiny. The most powerful man left will take over charge of the country, that is to say I, shall assume the duties of Governor. If you are court-martialled, as soon as order is eventually restored, I shall back you up to the best of my ability, and I shall prove to the prosecution that the action you took was the only one feasible under the circumstances, which would prevent a frightful catastrophe. Whatever your opponents say, all democratic people will support my point of view. And this will decide the case in your favour in the long run. I shall be grateful if you will now tell me which course you propose to take."

All the fire and obstinacy appeared to have left the Governor during the course of my speech. He was like a pricked balloon. He squirmed in his chair, scratched his bald head, and wrinkled up his face. He stuttered, choked on a hefty pull at the hubble-bubble, and spat in the fireplace. After more head-scratching he replied.

"You are right. I shall adopt the former course. I shall order the Mirs and Rajas to hold referendums in their respective States and Districts immediately. The results will then be forwarded to me. Captain Mathieson will hold a referendum in Chilas and the Revenue Assistant can deal with the Sub-division."

This was satisfactory, but I made no mistake and made him promise on his honour that he would take this action. He did so.

As soon as I returned to my bungalow I called Haider and informed him of the action I had taken. He entirely approved and seemed greatly relieved. I knew that by now the news would have been flashed to every corner of the Province by the Frontier Telegraph, so I breathed a deep sign of relief at the temporary respite.

In the evening I called on the Governor again to ascertain developments. The Governor told me that he had contacted the Mir of Hunza on the telephone. The Mir had informed him that both he and his people were very happy under the existing relations with Kashmir and they had no wish to join Pakistan. The Mir of Nagir had gone away on a shooting trip so it was impossible to hear his views.

The Governor had further decided that, before referendums were held in the Political Districts, he would like to discuss the matter with the Raja of Punial. He had therefore called the latter to Gilgit. All this sounded very suspicious, but I said nothing and excused myself.

I now decided to contact the Mir of Hunza myself and satisfy myself as to what exactly the position was. This meant going down to the Post Office in the bazaar as I had not yet fitted up an extension of the telephone in my bungalow. After collecting my greatcoat, as it was very chilly, I set off accompanied by Shukar Alt.

I soon realized that we were being shadowed by two people whom we could not recognize in the darkness. As we turned the corner at Haider's bungalow, I told Shukar Ali to slip over the wall, double back and discover who the gentlemen of the night were.

Shukar Ali eventually caught up with me again and reported that they were two Sikh linemen, employees of the Posts and Telegraph Department. This was very interesting, as there was no doubt now that they were watching our movements. What was even more interesting was that both were armed with *kirpans* – the traditional Sikh swords – and people did not usually wander about with swords in Gilgit unless they intended participating in tent pegging which is usually not indulged in at 10 o'clock on a winter's night.

"Were they going to bump us off?" I thought to myself.

As we reached the Mir of Nagir's town palace we quietly slipped into the compound, and by hopping over garden walls and slipping through a maze of back alleys, reached the Post Office. We entered.

I yanked the frightened Kashmiri Pandit Post Master out of his bed. He cringed and grovelled at my feet, and begged for mercy for any crimes committed. Catching him by the scruff of the neck and pulling him to his feet I demanded,

"Is the bloody Hunza line tapped?"

"Yes," he replied, shaking like a leaf. "All the lines are tapped to the Governor's bungalow. There is a Sikh linesman on constant duty up there, who listened to every conversation, and reports the interesting ones to the Governor."

"All right, all right, there's nothing to be frightened about," I said and turning to Shukar Ali, "get the Subedar Major quickly and tell him to bring two or three armed Scouts with him."

Shukar Ali departed and I slipped out on to the verandah, shutting the pathetic Pandit in his bedroom. I concealed myself in the shadows. I was taking no chances, but nothing happened until the Subedar Major soon arrived. I posted the Scouts round the building and explained the situation to Baber.

"I want you to speak to the Mir of Hunza on the telephone in Burushaski. Ask him whether he and his people wish to accede to India, Pakistan, or remain independent. Also ask him whether the Governor has telephoned him in this connection in the last twelve hours."

The call went through to Karimabad and presently the Mir came to the telephone. I plugged in the extension earphone so that I could hear the ensuing conversation. By now I could understand Burushaski but could not speak it fluently enough to cope with a situation such as this.

The conversation started with the usual greeting and questions regarding health and welfare. Baber's sister, of course, was married to the Mir of Hunza so they were closely connected by marriage ties. Baber then put the important question.

"Tell the Commandant Sahib," the Mir said, "that I am a Muslim and my people are Muslims. Are we unbelievers that we should join India or stay aloof by remaining independent? There is only one way for us to go and that is to Pakistan and we shall join Pakistan. I have had no telephonic conversation with the Governor today, and I know he has not been in touch with anyone else in Hunza or Nagir. Give the Commandant Sahib my very sincere regards and tell him that my services are always at his disposal. *Salaam Aleikum.*"

"*Wa Aleikum Salaam,*" Baber replied.

Click!

Baber now translated the Mir's message into Urdu. I don't think he knew I understood Burushaski, yet he gave me the Mir's message absolutely correctly.

"Right," I said. "Now do the same with the Mir of Nagir."

The Nagir telephone line is very bad. I heard the Mir's voice, which proved he was in Nagir, but it was impossible to hold a conversation. There seemed to be about six separate conversations, all in different languages, going on at the same time on the line. I told Baber to hang up. I had got what I wanted and I knew that Hunza-Nagir relations were so good nowadays that the two Mirs' sentiments would be the same.

DATTA KHEL must go through now, without a doubt, and the only question is to know when to strike. I had a strange inner foresight that zero hour would be intimated to me by someone or from somewhere at the critical moment. My luck would hold, I knew it. I must now just wait a little until the signal came.

On arrival home I drank a cup of steaming hot cocoa. There was a code message waiting from Jock; I decoded it and sorted out the string of letters to read:

To: KUKI
From: JANI   301900

I Cannot hold on much longer here – stop – situation is very grave – stop – message ends.

I replied:

Datta Khel very imminent – stop – for God's sake restrain Scouts till you get signal from me – stop – good luck.

This encoded and dispatched, I went to bed. I slept with a pistol under my bed. Munajat slept across the window: Shukar Ali across the door.

On 31 October I went on parade, and made my journey to the Lines via the bazaar. There was a strange tension in the air, no ostentatious excitement, no shouting of slogans, but the atmosphere was charged with that queer quiet stillness which fills the Scottish Border uplands before a raging thunderstorm breaks.

After parade, which was well up to a very high standard, I told Haider to clear the "bumph" from the office trays, and I rode up the hill to have my final interview with Ghansara Singh. It was short and to the point.

"You appear, Sir, to disregard my advice entirely," I said. "I want to make it quite clear that I cannot be held responsible for future events. In the event of the possibility of the situation getting out of control, I shall assume complete charge of the whole country from the Shandur to the Burzil. I am sorry our relationship has reached this pretty pass, but I have sincerely and honestly tried to help you out of an impossible position, without your losing face."

He writhed in his chair and screwed up his face.

The Gathering Storm (September to October 1947) 133

"You can go," he said.

I saluted smartly, turned on my heel, and departed. I returned to my bungalow with the intention of calling Haider and putting him in the picture.

There was a disturbance of some sort going on in my garden. I heard voices raised in anger, and through the now bare apricot trees I could see servants milling round the door of the verandah. As I approached, Mr Limbuwala shot out of the door. He was in a high state of excitement. His felt hat was on the back of his head, his eyes were flashing behind the thick lenses of his spectacles; in one hand he was brandishing his walking stick, in the other he was waving a piece of paper.

To: MAHARAJA OF KASHMIR
From: H.H. MEHTAROF CHITRAL

Chitral breaking off all relations with Kashmir Government – stop – neither my State nor Gilgit can accept accession of Kashmir to Hindustan.

This was Chitral's obvious preliminary to her now imminent attack on the Northern Districts of the Gilgit Province.

Haider soon arrived. I clearly explained to him the latest developments. He whistled through his teeth and looked worried. He stayed for lunch. After lunch I sent him off to check the Scout wireless, petrol stocks, ammunition, and rations. It would be wise to know exactly where we stood.

I read passages out of the *Seven Pillars*, until the *chikor* had had time to come down to the fields on the foothills for their evening meal. I then took my gun, cartridge belt, and game bag and whistled to the dogs who were playing in the garden. I climbed the steep hill behind my bungalow until I reached the main Gilgit water channel. I walked along the convenient path which ran beside it. There were plenty of birds. Sammy skirmished in front and put them up. Dinah remained at heel and retrieved when signalled forward. The trio of us worked perfectly as a team, and by the time we had passed through the suburbs of Naiqi and Naupore, and had almost reached Basin, the game bag hung heavy on my shoulders with six brace. A couple of rock pigeon and a painted snipe added variety.

I sat down above the entrance to the Kargah on the prominent mound which marks the site of an ancient Buddhist Stupa. I lit my pipe and rested. My mind wondered to the faraway days when the monks of the Buddhist Monastery must have gazed down, as I was doing now, on the Gilgit settlement spread out below. The view can have changed very little. In my daydreaming, I could almost see a procession of monks breast the hill; long robes swirled, and the mighty mountains echoed the hymn they were solemnly chanting. The Monastery bell pealed out clear in the thin air, and, even as then, the evening breeze now wafted up from the township the cries of children at play, the ploughman's shout of encouragement to his bullocks as he turned the last furrow for the day, and the crowing of the barnyard roosters, seeking their nightly perches in the trees.

It was getting late so I retraced my steps along the water channel. I dropped three more *chikor* on the way. One I lost in the rocks: even Sammy's keen nose could not trace it. It was dark by the time I reached my bungalow. I entered through the stables and noted that the ponies were well bedded down and comfortable. They whinnied into their nosebags, as I approached. I then entered the house and went through to the sitting-room.

Haider was waiting for me. He had shaved off all his hair in an attempt to prevent an imaginary tendency to baldness, and now looked rather comic.

I gathered up the rifle oil, flannelette and ramrod from the mantelpiece, and throwing the game bag on the floor, started to clean my gun. One of the many good rules in life, drummed into me from childhood by my father, was that guns must be cleaned immediately on return from shooting. Any delay whatsoever, whether it be to change wet clothes, to have a drink, or to have a short rest is inexcusable.

"And what can I do for you, Lieutenant Haider?" I asked jokingly, smearing oil over the flannelette.

"It's you who are fiddling now, fiddling out shooting while Gilgit burns, Sir," he replied with a nervous laugh.

He helped himself to a very large whisky and lit a cigarette with shaking fingers, stained yellow with nicotine. I grasped what he meant immediately. Although I knew it was coming any day now, I felt a momentary alarm grip me. In a flash I regained my composure.

"Right, let's have it," I said sitting down.

Haider began: "The Mullahs are preaching *jehad* in the mosques at this very moment. They are exhorting the people of the Province to rise up and massacre all Unbelievers. Many hundreds of people have come in to the bazaar from the outlying villages. They are armed with anything they could lay their hands on, rifles, ancient matchlocks, rusty swords, daggers, and agricultural implements. They are now roaming about in bands shouting 'Pakistan *Zindabad*'. The Hindus have mostly barricaded themselves into their homes, but a few have joined forces with the Sikhs. The latter have armed themselves, pretty well too from all accounts, and are intent on opposing the locals to the best of their ability. There's been no violence yet, but there will be any moment now. The Scouts are still under control and quiet. The Indian Officers have gathered in the Subedar Major's bungalow and are discussing the situation. They don't seem to be getting very far though and they are like a flock of sheep without a shepherd. Half the 6th Kashmir Infantry have crossed the Partab Pul and are marching towards Gilgit on the Governor's orders. Something will have to be done quickly or there's going to be a bust-up like nobody's business."

Haider's most enlightening report was interrupted at this stage by the entry of Shawar Din. Talking in Pushto, he told me that five or six people were prowling round the perimeter wall of the garden. They were Sikhs and they were armed with swords. My two linesmen friends of the previous evening were among them. Now it was not normal custom in Gilgit for the Commandant to have a Scout Guard on his bungalow. Much as I would like to have posted a guard here over the past few days, I had refrained from doing as the sudden change of policy would have aroused suspicion. There was therefore a certain element of danger now.

The Gathering Storm (September to October 1947)

I told Haider about the Sikhs. His face took a determined look and he shed his nervousness.

"Now look here, we are going to be bumped off if we are not bloody careful. Hang on here for a minute till I collect some kit, and then we'll try to make the lines. Take this, and use it if necessary," I said, loading and handing him my gun.

I slipped into my bedroom. Although it was pitch dark I had everything I required at my fingertips. I slipped into grey *partugs*, shirt, and pulled a *koi* over my head. I opened my private cupboard with a key I kept round my neck. I removed my service revolver (always loaded), automatic Colt (also loaded) in its shoulder holster, Pathan dagger, binoculars, water bottle, haversack (with usual contents), money belt, map case and briefcase with my private papers. I slung the equipment round me, and fixed it snug with a leather belt.

I also removed some Pakistan propaganda literature and a Muslim League shirt (green emblazoned with the Star and Crescent) and handed them over to Shawar Din with orders that they should be concealed under the floorboards as soon as I had left.

Then stuffing some spare ammunition in my pockets, I joined Haider, and almost got shot for entering the sitting-room without warning.

One orderly would accompany us unarmed. He would hand over his rifle and ammunition to Shawar Din, who along with the other orderly would be responsible for the protection of the bungalow, until I could send a Scout guard up.

It was now bright moonlight outside. Shawar Din would put on my greatcoat and shooting hat. He would then walk openly down to the front gate. The Sikhs, so I hoped, would mistake him for me and close on the main road in order to ambush me as soon as I passed through the gate. Shukar Ali would take up a position on the verandah with his rifle, and cover Shawar Din, should the Sikhs actually enter the garden. In the meantime Haider and I would slip out of the back gate and make a dash for the Lines.

The little scheme went according to plan. Shawar Din walked slowly down the garden path, the Sikhs congregated on the road; we made a dash into the fields and were soon well away, and good old Shawar Din bolted back into the bungalow. I had no qualms about leaving these two in the bungalow, as I was fully aware that they could quite well look after themselves.

Haider, Munajat, and I hared through gardens, over walls, across water channels, down back alleys, until we eventually struck the main road near the lines. In that mad point-to-point across country, I thanked God that I had previously taken the trouble to study the locality so that I knew it like the back of my hand. We kept in the shadows and gradually approached the Lines. We froze as a couple of armed gangs passed us, and then moved on again. These, coupled with the din which was going on in the bazaar, were quite sufficient to confirm Haider's report.

We entered the Lines by a back entrance I knew, and went straight to the Subedar Major's bungalow.

"Thank God, that's over," said Haider.

"So far, so good," I replied.

Chapter 4

The Coup D'état
(October to November 1947)

1. The Gilgit Agency Joins Pakistan

The Indian [that is to say locally recruited non-British] Officers rose to their feet and saluted as I entered and stood on the threshold until my eyes had become accustomed to the glare of the unshaded pressure lamp.

I motioned to the Indian Officers to sit down and sat down myself. They were all looking extremely worried. Baber gazed glumly at the floor muttering, *"bara mushkil.* Sahib, *mushkil"* which means "very difficult, Sir, very difficult."

"What, may I ask, is very difficult?" I said.

"Well Sahib," Baber began, "earlier in the evening, just as it was getting dark, I received a message from the Personal Assistant asking me to go and see the Governor. This seemed rather suspicious so I sent my orderly on ahead to spy out the land. You know the little lane leading off the main road to the Old Polo Ground? Well, he returned with the report that three Sikhs armed with swords were lying in ambush there. Their intention obviously was to cut me down as soon as I approached. So I did not leave the lines. Shortly before this, the disturbance had started in the bazaar. We had all gathered here, Haider Sahib was with us and he volunteered to go up to your bungalow, and explain the position."

I believed Baber's story about the attempt on his life. My belief was justified later when the incident fitted into the sequence of events correctly. I knew that the time had come for me to put my cards on the table. I explained to them that I was just as much in favour of the Province joining Pakistan as they obviously were. I explained to them that in my opinion the only way to prevent a blood bath in Gilgit, such as was taking place down-country, was for the Province to accede to Pakistan. And I concluded by stating that my immediate intention was to do everything in our power, but with minimum force and bloodshed, to ensure that the Province did become an integral part of Pakistan. No one showed surprise.

Haider said, "I thought so."

"Now that there are no doubts regarding my sentiments and intentions, I want to ask a few questions," I said looking at Baber. "Just how far are you people responsible for what is going on in the bazaar and what action do you propose taking now?"

"We are more or less responsible for the present situation," Baber replied. "Our intention is to stage a revolution in Gilgit in favour of Pakistan. We have not told you up till now, as we were not sure what side you would take. Tonight is the night fixed for the revolt. Our plan of action ..."

And here Baber's speech was interrupted by a sudden outburst of babble by the other Indian Officers. Each was shouting in his own language but I gathered through the din that there was considerable disagreement as to the plan of action.

"Shut up, all of you!" I bellowed. "Tell me," I continued calmly, "what part do the 6th Kashmir Infantry take in these fun and games?"

"I'll explain this," said Haider entering the conversation. "The Muslim company is in this up to the neck, under the command of Mirza Hussan. The Sikh and Dogra companies are on their way to Gilgit. The Muslim company is left in Bunji and tonight will secure the magazine and rifle *kotes* and will arrest any Sikhs and Dogras left behind. The operation will be carried out by Mirza Hussan; Colonel Majid will also be put under arrest."

"Are you certain about this?"

"Yes."

I had to accept it, but I would leave my plan fluid in case Haider's information was incorrect.

At this juncture a message came in to say that there was suspicious movement in the fields and trees in the vicinity of the magazine.

"Have you doubled the Guards?" I demanded of Haider.

"No."

"Well double them immediately."

Accompanied by Baber I ran round to the magazine. The report was correct. I fired a white Very light into the sky and by the light of it I saw several Sikhs and Hindus scuttling away towards the Hindu Temple. One dropped something. I ran forward and picked it up.

"A stick of gelignite, indeed!" I said, showing it to Baber. By this time the double guard had arrived. I ordered some extra stone sangars to be built at strategic points in the near vicinity, and to be manned. I also ordered a medium machine-gun to be put in position. I then returned to the Subedar Major's bungalow. "Now for some damned quick thinking," I thought to myself.

I gave the Indian Officers a letter I had recently received from the Inspector General Frontier Corps (by mistake I presume) which gave the dimensions and design of the new Pakistan flag. They crowded round it like a lot of children with a new novelty, and this kept them busy whilst my mind worked at full speed. I doodled with my pencil on a message pad for about five minutes and then issued these orders:

1. The platoons present in Gilgit, including headquarters, would be paraded immediately. Under my personal supervision each man would then swear allegiance to Pakistan on the Holy Quran. I made a point of adding that it would be a genuine Holy Quran this time. This brought a smile to the faces of some of the Indian Officers.
2. The three platoons present in Gilgit, Nagir, Punial and Kuh Ghizr, would be reorganized so that each platoon would contain one section of each tribe. This would guard against the possibility of treachery from one particular tribe.

3. One platoon, under the Subedar Major, would proceed to the Governor's house. The platoon would secretly take up positions in the garden, throwing a complete cordon round the place. The Subedar Major, would then enter and announce that he had come according to orders. Once admitted to the Governor's presence, he would draw his pistol, place the Governor under arrest, and bring him to the lines for protective custody. This platoon was allowed a medium machine-gun for an emergency.
4. One section would proceed to the Post Office and ensure that no messages were sent out of Gilgit until the telephone wires had been effectively cut in all directions.
5. Two sections would proceed to the wireless operator's bungalow to protect Limbuwala and his set.
6. One strong platoon under Jemedar Safiullah Beg, and with a medium machine-gun and ample reserves of ammunition, would proceed to Bhup Singh Parri and re-enact the massacre of 1847 by wiping out the Sikh and Dogra troops of the 6th Kashmir Infantry, now on their way to Gilgit.
7. The recruits, numbering about sixty in all, would be organized into two platoons under Jemedar Shah Khan. One platoon would clear the bazaar immediately and impose a strict curfew. The surplus folk who had come in from the villages would be collected on the Shahi Polo Ground until they could be disposed of later. The bazaar area would then be patrolled intensively with particular attention to the Hindu quarter. I made it very clear that if one Hindu or Sikh was killed unnecessarily or any property looted, there would be one hell of a row.
8. The remaining strength would remain in the lines with me as a mobile reserve. All permanent guards would be doubled. I did not omit to send a strong Hunza guard to my bungalow. I was damned if I would allow my bungalow to be looted, cause or no cause.

These orders were pretty clear and I think the only one which can be criticized is number 3.

Why did I not carry out this order myself or send Haider rather than entrusting the job to the Subedar Major? Well, there are several reasons. Firstly I did not yet entirely trust Baber, or any of the Nagir Scouts, which follows, of course, because the latter were completely under his influence. In my opinion as of that time, they were as likely to side with the Maharaja's cause as that of Pakistan. This test, however, would prove Baber's reliability. Despite everything, there was the faint possibility that the Scouts might turn traitor to the revolution at the last moment. Haider and I were the only two outsiders in the movement in Gilgit. It would be an intolerable situation if either of us went up and arrested the Governor and then found that we had not the support of the Scouts. In the event of the revolt petering out we would have a far better chance of escape from the Lines rather than caught between the two fires of the Governor and the Scouts up at Government House.

I had also noticed that when I was allotting reserve ammunition to the platoon proceeding to Bhup Singh Parri, Baber had urged me to issue an amount vastly in excess of that required. In fact he had tried to make me empty the magazine

The Coup D'état (October to November 1947) 139

completely. This was very suspicious. I had issued reserve ammunition according to my own reckoning, and had then locked the magazine and taken over the keys myself. I vowed then and there that no one should enter the magazine again that night, except by my order or, in the event of trouble, over my dead body. As things were, I dared not abandon this key position, the magazine, by rushing off to Government House. And lastly I thought that my sudden arrival at Government House at that time of night and under the present circumstances might quite easily lead to a little pistol duel between the worthy gentleman and myself. I did not want him to be killed under any circumstances. Whereas the arrival of Baber unescorted, in response to the summons and despite the fact that he was supposed to be waylaid on the road, would definitely catch the Governor off his guard.

To sum up, it seemed to me to be much safer from the point of view of the success of the revolt as a whole, and there seemed to be a much better chance of taking the Governor alive, if Baber went in preference to me, or Haider.

I could see, as I was detailing these orders, that they would be obeyed without hesitation. I felt I had a complete grip of the situation, which gave me a supreme sense of confidence.

"Any questions?" I concluded. "Right. The time is now 2100 hours. Lieutenant Haider is in charge of all further details. He will report to me as soon as everything is ready. Move!"

They filed out.

Now for Chilas. This was very easy thanks to DATTA KHEL being already cut and dried.

```
To:    JANI
From:  KUKI    312230

URGENT
Datta Khel – stop – count Muslim troops Bunji on our side – stop – good luck – stop –
message ends.
```

I encoded the message and gave it to the wireless havildar with orders to pass it as soon as possible.

Haider reported that all was ready. I went outside. It was now bright moonlight which lit up the parade-ground with a pale ghostly effect.

It was an impressive moment as the platoons moved out from the barrack rooms in single file and the men passed a given point where a Holy Quran was lying on a table. In turn, they placed their right hands on the Book and swore by Almighty God that they would be faithful to the cause of Pakistan. Nagir, Punial, Kuh Ghizr, headquarters, the recruits, they filed through – one after one and took their places in the new mixed platoons. It was all so silent, so mysterious, so ghostly – I felt as though it were a dream; but it was a sight which will remain in my memory for ever. They were like Caesar's troops massing on the bank of the Rubicon prior to the fateful crossing.

Platoon commanders issued orders and then reported "All well" to me.

"Carry on," I said quietly.

It was as though I had pressed a switch which put several sets of machinery in motion. Without a word the phantom bands peeled off and disappeared into the shadows. My heart was with the platoon which was going to Bhup Singh Parri, the lads who, if all went well, would repeat the traditions of their forefathers. I felt immensely proud of the clockwork precision with which this initial move had been carried out, and I silently prayed to God that the remainder of the operation would pass as easily.

There was trouble with the wireless. The Chilas signals were too weak to receive my message. The charging engine had broken down. They had repaired it and were charging a battery. I thought we could send the message over the telegraph as soon as we had secured the Post Office. It then turned out that the Chilas line was down somewhere near Theliche. So the DATTA KHEL message was not passed till midnight.

Reports started coming in now. The Post Office had been taken over, the Gilgit Bridge was held, Limbuwala's wireless was under protection, the bazaar had been cleared and the curfew was imposed. Shah Khan reported that the outsiders had been collected on the Polo Ground. Our strength was dangerously low for the commitments in hand so I handed over the responsibility of controlling this mob to the Sub-Inspector of Police and his merry men. This was a bad mistake as I discovered later. All seemed to be going well and the only thing that worried me was the lack of news from Baber.

Suddenly the night air was broken by a rifle shot from the direction of the Governor's house. This was followed by several more. They were not being fired from a .303. It was something heavier. Whilst the first volley was still re-echoing round the mountains, another followed. Then came two more deeper thuds of a shotgun. Now a .45 pistol was being fired – crack, crack, crack!

"There's a bloody battle going on up there," I said to Haider.

The firing then broke out again – a heavy rifle, a shotgun, a pistol but no .303. It was strange.

I was still reluctant to leave the nerve centre at the lines, especially as I wanted to ensure that the message to Chilas did go; so when Haider volunteered to go up to the Governor's House and find out what was going on, I agreed.

After about half an hour, during which intermittent shooting had continued, a somewhat garbled verbal message arrived from Haider by a runner. Evidently the Governor was resisting. All the shooting heard was being done by him. One Scout had been killed and one wounded.

Just then the wireless havildar reported that contact had been made with Chilas. I sent the runner back with orders to keep the house cordoned, to keep under cover, and do nothing till I arrived. I was desperately anxious to see that there was no mistake about the message to Chilas. It was much more important, actually, than the musketry competition going on up the hill. It took about twenty minutes to pass as signals were still weak, but I was satisfied that it had been received.

Just as I was leaving the wireless room there was a crackle of machine-gun fire from up the hill. At the same time the barely audible buzz of excitement coming from the Polo Ground rose to the wild mob fury which began to move in the direction of the Governor's House. This appeared to be the occasion for my intervention, so I collected a posse and climbed the hill. There were several more bursts from the machine-gun: in fact the thing was firing non-stop and must have been wasting thousands of rounds of ammunition.

I found the set-up like this. A machine-gun had been mounted on the top of the guard house. Belt after belt was being blazed over Government House for no apparent reason. Haider and Baber were crouching beside it, but they had taken the precaution of seeing that the two stone walls of the guardroom were between them and the Governor. The Scouts were in a cordon round the house but they too were taking no chances, and were making full use of cover from fire.

There were two corpses: one a Hunza lad and the other that of the Hindu Office Superintendent. One of my spare orderlies, Shafyo by name, had joined the fray to raise strength, and had got in the way of one of the Governor's bullets. He had rather prominent ears and a bullet had drilled a neat hole through the right one. I couldn't help laughing when I saw him. He laughed too. I don't suppose he'll ever be nearer to death again.

The most alarming side of the situation, however, was the howling mob of Gilgitis which had broken away from the useless police at the polo ground and were now fast approaching up the road. "Pakistan *Zindabad, Inquilab Zindabad* (long live the revolution), *maro, maro* (kill, kill), *Allah Akbar* (God is Great), *Zindabad, Zindabad!*"

Nearer it came, nearer and nearer. I was speechless with astonishment. Never did I believe that the easygoing Gilgitis would rouse themselves to such a maniacal frenzy.

"Kill the Governor, kill the Hindu pigs, kill, kill, kill!"

This was extremely serious. Some quick thinking was required; this fanatical mob had got to be stopped or else. And now from inside the Governor's bungalow a weird shrieking and crying started along with the banging and crashing of furniture being broken. Was all Hades let loose? Was this a frightful nightmare which would pass in a minute and I would wake up in bed? I suddenly became galvanized into instinctive action.

"Stop that bloody machine-gun at once," I shouted to Haider.

I stood up in the middle of the road to make myself seen and heard the better.

"Crack!"

There was a flash from one of the windows of Government House and a bullet passed dangerously near my head and embedded itself in a chinar tree. Thank God, I had the presence of mind not to duck or appear frightened as I undoubtedly was. However, I lost no opportunity in taking cover, but slowly and quietly.

I turned to Baber. "Stop that mob, if you possibly can, and turn it back to the Polo Ground."

I thought no power on earth, but a machine-gun, could stop it, but there was just the off chance. And then the unbelievable happened. Baber gave as smart a salute as I have ever seen and walked forward. The mob halted.

"Get out of here, and get back to the Polo Ground immediately," he shouted and followed this up by some unrepeatable abuse in Shina and Burashiski.

For a minute the crowd swayed backwards and forwards like the Tarquin hosts at the bridge of Rome when opposed by Horatius and his two gallant companions. The

Gilgitis then turned and scuttled back the way they had come. This was an object lesson to me, and one which I wisely remembered. I knew Baber had influence over the folk of the Sub-division as well as over his own Nagirwals, but I never realized that his control reached such astounding limits. Truly this was something to be reckoned with.

Order restored, except for the unearthly noise of shrieks and the smashing of furniture in Government House, I sat down with Haider and Baber and pieced together the sequence of events. Evidently Baber had led the platoon straight up to the house as if they were going to a tea-party. With the usual chattering, talking, and clashing of equipment, they had entered the garden and had lined up in threes on the lawn.

The Governor watched this little operation from a window and not unnaturally imagined they had come to liquidate him at the worst or capture him at the best. The old fighting blood of the Dogras flared up, and he determined to go down fighting.

With him in the house were his orderly, his Sikh servant, the Office Superintendent and a small Sikh boy. The latter two were insignificant. But the orderly was a real tough Dogra lad who was prepared to fight to the last round with his master. So the two of them collected all the arms available which consisted of a .318 Sporting Rifle, a 12 bore shotgun, and a Government .45 pistol. They loaded them, and laid out spare ammunition at vantage points.

When the Scouts in the garden had completed a smart drill movement of right dressing and standing at ease, Baber and Jemedar Shah Sultan of Nagir drew their pistols and entered the house. Guv and gang retired to the back bedroom. Baber and Shah Sultan carried out a systematic search of all the rooms and eventually entered the bedroom where the Governor was waiting for them. As they crossed the threshold, the Dogra orderly flashed a torch on them and the Governor let fly with his rifle. Fortunately for them he missed. Baber and Shah Sultan then took to their heels and must have broken all records for the hundred yards in a prudent dash for the safety of the garden.

The Governor and his orderly rushed through to the drawing room and belted indiscriminately through the window at the Scouts outside. The Scouts made a frantic dive for cover but the volley took its toll. A Hunza lad staggered, and fell stone dead with a bullet through his throat; Shafyo, my orderly, went out for the count from the shock of getting a bullet through his ear. The Scouts then took up positions round the bungalow. Wherever the Governor or his orderly saw a movement in the bright moonlight, they fired.

It must have been an overwhelming temptation for the Scouts to have riddled the house with machine-gun bullets, and, advancing under the covering fire, to have exterminated the Governor and his minions in revenge for their slain comrade. And they would have too, had it not been for the supreme control exercised by the Subedar Major. He implicitly obeyed my order that the Governor was not to be killed, he restrained the men with great presence of mind, and not a shot was fired in return.

After some time, a figure was seen leaving the house from the back entrance. He dashed through the Scout cordon, pushing aside a sepoy who tried to stop him. The Subedar Major clearly shouted to him to halt. He ran on. As he was obviously bent on a mission which might have unfavourable results, and as it was clear that he did not

The Coup D'état (October to November 1947)   143

intend stopping although he had been warned, the Scouts shot him down under the Subedar Major's orders. I approved the action whole-heartedly. Apart from it being most unnecessary, it was an apt opportunity to take an eye for an eye. It helped to safeguard against further violence in revenge for the poor Hunza boy.

About this stage in the proceedings, Haider had arrived. He soon struck on the idea of firing the machine-gun high over the house in the hope that this would force the Governor to surrender. The net achievement was that about ten thousand valuable rounds of ammunition were uselessly blazed off, with nothing to show except a few broken windows through ricochets, and what was more annoying, some broken windows in my own bungalow.

"And now," said Haider, "there's only one way left to force him to surrender. We must burn the house down and smoke him out like a rat. Shall I send down to the lines for some petrol, Sir?"

"Certainly not," I replied, "never under any circumstances will the old Agency House be burned down, and you can be quite sure of that. Do you hear that racket going on inside. Well, the old ***** has probably gone haywire. When the madness passes at dawn or in the early morning he will surrender. You see! Now the thing to do is to keep the cordon round the house and when he throws in the towel he should be brought to the lines with the full courtesy and dignity befitting his rank. A guard should be put on the house to prevent looting. Understand?"

I ordered that the body of the dead Scout should be removed to the lines, with special instructions that it should not be paraded in front of the recruits as this might affect morale.

Baber was left in charge and Haider and I returned to the lines. As we were leaving, there was another fusillade from the Governor, this time through the roof!

The first news now came in from the Bhup Singh Parri contingent. They had met a reliable and trustworthy man travelling from Jaglote to Minawar. He reported that he had passed the 6th Kashmir Infantry en route.

The contingent consisted of about two hundred Muslim sepoys under Colonel Majid and Captain Mirza Hussan. This was rather startling news. Evidently Majid had been clever enough to see the showdown that would result if he brought the Sikhs or Dogras to Gilgit; so on receipt of the message from the Governor he had set off himself with the Muslims. Majid, however, had far too much control over his battalion for my liking. The only way to paralyse the dangerous potentialities of the entire unit was to separate the Colonel completely from his men. So I sent back a message that the Colonel should be placed under arrest immediately and sent to Gilgit. The Muslim troops should remain at Bhup Singh Parri with the Scouts. It was imperative that I should see Mirza Hussan immediately so that we could co-ordinate a plan in the light of this new development. So I asked him to come with all speed to Gilgit.

This completed, I gathered a posse and went along to the Polo Ground to see the self-styled *Ghazis* (holy warriors). They were in a high state of excitement and gave me a tremendous greeting. They crowded round me, falling over each other to shake hands, and congratulated me on the downfall of Hindu Rule and the success of the revolt so far.

"Tell us what to do now, Sahib, and we'll do it."

"There's lots for you to do," I replied, "but you must do nothing without my orders. Keep calm and disciplined, and by the Grace of God, the All Powerful, we shall succeed."

I noticed, however, that this previously unruly and rowdy mob now showed signs of being under a semblance of control. And I soon discovered that this was in no small way due to the presence of Gushpur ex-Subedar Shah Rais Khan, younger brother of the Raja of Gilgit.

Now Shah Rais was a Shiah and he was closely related to Baber. I noticed that this Gilgit mob was also about ninety per cent Shiah, and, what was more important, Shah Rais appeared to exercise a complete control over it. He was an old acquaintance of mine so we chatted for a bit. He vehemently swore allegiance to Pakistan. He placed himself and his volunteers at my disposal. I told them to bide their time.

I then collected Haider. It was sunrise now and a beautiful one too. Saffron-coloured clouds floated over the Haramosh Range, now streaked with the rosy fingers of down. A belated star blinked out over Dubani. We silently gazed at this glorious spectacle for a moment.

Haider broke the quiet by exclaiming, "This is a dawn we'll never forget as long as we live."

"How very true," I thought.

We then patrolled the bazaar, paying particular attention to the Hindu quarter. The wretched Pandits were in a high state of panic, poor souls, and fully expected we had come to butcher them. We reassured them, however, and it was pathetic to see the faith they put in us. Their offers of protection money sickened me – a typical Pandit gesture. I could have collected four or five thousand rupees if I had wanted. The Sikhs, and more manly Hindus, were truculent.

I ordered Haider to open a Minorities Camp in the lines where all non-Muslims would remain until conditions had returned to normal. It was much safer, as a sudden rush of blood among the locals might lead to a disaster. Their houses would be searched and all firearms and warlike material deposited in the Police Station where proper receipts would be issued. I impressed on Haider the necessity of seeing that this camp was properly organized and run on orderly lines. I would attempt to get news through to India that there was a refugee camp in the Scout Lines and this might deter them from bombing us. All is fair in love and war.

A message came in from Baber to say that the Governor had not yet surrendered. I decided to go up myself but then glanced at my watch. It was 8.45 am.

At 9.00 am the wireless would contact Peshawar and I had a most important message to send through, the passing of which I must supervise personally. So I told Baber to hang on, and, accompanied by Haider, I went up to the wireless station. An interview with Limbuwala would do the now highly strung nerves of both of us good. Limbuwala certainly rose to the occasion. He was standing on his verandah in a gaudy dressing gown, his hair on end, and he was obviously much agitated. When he saw us the expected tirade started.

Haider broke out in a fit of hysterical laughter. I couldn't help laughing myself. The impossible situation was relieved by the crack of the discharge of a Very light from the direction of the Governor's house. A green signal shot up into the air, and faded away in a wide arc.

"The Governor's packed in," I said, "get along there, Haider, and superintend operations."

Haider departed at the double.

Limbuwala sat down at the set. He lit a cigarette which he dangled between his lips. He switched on the set, turned the tuning dial, and tapped out his call sign at an amazing speed, talking the while. I heard a high-pitched signal in reply through the earphones. It was very clear.

"That's bloody Donaldson in Peshawar," Limbuwala said, "a bloody good operator is old Donaldson. One of the old school. Only two of them left now. Him and me. Here, where's the message?"

I handed it to him. He started. I checked every letter but it was no easy task as Limbuwala's speed was remarkable.

To: KHAN ABDUL QAYUM KHAN PREMIER N.W.F. PROVINCE
From: MAJOR BROWN   010900
Revolution night 31st to 1st in Gilgit Province entire pro-Pakistan populace has overthrown Dogra regime – stop – owing imminent chaos and bloodshed Scouts and Muslim State Forces taken over law and order – stop – Scout Officers and Muslim Officers State Forces running administration temporarily – stop – request higher authority be approached immediately and reply through wireless – stop – can carry on meantime Commandant Scouts – stop – message ends.

This was a very carefully worded message and I had given much time and thought to the text. It was most necessary to guard against an impression arising that I had performed the *coup d'état* at the instigation of the British Government, so that the latter might once again stake a claim in this all-important part of Central Asia. This would have led the Pakistan Government to believe that the British were breaking their pledges of the Independence Act of 15 August. It was also unfair to buoy up in the minds of the people of the Province false hopes of a British come-back, which they might well, I suspected, have at that time welcomed. So it was most essential that any hint at egotism should be avoided. In order to prevent faction feeling and internal friction, however, it was also important that the honour of staging the revolt against Hindu Rule should be equally distributed between the influential and useful participants, whose vanity and prestige would be much enhanced, if their names were put up to the Pakistan Government as having struck a blow for Islam in faraway Gilgit.

I also sent a personal message to Colonel Bacon who was now Political Agent of the Khyber Pass and had his headquarters in Peshawar. I knew he would be of the utmost assistance in explaining the conditions of the little-known Gilgit Province to the Frontier Premier and to the Pakistan Government. He was the only real authority on Gilgit in Pakistan at that moment.

> To: COLONEL BACON
> From: BROWN   010900
>
> Coup d'état in favour Pakistan in Gilgit – stop – can carry on meantime but can you help – stop – Brown – stop – message ends.

Limbuwala's cigarette had now burned down to a short stub which dangled between his lips. The front of his dressing gown was covered with ash.

"Thanks a lot, old boy," I said, "Oh, by the way try and get through to Srinagar. Let me know if you manage it as I have a message for the Kashmir Government."

"Right you are, Major, always at your service. Good luck," he replied switching off the set.

As I was leaving the premises I ran into a gang of rowdies who had formed themselves into a procession and were patrolling the streets, brandishing swords and shouting slogans. They were mostly Gilgit polo players. They greeted me enthusiastically and congratulated me on the night's work.

"Shall we kill him?" they shouted.

"Kill who?" I replied.

"Limbuwala. Just tell us whom you want killed and we shall oblige."

"Certainly not," I said. "Nobody at all is going to be killed. Now you will kindly return home and put these swords away before somebody gets injured. And stay at home. Don't let me see you disturbing the peace again. In a few days we shall start polo, and you can kill each other to your heart's content during the game."

They looked sheepish.

"All right, Sahib, you know best."

The crowd broke up. This was the last unlawful gathering to parade the Gilgit streets.

I now received word through an orderly that Captain Mirza Hussan had arrived and was partaking of breakfast in Haider's bungalow. I went there immediately and found him tucking into scrambled eggs and toast. He stood up as I entered the room and greeted me effusively with a cry of:

"Pakistan *Zindabad!* Major Brown, it's good to know you are on our side too. Good show, good show!"

He was magnificently decked out in uniform and looked quite the picture-book general. He wore a smart barathea jacket with a distinct cavalry cut, and highly polished buttons. His Sam Browne belt had a high sheen on it in which you could have literally shaved. His lower half was clad in impeccable riding breeches and long brown field boots. On the table beside him lay a cheese-cutter cap of the Nazi General design and a pair of brown leather gloves. A riding switch dangled at his wrist, with which he slapped his right boot from time to time. He wore a Government .45 pistol and I noticed that he had removed the insignia of the 6th Kashmir Infantry from his uniform.

"Pakistan *Zindabad,*" I replied in return. "Now look here, Hussan old boy, you and I have got to get down to work if this revolt is going to be successful."

The Coup D'état (October to November 1947) 147

I then roughly sketched out my plans.

"Grand," he said, "that fits in with my plans perfectly. Bunji is already in our hands. About fifty Muslim sepoys under Mohammed Khan are left there. Last night they secured the magazine and rifle *kotes,* and have disarmed all the Sikhs and Dogras who are now under custody. Smart bit of work wasn't it? Colonel Majid is under arrest and is on his way to Gilgit. Incidentally he has the magazine keys in his pocket so there is not much to fear. I shall return to Bhup Singh Parri now, and as soon as you have set the administration going in Gilgit again, you can join me with reinforcements. We can both then proceed to Bunji and consolidate our position."

Mirza Hussan exuded confidence and I must admit I believed what he had just told me. I later discovered that, except for the bit about Colonel Majid, the rest was just a pack of lies. Fortunately my plans were elastic enough to deal with this situation.

Actually, as I myself had foreseen, the news of the revolt had not yet reached Bunji owing to the telegraph wires being out and all outward routes from Gilgit being effectively held by the Scouts. Life in Bunji was carrying on normally, with no one aware of what was taking place in the restricted area of Gilgit. This, therefore, was the last time I ever believed a word of Mirza Hussan's or relied on him to any extent whatever.

Thinking that everything was under control, I excused myself and returned to the Lines. I met Haider. He reported, "all's well."

It had been a difficult job getting the Governor to the Lines as the Gilgit people were out for his blood; but Baber and the Scouts had managed to restrain them. The Governor was now housed in the Indian Officers' Mess. I went to see him. He refused to speak to me, but I noticed that he was very comfortable and had all the necessities of life. I issued orders that his orderly should be allowed to move freely in the Lines, and should be given every facility for administering to his master and preparing his food. The orderly gave me a broad grin, as much as to say, "you're the winner!"

I then inspected the Refugee Camp as I had now named it. Thanks to Haider, it was running smoothly and everything was in order. Tents had been erected, latrines built, water laid on, firewood collected, and storerooms opened adjoining the camp to take the possessions of all the Hindus and Sikhs, to prevent the possibility of their being looted if left in the bazaar. The Scouts were throwing their backs into the work willingly, and now that the first flare-up of religious hatred had passed, it was strange to see large Hunza sepoys striding through the bazaar to the camp with laughing Hindu children clasped in their arms whilst the mothers followed behind.

Other Scouts could be seen hauling handcarts piled high with the household effects of the refugees, to deposit them safely in the Lines within the owners' reach. I saw my Sikh friends of the previous evening. They smiled at me obsequiously. I smiled back and asked them if they had any complaints regarding the camp. They were full of praises for the arrangements and thanked me very much. I am never able to raise any ill-will towards the vanquished; even when Haider asked me to come to the Police Station, when he had seen I was satisfied with the camp.

Here I was shown the pretty little armoury which had been collected from the houses of the minorities. There were about fifty modern sporting rifles, the same number of

Sniders, many bandoliers and boxes of ammunition, about twenty hand grenades, and large quantities of various types of explosives. I whistled through my teeth. There was sufficient here to have caused quite a nice little showdown last night if brought into use. We had nipped it in the bud. On seeing the willing way in which the Scouts had been helping the refugees, I had almost decided that a camp in the protection of the Lines was unnecessary. On seeing this warlike collection of missiles, however, I decided that it would be much safer to keep the Hindus and Sikhs in the Lines until things had returned to normal.

I now turned my attention to the hospital which must obviously be kept running. It was unsafe, from all points of view, to allow the Sikh and Hindu doctors to continue work. So I appointed the senior Compounder (an unqualified doctor; more a glorified orderly, who was capable of handling minor diseases and dressing simple wounds), Hamayun Beg, as Surgeon.

Hamayun, a Hunzawal of the Wazir family, was an excellent man in all respects, and despite the fact that he was not qualified, I considered him much more efficient than the doctors Kashmir produced for Gilgit. Not only did Hamayun fully justify my trust, but he proved loyal and faithful to me in many other ways during the days to come. To assist him he had Miss Miriam, an Indian Christian nursing sister who also proved a tower of strength in administering to the female population. Revolution or no revolution, babies continue to be born.

Now for the Treasury. I had full confidence in Haider's integrity so I made him responsible for this. I ordered him to go and check it with the books, every anna in fact, and then report to me. In future he would keep the keys himself and would have to answer for any losses. He eventually reported that eight lakhs of rupees were lying in the vault. I checked this up with the books and satisfied myself that it was correct. I told him that the Treasury should now be sealed and no transactions should be made without my orders. Haider did not betray my trust in any way and I was later able to hand over proudly to the Pakistan Government this tidy sum of £60,000: a somewhat different fate from that of the proceeds of the Mirpur and Baramula Treasuries which are now spread out the length and breadth of the barren hills of Waziristan and the Khyber Pass.

The work ahead of me seemed unending, yet I now felt possessed of a feeling that my body and brain were indefatigable. I felt no urge to eat, drink, or smoke. There was work to be done and I would do it until I was satisfied that all was shipshape. Any negligence or omission now might have untold consequences. Apart from the major tasks on hand I was besieged continually by people with minor reports which required immediate decisions. I dared not waver, I dared not lose control of the situation.

I proceeded to the late Government House. It was in a sorry state. *Sic transit gloria mundipads Britannicae.* The furniture was smashed and the carpets ripped up. The bare floors were covered with empty cartridge cases. A smell of cordite hung about the air. The windows were smashed, where the ex-Governor and his orderly had fired through them from our machine-gun. The ceilings were covered with bullet holes. Again my mind wandered to the good old days of Colonel Cobb and Colonel Bacon. But this was no time for day-dreaming. I packed up the Governor's kit, and placed it in his steel trunks. I carefully checked his arms and ammunition and packed them in their cases. I went through all the contents of the confidential safe in the office. They consisted of the files which had been handed over by Colonel Bacon.

I found them complete and dispatched them to my bungalow for safe keeping. I went through Ghansara Singh's personal correspondence. There was little of interest except a copy of a private letter to the Maharaja which showed that Ghansara Singh was not in entire agreement with the way in which the State of Jammu and Kashmir was being governed. He made reference to the rampant bribery and corruption among the officials. There was also a rather interesting pamphlet which traced the history of the Gilgit Agency and which concluded by stating that the entire area was unquestionably the right of the Maharaja. I eventually handed this pamphlet over to the Pakistan authorities. I wish I had kept a copy.

Having locked the house, I had the steel boxes loaded on a handcart and transported to the Lines. I then had them deposited in the mess. The Governor sat up and took interest. He went through the contents of each box, checked the arms and ammunition, and announced that all was complete except for one fishing rod in a tubular case. I gave him his private correspondence. He thanked me. He asked for the pamphlet on the history of the Agency. I regretted I must retain it. He sulked. As there was not sufficient room in the mess for the thirty-odd boxes, I suggested I should store them in the Lines. He agreed. He then turned to the wall and would not utter another word. I deposited the kit in a storeroom, locked it, and kept the key myself.

I then returned to Agency House (which I had now renamed it) and hunted high and low for the wretched fishing rod. It was not to be found. Somebody had got away with it, but it was a small price to pay for the safeguarding of the rest of the kit and arms, which might well have been looted in the general confusion of the morning.

I gathered that about 9.00 am Ghansara Singh had suddenly appeared on the verandah in his night shirt with his hands above his head in surrender. Baber had requested him to put on more suitable clothes before coming to the Lines for protection. Whilst this operation was taking place the Scouts had invaded the bungalow, curious to see what ravages had taken place during the night. So it was a great tribute that to the last stick of broken furniture all was correct except for the fishing rod.

Whilst on the subject of possessions and looting, I then returned to the refugee camp and carefully questioned each inmate as to whether he had received his kit intact. In every case I received an answer in the affirmative. I was very pleased.

It was next announced that ex-Subedar Shah Rais Khan waited on my honour for an interview. He was duly shown into the office. He started with a long discourse on the meritorious services his father and grandfather had performed on behalf of the British Government. He then went on to explain how loyally and faithfully he himself had served as a Scout Officer until he had been forced to resign on the grounds of ill-health. I chuckled to myself.

"Now," he said, "I have five hundred men of the Sub-division waiting at my beck and call. The Indian Army may invade Gilgit at any moment and you have not sufficient Scouts to resist. Enlist my men in the Scouts, arm them, from your reserve of rifles, give them ammunition and there you have all the reinforcements you want."

He then repeated the tiresome story of his ancestors' services. This all sounded very suspicious, but realizing how influential he was in the Sub-division, I saw that it was necessary to humour him rather than boot him out of the office.

"All right, Subedar Sahib," I replied, "a very good idea. We'll enlist your men. But of course before I give them proper rifles and ammunition, it is necessary to teach them rifle drill, musketry and so on. You as an ex-Subedar know this as well as I do. I shall issue them all with DP (Drill Purposes) rifles (castrated affairs which were quite useless for violence of any sort). They can then parade here for four hours every day under Scout instructors. As soon as they are qualified, I shall give them pukka (genuine) rifles and ammunition."

I would soon see from this whether Shah Rais' merry men wished to enlist in bona fide, in which case they would undertake this task willingly. If, on the other hand, they merely wished to lay their hands on my reserve rifles for some ulterior motive, these indolent Gilgitis would never suffer themselves to be hounded about the barrack square for days on end by Scout instructors. In actual fact the latter guess proved to be correct.

On the first day about five hundred men turned out for drill and tactical exercises. On subsequent days this number gradually dwindled, until all were back at the much more easy task of light pleasantry or gossiping at street corners. Before Shah Rais departed I tried one more ruse to test his reliability.

"Look here, Subedar Sahib, I want to send some ammunition out to my troops at Bhup Singh Parri. We are rather short of strength. Do you think some of your volunteers could manage this."

"Of course, Sahib," he replied, "I'll detail my most trusted men."

It was now becoming increasingly obvious that there was a good deal more going on than Pakistan proclivities, and the somewhat dubious situation was clarified to me some ten minutes later in a most interesting manner.

Hoping for a short respite now, I lay back in my chair and lit a cigarette. It made me feel dizzy, from lack of food no doubt. I threw it in the fireplace. The wireless havildar, Sher Ahmed, entered. He gave me a message which had just come in:

To: CS (Commandant Scouts)
From: ACS (Assistant Commandant Scouts)   011320

All well this end so far – stop keep w.t. constant contact – stop – best wishes to you and Haider stop have you contacted Peshawar – stop – message ends.

I reached for a pad to scribble a reply. The havildar shook his head.

"The set won't send," he said. "Some vital part is broken and there is no spare. I have done my best and cannot remedy it." I believed him. Sher Ahmed was a good chap.

"Get Limbuwala quickly and see what he can do," I said.

The havildar departed at the double. This was a blow, and knowing the Scout sets I was fully prepared for the worst.

The Coup D'état (October to November 1947)

The Subedar Major now arrived. He said he had been fortifying the perimeter wall of the refugee camp with stone picquets in case of an attack. I inspected his work later, and found it well done. He asked me if I would care to come to his bungalow for a minute. I agreed.

I found quite a gathering of the clans in the sitting room. All rose to their feet and saluted. I motioned them to sit down and took stock: Baber, Shah Rais, Mirza Hussan, Shah Sultan, and Jan Alum (eventually returned from retirement), representing the Shiah contingent, sat together. On the far side sat Shah Khan, Fida Ali (a Hunzawal but a Shiah), Jemedar Shah Zaman of Punial (just returned from leave), Police Inspector Hamid of Punial, and Jemedar Akbar Hussain, who commanded the Gilgit platoon and was the eldest son of the Maharaja of Gupis. His leave had not yet expired but he had evidently returned to join in the fun.

The atmosphere was tense. People gazed at the floor, fidgeted in their seats, and twiddled their thumbs. Haider entered and sat down beside me.

"Very pleasant to see everyone," I said. "We ought to have a polo match with such a fine representative gathering."

Shah Khan laughed. Baber cleared his throat.

Mirza Hussan rose to his feet and smacked his leg with his riding switch. He straightened his tie, rubbed his moustache and gazed round at those present.

"A speech!" I thought to myself. "Listen to the words of the oracle!"

Hussan started talking in his usual perfect English and I gathered he was addressing me.

"Now, Major Brown, we are all very grateful for the help you gave us last night. But you must understand that this blow and all succeeding blows are being struck in the name of Islam, and since you are a non-Muslim we regret that we cannot allow you to join our glorious band of *Ghazis* and take part in our *Jehad*. This of course applies to Captain Mathieson as well."

I sat back expecting a round of applause but there was only an embarrassing silence. Mirza Hussan continued.

"We know of course that you are loyal to Pakistan – all Britishers are – but it is not our intention to join Pakistan. We intend to set up an independent Islamic State called the United States of Gilgit, and although we shall keep the friendliest relations with Pakistan we shall in no way owe allegiance to that dominion."

I cocked up my ears, especially as I noted the Shiah contingent nodding their heads in approval. This was very interesting and fitted into the picture of my suspicions. So at least some of these people were out to seize complete power for themselves? So their motives were not to join Gilgit to Pakistan. Very interesting, very interesting indeed!

And now Mirza Hussan, in a sudden burst of wild oratory, proceeded to emulate Hitler in one of his more vociferous moments at a Party Rally. With a wild wave of his hands, which brought his sleek hair down over his eyes he thumped the table and bellowed.

"We shall start the new state off by hanging the Mirs and Maharajas over the Gilgit Bridge by their necks. We shall then cut the throats of all the Sikhs and Hindus in Gilgit and throw them in the river. We shall line up the non-Muslim element of the

6th Kashmir Infantry on the banks of the Indus at Bunji and mow them down with machine-guns. In the blood of the tyrants and Unbelievers we shall build up a new and glorious state!"

With this final burst of oratory and a flourish of his riding whip, Mirza Hussan sank bank in his chair, his face flushed.

"Hear, hear!" shouted the Shiah contingent, obviously overcome by this dynamic personality.

I turned to Baber.

"Perhaps you will be good enough to tell me just exactly who amongst you is connected in this little escapade."

Baber, Shah Rais, Shah Sultan, and Jan Alum spoke simultaneously.

"All of us present here are in it, and we mean to go through with it."

"They're in it too," said Baber pointing to the other Indian Officers at the far end of the room.

I turned to Haider, "And you too?" But the question remained unanswered through a sudden outburst from Shah Khan and others. A violent argument then started. Everyone appeared to be talking at the same time in Shina, Burashaski, and Urdu. It was obvious that all were not in agreement with Mirza Hussan's plan, possibly in part, maybe in whole. I held up my hand. The babble ceased immediately.

The sudden silence was most gratifying, as it showed I was still in control.

A multitude of thoughts now flashed through my mind in a matter of seconds. Hussan's plan was obviously a plot on behalf of the Shiahs to gain complete control of the Agency (henceforth I shall refer the country as the "Agency" again now that the Kashmiris and their term "Province" are out of the picture). They would then set up an entirely Shiah administration. The result would be civil war and absolute chaos. For all I knew, an Indian Army Expeditionary Force might at this very moment be setting out from Bandipur. It would make their task very easy, if they arrived to find the Agency engaged in communal strife. I was also not at all sure of the whereabouts of the Sikh and Dogra elements of the 6th Kashmir Infantry.

So instead, I decided to adopt a course of bluff, tact, diplomacy, and humouring which later proved to be much the wisest plan under the circumstances.

"Well it's been very nice of you to have been so frank with me," I said to Mirza Hussan. "It's always best to know where one stands."

I handed round a tin of Craven A cigarettes. Eyes lit up. There's nothing like a free cigarette. Shah Rais created a diversion by lighting the cork tip by mistake. He succumbed to a fit of choking. Smiles were playing round many lips now and the atmosphere was much easier.

"Now I shall put my cards on the table," I said, taking advantage of the favourable situation. "I have only one motive and that is to see the Gilgit Agency an integral part of Pakistan. As a matter of fact I sent off a wireless message this morning to the Frontier Premier, for passing to the Pakistan Government, to the effect that there has been a revolution in favour of Pakistan in Gilgit. I've no doubt the Government will be sending an observer shortly to report on the situation. I doubt if the Government would be very pleased if the observer reported that he found the Mirs and Maharajas dangling from the bridge with ropes round their necks. As for the massacre of the Sikhs and Hindus, I think I recall the Qaid-i-Azam always emphasizing in his speeches the necessity of safeguarding the life and property of the minorities. I've no doubt the Government would arrange to take pretty strong measures against those responsible for such atrocities. Here's a copy of the message."

I threw the message on the table. Mirza Hussan read it. It was a trump card all right. Faces fell, there were whispered consultations. I waited just long enough for the full impact to sink in and then I continued.

"Whatever way of it, I expect India has now heard about the revolt in Gilgit. Wireless messages can be intercepted you know. In fact I wouldn't be at all surprised if an Indian Army Expedition was setting out for Gilgit from Bandipur at this very moment. So if you people don't want to find yourselves dangling over the bridge, you had better get a move on and prepare your defences by consolidating your position here."

This bolt went home. The Indian Officers looked worried. Hussan sprang to his feet.

"Major Brown, you're right. We must consolidate. Let's start consolidating. I'm off to Bhup Singh Parri to consolidate. Goodbye everyone. Salaam Aleikum."

And with that he rushed out of the door, and we soon heard the sound of a galloping horse disappearing in the distance.

Mirza Hussan's method of consolidation was rather amusing, and might be described here as an interlude. Having reached some way out of Gilgit he halted. He removed his captain's badges of rank from his shoulders and replaced them with those of a general. On arrival at Bhup Singh Parri he announced that he had been appointed Commander-in-Chief of all forces in the Gilgit area. He then announced that on the morrow they would advance on Bunji and make a triumphant entry as the victorious army. The Indian Officer in charge of the Scout platoon seemed rather doubtful about this but Mirza Hussan dispelled all his fears by telling him that he had discussed the matter with the Commandant Scouts, who agreed.

As I left the conference room I found Limbuwala gesticulating and shouting at the wireless havildar in the middle of the parade ground.

"What's up?" I asked.

He then branched off into technical jargon from which I gathered that some vital part was broken which could not be replaced, and although the set could receive, it could not send. I accepted it philosophically – I knew Jock could work on his own in Chilas without prompting, and I knew he could be trusted to use his initiative under all circumstances.

"OK, Mr Limbuwala, thanks a lot for the trouble."

"Always ready to help, Major. By the way, come here."

He took me aside and whispered in my ear.

"Srinagar are calling me continuously. Give me your message and I'll pass it immediately."

I took out my pad and began to scribble a message. I was interrupted by the arrival of Colonel Majid, escorted by a posse of Scouts. He was accompanied by another officer, a foxy-faced, smart-looking individual wearing the uniform and insignia of the

Jammu & Kashmir State Forces. I did not recognize him but he did not leave me long in doubt. He jumped down from his horse, saluted, and grasped me by the hand. He then began talking in the most perfect Oxford accent.

"My name's Ihsan Ali. I think you are Major Brown. Most awfully glad to meet you, old boy. Always been wanting to. A bit thick, this business, isn't it? A fellow comes back on leave, years away from his native country and all that: then finds himself under arrest in the middle of some sort of revolution. Hardly cricket, what?"

It soon dawned on me who he was. He was one of the local Nagir lads, who had gone off to seek his fortune and had done well for himself in the State Forces. I gathered that Mirza Hussan had put him under arrest, evidently seeing in him a possible rival for Commander-in-Chief. However open custody seemed to me to be the appropriate answer at the moment, with the Nagir situation so tricky, so I made no effort to release him. He might be useful later.

"Look here, old boy," I said, "as you can see, I am up to the eyes in work. Do you mind very much taking Colonel Majid into the garden here – and waiting half an hour or so until I can straighten your affair out."

"Not at all, not at all, always glad to help. No chance of a beer, I suppose? I'm bloody well parched after that journey."

"Yes, I'll get you some beer," I replied.

"Grand, grand. If you've got any magazines, *London Opinion, Men Only*, that sort of thing, send them along. Pass the time, don't you know?" drawled Ihsan Ali shepherding Colonel Majid into the Subedar Major's garden. The last I heard was a feeble wail from Majid,

"I say, Brown, I really think this is past a joke."

"Don't you worry, Sir, everything will be all right."

I turned to Limbuwala, who was gazing goggle-eyed at the incident.

"Here take this."

And I scribbled out the message for Srinagar:

To: PREMIER OF KASHMIR STATE
From: GOVERNOR GILGIT   011830

Situation here hopeless – stop – entire population pro Pakistan – stop – am therefore withdrawing – stop – minorities safe in refugee camp in Scout Lines – stop – quite safe provided no offensive – stop – Ghansara Singh – stop – message ends.

Limbuwala glanced through it and strode off, twirling his walking-stick. I immediately detailed a trusted wireless operator to pose as one of the guards on Limbuwala's bungalow, and, by listening through the window of the wireless room, to ensure that this message and all subsequent messages were sent correctly. He would also ensure that no illicit messages were sent to India, should Limbuwala decide to double-cross us.

I now detailed Haider to take Colonel Majid and Ihsan Ali up to his bungalow and make them as comfortable as possible. A guard would be posted, but the only restriction was that they should not be allowed access to visitors.

The Coup D'état (October to November 1947) 155

Darkness was setting in as the Subedar Major rushed up to me in panic and reported that heavy firing had broken out at Jutial. I had not heard it, so I questioned the other Indian Officers. They swore they had heard it. I therefore gave my pony to a very reliable havildar, named Janan, who later became leader of my bodyguard, and told him to gallop out and make a quick investigation. He soon returned with the report that there had been no firing and that nothing untoward had happened. The Indian Officers were obviously beginning to feel the prolonged strain now and had started imagining things. To tell the truth, when Janan returned with his report I felt a sudden urge to burst out laughing. And I knew it would be hysterical laughter – the mad outburst of a body strained to the breaking point through mental and physical exhaustion. It was now high time we all got some rest, otherwise we could never tackle the tasks which were ahead of us.

With a last effort I organized a ration caravan to proceed to Bhup Singh Parri. I ordered several hundred cigarettes and extra blankets to be loaded on as well. When I had seen the pack ponies on their way I dismissed the Indian Officers and rode up to my bungalow.

How I was tired! I have never been so tired before. I was too tired to eat. All I could manage was a glass of Horlicks, laced with a dram of whiskey and a water biscuit. After a hot bath, shave, and change I felt better.

It was now about 10.00 pm. I sent for Haider.

He arrived in due course. He appeared haggard and drawn, obviously on the verge of exhaustion. I therefore treated him very gently. I gave him a very stiff brandy which brought some colour to his cheeks. He refused to eat. I stuffed down another biscuit with difficulty.

"I know why you've called me," he said.

"All right, let's have it," I replied.

"I'm not mixed up in this business of Mirza Hussan's at all," he said. "I've pretended I was up till now to prevent difficulties, but I'm not really. I'm not, I'm not, I assure you, Sir. All I want to see is Gilgit a part of Pakistan. I don't want any bloodshed. I admit we used to hold secret meetings before the revolt. I admit that everything was planned as you heard this afternoon. But my heart was not in it."

"And Said?" I asked.

"He's in it. He's supporting Hussan to the end."

I believed Haider, and I was justified as later events proved.

"Right, you'd better get some rest now, old boy. I believe you, rest assured of that, and if you and I work together we can see this thing through."

A couple of wireless messages now arrived from Chilas which required immediate attention.

"How long can I go on without passing out?" I wondered to myself.

To: CS (Brown)
From: ACS (Mathieson) 012100

Everything still going well – stop – self taking gasht 30 rifles 0500 hrs to hold RAIKOTE bridge and act as reserve for forward platoons – stop – must retain contact – stop – mounted messengers arranged this end – stop – message ends.

To: CS
From: ACS   012100

How do we stand with Bunji – stop – please reply immediately as information is essential – stop – message ends.

The only way to get a message through to Jock was by mounted levy now. So I sat down and composed a long letter giving him as many details of the situation as were at my disposal. By midnight I had completed it. I then sealed it, and handed it over to two levies whom I bade make all haste down the Chilas line and deliver it to Captain Mathieson as quickly as possible. They galloped off into the darkness. Actually this message and subsequent messages never reached Jock. The bearers were detained at Bhup Singh Parri by Mirza Hussan who intercepted the letters and destroyed them. I did not realize this till later, but thanks to Jock's good common sense and initiative – no harm was done.

I then collected a small patrol of Scouts and inspected all guards and picquets in the in-lying area. They were on their toes, but there was still much work to be done by me; strength to be increased here, strength to be reduced there, a machine-gun to be sited in such and such a place, a stone block house to be built in another; the tasks were endless and dawn was breaking as I returned to the bungalow to snatch a couple of hours' sleep before being up and about at 8.00 am.

The sleep worked wonders and I felt much refreshed. My appetite had returned and for breakfast I easily disposed of two roast *chikor* and four fried eggs, along with large quantities of scones and marmalade. As was my wont, I planned the day and issued my orders to waiting orderlies over the last cup of breakfast coffee and cigarette.

I have never been imbued with a spirit of false bravado, and I now fully appreciated the danger I was in. At every move, I was thwarting Mirza Hussan and his satellites from their dream of a United States of Gilgit. If I could be disposed of, however, they would be free to pursue their nefarious plans. So the first thing I did was to organize a strong Scout bodyguard for myself, of chosen men from different tribes, on whom I placed full confidence.

Havildar Janan was appointed leader. He belonged to Nagir, so this may seem a strange choice. However I knew that Janan was one of the most loyal people in the whole country to me. There was no doubt that he would lay down his life for me and I had the utmost confidence in him. I knew he would fear and obey the Subedar Major to the extent of reporting to him all that I did and all that went on in the bungalow, but this was all to the good as it would show Baber that the cards I had put on the table were definitely genuine.

A trustworthy Hunza lad was appointed as second-in-command. We later nicknamed Janan the "*Bara* Gushpur" (the senior nobleman), and the Hunzawal the "*Chota* Gushpur" (the junior nobleman). In future half the bodyguard always remained at the bungalow day and night, whilst the other half accompanied me wherever I went.

This organized, I issued orders for a flag raising ceremony in the Scout Lines at 9.30 am.

As I arrived at the Lines to superintend this ceremony I noted that a goodly crowd had gathered, and what was most gratifying was that many Hindus had left the safety of their camp to be present and were mingling unmolested among the Gilgitis. There were no Sikhs, however, and this was just as well. Baber had made good arrangements under the circumstances. The crowd was grouped in a semi-circle round the ancient tower of the original Gilgit Fort. In front there were chairs for the privileged classes. A small guard of honour of Scouts was drawn up under the Tower with an Indian Officer in charge. There was little of the splendour and glamour of the normal ceremonial parade in Gilgit, but the little show served its purpose to boost up morale and to show the people that the situation was well under control, despite the recent revolution.

At the stroke of 9.30 am on the Quarter-Guard gong, the guard of honour presented arms, the bugles played the Royal Salute, and the flag of the new Dominion of Pakistan was hoisted on the old tower. There was a quick breeze blowing and as the white Star and Crescent on the green background (the Scout tailor had done a good job of work) broke against the sombre hue of Konidass, a great cheer broke out from the multitude,

"Allah Akbar, Allah Akbar, Pakistan Zindabad, Qaid-i-Azam Zindabad, Zindabad. Zindabad!"

As the last echoes of the cheers rolled back from the hills and the frenzied crowd calmed down, I breathed a sigh of relief. A very definite step had now been taken against Mirza Hussan and the gang. Let him dare to remove the Pakistan flag and replace it with that of his United States.

I looked along the spectators. They all seemed wildly happy. So were the Indian Officers – even the Nagir contingent. I wished I had the power of thought-reading. The only glum corner was where Sahdev Singh and the rest of Guv's gang were sitting. They sat with pained expressions on their faces.

"Where's Guv?" I asked Haider.

"In bed, sulking," was the reply.

Before the dancing started Baber made what turned out to be an extremely nice gesture, though I must admit I was very suspicious at first. He asked if a Mullah could be asked to lead a short prayer for the soul of the Scout who had been killed the previous night. I couldn't very well refuse. The priest came forward and faced the crowd. He was a young man, dressed in grey clothes. He wore rubber Plimsoll shoes on his feet, which he removed, and he had a fur hat on his head. A thin wispy beard grew on the end of his chin. He raised his hands in supplication and gazed towards Heaven.

"In the name of God, the All Compassionate, the All Merciful. We beseech thee, the only True God, to have pity on the soul of our departed brother who has sacrificed himself In the cause of Islam, and to accept him in Your Fold. A worthier death no man can have than to die as a *Ghazi* of the True Faith. And for us Almighty God, help us we beseech thee, that we may do better in Thy Sight so that we may take our place with all true Muslims on the Judgment Day. Teach us tolerance and give us strength to support the glorious Islamic State of Pakistan. There is no God but God and Mohammed is his Prophet. Amen."

People may scorn mass emotionalism. Outsiders may wonder how it is that the Mullahs wield such power on the Frontier. All I can say is that this insignificant priest had his audience completely in his power, and even I felt myself overcome by a certain hypnotic attraction. I was glad when it was over. I had a lump in my throat. He had not preached *Jehad*. I marked well the reference to tolerance and decided that any trouble henceforth would spring from a material source rather than from a spiritual one. I had suggested to Haider on the previous day that he might tackle the Mullahs on the question of preaching tolerance and he had evidently done his job well.

Baber with one of those strokes of genius, which he sometimes produced, now suggested that I should address a few words to the crowd. It was all that was required to break the spell.

I spoke briefly in Urdu. I congratulated the people on overthrowing Hindu Rule, and casting their lot with Pakistan which was the true course for all Muslims. I exhorted them to remain calm, and to show the utmost tolerance towards the minorities. I finally pointed out that they must forego faction feeling and petty jealousies and unite as one, if they were to withstand a possible counter-attack by India. I assured them that if they did so, they would undoubtedly emerge victorious to become useful citizens of their own State of Pakistan.

"And now, on with the dance," I shouted as the band struck up amidst rousing cheers.

"This will do all the good in the world," I thought to myself as I allowed the festivities to continue for a couple of hours.

And I think it did. I think that but for this jollification things might have been a lot more awkward than they were.

The bazaar was still closed. It was imperative that it should be opened so that normal life could start again. So I called the main Muslim shopkeepers and asked their views. They said they were very ready to open their shops but they pointed out that the bulk of the shops belonged to Hindus who were now lodged in the refugee camp. They promised to take full responsibility for the life and property of these Hindus if I released them. I agreed and in the evening when I rode home through the bazaar I was pleased to see the place functioning as usual, with thriving trade being done in Hindu and Muslim shops alike.

In view of what I had seen and heard during the morning, I intended releasing all Hindus gradually from the refugee camp and letting them return to their various jobs. The Sikhs and Guv and gang would have to remain in custody however. They were too tempting bait, despite the fact that religious hatred had now completely disappeared.

This completed, I scanned three messages which Limbuwala's messenger had just brought:

To: MAJOR BROWN
From: ABDUL QAYUM PRIME MINISTER

Have repeated your telegram to Pakistan Government whose orders should be awaited – stop – meanwhile grateful for any support you can give in maintaining law and order.

This was satisfactory. I folded it and put it in my pocket.

To: BROWN
From: COLONEL BACON

If in danger go to Hunza – stop – will try and contact you through Swat and Chitral – stop – is Gilgit safe for aircraft – stop – how is petrol.

I dictated the reply and dispatched it.

Am in no personal danger – stop – landing ground safe – stop – petrol stocks OK – stop – message ends.

To: GOVERNOR GILGIT (Ghansara Singh)
From: PRIME MINISTER OF KASHMIR

Your action approved – stop – signal whereabouts and intentions of State Forces Battalion.

"No reply," I said to myself, tossing the message in the waste-paper basket.

I then attended to a few minor reports, and sent off some volunteer linemen to repair the telegraph wires to Hunza and Nagir and those on the Gupis-Yasin line. Though they presented themselves as volunteers, they demanded huge sums of money to do this job. An appeal to lend their free services in the interests of Pakistan cut no ice. Everyone was out for themselves – Pakistan seemed to be a convenient means and a secondary consideration.

Time had been flying; it was now getting late. I took final reports for the night from my staff and departed. On the way home I visited the refugee camp, bazaar, post office, treasury, and hospital. All was well.

Haider came up for an early dinner. He talked much about his home and family. He left about 9.00 pm and I went to bed, determined to get a good night's sleep.

Half the bodyguard slept in the adjoining room. They chattered like a lot of monkeys before they eventually bedded down on the floor and on my beautiful spring divan – the only one of its kind in Gilgit. I heard some rude jests being made about it.

I woke up about midnight – I have a convenient knack of waking up at whatever time I decide to before falling asleep – and roused the sleepy bodyguard. Escorted by them, I made a quick tour of the guards and picquets which were all in order. I felt very safe surrounded by my own hand-picked men. Over the breakfast table on the following morning, which was 3 November, I studied some wireless messages which had come in from Chilas. They mostly contained request for news details which I had already given in my letter. In my estimation, the letter would have reached Jock after the messages had been passed, so I made no effort to reply. The news then came in that Said had arrived back from Kalamdarchi and that Mirza Hussan had returned from Bhup Singh Parri.

Said and Haider eventually arrived at the bungalow; the former was very affable and submitted a very satisfactory tour report. The Hunza platoon should arrive in a few days. Said had hurried back alone when he heard of the revolt in Gilgit, and was now ready to lay down his life for the cause and all that sort of thing. I suggested we might go down to the post office and check up that everything was all right there. I also suggested that some of the native Officers might accompany us. I did not say, however, that the telegraph line to Bunji had been repaired and that if my reckoning and Jock's plans were correct, we should be hearing some very interesting news over the buzzer.

On arrival I looked around, found a few minor faults with the guard, and then entered the telegraph room. The quaking Pandit operator was summoned and told to connect up with Bunji. As soon as he pushed the plug home the needle on the registration dial started flickering, showing that the Bunji operator was calling Gilgit. My companions were fascinated.

Dot, dot, dot, dash, dash, dash, dot, dot, dot, SOS, SOS, SOS.
"Go on," I said to the Pandit, "call him up and take the message down."
The Pandit complied with a shaking hand.

> To: GOVERNOR OF GILGIT
>   3 November 1947
>
> Hostile tribesmen attacked our picquets Jaglote and Parta Pul at dawn – stop – both picquets wiped out – stop – bridge destroyed and ferry boat set adrift by raiders – stop – Ramghat held by enemy – stop – we are therefore completely cut off – stop – situation hopeless – stop – Baldev Singh – stop – message ends.

Now the psychological effect on the little gathering when the news of the first blood had sunk in was most interesting. The Pandit collapsed on the floor with tears flowing down his face. Haider looked startled but with an effort controlled himself. Said looked wildly about him as though searching for support – there are heavy penalties for high treason especially when units of the State Forces are liquidated in the process; and his family was still in Jammu. The Indian Officers, except in a very few cases, looked extremely anxious. This was the first organized act of violence on any scale which had taken place in Gilgit in their memory.

The *Jehad* was on now all right and the opponents were not defenceless clerks and shopkeepers. I must say I felt extremely callous and cold-blooded about the whole thing. I had contracted to serve the Maharaja faithfully. I had drawn his generous pay for three months. Now I had deserted. I had mutinied. I had instigated the Scouts to mutiny. I had ordered the Scouts to annihilate a unit of the Maharaja's State Forces, which they appeared to have done successfully. All this had happened after the State of Jammu & Kashmir had acceded to and had been accepted by India, which was one of His Majesty's Dominions. My actions seemed to possess all of the ingredients of high treason, amounting to waging war against the King Emperor. Yet I knew in my mind that I had done what was right. I was still confident that the killing of the few in fair military battle would eventually save the lives of many. I felt no remorse.

The little gathering of people broke up and left in small groups, whispering amongst themselves.

I then made a rapid appreciation of the situation.

It was obvious that the Sikhs and Dogras were in control in Bunji. The message had been sent by Baldev Singh. Their morale was low and there was no doubt that they were cut off as they stated. With the Partab Pul bridge destroyed, and the Ramghat bridge held by the Scouts, they could not move out of the Bunji plain area, except by crossing the high mountains into Baltistan. With the season so far on and so much snow on the uplands this would be a superhuman task. A few of the braver and tougher might get through, but they would never manage to take their supporting weapons with them. No, the Sikh and Dogra companies were no longer a factor to be reckoned with. Bottled up like sheep in a pen they were there for the taking and only a careful plan was required to complete their final destruction without a regrettable incident of any sort.

Just such a plan was forming in my brain when a message arrived from Haider to say that the *Ghazis* were holding a conference in the Subedar Major's bungalow. He thought I might like to attend. I certainly did, and as delay could in no way now endanger the final disposal of the Sikhs and Dogras, I shelved the half-formed plan at the back of my mind and proceeded to the Lines.

There was a racket going on like the Tower of Babel in Baber's sitting room. Silence fell as I entered and everyone saluted me. Shah Rais was very friendly and sat beside me. The same crowd was present as at the previous meeting with the addition of Said.

I deemed it wise to lead off, so I showed them the reply I had received from the Frontier Premier. This would leave no doubt in their minds regarding the fact that the Pakistan Government was fully aware of what was going on in Gilgit.

Said and Mirza Hussan took the floor as joint spokesmen.

They addressed me: "We have changed our plans after much discussion. We have decided to spare the Mirs and Maharajas, and we have decided not to kill the minorities. The Governor and all Sikhs and Hindus must be protected. Tolerance is a very good thing."

"Very good thing, very good thing," repeated Shah Rais solemnly. "It is our duty now to capture the Sikh and Dogra companies in Bunji without further fighting. It is very regrettable that fighting has taken place at Jaglote, and the picquets massacred. You, of course, Major Brown, will have to take full responsibility for this in the event of an inquiry afterwards. We had nothing to do with it."

"And now," continued Said, "We have decided to form a Provisional Government to rule the Gilgit Agency. The word of the Government will be law, and if a representative of the Pakistan Government does arrive he will be allowed no hand in dictating policy, but will be treated as a mere observer."

"Oh yes," I said, "and what is the Provisional Government going to consist of and whose going to be in it?"

Mirza Hussan jumped up, General's badges flashing.

"I shall be in it as Commander-in-Chief. I shall be Field Marshal and control all troops in the area. We shall be called the Gilgit Azad (Free) Forces. There will also be a President, a Chief of Military Staff, a Commissioner, and a Chief of Police."

"Pray who will fill these posts?" I asked innocently.

I evidently exploded the detonator. Bedlam was let loose. Hussan shouted about leading his gallant forces over the Burzil Pass and saving Kashmir.

"I'm off to spend a penny," I said to Haider, "coming?"

We went outside.

"Now look here," I said, "as an unwanted outsider I shall not be offered, and would not accept anyway, a position in this comic opera government. I have my own plans which will be successful in the long run. But you've got to do one thing.

Whatever happens you must become Commissioner, because as such you will be responsible for the Treasury and will retain the keys. I don't care how you do it, but do your utmost to get that position in the Government. If you fail, I shall have to use force to safeguard that money (eight lakhs), and I want to avoid violence if it is humanly possible."

"Right, Sir," he replied.

I returned to my bungalow for roast *chikor*, chipped potatoes and carrots, washed down by an excellent pint of Pilsener.

After lunch I wrote a letter to Jock giving him the latest "gen" on the situation. I told him not to worry about the Sikhs and Dogras in Bunji, apart from maintaining the blockade he had already established. I sealed it and gave it to a mounted levy with instructions to deliver it to Captain Mathieson whom he would find in the Jaglote or Rainkote areas.

This was another futile effort which never reached Jock but the fate of the letter was rather interesting. The levy's pony had cast a shoe so he went straight away to the local smithy in the bazaar. Whilst the smith was at work, the levy hung his belt with the dispatch pouch on it on the pommel of his saddle. Some smart individual took advantage of the smith blowing his bellows and the levy chatting to a friend, to remove my letter from the pouch and replace it by an empty envelope. In due course the levy mounted and made all haste to Theliche, where he proudly presented Jock with the empty envelope. I wish I could have seen Jock's face – and the levy's. We laughed about it later.

The letter dispatched, I mounted Roshan with the intention of returning to the Lines as I had some important work with the Governor. As I reached the corner of the road, I ran into a half platoon of Scouts led by Havildar Firdos Ali Khan, who was Shah Rais Khan's son.

I scented trouble so I halted some distance off, unobtrusively loosened my .45 in its holster and pressed my left arm against my side to receive the comforting sensation of feeling the Colt in its hidden shoulder holster.

The Scouts advanced. I backed against the wall. I would go down fighting, if I had to go down. Firdos gave me a message from the Subedar Major. I gathered from it that a Mullah in the bazaar was exhorting the locals to kill me as an Unbeliever in this new Islamic State. My life was therefore in danger, and I should remain in my bungalow under the protection of Firdos and his men until the situation was under control.

I understood immediately that Said and Mirza Hussan had appreciated that they could make little headway with their Provisional Government so long as I was present. The Indian Officers, and even Baber and Shah Rais to a certain extent, were under

The Coup D'état (October to November 1947) 163

my influence and turned to me when a decision was required rather than to Hussan, so the latter had persuaded the gullible Baber to send the note I was now reading. The best course seemed to me to be to let them wrangle all afternoon among themselves. The more disagreement the better. The policy of "Divide and Rule" often pays good dividends.

But to return to the bungalow immediately, escorted by the Scouts, would have shown a fatal weakness and fear. I urged Roshan forward slowly, though the Scouts were barring my way. One Nagir had the nerve to grasp my rein. I was just on the point of kicking him in the teeth as hard as I could, when Firdos forestalled me by bashing him in the eye with his clenched fist. I never forgot Firdos' action and before I left Gilgit I promoted him Jemedar in recognition. I then rode straight down the road without looking back, and having doubled round by the hospital, returned to the bungalow. That showed my complete independence all right. Firdos was very friendly but rather worried. I assured him I would see that everything was all right, and told him to wait in the garden with his men until the incident had blown over. I arranged tea for them, which kept them happy. The last I saw, as I shouldered my gun and whistled up the dogs for an afternoon's shooting, was the unfortunate Nagir sepoy nursing his bruised eye with one hand and stuffing cakes down his throat with the other.

There was one amusing repercussion to the incident, however. Limbuwala from his garden witnessed the first act. Without waiting to see more he had rushed to his set and had logged a message to Peshawar to the effect that Major Brown had been put under arrest and the situation was very serious. No harm was done – good if anything as it impressed upon the Pakistan Government the necessity of sending an observer quickly. It did cause some unnecessary worry to my friends in Peshawar though.

[Editorial note. In later years this misleading message was to be used in support of the argument that Major Brown had not in fact played a significant part in the events described in this narrative.]

I had a pleasant and relaxing afternoon at the *chikor*. Half a dozen dropped to the gun along the water channels. The dogs were working well after their enforced rest. Sammy bustled about among the bushes like a bumble bee. Good dog work is half the pleasure of a day's shooting.

I walked home through the bazaar, and passed the time of day with some of the Mullahs who were gathering at the mosque preparatory to evening prayers. They were all very friendly, and they assured me that there would be no further religious outburst. I bade them goodnight and went on my way. I stopped at Abdul Jabbar's shop and brought some cigarettes. He was the Scout ration contractor so we took the opportunity of settling some minor business. I then returned home in the gloaming.

With my gun cleaned, and dogs fed, I sat down in front of a roaring fire whilst Shawar Din brought tea. Baber then arrived looking very worried.

"There was an awfully serious situation this afternoon, Sahib," he began. "A Mullah from Gulmutti in Punial appeared in the bazaar brandishing a sword. He collected the people and urged them to kill you. They were all ready to do so. You know what these jungly (wild, uncivilized) people are. Fortunately Shah Rais and I rushed to the scene, and by what almost seemed a miracle managed to dissuade them. I then sent the guard up to your bungalow. I thought it was better you should not appear in public until everything was under control again."

"Quite," I said, "I seem to have had a narrow escape, and I appear to owe my life to you. I can't thank you enough."

The next visitor was Haider. He helped himself to a large whisky and water on my suggestion. I joined him.

"Well, what's the news?" I asked.

"OK," he said, "the gang met this afternoon. You were wise to lie low. They have now formed their Provisional Government. There was a frightful showdown of haggling and arguing but the final result was as follows. Shah Rais is President, Hussan is Commander-in-Chief, Said is Chief of Military Staff, Hamid is Chief of Police, and I am Commissioner."

"Good work," I said, "and Baber?"

"Baber is simply a gullible fool," Haider replied. "Hussan," Haider went on, "is merely using Baber as a tool, just as he is using Shah Rais too. Baber has been promised the post of assistant Commander-in-Chief. Hussan knows that Baber has complete control over the Gilgit and Nagir platoons. He is banking on the support of these platoons in the event of a showdown, so he is out to keep Baber happy at the moment. The same with Shah Rais who has influence over the Sub-division mob. Hussan will use these two until he has set himself up as Military Governor of the whole Agency and Wazarat, and he will then throw them away like old gloves. But both are such idiots they cannot see this. They are both preening themselves now at the exalted positions they have attained."

"I couldn't agree with you more," I said.

This fitted into the picture perfectly.

"And me? What do I and Jock do?" I asked.

"Oh, you have been appointed Chief Military Adviser to the Commander-in-Chief, and Jock is your assistant," Haider replied with a laugh.

We chatted for a time, had some dinner, and then toured the guards and picquets.

I meanwhile received a message that the telephone lines to Hunza, Nagir, and Gupis were in order; so whilst at the post office I put through some calls. The line was bad, but I gathered from the Mir of Hunza that he had dispatched that day a written instrument of accession to Pakistan which he wished passed on, over the wireless, to the Pakistan Government. I assured him that all was well, and he gave me his heartfelt thanks for all I had done. He then wished me the best of luck and rang off.

A similar conversation took place with the Mir of Nagir. He was very worried regarding the whereabouts of the Sikh and Dogra element of the 6th Kashmir Infantry. I assured him they were in no position to attack Nagir. I heard an audible sigh of relief over the phone.

I then contacted the Governor of Kuh Ghizr who conveyed to me verbally, on behalf both of himself and of his people, the desire to join Pakistan, with the request that this should be passed on to the Government by wireless.

Telegram by Wireless Telegraph Gilgit.
Dated the 3rd November 1947.
. . . . . .

Qaidi Azam,
    Governor General Pakistan.

I declare' with pleasure on behalf of myself and my State accession to Pakistan.

Mir of Hunza

666

Camp Gulmit the 3rd November 1947.   Mir of Hunza
                                               Camp Gulmit.

. . . .

Copy to the:/

1. His Highness Sir, Aga Khan C/O Aga Majid Khan
   Aga Saloon Bombay.
2. Colonel R.N. Bacon Political Agent Khybar,
   Khybar House Pehsawar.

May be released to the press.

. . . . . .

Facsimile of the Mir of Hunza's telegram of 3 November 1947 announcing his accession to Pakistan. The original is in the possession of Margaret Brown.

To KHAN ABDUL QAYUM KHAN   Urgent 1
    PRIME MINISTER NWFP
        PESHAWAR

REVOLUTION NIGHT 31ST TO 1ST IN GILGIT PROVINCE ENTIRE PRO PAKISTAN POPULACE HAVE OVERTHROWN DOGRA REGIME STOP OWING IMMINENT CHAOS AND BLOODSHED SCOUTS and Muslim elements State forces TAKEN OVER LAW AND ORDER STOP SCOUT OFFICERS AND MUSLIM OFFICER STATE FORCES RUNNING ADMINISTRATION PROVISIONALLY STOP REQUEST HIGHER AUTHORITY BE APPROACHED FOR ORDERS STOP CAN CARRY ON MEANTIME IMMEDIATELY AND REPLY

To COL BACON
    PA KHYBER   Urgent 2
        PESHAWAR

COUP DETAT IN FAVOUR PAKISTAN IN GILGIT STOP CAN CARRY ON MEANTIME BUT CAN YOU HELP

Brown

The Coup D'état (October to November 1947)

TO COL BACON PESHAWAR

Doing utmost to keep situation under control but cannot do so indefinitely owing excessive internal intrigue stop imperative yourself or other representative from Pakistan arrive immediately stop moral effect of even short visit would reassure population

BROWN and MATHIESON

Unclass/8 (aaa) Your telegram WB1 Nov first aaa Have referred your telegram to Pakistan govt whose order should be awaited aaa Meanwhile grateful for any support you can give to Provisional administration in maintaining law and order

Prime Minister

Facsimiles of four telegrams between Major Brown and Peshawar between 31 October and 2 November 1947.

168   Gilgit Rebellion

The Governor of Yasin was also in Gupis. I spoke to him and he expressed similar sentiments. The Raja of Punial had beaten it back to his fief when the fun started and there was no telephone in Sher Qila.

When I arrived back at my bungalow I found messages waiting from Hunza and Nagir. I took the sealed envelopes, and sent the messengers round to the kitchen for their supper.

I opened Hunza's epistle first. It was the typewritten accession on crested notepaper and ran as follows:

Hunza State
Telegram by Wireless Telegraph, Gilgit. 3 November 1947
To: Qaid-i-Azam
Governor General Pakistan
I declare with pleasure on behalf of myself and my State accession to Pakistan.
    Mir of Hunza
Signed: Mohammed Jamal Khan
    Mir of Hunza
Camp Gulmit 3 November 1947

Copy to:
1. His Highness Sir Agha Khan C/o Agha Majid Khan, Agha Saloon, Bombay
2. Colonel R N Bacon, Political Agent Khyber, Khyber House, Peshawar
May be released to the Press

The Mir of Nagir's instrument was written on plain paper in Urdu characters. It was addressed to the Qaid-i-Azam and simply said that he and his people acceded to Pakistan, signed, Shaukat Ali.

I then made out wireless messages on behalf of the two States and the two Districts, addressed them to the Pakistan Government, and dispatched them to Limbuwala for passing to Peshawar first thing in the morning. I kept the original Hunza and Hunza and Nagir instruments myself.

It was 2.00 am by the time I turned in to my cosy sleeping-bag.

2. The Defeat of the 6th Jammu & Kashmir Infantry

On the morning of 4 November 1947 I had an early breakfast, and had disposed of routine reports and orders by 9.00 am.

I then paid a call on Ghansara Singh; he was extremely uncooperative and refused to speak to me at first. He was in bed and he turned his face to the wall and pulled the sheets over his bald head. In fact it was not until I hinted what might happen if the Gilgit mob got out of control again that he sat up and took interest.

"What do you want?" he asked.

"Merely to write something for me. Here is paper and a pen," I replied. "Now write as follows. Address it to the Officer in Charge of the State Forces in Bunji and say: I hereby order you and your men to lay down your arms, raise a white flag, offer no resistance, and surrender to Captain Mirza Hussan: he guarantees to treat you with all the respect due to prisoners of war. Then sign it."

"No, no, I can't possibly do that," Ghansara Singh wailed.

"I'll tell you the alternative," I replied. "Bunji is completely surrounded by the Scouts and your Muslim troops. Five thousand tribesmen, armed with modern rifles, have come down from Darel and Tangir. At a signal from me the whole shooting-match will attack the Sikh and Dogra troops in Bunji. The latter will not have an earthly chance. The most dreadful atrocities imaginable will follow, when these uncivilized people get loose. Those of your Sikhs and Dogras who die a quick death will be the lucky ones. The others will be rounded up, mutilated, and carved to bits alive. Is it worth it? It can only be prevented if you write this order."

Ghansara Singh thought for a minute and then wrote out the surrender order as I dictated it. He signed it.

"You're a wise man," I said, "thank you."

I then rode up to Haider's bungalow.

"Where's Majid?" I asked.

"Up on the verandah meditating."

I found him sitting in a deck chair, muffled up to the neck as though he were at the North Pole.

"Good morning, Sir. Would you mind reading this and writing at the bottom that it has your approval, and then sign it."

I gave him Ghansara Singh's surrender order. He read it slowly. He put on his spectacles and read it again.

"Really, Brown," he began feebly, "I've got a pension coming to me."

But he took out his pen and wrote and signed as I had ordered. He was clever enough to see that this was the only way to prevent the remnants of his battalion meeting a very sticky end.

Ihsan Ali had been watching the little scene with interest. As I left he breezed away again.

"Bit hard on the old boy, aren't you? Hardly playing the game this sort of thing. He'll lose his pension for signing that."

"To hell with his pension," I thought. "Everything will be all right," I said, "don't worry."

I then rode back to the Lines. From the racket going on in the Subedar Major's bungalow, I gathered that the new Cabinet was in session. The Chief Military Adviser would obviously be required, so I entered.

A heated argument was taking place about something, but a hush fell when they saw me.

"Major Brown," Hussan began, "you may have heard, or you may not have heard but we have formed a Provisional Government," and he looked round at those present. "You must understand that it is impossible to appoint you or Captain Mathieson to an executive post in an Islamic State as you are outsiders by religion. We have therefore decided that you will be Chief Military Adviser and Assistant Adviser respectively. You will hold the rank of Major-General, and Mathieson that of Brigadier. I am now

Field Marshal," and he looked round at his shoulders to see that the badges had not fallen off.

"That's all right by me," I replied. "Give it to me in writing some time, so that in days to come I can claim I was a real live Major-General in the Gilgit Azad Forces. I presume of course I shall draw the pay of rank, let's see, that will be about three thousand rupees or so."

Mirza Hussan treated my banter with all seriousness.

"We are sorry, Major Brown," he said, "but our funds do not rise to this. We regret you will have to continue drawing your present pay. You must look on it as your personal contribution towards Pakistan."

"And your pay?" I asked mockingly.

"Well, that's different. You see I am a Muslim."

"Now to work," exclaimed Said, trying to change the conversation.

I was sorry. I had been enjoying myself.

Said piped up again: "The first item on the agenda is to choose a suitable tide for our President, Shah Rais Khan."

It was getting near lunch time, so the other Cabinet members, after some animated debate, decided to settle the question by agreeing that Shah Rais should be officially dubbed "Nawab".

Before leaving I called Mirza Hussan outside, and had a little private talk with him. I pointed out the necessity of rounding up the Sikh and Dogra element of the 6th Kashmir Infantry. I laid it on good and thick what would happen if these troops did manage to cross the river and attack Gilgit. Mirza Hussan obviously appreciated my point of view and greed that the companies must be disarmed immediately and the men put in custody. I then produced Ghansara Singh's surrender order which, I said, I had procured as one of my duties as Military Adviser. Hussan was much impressed. He clearly imagined himself making a triumphant entry into Bunji and accepting Baldev Singh's sword as token of surrender.

"Good work, Major Brown," he said. "Give me the message and I'll capture Bunji. The Sikhs and Dogras will be in the bag before you know what has happened."

And this suited me perfectly. The non-Muslim troops would surrender, without a doubt, on seeing Ghansara Singh's message and knowing that they were surrounded. Hussan would disarm them and take them over as prisoners of war.

He wrung my hand, shoved the message in his breast pocket, mounted his horse, and galloped off towards Parri. He was not seen in Gilgit again for quite a long time.

We had a very awkward afternoon. Every unemployed Gushpur and ex-Government official in the Agency arrived in Gilgit and demanded well-paid jobs under the new Provisional Government. They made it quite clear that they considered the new Government an entirely Shiah-sponsored concern and they urged its immediate dissolution and die formation of a representative administration. The Cabinet disappeared, as it always did on such occasions, and left me and Jemedar Shah Khan to cope with the trouble. After a great deal of discussion, which taxed our diplomacy and tact to the utmost, Shah Khan and I managed to persuade the disgruntled Gushpurs to return home and await future events, which we assured them would be

The Coup D'état (October to November 1947) 171

quite satisfactory as soon as Pakistan had accepted the accession of the Agency. But the seeds of Sunni-Shiah faction feeling were above ground now, and I realized I would have to be most careful if a regrettable incident was to be avoided.

In the evening I toured the refugee camp, post office, treasury, and bazaar in the company of Haider. All was satisfactory. On the completion of the inspection, I suggested we should go and get a free tea from Baber, so we entered his bungalow. The Provisional Government had thought likewise and were tucking into cakes and hot tea when we arrived. The conversation veered off present-day events entirely and we were soon chatting merrily about polo and shooting.

Ex-Jemedar Nasir-ud-Din, son of the Raja of Punial and heir apparent, arrived and gave me the written instrument of accession of Punial to Pakistan, signed by his father. I transcribed it on to a message form immediately, and sent this up to Limbuwala for onward passing to Peshawar by wireless.

Ishkoman, only, remained now. But I knew the Raja would lie low and say or do nothing. This was the policy he had found was the best and easiest during his monotonous and uneventful life.

Time passed quickly in the relaxing atmosphere of anecdotes and stories of the good old days, and it was almost 6.30 pm when a Chilas levy was announced. He gave me a message from Jock.

```
To:       CS
From:     ACS
Theliche  031400
```

D day – stop – 0100 hrs received DTK message and set about arrangements accordingly – stop – 0530 hrs sent off gasht number 1 with 65 rifles + MMG (medium machine-gun) with instructions according to previous plan to overcome all opposition in taking Partab Pul – stop – tel wires also cut by gasht to prevent warning being given by Chilas Hindus 0800 hrs rearranged remaining strength into reserve of 50 rifles (two platoons) + MMG and HQ defence platoon of 25 rifles + MMG – stop – carried out complete siege arrangements including ration and water supplies – stop – mobilised all local transport and put it at disposal of Scouts no contact on wireless from you and no answer to my many messages therefore extremely worried locked all premises of Hindus and moved latter into barrack inside fort – stop – D+1 – stop – 0500 hrs intended setting off with gasht but received report that Hindu houses outside wire had been raided by Soniwals – stop – carried out immediate barampta (counter raid) and placed in Q guard two lumbadars (headmen) and three levies who had been involved – stop – 0700 hrs set out with gasht 26 rifles +Raja Orderly + 4 levies as messengers to advance up to and hold RAIKOTE BRIDGE and small bridge on Bunji road and to act as reserve to no 1 gasht – stop – both gashts carried five days rations and no 2 gasht brought four days spare rations for both gashts stop 2200 hrs arrived at Raikote with party of mounted levies – stop – 2230 sent off message to give you verbal sab achcha (OK) – stop – D+3 set off from Raikote Bridge 0530 hrs with RO, levies, and four mounted Scouts – stop – reserve rations for no 1 gasht + 4 rifles following on foot – stop -arrived Theliche 0800 hrs and established HQ – stop – so far no news whatever from no 1 gasht but post levy havildar reported that about 0500 hrs he saw a glow in the sky in the direction of Partab Pul –

stop – have sent out more people to bring back reports and am awaiting these – stop – last report re enemy 18 Sikhs + MMG in Jaglote so conclude there has been a battle of some description – stop – am still not completely in the picture – stop – extremely difficult up to now knowing who friend and who enemy – stop – where is Mirza Hussan – stop – is he with us or against us – stop – where is Majid – stop – where is Governor stop – has reply been received yet from Pakistan – stop – before departing Raikote this morning 150 armed men arrived from Gor to help the British sirkar (government) – stop – these were thanked and sent back – stop – have just sent Havildar Mir Baz back to Chilas to report on situation – stop – have ordered him to direct his own following of thirty to sit at Raikote and assist Scouts if necessary – stop – Sikh picquet of 10 rifles and LMG (light machine-gun) were reported and confirmed at Ramghat Pul – stop – have just observed them from here retiring with all speed towards Bunji – stop – if no 1 gasht reports success and no rifles required RO will return to Chilas tomorrow – stop – hope all well your end – stop – make every effort to clarify situation earliest possible as am completely out of picture – stop – Darel and Tangir wished to be amalgamated to Chilas in Pakistan – stop – send reply with bearer of this – stop – all the best.

I formed two immediate conclusions; Jock had not received my messages; the time had now come when we both must join forces at the very earliest opportunity. I then took immediate steps to prosecute the latter. A quick mental appreciation followed. I would travel now and very quickly. I would ride so fast that even a mounted escort would be unable to keep up with me. I would therefore travel alone. From the fact that Jock had received no word from his no 1 patrol it seemed possible that the Sikh and Dogra troops had managed to cross the river and had wiped out the Scouts.

If this was correct, then the journey would be extremely dangerous. It did not matter. I knew I could get through on my own. The only thing that mattered now was that Jock and I must meet immediately and co-ordinate a plan. It was too dangerous to order an Indian Officer to accompany me. I had a better chance alone anyway. I would probably kill the horse I rode through hard riding.

"I'll not take my own, I'll take Majid's Government charger, poor beast," I thought to myself.

I then announced that I was leaving alone for Theliche immediately. There was an awestruck silence. All were well aware of the possible consequences of this decision.

"Subedar Major, Sahib, get Colonel Majid's horse saddled at once. Said, you are in command here till I get back. You are fully responsible and you will answer to me for all that happens. First thing in the morning send a strong platoon under an Indian Officer, and supported by a machine-gun to Haramosh. It will hold the gorge where the Indus debouches from Balustan and prevent all movements towards Gilgit."

I would feel much safer with the back door locked. I threw my haversack over my shoulder and buckled it under my belt. I was now ready.

Baber returned and came out with the somewhat astonishing announcement that he wanted to accompany me.

"Two is better than one in a tight corner Sahib," he said.

I was suddenly filled with a great admiration for his spontaneous courage; furthermore I knew he was right. There is an unwritten rule on the Frontier that the minimum strength of an operational unit is two.

"All right," I said, "get ready."

"I doubt if you will make it through," I thought.

I was wrong.

We said goodbye to the other Indian Officers and Shah Rais. They prayed God to protect us.

"We'll need it," I almost added.

Haider looked very sad. I punched him lightly on the shoulder and gave him a slip of paper with my home address on it.

"Next of kin, you know the drill," I said. "Come on outside and see me on my way."

We both went out together and as I was leaving I noticed Baber giving Shah Sultan an envelope.

"Another last message," I thought grimly. "I devoutly hope that it won't be necessary to deliver them."

It was a sharp winter night. There was no moon but the clear starlit sky made visibility reasonable. I turned to Haider. He looked very young.

"I'm relying on you to keep the flag flying," I said, "keep the place under control and keep me posted with all the news."

"I'll do my best; I won't let you down," he replied as I swung into the saddle and urged the little mare forward. "*Khuda Hafi!*" (God protect you).

We cantered out the road to Sonekote at a brisk pace and eased the ponies up the hill to the forest nursery at Jutial. At the customary place we dismounted, and facing the famous shrine on the far side of the river at Dhanyor, offered a silent prayer for the soul of the departed saint whose bones lay there. For a minute we stood in silence, each in our own thoughts; then we mounted and jogged down the long incline to Sakwar. I now set the pace which was a fast one and the milestones flew back one after another at about seven to the hour.

As we galloped across the sandy waste before Ninawar, a serious mishap occurred which might have had grave consequences. My pony, whose long hooves, badly required paring, stumbled.

"Hold up," I shouted giving her rein, but the next minute we both bit the dust in a crashing purler. I felt the cool sand against my cheek, then a flying near hind hoof swung round and caught me a stunning gliff on the back of the head. Everything went black and the next thing I knew I was in a dark tunnel. At the end of the tunnel I could see the night sky with twinkling stars. There was a rope which seemingly led to the mouth of the tunnel. I grasped it and tried to drag myself toward the opening. But my limbs had that awful feeling of helplessness which one sometimes experiences in dreams. With a final effort I emerged, and found myself lying on the sand. The rope was the reins which I held on to instinctively, thank goodness, otherwise the pony would have been over the hills and far away by now.

Baber had been unable to stop immediately but was now pulling up some hundred yards ahead. There was a searing pain shooting through my head, and my whole body ached as though not one single bone was left intact. Spurts of red flame danced in front of my eyes. I felt unconsciousness coming over me again.

"I must not go under, I must not go under," kept repeating in my brain.

We both remounted and I let Baber set the pace for the next ten miles. I felt absolutely on top of the world. One and on we galloped, with never a halt, past Minawar with the watchdogs barking, past Parri – more dogs and a cock crowed thinking it was dawn. Baber was standing the pace well. I was very surprised. I took the lead again as the road narrowed to a mere ribbon stuck on the sheer cliff-face of the gorge where the river was spanned by the Partab Pul Bridge.

The starlight showed the bridge clearly, or rather what was the bridge. All that was left was a few strands of steel cable stretching from pillar to pillar. There was no necessity to descend and examine it closer. A single man might cross by a highly dangerous acrobatic feat but certainly not half a battalion of fully equipped infantry with supporting weapons. The only disturbing factor was that there was no Scout picquet on the remains of the bridge. Possibly the senior Indian Officer had considered it unnecessary. At least I hoped that was the reason. I sincerely hoped that the lack of a picquet was not due to the fact that the Sikhs and Dogras had crossed by some means or other and had liquidated the Scouts.

We trotted on round the dangerous curves and precipices and eventually descended to the sandy waste below Jaglote grass farm.

As we climbed on to the Jaglote plateau, I started moving warily. There was deathly silence, except for the dull booming of the Indus far below. Every house and hamlet was deserted. I looked at my watch. It was 11.00 pm. Thirty miles in four hours was satisfactory going. Keeping in the shadows of the trees we gradually approached Jaglote Chowki. I was expecting to hear the challenge of a sentry any moment now – a Scout sentry I hoped. The Chowki was certain to be occupied by the Scouts, unless a regrettable incident had taken place. Ah, a camp fire. I had visions of a great welcome. Probably Jock would be here too.

But we did not relax our precautions. We dismounted and approached nearer and nearer. There was still deathly silence – a horrible weird silence which made my blood freeze. A slight gust of wind rattled the dead leaves which still clung to the chinar trees. The ponies threw up their heads, nostrils twitching, and a distinct smell of burning flesh was wafted towards us. It took me back to my childhood days, when I had seen a gallant groom enter a burning stable to rescue a horse. The roof collapsed on him before he could loosen the head rope.

We moved round to the west slightly in order to approach closer under cover of the trees. Jaglote was a camp of the dead – death was in the air, over all hung the odour of death like the smell of decaying leaves and vegetation in a forest in autumn.

I was desperately frightened. I felt my hair rising and a cold chill ran up and down my spine. Baber was no better.

"Let's get out of this quickly," he whispered.

I had to investigate. It was imperative. Who was dead? Was it the Scouts or the Sikhs? Or both?

I threw my rein to Baber and told him to mount so as to be ready for a quick getaway if necessary. I drew my pistol and crawled forward, hugging the shadows.

I investigated the fire first. An old three-sided lean-to hut was burning fast. On the roof lay the naked body of a Sikh. It was a funeral pyre, and the body was being consumed to ashes in accordance with the laws of the Sikh religion. What alarmed me was that the fire had not yet reached the body. Some co-religionist had obviously been here very recently – in the last quarter of an hour in fact – to arrange the rites of his departed comrade in accordance with the correct observances. He might even be watching me now. Out of the corner of my eye I saw a wild dog slink off into the darkness from the far side of the camp.

I did not feel at all frightened now that there was work to be done. I glided over in that direction. There was a long shallow trench, lined by poplar trees, and it was filled with naked corpses. I moved closer and gave them a quick check with my shaded torch. They were all Sikhs and Dogras. At the end of the line were two Muslim bodies. I examined the faces of the Muslims closely. They were definitely not Scouts. The features were those of Kashmiri Muslims. Poor souls, they must have fallen fighting alongside their Sikh and Dogra comrades.

"Now for the telephone room," I thought, "and then I shall get to hell out of this."

I quickly slipped across the open space and entered the verandah. The door was stiff. It opened with an eerie creak. I stepped on something wet and sticky. The shaded torch revealed the body of a young Sikh bugle boy – he couldn't have been more than fifteen years old – twisted in a grotesque position in the middle of a black pool of congealed blood. He was wearing a uniform which was pierced in a dozen places by bayonet stabs. His bugle was still clutched in his hand. It later turned out that he had attempted to conceal himself up the chimney. The Scouts discovered him, however, and had emptied a rifle up the flue. As the body came crashing down, they bayonetted it in a wanton fit of fury.

The telephone was hanging uselessly from the main wire. I replaced it and clicked the receiver which responded.

It was now high time to clear out of this before something else happened. I doubled across to where Baber was waiting with the ponies.

"Let's go," I said vaulting into the saddle.

Baber was off like a Derby winner. I followed him but as I reached the edge of the oasis I felt my near stirrup leather slip out of the safety catch. I pulled up to adjust it and before I started again I took one last look at the death camp.

We made all haste to Theliche. As we rode onto the long straight parri, directly opposite Bunji, I ordered Baber to ride a couple of hundred yards behind me. If the enemy had a machine-gun fixed line on the road there was a better chance of one of us escaping. At one point the settlement seemed very close – so close indeed you felt you could toss a pebble on to it over the river. It was quite silent and not a light showed. From a hill above a signal lamp was flashing SOS towards Jaglote. We presently approached Theliche which was also blacked out, but we were left in no doubt as to proper defence arrangements and protection. Jock was definitely here.

"Halt! Who goes there?" snapped a sentry in a low tone.

"Friend."
"Advance friend and be recognized."
"Password?"
"Datta Khel."
"*Salaam Aleikum*, Sahib. Welcome. I hope you had no trouble on the journey."

Levies ran forward to catch our ponies and we entered the compound. A figure appeared at the shaded kitchen door.

"What's all the noise about? Willie!"

And the next minute Jock and I were pumping each others' hands.

"It's good to see you," we said simultaneously, and then for a second or two gazed at one another in silence.

Baber and Muzaffar were carrying through the same performance. We then changed partners and exchanged further greetings.

"We'll let Baber and Muzaffar have their pow-wow in one room, and we'll get down to business in the other," said Jock, leading me inside.

"I had really begun to think that the whole show was a false alarm. I fully expected to see an irate Guv and Colonel Majid come galloping down the road any minute, to demand an explanation as to why I had started destroying their battalion. I can hardly say I had a ready answer on the tip of my tongue."

This was Jock Mathieson's account of events in Chilas.

"I received your DATTA KHEL message soon after midnight, and it was about time too as the place was like an erupting volcano. Despite this, however, when I tackled the Senior Subedar at Chilas, Subedar Jamshed of Hunza (whom Brown and Mathieson had privately nicknamed Champagne Charlie), and told him what was going to happen, I discovered he hadn't a clue. When the impact of my orders struck home, he was visibly shocked. To think that he should live to see the day when British Officers turned revolutionaries. Really this was too much! So I wrote him off for that night as useless and ineffective. He pulled himself together the next day and proved a real tower of strength in organizing siege arrangements."

"The next really serious incident was when *gasht* number 1 had fallen in prior to departure. An attempt was made by some subversive to prevent the patrol setting out for Jaglote. They were told that the whole show was a trap arranged by you, me, and old Guv (Ghansara Singh). At some point on the road the 6th Kashmir Infantry were lying in ambush and would fall on the Scouts and wipe them out to a man."

"I made a public speech and turned on the persuasion tap. I pointed out to one and all that this story was absolute nonsense, etc, etc. The only people really affected by the ambush business were the Nagir men, but I eventually turned them to my way of thinking. From all accounts Havildar Nadilo of Nagir put up a damned good show at the Battle of Partab Pul and proved the hero of the day. He possesses the most complex character."

"Well, that settled, the *gasht* departed. We had a Quran Sharif at the main entrance to the fort. It was a most impressive sight as the men filed out under the old archway, swore their oath of allegiance to Pakistan, and passing out through the perimeter wire, disappeared into the shadows cast by a pale crescent moon."

The Coup D'état (October to November 1947) 177

"After that events took place as described in the message which brought you here. The only information, I have to add, is with regard to what happened at Jaglote and Partab Pul. Full reports have not come in yet; but as far as I can gather the Scout attacks were perfectly successful and the bridge went up in flames according to plan."

"My present dispositions are as follows. Number 1 *gasht* is at Jaglote. Up to this evening it was holding Jaglote Chowki and Partab Pul. Mirza Hussan arrived about 6.00 pm with your Bhup Singh Parri *gasht* and his Muslim troops. He then took the whole shooting match, including my *gasht*, up on to the tops of the hills above the grass farm. Why, I can't imagine, unless he feels safer among the mountain tops. I also have a couple of strong sections under Havildar Faiz Axnan of Yasin at the vital Ramghat Bridge which has gone up in flames, and a section at the Raikote Bridge – still intact. The Sikhs and Dogras are bottled up in Bunji and are completely cut off; I gather they have disarmed the Muslim sepoys who were left behind and that signal lamp blinking SOS is probably a message from some of the latter who have escaped to the foothills under cover of darkness."

"Right," I said, "that pretty well fits in with what I have seen on my way here and I think we may take it as a correct picture of the situation. By the way, what is your strength here?"

"A weak Scout section and a section of levies."

"I would feel much safer, and much more aggressive if we had a decent force here. You'll understand what I mean when you hear my story," I said. "Send a message off now to Subedar Sher Ali and tell him to withdraw the Chilas number 1 *gasht* here immediately and to bring the machine-gun with him. He must be here before dawn. I am aware they are tired but it can't be helped."

"OK," said Jock reaching for the message pad.

Whilst he was dispatching the message I got the other side of another cup of tea and a large slice of cake, which were excellent.

"Now for my story," I began. "It is obvious that you have received none of the messages both on account of the wireless defect and interception. It was no wonder you were in a flap. Your thoughts of Guv still reigning supreme in Gilgit whilst you were wiping out his battalion down here must have been alarming."

I then gave Jock a very comprehensive account of the course of events at my end from D day to our recent historic meeting at the door of Theliche Rest House.

We then discussed the military side of the operation up to the present. The conclusion we reached was that the operation had gone according to our fluid plan and that it had been entirely successful. The only defeat had been in intercommunication and we noted it well for future enterprises of this sort. For what it is worth, we give our advice to others who contemplate campaigning among these mountainous areas. Never rely on visual telegraphy, line, or messenger. Wireless telegraphy (morse) or better still radio telegraphy (speech) is essential to the successful prosecution of a campaign. Modern sets are imperative to the successful prosecution of a campaign. There must also be a large stock of spare parts and reliable, and portable, battery-charging engines. The No 19 set at present used by the Frontier Corps and Constabulary is excellent in all respects and the No 48 set might also be used to advantage for shorter distances.

It is much lighter and could be used for contact between picquets at high altitudes. I cannot, however, emphasize too much the necessity for reliable intercommunication.

We now discussed and appreciated the present military situation. We then divided it into two phases – the immediate future and the more distant future when the passes opened next June. If India decided to send an expeditionary force now to capture Gilgit there was still not sufficient snow on the Burzil Pass to prevent troops crossing it. The Kamri, the Babusar, Kamakdari, and Barai Passes leading into Chilas were now effectively closed. We must therefore concentrate on the Burzil route.

It was decided to send one strong platoon to Burzil to carry out a thorough reconnaissance and to act as a listening post. They would be in touch with Gilgit by telephone. In the event of an invasion by the Indian Army, we would make the narrow defiles of the rugged country between Astore and Ramgaht our battleground. Our hardy mountaineers would be in their element in this type of country. If necessary, we could fall back on the Indus as the natural line of defence and still hold the Agency secure.

At the same time there was a danger from the north. If Pakistan refused to interest herself in the Gilgit Agency and refused to accept the accession, there was every possibility that the Mehtar of Chitral would pursue his former intentions and annex Kuh Ghizr and Yasin. A force would therefore have to remain in Gupis. It would also be unwise to reduce the garrison in Chilas, surrounded as it was by the tribal territories of Jalkot, Darel and Tangir, where people were always ready for the chance of loot. And there was also the formidable threat from the Wali of Swat. To cope with these commitments our little force of six hundred strong seemed pitifully small. We could do it all right, but there would not be one single man to spare. Yet there were two external tasks which required immediate attention.

There was a State Forces post at Shardi on the Kashmir side of the Kamakdori Pass which leads into Chilas. Despite the fact that the pass was now more or less closed, this post had to be investigated and the strength and religion of the garrison ascertained.

We decided to send a tribal *lashkar* from Chilas. In actual fact this *lashkar* did its job only too well. On arrival at Shardi it bumped into a platoon of Sikhs from the Kashmir State Forces and wiped them out to a man. The Chilasi lads were very pleased with themselves when they returned to Chilas, after a desperate struggle through a blizzard on the divide.

The second important external consideration was Skardu in Baltistan, some seventy miles from the borders of the Gilgit Agency. Skardu is a small garrison town consisting of the fort, perched on a high mound, around which the hamlets of the village cluster down to the bank of the Indus. The valley broadens out here and both banks of the river consist of wide sandy flats. A route comes in from the Burzil Pass on the left hand bank of the Indus, and an extremely difficult one from Nagir via the Hispar and Chogo Lungma Glaciers on the right-hand bank. The State Force Battalion stationed in Leh normally finds a two-platoon garrison for Skardu. Our information was that the strength at the moment was one Muslim platoon and one Dogra platoon under Captain Nek Alum, who had previously been in Bunji.

The route from Skardu to Haramosh in the Agency, though difficult, is open throughout the year. The town would therefore make a very fine springboard for an

The Coup D'état (October to November 1947) 179

attack on Gilgit. As soon as the news of the revolt reached Leh, reinforcements of Sikh and Dogra troops would be sent to Skardu by the Commanding Officer who was a Dogra himself. The Muslim troops would be disarmed or liquidated. It therefore seemed to us imperative that we should forestall this by securing Skardu first.

But where was the strength to come from? I was loath to reduce the Scout force in the Agency by sending some of them. The Scouts were also a militia, and there was no saying how they might conduct themselves so far away from home, especially since there was no really reliable commissioned officer to send with them. Lastly, the Scouts might run up against serious opposition from Leh, armed with light automatics, mortars, and grenades and it would be no easy task to combat this with only rifles, when an actual place was being disputed rather than an area.

After thought, we decided that the answer was to send the Muslim State Troops to save their comrades and to hold the fort. The Muslim sepoys had nothing to lose now. Having mutinied, they dared not return to their homes in Kashmir; we had not sufficient rations in the Agency to feed them. Trouble-makers such as Mirza Hussan and Said could lead the force and this would rid the Agency of them. They would get plenty of scope for *Jehad* in Skardu with a Dogra platoon to dispose of and a Treasury to loot. As a defensive lay-back for this force, I would keep a strong platoon, supported by the medium machine-gun, at the extremity of Haramosh where the Indus emerges from the Baltistan defiles into the Gilgit Agency.

This disposed of immediate threats. If the Indian Army did not invade the Gilgit Agency now, before the Burzil became impassable, then an expedition would most certainly set out in the spring when the snows melted. And this expedition would most certainly approach all the entrances to the Agency from the Haramosh down to the Babusar Pass. Six hundred Scouts could never cope with such a commitment whilst at the same time keeping an eye on the northern frontier. But fifteen hundred Scouts, armed with light automatics, mortars, grenades and every kind of modern infantry weapon, backed by the support of a battery of mountain artillery, could stop anything from entering the Agency.

So we decided that as soon as the present operations were in the bag, we would draw up an immediate scheme for the expansion of the Scouts.

We also reckoned that if, by the spring, the Pathan tribesmen had been unable to advance from Uri towards Srinagar, they would undoubtedly try a by-pass and advance up the Kishenganga Valley via Titwal. In the event of this being successful, they would naturally hold the Gurez Valley which would prevent India sending a force against the Agency by the Burzil Route. The only route left to them then would be from Srinagar over the Zoji La Pass into Ladakh and thence down the Upper Indus through Skardu to Haramosh. This strengthened our contention that Skardu must be secured and held.

We did not entirely disregard the possibility of an air attack and the dropping of paratroops. Paratroops would have little chance in a strange, mountainous country such as this, provided we were prepared for them, and had strong mobile reserves ready to move to the limited dropping areas. Readiness for immediate action was all that was required on our part to deal with this menace. As for air attacks, as soon as we returned to Gilgit we would scatter the magazine and petrol stocks over a wide area so as not to have all our eggs in one basket. Also the fact that India knew that we held the Sikhs and Hindus in the Lines might prove a deterrent.

To be quite frank we considered the possibilities of air attack negligible owing to the difficulties of the flight. And we made a mistake, which we frankly admit. In 1948 the Royal Indian Air Force bombed and strafed Gilgit and Chilas on several occasions, and anyone who knows the enormous dangers involved in the flight from Srinagar will appreciate that this is one of the most outstanding feats performed in modern aerial warfare. I personally have had greatest admiration and respect, from a professional point of view, for the pilots who carried out these raids. It may be said they performed the almost impossible.

As the first light of dawn cast grey streaks across the floor, we appreciated and reached conclusions on the political situation. The Gilgit Agency was not nearly ready for self-government, and the continuance of the present so-called Provisional Government would only lead to anarchy in a violent outburst of faction feeling. If peace and tranquillity were to be maintained, an alien dictator must assume complete power, a dictator such as the Political Agent was before Partition.

Could I do this job? If Pakistan decided to interest herself in the Agency by taking over the administration on the grounds that her interference was necessary to maintain law and order and to prevent the useless loss of life, and appointed me as Political Agent, with her full support, then I could undoubtedly justify her decision. But the appointment by Pakistan of a British Officer to rule disputed territory, on her behalf, would most certainly prejudice her case when the entire Kashmir question came before UNO as it eventually would.

Furthermore the British Government would never agree to the embarrassing situation of having her subjects concerned in the Kashmir dispute. She would soon bring pressure to bear on the Britishers who held key positions in Pakistan to have me removed from Gilgit immediately. The Pakistan Government would naturally agree to this in order to prevent undesirable friction with the Mother Country. So it was most improbable that Pakistan would appoint me as Political Agent – rather she would send a Pakistani representative, under the title of "observer," who would in actual fact govern the country as a Political Agent. Such a representative would be welcomed by the majority of the people who were well aware of their own failings and inability to establish self-Government.

But supposing Pakistan refused to interfere in Gilgit affairs. Then I would have to set myself up as a despot. Our conclusion was therefore that it was imperative that Pakistan should send a Pakistani representative at the very earliest opportunity, who would assume the appointment of temporary Political Agent. We could then plan our own future, which unfortunately would probably be a fade-out from the picture.

The night's work completed, we rose, stretched ourselves, and gazed in the large mirror above the fireplace. Dawn, after an all-night session, does not normally flatter one. We were no exception to the rule. We looked frightful – haggard, unshaven, and bleary-eyed.

The Coup D'état (October to November 1947)   181

It was now broad daylight, but as yet there was no sign of the Chilas number 1 *gasht*. So we went outside, and from a position in the rocks studied the road to Jaglote through binoculars.

Baber and Muzaffar joined us.

I noted with satisfaction the excellent defence measures Jock Mathieson had taken by throwing up stone *sangars* at tactical positions round the perimeter of the oasis. They were very well sited and I think would have pleased our former critical taskmaster, Colonel Sandison of the Tochi Scouts.

We could see no sign whatsoever of Subedar Sher Ali and his lads but our attention was presently diverted by a white flag flying over Bunji.

Soon afterwards there was a crackle of rifle fire from the direction of Partab Pul. A long thin column of troops then wound its way out of Bunji like a snake, and moved slowly down the far bank of the Indus toward Ramghat. This was extremely interesting and we watched developments through our binoculars. When the column reached a point almost opposite us we could discern more details.

There were about one hundred and fifty men. Half that number wore the prominent *puggris* (turbans) of the Sikhs so we concluded that the people without beards were Dogras. They were fully equipped and carrying light automatics and mortars. Every second man carried a large bedding roll. As we gazed, the column started ascending the prominent feature between the Shaitan Nullah and Ramghat. Oh for the fire of the Chilas platoon and their machine-gun! The enemy knew that their position was hopeless and that they were cut off. A few strong volleys from our side of the river would have soon made them throw in the sponge as their comrades had obviously done who had remained behind in Bunji.

We mustered some half a dozen rifles and took up positions in Jock's sangars. We then opened up a sporadic fire on the column across the river. Faiz Aman at Ramghat took his cue and did likewise. The range was long – fully sixteen hundred yards – so we can't have done much damage. But it helped to infuse in the Sikh and Dogra troops the idea that their position was hopeless and that they were surrounded from all sides. It was also most amusing to watch them get off their marks like lightning and sprint up the steep side of the ridge like frightened ibex, when the firing started.

One Subedar (somewhat overweight) missed his footing in his frantic efforts to reach the summit, and rolled back to the foot of the ridge like a sack of potatoes. We all fired at him but we were well aware we would never hit him at that range.

We amused ourselves at this game for an hour or so. I was very worried regarding the platoon I had recalled from Jaglote, and of which there were no signs at all. Jock dispatched another mounted messenger. We then left the Scouts and levies to carry on the target practice and along with Baber and Muzaffar sat down on the lawn of the rest house to discuss the situation.

It was a glorious day – we basked in the comfortable warmth of the sun after the crispness of the early morning, whilst Nanga Parbat clad in a robe of sparkling satin seemed to smile down on us. But it was a sarcastic smile, as much as to say, "Now, what are you going to do?"

When our pipes were lit, we attempted to draw out Baber and Muzaffar, by making them do some straight talking regarding the situation and their intentions. They were both extremely reticent, but this, I think, was due to their inability to reach a decision on their future course of action rather than an attempt to hide anything. This much I did gather, that Muzaffar was entirely loyal to both of us and had absolutely no time for Mirza Hussan and his United States of Gilgit. Obviously this was the bone of contention between the two brothers.

The warm sun was making us all drowsy and sleep was fatal. So we rose to our feet and I decided we should saddle up and march to Jaglote, as there were no signs of Subedar Sher Ali and his men. Just as we were preparing to mount, the levy whom we had dispatched in the morning arrived back with a message from Mirza Hussan:

To: HQ GILGIT
From: OP HQ   Theliche
Bunji position captured – stop – all OK – stop – Muslims no casualties – stop – one Scout only killed – stop – Sikhs run away in panic and disorder – stop – Ram Got (Ramghat presumably) in our possession hence all will be killed when reach there – stop – send all available troops immediately Jaglote – message ends.
Signed: Hussan MC
Field Marshal

It was obvious what had happened. Mirza Hussan had intercepted our messages to Subedar Sher Ali with the result that the latter had not withdrawn to Theliche as we had hoped he would. Hussan had then managed to send Ghansara Singh's message to the senior officer in Bunji. At dawn the Sikhs and Dogras had raised the white flag as ordered, whereupon the Field Marshal along with his troops had crossed the river on skin rafts. They formed themselves up on the far bank and had made a triumphal entry into Bunji as victors of a hard-fought campaign.

While they were engaged thus, the Sikh and Dogra troops in the upper Lines, fearing worse to come and a complete breach of the surrender terms, quietly slipped out of the settlement and made their way towards Ramghat. And now they were sitting opposite us on the ridge above the Shaitan Hullah. At this time this was only a surmise as to the course of events, but it later proved to be perfectly correct in every detail.

We then decided that Muzaffar had better go back to Chilas and hold the fort there – a task we knew he could be trusted to carry out to the best of his ability. I gave him a temporary commission in the Scouts – a very necessary step – and dubbed him Subedar before we bade farewell and proceeded in opposite directions.

We reached Jaglote shortly after lunchtime. It was not a pleasant journey with the knowledge that the road was a death trap, should the troops on the far side of the river open fire with light automatics. So we travelled fast in extended formation; but not a shot came our way.

Subedar Sher Ali and the number 1 Chilas *gasht* were waiting for us at the Chowki and he explained that Mirza Hussan had told him that Major Brown had issued express orders that the *gasht* was not to proceed to Theliche. He had received none of our messages. I don't think I have ever seen troops so glad to see their Commanding

Officer as these lads were. They crowded round me, each eager to shake me by the hand and hear the news. It was no wonder either. They had now been out in the blue for days on end, they had fought a strenuous and successful action; and then Mirza Hussan had arrived on the scene, messed them around, and had made disparaging remarks about their achievements in a wild fit of jealousy at not having led the operation himself. He had then left them at Jaglote with no rations, blankets, or orders regarding their possible relief.

Jock and I gave them a short pep talk to boost morale, and heaped congratulations on them for their excellent work. This did the trick all right, and when a dozen donkey loads of rations arrived through the kindness of the people of Gor, the lads were on the top of the world again.

We then surveyed the battlefield. The once pleasant little oasis of Jaglote Chowki had been reduced to a shambles. The walls of the Polo Ground had been ripped down by attacker and defender to provide cover. The branches of the chinar and fruit trees had been shorn off by machine-gun fire and the bare trunks only were left, raising the stubs of their shattered limbs in the air. The plastered walls of the stone police post were perforated like a cartridge counting board with bullet-holes.

The head constable's newly constructed house had obviously borne the brunt of a heavy attack as it was in ruins. Several of the outhouses had been destroyed by fire and the funeral pyre smouldering round the unconsumed lower trunk and limbs of the sepoy served as a reminder of my grisly experience of the night. Over all hung a slight haze and the air was full of the smell of death.

Sher Ali then took us over to the perimeter of the camp where the remainder of the corpses lay in a long shallow water channel. They had obviously been collected here by the Scouts in an effort to clear up the dreadful mess. They had been stripped of every inch of clothing and lay in grotesque positions like stunted tree roots in the depths of a forest. Each body was covered with bayonet slashes but I was glad to see there was no mutilation. The Scouts had obviously behaved themselves and had done only what was necessary. There were fourteen bodies altogether – mostly Sikhs – and at one end of the grisly line I noticed the figure of the fat Subedar who had been commanding the post. His stomach had been ripped open by wild dogs and a couple of mangy-looking curs were fighting over the strings of guts lying about on the ground. I tossed a stone at them and they slunk away.

The picture was even more gruesome, because of a host of horrible-looking vultures which sat on the sand some distance away and watched our every movement with their beady black eyes. They were only waiting for us to leave; then they would swoop across to their banquet with delighted squawks.

"Who stripped the bodies?" I asked Sher Ali, "the Scouts?"

"No," he replied, "those Sai did it when we moved up to Partab Pul to consolidate after the action. They took everything – uniform, equipment, rifles, ammunition and the magazine. They even stripped the corpse of our one Scout who was killed in action, the sons of devils that they are. They hung about in the background while the fighting was in progress, and as soon as we left they came down like a shower of these," and he nodded over at the vultures. "I have been able to recover most of the arms and ammunition but there is still quite a quantity missing."

I turned to Wazir Abdur Rahman, leading headman of the Sai Valley, who had appeared on the scene.

"Wazir Sahib, I want every rifle, every Sten Gun, every Bren Gun, every grenade, and every round of ammunition, which your people have looted, returned here by tomorrow morning. And make no mistake about it. They can keep the uniform."

"All right, Sahib," he said, "I'll see to it," and I knew my old friend would do his best.

"Seriously, Willie," Jock said, "we'll have to dispose of these corpses quickly. Otherwise disease will break out."

"I know," I said, "we haven't got the time or facilities to burn them as their religion demands. Anyway their souls have gone to their Paradise by now and it doesn't really matter what happens to their remains provided they are not eaten up by dogs and vultures. I am not at all keen on burying them. They'll have to go in the river and the Sai people will throw them in the river. Abdur Rahman! Kindly arrange this immediately and see that every corpse has been thrown into the middle of the Indus by the morning. I don't care how you do it but get it done!"

"Right you are, Sahib," Abdur Rahman boomed, "I'll fix it," and he departed with a cheery wave of his hand.

We now sat down amongst the carnage and, with the help of Sher Ali, reconstructed the Battles of Jaglote and Partab Pul.

Subedar Sher Ali and his patrol of sixty rifles supported by a medium machine-gun arrived in the vicinity of Jaglote Chowki during the night 2/3 November. He immediately contacted several reliable ex-Scouts who lived in the nearby villages of Damot and Chakarkot. From them he ascertained the routine, dispositions, and strengths of the Kashmir Infantry picquets at Jaglote and Partab Pul Bridge, which were one Indian Officer and seventeen other ranks at the former; twelve other rank, under a havildar, held the latter. Both picquets were well armed in comparison to the Scouts and had light automatics, Sten guns, and grenades.

He then ordered the ex-Scouts to slip down quietly to the landing stage on the banks of the Indus and to remove the ferry boat some four or five miles downstream where it was not readily accessible. Thirty rifles under a havildar were sent to the Partab Pul Bridge with orders to lie up in the hills above it till first light when they would occupy the post. The remaining strength, under the Subedar, remained at Jaglote.

Under cover of darkness they surrounded the Chowki and, as first light streaked the eastern sky, they started moving in. One section blundered rather near a Sikh sentry post. The sentry, hearing the movement and being suspicious, raised the alarm. The next minute the picquet opened up with every weapon it possessed in every direction. The air was full of bullets and ricochets and little spurts of red flame darted here and there like demons' tongues, from the muzzles of the various firearms. Half a dozen hand grenades exploded with the usual dull thump. "Hell was suddenly let loose," to quote Sher Ali's own words. Dawn had come in quickly and it was soon light enough to take aimed shots.

Sher Ali realizing that all chance of a surprise attack had failed, withdrew his men to tactical positions round the oasis. It was quite impossible for the moment to advance under such heavy fire with only rifles and one single medium machine-gun for support.

The Sikhs had meanwhile occupied the Polo Ground and were continuing a withering fire from the excellent protection of the walls. Sher Ali, therefore, wisely decided that this was the first objective he must take by sheer and sudden force. He sited the machine-gun to give covering fire and gave the signal to advance to the two sections he had detailed for the task. The sections rose up from their cover and prepared to move forward. But unfortunately the heavy fire of the defenders was too much for the nerves of some of the younger lads. One cannot altogether blame them. They had never been in action before and this was probably the first time they had ever heard a shot fired in anger; and, by the looks of it then, a really hard battle was boiling up. But it left Sher Ali in an awkward position.

The tough little Yasini never wavered however. Grabbing a rifle which an absconder had thrown away, he fixed bayonet and charged at the Polo Ground position single-handed. An ex-Scout and old friend of mine, Najum Khan of Damut, followed close on his heels, and behind them charged a handful of older and more experienced Scouts, inspired by this gallant leadership. On reaching the objective they went in with the bayonet with wild yells of "Allah Akbar." In a flash they had effectively disposed of eight Sikh sepoys. Only two managed to escape and doubled over to the protection of the police post.

They quickly consolidated their position, in the course of which action Najum Khan hit the dust with a burst of Bren Gun fire through his arm. Fortunately it was not serious. Sher Ali then waved forward his sections on the far side and every man responded.

The two sections advanced on the main block of buildings in a wild rush, carrying everything before them. The defenders stood no chance at all and were indiscriminately slashed to pieces with bayonets. It was at this point that the bugle boy was shot from the chimney, like a nesting jackdaw, and wantonly stabbed to death on the floor. It was also in this encounter that the two Muslim sepoys of the Kashmir Infantry met a violent death which shows the state of fury the Scouts had reached.

Only one point of resistance remained. The Dogra Subedar and three Dogra sepoys had taken up a position on the roof of, what was, the Head Constable's house. They had obviously decided to fight it out to the last man and the last round from here, and they could not be dislodged. Any attempt to advance on our part was met by a hail of lead, and one Scout went down with a bullet through his head before Sher Ali decided that a frontal attack was out of the question. He was, however, most anxious to decide the final issue quickly as he wanted to cross over to Partab Pul Bridge in case reinforcements were required there, to prevent the remainder of the Battalion forcing their way over into the Gilgit Agency. So the Scouts battered the position with rifle and machine-gun fire until the house was little more than a ruin. The three sepoys were dead by now but the Subedar hung on, meeting fire with fire, and putting up the most gallant resistance. He held the Scouts off for at least half an hour single handed. Sher Ali then decided that something must be done he once again led a frontal attack personally on the position. The Dogra Subedar was dead by the time he reached the position – mown to bits by a burst of machine-gun fire.

Subedar Sher Ali lost no time in consolidating his position and reorganizing his troops. He wisely decided that he must send all available strength to the vital position of Partab Pul. But he made the mistake of not leaving a section to guard the spoils of war at Jaglote. He trusted his fellow countrymen, the Sai folk, to do this for him. As soon as the action was over they had appeared on the scene in large number, full of the desire to help in any way they could. As soon as Sher Ali's back was turned they looted every possible thing they could lay their hands on and bolted back to Sai. The only useful act they did was to hunt down two sepoys who had escaped; but again the motive was loot and nothing else.

And now we turned our attention to the action at the Partab Pul Bridge. The patrol of thirty rifles under the command of Havildar Nadilo of Nagir moved across country and were in position above the bridge before dawn. The State Force picquet guarding the bridge was housed in a small guardroom under the right-hand pillar. Only one sentry was posted and he stood at the entrance to the bridge. There were no sentries at all on the high ground, so this made our task comparatively easy. In fact the patrol was within fifty yards of the bridge when the sound of firing was heard from the direction of Jaglote Chowki at first light. Nadilo and his men immediately shot down the Sikh on guard. He threw up his hands and fell backwards over the rail of the bridge into the swift-flowing river below. There was a splash, a dark patch of blood stained the green water for a moment, and then faded into the swirling foam. Mother Indus claims her victims quickly. The remaining sepoys of the garrison were caught in their guardhouse like rats in a stack on threshing day. And like stack-yard rats they behaved too. In wild panic they rushed from the house and bolted across the bridge. They were instantly shot down and their bodies joined that of their comrade in the water below. Some of the sepoys attempted to make good their escape by diving into the water and striking out for the far bank. They were soon caught out in the fast current and carried off downstream; but the Scout marksmanship, well practiced on moving targets on the range, soon hit the figures in the water.

One sepoy remained behind in the house. As soon as the Scouts' attention had been diverted by the targets in the river, this lad threw a goat's skin over himself and proceeded to crawl across the bridge on all fours. He had almost reached halfway when the Scouts realized that it was a mighty strange goat crossing the bridge. They opened fire but the sepoy rose to his feet and completed the remaining distance unscathed in a wild zigzag run. He was the only survivor of the Jaglote and Partab Pul garrisons who reached Bunji to tell the tale.

It was at this point Nadilo noticed a force about one hundred and fifty strong emerging from Bunji and making all haste towards the bridge under cover of medium machine-guns and light automatics which were bringing heavy fire to bear on the Scouts. Nadilo, aware of his orders that the Sikh and Dogra troops were on no account to enter the Agency, acted calmly and quickly. He sent two sections up on to the high ground to return the fire. Taking the third section and the three tins of precious petrol, brought for the purpose, he advanced onto the bridge which was now under heavy

The Coup D'état (October to November 1947) 187

fire. They quickly doused the woodwork with petrol. Nadilo then signalled the section back to the safety of the rock, and taking handfuls of petrol-soaked tow, lit them and rammed them between the cables and the planking in several places. He then doubled back onto the Gilgit bank and joined his patrol. The dry wood of the bridge went up in flames like celluloid. Huge tongues of flame shot up in the air and the heat at close quarters was unbearable. In less than a quarter of an hour the conflagration subsided; all that was left of the Partab Pul Bridge was the bare skeleton of the cables on which no one could possibly cross. The opposing forces had stopped firing and now gazed at each other in awe-struck silence across the ruined superstructure. The Scouts collected the spoils of war – a small haul as most of the arms and ammunition were now lying on the bed of the Indus – and slowly climbed the rough hillside to the summits. The Sikh and Dogra troops on the far bank about-turned and slowly made their way back to Bunji. Not a shot was fired.

Thus ended the Battles of Jaglote and Partab Pul – the baptism of the modern Gilgit Scouts. No particular tribe could be noted for outstanding bravery. All those who remained fought equally well and the heroes and the deserters were evenly distributed among all the tribes concerned. This much was proved, though, that the older and more experienced Scouts were definitely a force to be reckoned with in action, and that all the younger lads required was a little more practice under fire.

We gathered that Mirza Hussan had taken Jemedar Safiullah Beg and the Gilgit number 1 *gasht* over to Bunji with him. It was imperative that I should see them and also become fully acquainted with the state of affairs on the far side of the river.

So about 3.00 pm Jock and I embarked on a raft consisting of a wooden frame of bamboo poles slung on to four inflated buffalo skins, and sailed across the Indus with a bearded old raftsman at the helm. About half a dozen of these rafts had been collected so our entourage, including my bodyguard which had arrived from Gilgit, followed in our wake. Baber had a raft to himself. It seemed safer. On the far side we ascended the steep sand dunes and gradually reached the outskirts of the settlement.

As we approached, we realized that the place was in a most incredible state of disorganization. No attempt had been made at consolidation. No arrangements had been made to cope with a counter-attack from the Sikh and Dogra forces which had escaped to Ramghat. The sides of the road were littered with arms of every description: boxes of ammunition, bedding rolls, and even bagpipes and drums. Dejected little groups of sepoys of all religions hung about in bewildered abstraction. The place was in complete chaos.

We made our way to what had been the quarter-guard of the battalion and searched for someone in authority, who was not engaged in looting.

Suddenly a small figure bounded up to us and, grabbing me round the neck, smothered me in embraces. He then turned his attention to Jock who had been watching my embarrassment with some amusement. It was my turn to laugh now. This was Mohammed Khan, who had been previously in the Scouts. Mirza Hussan, since his triumphal arrival, had been threatening the little man with all sorts of dire punishments for being a traitor. So his unbounded relief on seeing us was not difficult to imagine.

Just as we were beginning to hear Mohammed Khan's story, Mirza Hussan, in the full uniform of a Field Marshal, appeared at the top of the parade ground with Jemedar Safiullah Beg and came stalking down towards us.

Mirza Hussan saluted first.

He then wrung Jock and me by the hand and burst out: "Major Brown, I've conquered Bunji! Tomorrow I shall march on Kashmir. In a week I shall have captured Srinagar, and shall be sitting on the throne in the palace of the Maharaja. I shall make military history. I shall save the Muslims of Kashmir from the extinction by the Hindus."

We all went and sat on the mess lawn, which overlooked a deep gorge separating the settlement from the Bunji plain. We sat in a semi-circle – Hussan, myself, Mohammed Khan, Jock, Baber, and Safiullah Beg.

"A perfect day," explained Hussan, leaning back in his chair, and closing his eyes in the hot sun.

"Look at old Nanga Parbat, isn't she lovely?"

"Tak doom!"

A shot rang out from the far side of the gorge, and a bullet cracked over our heads at not more than a foot's distance. It embedded itself in the whitewashed mud wall of the mess with a dull thud. I have never seen people move so quickly. Tough old Safiullah Beg looked startled but remained in his chair, waiting to take the lead from us. Jock and I also felt a strong desire to beat it quickly but this would have been fatal for our prestige, especially as our bodyguard and retinue were convulsed with laughter at the antics of the others, from a safe vantage point behind an aiming wall.

We rose to our feet, lit cigarettes, and strolled over to the parade ground. But we unostentatiously made sure that a high bank came between us and the far side of the gorge at the first opportunity. A couple more bullets whined over our heads.

"That was a bloody narrow escape!" I said.

Safiullah Beg grinned. He understood English. At the same time desultory firing broke out from the ferry and from the higher ground to the east of the township.

"Come on! Let's see what's happening," I shouted and we doubled off to a point on the perimeter where the trees gave way to rocks and sand.

Going in opposite directions we carried out our reconnaissances and returned to a prearranged rendezvous to pool our information and appreciate the situation. We discovered that about ninety per cent of the Sikh and Dogra troops had absconded to the hills. The Ramghat force had returned to the near vicinity with the result that about two hundred and fifty of them now surrounded Bunji.

The question now arose whether we should recross to Jaglote or spend the night in Bunji as the day was rapidly progressing. We eventually decided that we would spend the night here. The two of us could have crossed in the short space of daylight left; but the Scout platoon could never be ferried across in so little time.

As soon as our decision was reached, Jock methodically set about the task of perimeter defence with the thirty-odd Scouts we had at our disposal. He wisely narrowed the radius to a small area round the mess, as it was obviously a case of self-defence and nothing more.

When our guards and picquets were ready, Jock reported to me; I made a brief inspection. The arrangements were very sound and required no improvements. I merely had to give the men a word of encouragement and their morale, which had reached rock-bottom under the mad Field Marshal, rose again. We both agreed that if we did go down that night we would go down fighting, and with that determination in our minds we returned to the mess to join the others. It was almost dark now. The desultory firing continued.

Jemedar Shah Khan had arrived from Gilgit. I had called him purposely to act as "Aide-de-Camp" to the Field Marshal. The latter was much flattered and thanked me profusely.

There was little news from Gilgit – the situation seemed to be under control still, but faction feeling was increasing and there was every danger of a serious clash in the near future unless something was done about it.

"We're spending the night here," said Jock to Hussan.

"And now to business," said Hussan, putting the hurricane lamp on the table and pulling up a chair.

Jock and I sat down but we took the precaution of keeping away from the windows.

"Bloody awful to stop one in here," said Jock with a laugh.

"Nothing to worry about, don't be afraid," breezed the Field Marshal. "Those pigs will never fire on us. They know I'll machine-gun the lot of them if they dare."

But we never heard his plan. There was a "rat-tat-tat-tat-tat" of a machine-gun at close quarters; there was a shatter of breaking glass; and the wall at the back of the room was scored by a burst of bullets. Little bits of white-washed plaster trickled to the floor.

There was immediate pandemonium. The hurricane lantern rolled into a corner. There was a heavy volley of fire from the Scouts on the perimeter defences in reply. Firing broke out all round the camp. Another burst from the hostile machine-gun wrecked the second window.

"Looks like a counter-attack," said Shah Khan.

"We'll soon know," I replied grimly.

Jock lounged over and righted the furniture. He picked up the lantern and, lowering the wick slightly, placed it in the middle of the floor out of sight of the windows.

"That will teach you to take cover when you're told to. Just wait till they get their mortars ranged on us."

I chuckled. Shah Khan wanted to do so too, but did not dare for the effect it might have on Hunza-Nagir relations.

With a few solitary rifle shots from the north of the camp, the firing gradually faded away, except for the echo and re-echo among the mountains. Then complete quiet reigned again.

The three of us held a quick consultation in the corner. We agreed that the enemy's firing had probably been a bait to discover whether we were still engaged in collecting and dividing the loot in the abandoned orgy which usually follows a barbaric victory. From the sound, the Scouts appeared to have shown their hand all right, so the chances were that the Sikhs and Dogras would not risk a counter-attack, knowing full well the consequences if they failed. But we dared not take chances so I ordered Shah Khan to tour the defences and to impress on everyone the necessity of keeping on their toes throughout the night. Poor chap, he was bitterly disappointed he had not been present at the Battles of Jaglote and Partab Pul and was even now spoiling for a fight of some sort.

"And now to business," I said.

The Field Marshal remained sitting on the floor, his back propped up against the wall.

"When are you leaving for Srinagar?" I asked.

"Well, I think under the circumstances I have decided not to proceed quite as far as that. In a few days I shall tour as far as Astore to let the people see their new Commander-in-Chief. There's also a Treasury there which I must check. And then, Major Brown, I shall return to Bunji and set up my headquarters here."

"The Sikhs and Dogras are going to be rather a thorn in your flesh, aren't they?" I said.

"Yes" he agreed.

"What do you think, Major Brown? How can we round them up?"

"I personally don't think there will be any trouble about that," I replied. "After a bloody cold night in the mountains on short rations, I quite expect the lot will come in here in the morning and surrender. But to make quite sure that none of them attempt to escape over the hills to Baltistan and Ladakh, I suggest you take out a strong patrol now from your Azad Forces (henceforth I shall refer to the Muslim element of the now non-existent 6th Kashmir Infantry as the Azad or Free Forces: this was the name given by Provisional Government) and completely circumvent the enemy positions in the mountains. When dawn comes in they will find you sitting on the top of them, and I bet my boots they will surrender without a squeak."

"An excellent idea, Major Brown, but the only trouble is that we are all too tired to do such a thing. Couldn't you take the Scouts instead?"

"Yes," I replied, "I can take the Scouts and will take them. But our strength is much too low to undertake such a task in which failure will be fatal, so I'll ask you to lend me half a dozen Bren Guns with gunners to accompany my patrol. I would also like a few Sten Guns and a bag of grenades."

"Oh no, Major Brown, I can't possibly do that," Hussan replied, "you might lose some of the arms and I have to answer for them. No, it's quite out of the question. All the enemy will surrender in the morning. You see if they don't."

"All right, it's your pigeon," I replied. "I'm crossing the river tomorrow, and I don't give a damn what happens on the Bunji side after that."

Actually Hussan's assurances were far from correct. In the morning about two-thirds of the Sikhs and Dogras did in fact surrender; but one third took to the hills. The latter caused endless trouble in the Wazarat by ravaging villages in search of food, and sniping at camps and convoys. Admittedly it was not long before they died of starvation and exposure.

The Coup D'état (October to November 1947)   191

A few made a gallant attempt to cross from Bunji into Baltistan and we later found their frozen bodies high up on the snowy divide. Their rifles were lying beside them but the bolts were missing.

We gradually veered round to Skardu. I put my cards on the table. I pointed out to Mirza Hussan the vital importance of holding Skardu and I also pointed out the considerations affecting the object of taking and retaining the garrison town, according to the discussions which Jock and I had held on the previous night. I concluded by saying:

"My suggestion amounts to this. You reorganize the Muslim element of the old Kashmir Infantry into a fully equipped battalion again. Take Ihsan Ali, Mohammed Said, and Mohammed Khan as your officers, and promote local Officers to fill the other vacancies. You must be in supreme command, however. I shall give you a small hand-picked skeleton force of Scouts to act as guides, interpreters, and skirmishers. You can appreciate why I can't spare more. Then you push off with this force through Haramosh and Baltistan to Skardu. If you set off immediately and move quickly, you will meet no opposition there. On the contrary, you will be welcomed by Nek Alum and his Muslim platoon and your combined force should have no difficulty in disposing of the Dogra platoon which is also there at present. Skardu is easy to hold provided you make careful defence arrangements, and you have a full complement of modern weapons to support you. On the other hand if you delay, you will give the enemy a chance to send reinforcements from Leh; and once a strong force of them is established in Skardu you will find it mighty difficult to dislodge them. In fact it will take months and months of starving them out; for I assure you, you will never take the fort by assault, if it is strongly held. If you decide not to go, then I shall go myself; but I cannot go until I have completed my plan of doubling the present strength of the Scouts. As you will appreciate, this is a big task and will probably take three to four months; by that time Nek Alum and his Muslim lads will be dead and gone and I shall run up against no mean opposition from Dogras and Sikhs. A protracted siege is the most I can hope for. So there's my plan for what it's worth, and what you do about it, is entirely your business. I can only suggest, and I suggest you go, and go quickly."

Mirza Hussan did not take his Azad Forces to Skardu immediately: in fact he never took them. Owing to my subsequent recall, I did not go to Skardu either. The expedition was delayed and procrastinated, after I left, throughout the winter till the late spring of 1948. As I had envisaged, the force which eventually proceeded ran into heavy opposition. A protracted siege ensued. It was not until well on in the summer that the supplies of the defending troops became exhausted and they surrendered. There is no doubt at all that if Hussan had taken Skardu when I suggested he should, then, with the help of the Frontier Constabulary and Chitrali reinforcements which arrived in the spring, all Baltistan and Ladakh – in fact all the country of the Indus basin up to Leh and Zoji La Pass, would have been in our hands by the middle of the summer.

Instead of that the long siege of Skardu gave the Indian Army a chance to secure the Zoji La, which made possible their historic tank advance over incredible country resulting in their securing the major portion of Ladakh, including Leh, which they held up to the cease-fire on 1 January 1949.

There was another burst of firing outside and when it stopped Mohammed Khan showed his head round the door to announce that dinner was ready.

"Bring it along," ordered Hussan and turning to us, "I told him to prepare a good vegetable soup, roast lamb with roast potatoes, and stewed apricots. We ought to feel better after that."

We squatted on the floor and dug in with our hands. The others followed. The platter was presently cleaned to the last grain of rice.

It was now well past midnight, and high time we got some rest. The others were already making preparations. Jock and I went outside to look at the night and to hold a last check-up on our perimeter defences. Now that the firing had stopped it was very still. The sky was clear and starry, the strong wind blowing down the valley had a bitterly cold edge to it and cut one's cheeks like a whiplash.

"I'm sorry for those poor ***** in the mountains tonight," said Jock as we re-entered the stuffiness of the mess.

As was our wont when in the field, Jock and I rose an hour before dawn. It is during that hour that things happen if they are going to happen. After touring the defences, which were in order and on the "qui vive," we sat on the verandah and waited. Presently the cocks started crowing and the voice of the muezzin rang out, thin and clear in the morning air. "Come to prayer, come to prayer; prayer is better than sleep."

We stood up and watched another glorious sunrise on Nanga Parbat, whilst I quoted the first few stanzas of the "Rubaiyat". It was now broad daylight and we breathed a sigh of relief, as we knew that the danger period was passed and it was unlikely that anything would happen now of a serious nature. We bathed our faces and hands in the ice-cold water of the irrigation channel, adjusted our dress, and then felt very ready for another day and whatever it would bring.

Just as we were returning to the bungalow, we saw a figure in blue striped pyjamas dashing along the verandah.

"Hullo, Mohammed Khan," I said, "where are you going?"

"Off on a dawn patrol, Sir," said Mohammed Khan with a quick salute.

"Hi, come here," I shouted at him as he disappeared round the corner of the building.

He doubled back and saluted again.

"Look here, Mohammed Khan. Take fifty Muslim sepoys and supporting weapons. Go and clear the entire area in the vicinity of the ferry, and then occupy the tactical features above the river. Stay there till the evening and then withdraw."

"Very good, Sir, but what if the General, I mean Field Marshal Hussan ..."

"Don't worry about that, old boy. The Field Marshal is going to be much too busy today to care what you do."

"All right, Sir. Goodbye, Sir," and the little figure dashed away.

Mohammed Khan complied with my orders to the letter, with the result that our lines of communication with Gilgit were secure throughout the day. In consequence of this, much invaluable work was carried out, not the least being that Jock and I were

The Coup D'état (October to November 1947) 193

able to regain our own bank of the river without the danger of being sniped during the crossing.

Mirza Hussan came up to us. We told him that we were leaving for Gilgit immediately.

"By the way," I said to him, "the magazine here is going to be a bit of a liability to you. I doubt if you have sufficient troops to safeguard it and at the same time guard the prisoners of war, who seem to be quite numerous. If the latter get their hands on it, you will be up a gum-tree. Why not hand over your entire reserve stocks of ammunition to me. I shall take them to Gilgit and keep them in the Scout magazine for you."

"Yes, yes," Hussan relied, "take anything, take anything you want. Only leave me to arrange the surrender."

"The keys?" I asked.

"Here you are."

And he took a large bunch out of his pocket.

"I don't know which is which, but you had better take them all."

"Thanks," I said.

"One thing, before you go," Hussan continued. "Captain Mathieson, I am appointing you sector commander. You are responsible for all troops in this sector."

And he waved his left had vaguely in the direction of Nanga Parbat and his right towards Haramosh.

"I am far too busy to attend to such details just now. Now goodbye, Major Brown; goodbye, Captain Mathieson."

With that he resumed his work of accepting the surrender of the remaining Jammu & Kashmir State Forces.

"My sector," Jock observed, "seems to include half the world. That was a stroke of genius, getting the keys to the magazine."

"Yes," I replied, "let's see what's in it."

We made our way over to the square grey dressed stone building which was the magazine. There were two heavy padlocks on the door. Keys fitted them and the strong reinforced door presently swung open on well oiled hinges, whilst that strange musty smell, peculiar to magazines, rushed out to mingle with the fresh air. We entered and a glance was sufficient to see that the stocks of ammunition had not been tampered with. Jock quickly checked the registers with the ground balance and found all in order. There were 119 boxes of .303 rifle ammunition containing in all 117,127 rounds as well as quantities of grenades, mortar bombs, and Sten Gun ammunition, etc.

I turned to Jemedar Safiullah Beg.

"You are responsible for getting all this ferried across the river today, and transported to Gilgit tomorrow. You have your *gasht* to help you and to act as escort. I shall arrange extra rafts and pack transport. I want delivery made as per register. Also collect all those stray boxes of ammunition which are lying around the camp here and bring them along too. Shah Khan will give you a hand, unless he is required for ADC duties. Are there any questions?"

"No."

"Then carry on."

He did, and with the exception of some small losses, brought about by the vicissitudes of the journey, the Bunji magazine was in Gilgit on the evening of the following day, escorted by the original patrol which had set out for Bhup Singh Parri at the beginning of the revolt.

With these arrangements completed, we collected Baber and the bodyguard and descended the sand dunes to the landing stage where the rafts were waiting for us. We noted through our binoculars that Mohammed Khan's "dawn patrol" was in position, so the crossing was not quite so risky as it would have been otherwise.

We were welcomed at Jaglote by Subedar Sher Ali and Wazir Abdur Rahman. I was gratified to note that the latter had kept his word and that the corpses had been removed. He had also recovered a quantity of the looted arms and ammunition, which, though not complete, certainly represented the bulk. We could recover the remainder later by surprise raids on the Sai villages, and woe betide those found in possession of them.

As a temporary measure I allocated Sher Ali the area from Partab Pul to Theliche, and posted picquets at Partab Pul, Jaglote, and Theliche. He would have his headquarters at Jaglote where the telephone was now in working order and which would be a useful vantage point for watching activities across the river.

The morale of the men was high but they were obviously tired from so many days in the field under irregular conditions. So I determined I would relieve them by fresh troops from Gilgit and Chilas at the first opportunity.

I ordered Abdur Rahman to return to Sai immediately and requisition another six rafts to be assembled ready for use down at the ferry. I made enquiries regarding the boat but discovered that it had run aground and required repairs.

In the meantime Jock had been nosing around and presently returned with the good news that there were thirty mules with drivers of the old 6th Kashmir Infantry encamped at the far end of the farm. So our transport difficulties for the ammunition were over.

Everything seemed to be under control now, so, with a feeling of relief, Jock and I sat down on a heap of rations for a smoke.

The Sai band had arrived, and they played selections whilst some of the Scouts cut a long willow wand. They attached it to the Pakistan flag which Jock had brought from Chilas with him, and amidst great cheering they raised it in the middle of the camp. Fortune was smiling fairly and to crown all a mounted levy arrived from Gilgit with a haversack of provisions for us, which good old Shawar Din had thoughtfully sent. We opened it on the grass and found two flasks of piping hot tea, cold *chikors*, sandwiches, sausage rolls, and curry puffs. We set to with zeal and presently all that was left was a small heap of bones and the wrapping paper. We now felt ready to tackle the thirty miles to Gilgit and about noon I gave the order to saddle up. As an afterthought before leaving, I selected a Sten gun from the spoils of war, loaded the magazine, and slung it round my shoulders. Who knows? It might be useful.

Waving farewell to Sher Ali and his lads, our little troop cantered across the farm and turned the horses' noses towards Gilgit and home. We were all well mounted, Jock was on Bimbo, Samarkand had been sent out for me (a welcome change after the battalion nag which had almost killed me) Baber had his own horse, and the bodyguard had a motley collection of beasts of different shapes and sizes. Janan had Ghansara Singh's massive eighteen-hander and gazed down at us from the heights in a supercilious way. There were many jests about the distance he had to fall.

I set the pace and we soon had the milestones flashing past us at a good six to the hour. We stopped for a short halt at Parri where a kindly family of Pathan settlers brought us refreshing cups of tea. They treated us as heroes and were anxious to hear the latest news, which we gave them.

With a cheery farewell we swung out onto the road again and started on the last lap. Between Bhup Singh Parri and Minawar the others began to tire and presently Jock and I found ourselves alone, about half a mile ahead.

Bimbo was an amazing little pony. Despite his size he plugged along behind me as though his life depended on it. In order to keep up with the long graceful strides of Samarkand, his little furry legs were going at a tremendous pace – so fast indeed that it looked as though the pony was legless and was running on a wheel attached under his belly. The only mishap occurred when we passed a road gang mending a breach. I cantered past with a wave and shout of encouragement. I presently heard behind me a string of oaths, followed by a shout of help from Jock. I pulled Samarkand up on his haunches and turned round to discover what had happened. Evidently Bimbo had taken a strong dislike to a shovel being wielded by one of the coolies. He had stopped suddenly and Jock had been jolted over the high pommel of the local saddle and was wedged there between it and the neck. Bimbo had decided to carry on and Jock in desperation had grabbed the animal's ears in both hands, as the only handy protection to prevent himself falling off. Bimbo stopped as soon as Samarkand did, and I roared with laughter as Jock extricated himself from this ridiculous position and regained the saddle.

Between Minawar and Gilgit we noticed a number of Scout stragglers making their way across country. We rounded them up and discovered that they were some of the men who had run in the initial stages of the Battle of Jaglote. We waited until the others had caught up with us and then detailed some of the bodyguard to escort them to Gilgit where the guardroom was ready for them.

On the long pull up to Jutial I noticed that several people in our party, including Baber, were standing up in their stirrups as they rode – a sure sign of saddle soreness, so I slackened pace a little. It was just in time too, as the girths of Janan's saddle broke. He rolled off his high perch and bit the dust which fortunately was soft so no damage was done. Hoots of derisive laughter greeted him from the rest of us, in which saddle sores and tiredness were forgotten.

Dusk was fast approaching as we watered our horses and stretched our stiff legs at Jutial. We walked down to Sonekote. Presently we heard the distant strains of the pipes and drums playing the Blue Bonnets and we could make out a vast crowd of people waiting at the entrance of the Scout Lines.

"A welcome?" said Jock.

"Seems to be," I replied.

"All right, let's make it a triumph, then."

We quickly cut a long willow wand and attached the Pakistan Flag to it. We made Janan, on his big horse, standard bearer. We told him to ride in front. We then formed ourselves into sections of threes behind him, and roused our tired ponies to a jog-trot. With three-day's growth on our faces, our clothes and bodies travel-stained, our miscellaneous collection of arms, our ponies lathered from head to foot, we must have looked a formidable but glamorous company of Moss Troopers. As we neared the gates of the Lines, the local band struck up too. The "Welcome" tune reached a wild crescendo and a continued burst of cheering broke from the assembled crowd.

We reined in our ponies with a flourish; the multitude surged forward and enveloped us; they almost dragged us from our horses in their efforts to congratulate us and shake our hands.

"Pakistan *Zindabad,* Pakistan *Zindabad!*"

"*Zindabad, Zindabad!*" we shouted in reply, waving our whips in the air in the intoxication of the moment.

"What news, what news?" they shouted.

Any reply would have been drowned in the cheering so I merely waved back again. They took this as a sign of success evidently, because the excitement redoubled.

They were starting to throw flowers and streamers at us now. Fearing lest some accidental physical damage should be done, I signalled to Janan to move forward and his big horse soon cleft a passage through the crowd for us. We entered the Lines with a sigh of relief and dismounted quite exhausted in front of the Subedar Major's bungalow.

The officers were waiting for us. Haider embraced me. Said also seemed pleased and relieved to see me, as was the case with the remaining members of the Provisional Government. Gilgit was wildly mad with excitement, to a pitch I have never seen before – even at a polo final.

We decided to wait in the bungalow until the crowds had dispersed. It was quite impossible to talk seriously, as we were bombarded with questions, which we did our best to answer. Presently Baber's orderly appeared with a huge platter laden with fried eggs on fried chappatis. We didn't really realize how hungry we were till the aroma invaded our nostrils. Then we tucked in and did full justice to Baber's hospitality. We shovelled the repast down our throats in silence, except for an occasional mutter of "this is good".

Jock and I then excused ourselves and slowly hacked up the hill to my bungalow. The trusty Shawar Din was waiting for us on the doorstep with a string of welcomes.

"Sikhan suh shoo?" (what's happened to the Sikhs? [Pushto]) he asked with a laugh.

"Do shoo" (In the bag [lit. "finished" in Pushto]) said Jock, putting his arm round the old boy's shoulders.

Chapter 5

The End Game
(November 1947 to January 1948)

1. Consolidation

On the morning after our arrival we both went down to the Lines early. The first person we met was Subedar Ghulam Murtaza, who in our absence had arrived from Kalamdarchi with his platoon. He was a first-class Indian Officer and an old friend of mine. We gave each other a warm greeting. I was greatly relieved to have him with me, as he was one of the few on whom full reliance could be placed. His platoon was busy cleaning the reserve rifles so I went along to welcome them all back. I knew every one of these Hunza lads personally. It was grand to meet them again and I spoke a few words and shook hands with each individual. One boy doubled across to the platoon barrack-room and presently appeared with a brown paper parcel, which he handed to Ghulam Murtaza. He, in turn, reverently presented it to me. I opened it curiously and discovered it contained a Union Jack – the last Union Jack to fly on Kalamdarchi, one of the highest outposts of the Empire.

A lump rose in my throat which became even more troublesome when Ghulam Murtaza said, "We never lowered it, Sahib, till we evacuated Kalamdarchi for good. We failed to comply with your order to replace it by the hateful tricolour of Kashmir on 1 August. Kalamdarchi at any rate remained British to the end," and there was a murmur of approval from the lads standing round.

"You *badmashes*" (scoundrels), I said, as a feeble attempt at a joke to cover my heartfelt emotion at the loyalty of these simple Hunza folk.

We returned to the parade ground to find that Shah Rais, whom we had nicknamed "Archie", had arrived.

"How are your Local Defence Volunteers getting on?" I asked.

"As a matter of fact this is a bad season for training," said Shah Rais in all earnestness. "They have all returned home to attend to their crops. They may return for parades again after Christmas. These are the only two on the roll at the moment. One seems to be rather old. The other has something wrong with his leg but no doubt the doctor can give him some medicine to cure it."

"Now I must be off to a Cabinet meeting," said Shah Rais importantly. "Are you coming?"

We excused ourselves from what we knew would be a rabble of dissension. There was real work to be done – there was a great deal of work to be done.

For the next week or so Jock and I toiled like slaves. Subedar Ghulam Murtaza's platoon was re-equipped and issued with snow kit. They were dispatched to carry out a comprehensive reconnaissance of the Gurez and Tragbal areas. They were then to return to a position on the top of the Burzil Pass. Contact would be maintained by telephone and all reports regarding Indian troop movements and the condition of the passes would be sent to Gilgit. They also had orders to seize all northbound caravans and escort them to Gilgit. I knew that several caravans had set out from Bandipur with vital stocks of salt, sugar, and cloth for the bazaar. I was much afraid they would refuse to continue their journey as soon as they heard about the revolt in Gilgit, or that Hussan would waylay them and dispose of the goods to his own advantage. Lastly Ghulam Murtaza was ordered to make every effort to trace four pony loads of liquid refreshment, beer, whisky, gin and champagne, which were on their important way for B and M's Christmas and New Year. I had implicit faith in Ghulam Murtaza which was fully justified. He did everything required of him – even to the tracing of the hooch. At least he found the empty bottles littered about the Doian Rest House amidst every sign of a wild drunken debauch. He arrived too late.

Mule load after mule load of ammunition was pouring in from Bunji. Every single round had to be checked and I know that Quarter Master Jemedar Fida Ali was working twenty hours a day at this task. He was almost asleep on his feet but not one single mistake did he make. We took it in turns to help him – even the faithful Humayan Beg came down from the hospital in his spare time to lend a hand. As soon as batches were checked, they were sealed and widely distributed among the various guards and picquets in the settlement, so that all our eggs would not be in one basket in the lines. We did the same with our own magazine.

Limbuwala was frantic because his stocks of petrol for his engines were exhausted and he imagined there were no more this side of the Passes. So to his delight and surprise, I unearthed my hidden stock from the godown at the aerodrome. This consisted of a hundred gallons of high octane petrol, and strange to say the drums were shown as empty in the ledgers. It was only through a stroke of luck that I happened to check through the stocks of supposedly empty drums one day, and found fifty full drums of two gallons each hidden under the rest. I earmarked twenty-five gallons for Limbuwala – he complained at first that high octane juice would spoil his engines. I told him he was bloody lucky to get any at all and to get on with it. The remainder I kept in reserve in the event of air movement later.

I was glad I did so, too. All the petrol was widely distributed in the same way as the ammunition.

The Scouts who had been in the field since D day were relieved by fresh troops as far as possible, and withdrawn to their respective Headquarters in Gilgit and Chilas.

Recruits who had not yet completed their course were posted to their platoons to keep strength up. As soon as platoons returned, their kit and equipment had to be checked. Shortages were many, I am afraid, but this was natural considering that it was the Scouts' first taste of active service and they had not yet learned to look after themselves under active service conditions. Minor losses I overlooked, and issued replacements. But Courts of Inquiry had to be held regarding the more serious deficiencies, and this kept Said and Haider busy for many days. The Quarter Master's store was working at full speed and the tailors and shoemakers shops were also a hive of industry.

I have never seen such activity in the Scout lines and it did my heart good to see the way that everyone concerned threw their backs into the job. As soon as relieved troops were completely re-equipped, they were given two days' rest to clean up and get themselves in order for further duty. Then normal parades started again, but a little more emphasis than usual was put on barrack-square drill, and line discipline was more rigidly enforced than previously. We saw that this was the only way to boost morale and to prevent a rotten disintegration setting in, which was quite possible under the unsettled and disturbing conditions. After about a week we were glad to notice the results of our labours and we agreed that the Scouts were back to normal again.

But normal was not sufficient now. A scheme was simmering in my brain for raising the Corps to a modern fighting force of fifteen hundred men, which could resist all aggression from outside. As usual Jock was confining himself to details, at which he was an expert, as he could appreciate what was required down to the last *chapli* nail. I, on the other hand, was considering general policy and organization on a much wider plane. The present 600 Scouts, I was thinking, would be the backbone and nucleus of the new Corps. So it was imperative that they were trained to a high standard of modern warfare immediately.

We had a quantity of modern weapons captured at Jaglote, some half dozen Bren Guns, double that number of Sten Guns, a three-inch mortar, and there were unlimited stocks of hand-grenades among the Bunji reserves of ammunition. I handed the question of training over to Jock and told him to get on with it.

"Instructors?" he asked.

"Phone up Mirza Hussan," I said. "Turn on the charm tap, tactfully flatter him, and ask him to send us six first-class Muslim instructors from his Azad Forces."

"Right," said Jock, and I knew it would be done.

I left it at that. A few days later, when I went on parade in the morning, I found the ground in a feverish state of activity. In one corner a Bren Gun Course was in full swing. A smart Kashmiri havildar in battle-dress was busy demonstrating how to strip and reassemble the gun. In another corner a dozen NCOs were poised in pugnacious attitudes with Sten Guns whilst an instructor demonstrated the various firing positions. In the centre a mortar team were kneeling in position round the three inch mortar, waiting for the order to fire. They looked exactly like old hands at the job. On the football ground a line of lads were busy throwing dummy grenades over a high wire. Jock was dashing about from group to group – a reprimand here, encouragement there, help and advice somewhere else.

"Keep them at this for a day or so," I said, after taking a look at each group. "Then get them working behind natural cover. Close supervision is necessary but you can't spend all your time here. What to do? Haider is up to the eyes in Q work. Said is much too busy with the Provisional Government to devote the attention required for the courses."

Jock thought for a minute and then exclaimed, "I have it. Ihsan Ali."

Ihsan Ali agreed readily when approached.

"Rather, old boy, only too ready to do anything to help."

So he became chief instructor and a first-class one at that, as I soon discovered. He threw his heart into the job and raised so much enthusiasm that all thought of political intrigue was forgotten.

Nothing could be left to chance in the way of protection and defence. We would have plenty of warning of a land invasion through Ghulam Murtaza. But there was also the possibility of an air attack, the landing of airborne troops, or the dropping of paratroops. And if these came, they could come be surprise, and would probably be directed at the township of Gilgit itself. So we worked out elaborate plans for the defence of the settlement. We threw up strong picquets round the landing ground and at various strategic points on the wild plain between Gilgit and Nomal. We posted permanent guards at the aerodrome. We threw up perimeter defences round the entire settlement and linked it up with the aerodrome by a series of lay-backs. We practiced the Scouts till the scheme was cut and dried, and worked like clockwork when the alarm was sounded.

We decided that my bungalow would become GHQ in the event of the balloon going up. It was completely hidden from the air by the large chinar trees surrounding it. It was large and had quite sufficient room to house Limbuwala's wireless set as well as the rest of the paraphernalia and troops required in a General Headquarters. Situated as it was on the fringe of the settlement there was only one track which had a covered approach. On the other hand there were numerous getaways which I had studied carefully in moments of leisure and which would be an invaluable advantage if the worst came to the worst. Jock and I spent one afternoon personally arranging the defences of the bungalow. No thought was required as such tasks came to us instinctively now. When the last box of ammunition had been checked, and the last fire-bucket with stirrup-pump was in place, we stood back and surveyed our work. The bodyguard was thrilled and examined our handiwork with great interest.

As we carried out a last check-up, I observed, "Well, this is the place where we shall be fighting it out, if we are cornered by enemies from within or without, and by the looks of it we ought to be able to give them a run for their money."

We cleaned our armoury that evening, and put in a little combined practice against an imaginary mob with our Sten guns – backs against the wall, the one firing short bursts at different points whilst the other loaded; then a quick change-over. It kept our eyes in.

In the morning, whilst we were discussing our plans for the day over breakfast coffee and cigarettes, an official courier arrived from Bunji bearing an important-looking letter all sealed and signed.

"With the General Sahib's compliments," said the individual.

Did I notice a touch of sarcasm in his voice? He saluted and was shown out. I opened the envelope and extracted a badly typed sheet of poor quality paper.

"Daily Orders by General Mirza Hussan Khan, Commander-in-Chief Gilgit Pakistan Forces Bunji Cant. (Civil Administration)."

"Read it out," said Jock.

Most of it was unintelligible nonsense, so I confined myself to the more interesting portions.

"Dated 7.11.47. Office will resume work with effect from yesterday. The boys school to start from tomorrow properly. The Police Head Constable should investigate one theft case which has taken place in the Bunji bazaar. Sikh surrendered. The public is hereby warned not to obstruct the Sikh who have surrendered and are coming back to HQ. Any living Army Sikh hiding himself is seen by any local will be directed by him to report with his arms and ammunition to the Pakistan Forces HQ Bunji. Warning. Army Sikh had taken away arms and ammunition with them at the time of desertion from the Camp on 4 November 1947 by 2200 hours. I believe that most of the personnel have thrown their arms and ammunition within the limits of Bunji plains including Bunji Hills. Any local who finds the Govt, articles is warned to deposit at once with this HQ otherwise he will be shooted for this offence. Kashmir Army Sikhs and Dogras are warned to surrender their arms and ammunition, equipment and themselves before 1700 hours 7 November 1947. Their life safety is guaranteed. Failing to obey this order will result in a mopping up operation after the given hours. All troops have been informed not to fire on any person without previous warning. Deserters must raise white flags when they approach to the Camp. Murder, arson, treachery to the country in nation are offenders punishable with death or transportation for life. All movable and immovable property of the enemy agents will be forfeited to the Govt, forthwith on proof by competent Army Court. The final appeal to C-in-C only. All minorities are warned that their safety of lives lies in their strict allegiance to the new Govt. Their property, lives, and religious liberties shall be respected by all residing within the precincts of dominion of the new Govt. Any one found infringing these orders shall be dealt with severely. Signed: Mohammed Khan, General. For C-in-Chief, Gilgit Pakistan Forces. Bunji."

"Mohammed Khan is a General now too," said Jock.

"Let's speak to the courier."

He was duly ushered in.

"How's the General Sahib, these days?" I asked.

"Oh, very well."

"What's he doing with himself in that dull place?"

"Oh, he's busy collecting subscriptions from the local population for the Qaid-I-Azam Fund."

"That's nice of him. Has he collected much?"

"About six or seven thousand rupees."

The pressure of Scout work had been so heavy recently that I had gravely neglected political considerations. The results of a rapid appreciation of the situation were far from satisfactory. The *coup d'état* had taken place eight days ago. Apart from the Frontier Premier's message of the 3rd (November) to say that my message had been passed on to the Pakistan Government, nothing further had been received. Was it possible that Pakistan did not wish to intervene in Gilgit affairs? Had she enough on her hands as it was with the Kashmir debacle? The ambitious in Gilgit were now preparing for the inevitable scramble for power which would result if Pakistan did not decide to interfere. Political factions, religious factions, blood factions, and tribal factions were gathering their forces and planning their campaign of action. Tension was increasing, and these forces might be released any moment now in a savage welter of internecine strife. I must strike first, but I did not wish to strike if Pakistan did in fact intend intervening. It was therefore imperative that I should know Pakistan's intentions at the earliest possible moment. So on 9 November I dispatched a wireless message to Colonel Bacon, the only person in Pakistan at the time who could really appreciate the situation:

To: COLONEL BACON
From: BROWN   091000

Doing utmost to keep situation under control but cannot do so indefinitely owing excessive internal intrigue – stop – imperative representative from Pakistan arrive immediately – stop – moral effect of even short visit would reassure population.

The news from Kuh Ghizr and Yasin was also disturbing. The claimant to the throne of undivided Yasin and Kuh Ghizr was a young man named Ghulam Dastgir, son of Shah Abdur Rahman, who was the Khushwaqt Governor of Yasin from 1923 till his death in 1933. The presence of Ghulam Dastgir in Yasin had seemed to me to be imprudent at this juncture, so as soon as the *coup d'état* had taken place, I banished him to Ishkoman to remain in the care of his cousin the Governor, until the situation was more stable. The news that I now received was that the "Young Pretender" had fled from Ishkoman and had crossed into Chitral in the company of a brother. Would he be returning with a Chitrali army to reimpose, by force, Khushwaqt rule in the northern districts? I reckoned he most certainly would, unless Pakistan intervened by interesting herself in the Gilgit Agency. I was therefore again faced with this most awkward problem and I decided that the only temporary solution was to adopt "delaying" tactics. I dispatched the following wireless message:

To: MEHTAR OF CHITRAL
From: MAJOR BROWN   100900

Owing recent overthrow of Kashmir rule and declaration for Pakistan by entire Gilgit Province situation here at present unstable and administration extremely difficult – stop – grateful therefore for any help by you in preventing political strife in Kuh Ghizr and Yasin until such times as negotiations can be entered into – stop – please instruct Ghulam Dastgir Mohammed Wazir etc to return to Ishkoman and refrain from political activities meantime.

This message had exactly the desired effect. On 11 November I received a reply:

To: MAJOR BROWN
From: MEHTAR OF CHITRAL   110900

I am ready to give every help on instructions from Pakistan Government – stop – please approach Pakistan Government on this subject also please inform whereabouts of Ghulam Dastgir and Mohammed Wazir.

The End Game (November 1947 to January 1948)   203

I took no action at all on the message. It was however significant to note that on that very day Ghulam Dastgir and Mohammed Wazir crossed the Shandur Pass from Chitral. Two days later they were back in Ishkoman and stayed there. On 12 November I received another message from His Highness:

To: MAJOR BROWN
From: MEHTAR OF CHITRAL   120900

Your telegram of 10th not well understood – stop – please inform whether the Scouts have joined Pakistan or not.

Again I did not rise to the fly by replying.

The Mehtar was in a state of doubt and it suited me he should remain guessing in the meantime. I felt somewhat immoral at bluffing my old friend, Muzaffar, this way but all is fair in this game, and I also had every reason to believe that there were other, and undesirable, Chitrali fingers in this particular pie.

On the morning of 10 November I was tinkering with a charging engine inside the wireless room. I suddenly heard the sound of Limbuwala's voice raised in anger outside. Then I heard Jock talking to him. This was followed by another tirade. Eventually, I heard Limbuwala exclaiming,

"Where's Brown? Why isn't he here? What's he doing?"

I emerged.

Limbuwala looked all round suspiciously. "Come here," he said and entered the wireless room. "Can anyone hear us? Can anyone see us?"

I reassured him.

"Well read that," he said, surreptitiously removing a folded piece of paper from the inner pocket of his immaculate pinstripe.

I read it whilst Limbuwala watched the door, as though in terror of his life. It was a wireless message just received from Peshawar:

To: BROWN
From: ABDUL QAYUM   10090

Mohammed Alam being sent to you as soon as possible with instructions.

I felt very relieved. A Pakistan representative *was* coming. Pakistan *was* interested. Our immediate difficulties were almost over.

"Thanks a lot," I said to Limbuwala.

"Not at all, Major. Always at your service," he replied with a tweak at his mauve bow-tie.

We immediately released the news and knew that it would be broadcast to the ends of the Agency before the day was out. It was now only necessary to keep the wheels turning until Mohammed Alam arrived with his instructions.

I settled down to writing a long and comprehensive report on the events in the Agency, which would help Mohammed Alam to grasp the situation on his arrival. Jock settled down to sketching out preliminary details of the new Corps of Scouts. One evening I glanced up from my typewriter.

"You know, Jock, I am not happy about the Hindus and Sikhs here. There is nothing to worry about the Hindus who are domiciled in Gilgit, the traders I mean. They can all look after themselves, and I've no doubt they have already deposited the bulk of their wealth with their Muslim counterparts, such as Abdul Jabbar. But the Hindu clerks and all Sikhs are going to be a liability. As I see it, the Kashmir war will probably be a long-drawn-out affair now, and Gilgit might well become a base for operations. The Hindu clerks are useless under such conditions. They are forever worrying about their homes and relations. And furthermore they are always a temptation to the more unruly elements. As for the Sikhs, after the Punjab atrocities, it is like showing a red rag to a bull to show a Sikh to a down-country Muslim. And that attitude will spread here in due course. I think they are definitely in danger. It would be perfectly all right if there was no war in Kashmir, and if relations between the two Dominions were not so tense. So I think it would be a good idea to arrange a refugee column which should proceed via Chitral to Peshawar where there are proper arrangements for the reception and rehabilitation of refugees. Protection can be organized quite easily under arrangements with the Mehtar and the Peshawar authorities. We cannot of course force people to go against their will, but we can point out that those who stay behind, do so entirely at their own risk. We shall then be satisfied in our own minds that we have done our best for them."

The following day we discussed the matter with the Hindu clerks and all the Sikhs. We explained the position very clearly, we pointed out the futility and possible danger of staying. But to a man they adamantly refused to go.

"Let us rather bear those ills we have, than fly to others that we know not of. Kill us, loot us, throw us in the river. We shall not move from Gilgit."

They would not move. There was nothing we could do. Perhaps they would change their minds later so I left the offer open. I personally still thought there was no immediate danger – it would come in the spring if Gilgit became a base for operations.

We did not know Mohammed Alam, but it was befitting and most necessary that the Pakistan representative should stay in Agency House. We also thought that there was every possibility that Colonel Bacon might be accompanying him – in fact the current rumour in the Agency was that Colonel Bacon was returning as Political Agent. But this was only wishful thinking and had no element of truth in it. Jock and I spent an afternoon and evening clearing up the shambles in Agency House. We mustered the levies and the old complement of servants of pre-partition days, and we all set to with a will.

By evening they had performed wonders, and the old house almost looked itself again apart from the battle scars of shattered windows and ceilings. We requisitioned some extra carpets, curtains, ornaments, and pictures from the spare stocks kept in the Treasury, and arranged them to fill gaps. We went out to the garden and gathered large bunches of bronze-gold chrysanthemums for the flower vases. The garden had been sorely neglected, I fear, so the old gardeners were called and set to work. The whole place was a carpet of fallen leaves but the malis, glad to be back in their domain again, started work enthusiastically. We noticed a great change by the following morning. Just as we were about to stand back and admire the afternoon's work in the house, the levy Jemedar came struggling in with a huge picture. It was an extremely good old portrait of HM King George VI, which prior to 1 August 1947, had hung in the lounge of Agency House.

"Hullo," I said, "where did you get that from, Jemedar Sahib?"

"Those Kashmiri ***** threw it in the cellar," he replied indignantly. "But now we have got rid of those sons of pigs our Badshah (King) shall return to his rightful place."

With that he reverently polished the glass and frame and hung it up on the wall in the place I had known it for so many years.

"God protect our King," murmured the other levies and servants standing around.

I again felt a lump rising in my throat.

On the afternoon of 11 November we were disturbed at tea by Limbuwala.

"Read that," he shouted jubilantly, waving a message in our faces:

To: BROWN
From: BACON

Pakistan representative arriving Gilgit by air approx. 1000 hours 16 November – stop – suggest Mirs and Rajas be asked to meet him in Gilgit as soon as possible after arrival.

I quietly put the message in my pocket. Limbuwala swilled down a cup of tea and departed. The first thing we did then was to call a meeting of the Provisional Government in Baber's bungalow. When all were present, I announced the news.

It was amazing to see the look of relief which came over the faces of those erstwhile supporters of the independent United States of Gilgit.

"It is God's Will. God is Great," murmured Shah Rais.

"Amen," repeated the others in chorus.

The news was then announced in the bazaar by beat of drum, and orders were issued that a royal welcome should be accorded to the Representative of the Dominion of Pakistan who was arriving on the morrow. I meanwhile had telephoned the news to the Mirs and Rajas. They were overjoyed to hear it, and promised they would make all haste to Gilgit.

2. The Arrival of Sardar Mohammed Alam

The morning of 16 November dawned dull and cloudy. As I gazed out from the bedroom window I noticed that snow was falling in the deep cleft of the Barmas Nullah directly behind the bungalow.

"It's doubtful if the plane will make it today," I said.

Limbuwala had been keeping his set open from dawn and at breakfast a message arrived to say that one aircraft had left Peshawar at 0800 hours with an estimated time of arrival at Gilgit as 1030 hours.

We saddled up at 9.30 am and, accompanied by the mounted bodyguard, rode down to the bazaar. I noted with pleasure that it had been well decorated with flags, bunting and strips of coloured cloth. Triumphal arches of green juniper had been erected at either end of the bridge. We were met by the Provisional Government and other local notables. They were all dressed in their best clothes and mounted on the best horseflesh available – overfed polo ponies which had not been exercised for some considerable time now. We turned our ponies and jogged across the sandy plain.

When we had covered half the distance, a faint buzz of aircraft engines reached our ears. The noise gradually increased and presently a speck appeared in the sky. This too increased until we could make out the outline of a small yellow Harvard aircraft. Descending slowly it circled above the settlement on the far side of the river and then made the run-in preparatory to landing. Appreciating the anxiety and embarrassment of Mohammed Alam, should there be no one waiting to meet him, I flicked my pony, Roshan, with the spur and in two strides he was in full gallop. I gave him his head and we reached the landing ground alone just as the plane was taxiing up to the Rest House. Scouts hurried forward with undercarriage chocks whilst the remainder of the contingent I had sent out kept guard on the surrounding hills.

I pulled Roshan back on his haunches as Mohammed Alam divested himself of his parachute and descended from the passenger's cockpit.

He was a small squat man with a prominent bushy moustache. He was wearing a large fur-lined flying jacket over a warm serge suit. His head was swathed in a blue and white Peshawari *lungi* (turban) round a *khulao* f gold thread. A Pathan of the Hazara tribe, he seemed of a determined and strong character, as he swung his Luger machine pistol over his shoulder and advanced to meet me. Introductions were unnecessary. We shook each other warmly by the hand. Squadron Leader Ahmed of the Royal Pakistan Air Force jumped down from the cockpit, introduced himself, and made some suggestions regarding the protection of the "kite". I passed these on to the Jemedar in charge of the Scout contingent. Ahmed then went off to carry out his routine check.

I then invited Mohammed Alam to inspect a small but smart Guard of Honour of Scouts, which he did most graciously. Our attention was suddenly attracted by the thundering of horses' hooves. We turned round and what looked like the Charge of the Light Brigade breasted the brow of the road. In the lead was Shah Rais Khan. His horse completely out of control, he had thrown the reins to the wind, and was hanging on to the pommel of the saddle with both hands for all he was worth. At the top of his voice he was bellowing imprecations to Allah to save him from violent death. Running a close second was Jock. Behind them followed two or three loose horses in a whirligig of flapping reins and stirrup leathers. Then followed the rest of the field in various stages of falling off or attempting to regain the saddle.

"Good Heavens!" exclaimed Mohammed Alam, "what's this? The first fence over Aintree?"

"No," I replied with a sarcastic chuckle, "your civic reception, out of control."

We both laughed.

"Who on earth's that fellow in front? A Cossack trick-rider?" asked Mohammed Alam.

"That is the Nawab of Gilgit," I replied.

I think it was these few words which cemented an invaluable friendship between us. I saw he had a keen sense of humour after my own heart, and there can be nothing fundamentally wrong with a man who has a sense of humour. We both laughed till the tears ran down our faces.

The receptionists gradually dribbled up in various stages of deshabille, and with all due courteousness I introduced them to Mohammed Alam as though nothing had happened.

By the time this was finished most of the loose horses had been caught. So we remounted, and forming procession rode back towards Gilgit. The Police Inspector rode in front on a handsome white stallion, bearing aloft the Pakistan flag. He had strict orders from me that he was not to move out of a walk on any account. Behind him followed Mohammed Alam mounted on my quiet Tadjik, not that this was necessary as I soon saw he could ride all right. I rode on Mohammed Alam's right and Jock on his left. We both kept these positions throughout the journey, pressing a little closer through the bazaar just in case. The remainder followed behind.

Leaving sufficient Scouts to guard the aircraft, I signalled the remainder to close on us. They then formed a flanking escort, bounding and leaping from crag to crag as only born mountaineers can. Mohammed Alam was much impressed.

As we rode along I attempted to give Mohammed Alam a brief outline of the recent course of events though, as I explained to him, it was impossible to give details of the ramifications and complications except under more tranquil conditions. He was much interested for, as he explained, no news whatsoever had yet filtered down-country.

As we approached the bridge, it was evident that Gilgit had risen to the occasion and the Pakistan Representative was about to be accorded a right royal welcome. The local band was playing the Welcome tune and as we swung into the bazaar, under the triumphal arch, we were joined by the pipes and drums of the Scouts in full ceremonial dress. The streets were lined with cheering crowds, restrained with difficulty from invading the route.

"Pakistan *Zindabad! Allah Akhar!* Mohammed Alam *Zindabad! Qaid-i-Azam Zindabad! Zindabad! Zindabad!*"

Despite the apparent rejoicing, I was in deadly fear that there might be a regrettable incident, and I prayed that we might reach Agency House safely without anything untoward happening. Mohammed Alam was quite taken aback at first. He had never imagined a welcome such as this. He told me afterwards that he fully-expected a state of anarchy, such as that in the towns of Kashmir which had been captured by the tribesmen. This was obvious from his observations, but it was not long before those ideas were dispelled. He noticed with interest two Sikh shopkeepers, standing in front of their open and well-stocked shop, joining in the fun as much as anyone else.

"You know," he shouted in my ear above the din. "A Sikh cannot appear in public in Pakistan now, after the atrocities they committed on Muslims in the Punjab."

He raised his eyebrows again when fat old Bishambar Dass folded his hands on his breast in the Hindu expression of greeting, as he mingled with the crowd at Abdul ner – Bishambar Dass, the richest Central Asian Trader, who had started ... as pantry boy in His Britannic Majesty's Consulate at Kashgar.

As we rode up the hill I pointed out the Treasury.

"Not much use with no money in it," said Mohammed Alam. "As a matter of fact I have brought two lakhs of rupees with me as I knew the Treasury would have been looted as happened at Mirpur and Baramula," and he tapped a paper parcel, carefully sealed, which he had been clutching under his arm since his arrival.

I grinned. "The two lakhs will be a useful addition but they are not essential. There were eight lakhs in the Treasury in the night of the revolt and there are still eight lakhs there. The books have been checked with the cash and the total is correct to an anna. My good friend Haider here will be pleased to check the books and cash with you any time you want, and I can assure you that all will be in order."

Mohammed Alam gave a start of astonishment; his moustaches visibly shot up.

"Incredible," he muttered, "quite incredible."

We eventually reached Agency House, and rode through the gate whilst the guard turned out and presented arms. Mohammed Alam ascended the front steps and with a few well-chosen words thanked the multitude for their rousing welcome. He was greeted with another burst of *Zindabads* which he acknowledged with a wave and entered the house.

"There seems to be no doubt about their sentiments anyway," said Jock to me quietly as we followed.

"They're all Sub-division folk," I replied, "and the Sub-division is fickle and easily influenced. We must not relax our precautions. We must not take one single chance."

But for all that, I breathed a temporary sigh of relief.

Lunch was ready and an excellent one at that. We were soon tucking into a fine hot vegetable and chicken curry. Mohammed Alam seemed a good trencherman, and Jock and I did full justice to the meal too, with appetites well sharpened by the cold day.

After lunch I had a word with Ahmed, the pilot. I expressed a quiet word of admiration at his undertaking and successfully completing the flight on such a bad day. I could see he appreciated this, coming as it did from one who realized the difficulties involved. I also congratulated him on being the first pilot of the Royal Pakistan Air Force to land at Gilgit.

We agreed that, in view of the weather, it would be inadvisable to make the return flight that day and I suggested he should leave at sunrise on the morrow. Haider very kindly offered to put him up for the night.

Mohammed Alam and I then went into secret session in front of a roaring fire in the drawing room. He first of all showed me his credentials which I checked very carefully. They were in order. From them I gathered that the Pakistan Government had taken a very sensible course of action under the circumstances. It had been proved that the Kashmir Government was incapable of governing the Agency. The Indian Government had made no effort to apprise itself of the situation in any way, nor was it in a position to do so if it had wanted. The present uncertain state of complete independence in the Agency would undoubtedly lead to confusion. It therefore was the moral duty of Pakistan to interfere in the affairs of this predominantly Muslim country and prevent

The End Game (November 1947 to January 1948) 209

the rapidly approaching chaos. The Pakistan Government had, therefore, appointed Sardar Mohammed Alam as an agent who would administer the Gilgit Agency and maintain law and order until the eventual fate of the area was decided. It seemed to me a perfectly logical point of view.

Mohammed Alam had been a *tehsildar* or sub-collector of revenue in the North West Frontier Province. This is a comparatively junior appointment. But evidently the Pakistan Government had decided that he was the right man for the job in the Gilgit Agency, and the more I saw of him, I too was inclined to agree. I spent the whole afternoon describing the general conditions in the Agency, the events leading up to the *coup d'état*, the revolt itself, and the present situation. I could see by the intelligent questions he was asking that my words were not falling on deaf ears. He was quick on the up-take and quick at appreciation. I concluded by advising him that he could not do better for the present than to model his administration on that pursued prior to 1 August.

Mohammed Alam rose and with a quiet smile said, "Well, Major Brown, though you don't know it I was briefed by Colonel Bacon before I came here. His advice and yours tally and I propose accepting it."

We then went through to the office and I handed him over the keys to the confidential safe. We checked through the confidential records which were correct and I also gave him the papers and letters of Ghansara Singh. I gave him my report on recent events and suggested he might like to study it at his leisure.

Jock joined us for tea. He had spent the afternoon arranging and checking up on the protection arrangements for Agency House. I doubt if a Viceroy has ever been protected better than Mohammed Alam was for the first week after his arrival in Gilgit. As well as a strong force of Scouts, trusted plain clothes men were on duty day and night. Nobody was allowed to enter the gates of Agency House without first being vetted by Jock or me. Havildar Janan and another trusted member of my bodyguard had orders that they must not allow Mohammed Alam out of their sight by day or night unless he was in our company. We both moved into Agency House and camped in the guest room. We intended staying there until we were certain that there was no danger; and we had the connecting doors so arranged that we could reach Mohammed Alam's room at a moment's notice by night. The whole place bristled with arms and armed men.

On the morning of 17 November we found ourselves drawn up on the lawn of the Agency House in the same positions as on the fateful 1 August. The Guard of Honour was there, spick and span in full ceremonial dress, with pipes and drums at the rear.

Only this time there were no State troops to spoil our precision arms drill. The Officers and notables were in line as before. But opposite us, in place of Colonel Bacon and Ghansara Singh, was Sardar Mohammed Alam looking most distinguished in a black achkan and white pyjamas.

On the stroke often, the Guard of Honour presented arms, the pipes and drums struck up the Royal Salute, and the white Star and Crescent on the green background with the broad white stripe, the flag of the Dominion of Pakistan, was slowly run up on the flag-staff. For me it was a supreme moment. It was the realization of all that we had striven for since that memorable night in Chilas when we decided to cross the Rubicon. The Gilgit Agency had been accepted by Pakistan. And as the flag reached the pole-head on the last bar of "God Save the King," I felt fully justified in what I had done; I felt I had done my best to follow in the worthy footsteps of those gallant British Officers who had served the Agency in the past, whose traditions I could never hope to equal but which served as an inspiration to do what is just in God's sight. As we broke off, I gazed once again at the Pakistan flag, now full-blown in the ice-edged wind, and the prophetic words of Colonel Bacon, on our last night together, came back to me:

"I give the Kashmiri administration three months in Gilgit."

We made merry for the rest of the morning in dance and song on the lawn. The Scouts and locals threw their hearts into the festivities in a burst of pent up spirits after weeks of uncertainty.

We declared the afternoon a holiday.

On the following morning, I took Mohammed Alam on a tour of the various departments and public institutions of the township – the hospital, the Scout Lines, the school, the Post Office, the bazaar, the law courts, the police station, the Public Works Department and the Treasury. The more he saw, the more amazed he became at how each was functioning normally and was busily engaged in the day's work.

He had an interview with Ghansara Singh, who had now decided to accept the situation and was in good spirits. They both seemed somewhat embarrassed to see one another, so after some small talk I suggested to Mohammed Alam we might continue the tour, as there was still much to see. As we climbed the hill, on our return to Agency House, Mohammed Alam exclaimed,

"This is incredible, Major Brown. I arrived here expecting to find a war-torn ravaged country and instead of that it seems as though nothing had happened at all. Incredible, incredible."

I smiled grimly as I cast my mind back over the past few weeks.

"Well, it's all yours now," I said, turning to Mohammed Alam. "There are sufficient local Muslim clerks to open the Agency Office and I can recommend an excellent temporary Superintendent, Abdul Latif, one of the few educated Chilasis. He taught me Shina. But I would advise that you make immediate arrangements for a Pathan staff to be sent up from Peshawar. Five are required: an Assistant Political Agent, a Tehsildar, a Naib (Assistant) Tehsildar, a Treasury Clerk, and a Personal Assistant. That is a sufficient number of neutral outsiders and with them you'll soon have your administration functioning like clockwork."

In the late afternoon the sound of drums from down in the valley announced the fact that the Mirs and Rajas were arriving. According to custom I had sent out small Guards of Honour of Scouts to welcome their respective Chiefs. The Subedar Major toured the various camps on my behalf, presented my compliments, and asked whether there was any assistance I could render. I sent them large baskets of fresh vegetables from the Scout garden and detailed two local, or "Indian" (in future it would be proper to designate these "Indian" Officers of the Scouts as Pakistani Officers) Officers as Aides-de-Camps to the Mirs. The throbbing beat of the drums continued far into the night.

In response to my request, the Mirs and Rajas came to Agency House at 10.00 am on the following morning.

The Mir of Hunza arrived first. I met him at the top of the steps, ushered him into the lounge, and introduced him to Sardar Mohammed Alam. Jamal was in good health, and we were both very pleased to see one another.

Shortly afterwards Nagir followed, a little excited and jumpy.

Then came the Rajas in order of seniority.

I met them at the door as demanded by custom; Punial looking tired, old, and somewhat sinister; I could not help speculating on the thoughts in the mind behind those long moustaches; Gupis, quiet and dignified with a very warm welcome for me; Mahboob of Yasin, the same as ever, wearing a bright multi-coloured necktie. The Raja of Ishkoman had not come to Gilgit. He was sick and I have reason to believe that this was true, rather than some Khushwaqt intrigue which was the first thought that struck my suspicious mind.

Mohammed Alam then held private individual interviews with each of the Mirs and Governors in the drawing-room, whilst I entertained the others. Their overwhelming gratitude for the way in which we had steered the ship through the turbulent waters of the past weeks was most embarrassing. So we swung the conversation away from politics to the evergreen topics of horses, hawks, and sport of all kinds. There was no possibility of the talk flagging then and before we knew what had happened it was lunch-time and the interviews were completed.

The Mirs and Governors took their leave and departed in a cordial and happy atmosphere.

Mohammed Alam looked extremely pleased. I raised an enquiring eyebrow as we lit cigarettes.

"Very satisfactory, Major Brown, very satisfactory. There is no doubt at all about the Pakistan sentiments of the Rajas. The Mirs have both signed official instruments of accession to the Dominion of Pakistan," and he tapped a large white envelope. "The Governors have pledged unconditional fealty to the Dominion. The only thing I am a little worried about is whether the Chiefs' sentiments represent the will of their peoples." [Note by W. Brown: since the Political Districts have always been under the direct suzerainty of the paramount power and not through treaty obligations, as in the case of Hunza and Nagir, the question of signing an instrument of accession did not arise.] "I can assure you," I replied, "that in this case the Chiefs' sentiments are in entire agreement with the will of their peoples and that there is absolutely no question of coercion in any way."

"I am glad to hear that," said Mohammed Alam, "and I unquestioningly accept what you say."

After lunch the Provisional Government appeared on the scene, led by Mirza Hussan and Said. Mohammed Alam granted them an interview.

It transpired that Mirza Hussan had arrived in Gilgit the previous evening from Bunji. He had immediately called a meeting of the Provisional Government. He pointed out to the members that the powerful duo of Mohammed Alam and Brown, working in close co-operation, spelt the doom of the Provisional Government and all their aspirations towards absolute power in the independent United States of Gilgit. He therefore suggested that the Scouts should be instigated to mutiny against me immediately. They should be ordered that on the morrow both I and Jock should be denied access to the Lines and that we should not be paid our due respects. The members of the Provisional Government would then approach Mohammed Alam. They would inform him that although he was the Pakistan Representative, it was the Provisional Government which held absolute power in Gilgit. He must therefore make no decision without first receiving their approval, and that he further must obey their orders in all matters.

Their first order was that Major Brown must be instantly relieved from his appointment of Commandant Scouts, since he obviously could not now hold the position when the Scouts had mutinied against him. Mathieson must go and Mirza Hussan and Mohammed Said should be appointed Commandant and Assistant Commandant respectively.

Needless to say, Hussan was well supported by Said during this speech. When Hussan had announced this plan, Ghulam Haider jumped to his feet.

"You can count me out of this. I'm for Pakistan!"

And with that he left the room.

"We'll fix you later, you traitor!" shouted Hussan.

But Hussan had managed to convince some of the other members that this was a sound plan.

The first part of the scheme miscarried completely. The Scouts, when approached, pledged unanimous and unswerving loyalty to Mohammed Alam and myself. They downright refused to countenance such a nefarious plot in any way. The second phase fared much the same. Mohammed Alam let them have their say. Then, disregarding Hussan and Said, he turned to the others.

"You are a crowd of fools being led astray by a madman. I shall not tolerate this nonsense for one instant. Another squeak out of you, and Major Brown and myself will pack up and leave you to your own devices. You have already seen the beginnings of the chaos which will ensue from your so-called independence under your so-called Provisional Government. It will not be long before the country is plunged into civil war. And when the Indian Army starts invading you, there will be no use screaming to Pakistan for help, because you won't get it. And as for you," he said turning to Hussan, "you clear out of here and get back to Bunji immediately. And in future don't show your face this side of the river without my permission."

He rose to show that the interview was finished.

From all accounts, the members of the Provisional Government then went to the Mir of Hunza and asked him to help them.

"What sort of help I could not understand," Jamal told me afterwards.

Anyway he sent out a message to them that unless they left his compound immediately, he would have them thrown out. This was the last that was heard of the Provisional Government.

Hussan had one last abortive fling to disrupt the status quo. The former telephoned Subedar Sher Ali in Jaglote and told him that Major Brown had issued orders that he was to escort the Sikh and Dogra officers, who were at present prisoners in Bunji, to Chilas. I have every reason to believe that this order, had it been carried out, would have been followed by another in my name to the effect that the Officers should be shot and their bodies thrown in the Indus. Fortunately Subedar Sher Ali demanded personal confirmation by me before he acted.

Mirza Hussan then returned to Bunji. He paraded his Azad Forces and produced a Holy Quran. He informed them that they would swear on oath that they would march to Gilgit under him and liquidate Mohammed Alam, Mathieson, and myself. To a man they refused. Completely frustrated, Hussan gave up the struggle.

Meanwhile I had left Mohammed Alam to find his own feet as Political Agent, which he soon did. He never hesitated to ask questions and he followed advice. This made our task easier and left us free to get on with our work with the Scouts. We had now returned to my bungalow, though we usually paid at least two visits a day to Agency House and often stayed for meals.

The task of paramount importance on our hands was the preparation of the plans for increasing the strength of the Scouts to 1,500 and equipping them in such a way that they would be an independent Corps d'Elite of Central Asia, capable of stemming all aggression against the Agency. Every evening after dinner, the papers and files would be brought out. We were now detailing on paper the combined schemes of higher policy and minute detail which had been maturing in our respective brains. With sheaves of both our notes in front of him, Jock compiled the scheme, which we named JALER, after a certain picquet in North Waziristan where we had both once served together. He occasionally glanced up to ask a question of me, whilst I remained sunk in deep concentration on some difficult point. Wireless, pack-mules, mounted infantry, mountain batteries, light automatics, heavy machine-guns, mortars, uniform, and so on down to the last horseshoe nail and *chapli* stud; we made provision for everything.

The general burden of work was so heavy these days that we had staggered our working hours. After midnight I would doze off to sleep in my chair, whilst Jock continued with the preparation of the scheme.

He would waken me with a kick on the shins if there were any important points to be discussed. At about 4.00 am Jock would go to bed and sleep till about 9.30 am.

I would doze on in my chair till dawn when I would wash, shave, put on uniform, breakfast, and proceed to the Scout Lines. I always liked to get my orders for the day issued as early as possible and to see them put in motion personally. Then came parades and fatigues to supervise, all of which would have become idle and slack had I not given them my personal supervision. Then Jock would join me, and we would continue with the rest of the work of the day. We found this plan worked admirably under the present circumstances. I, for my part, was beginning to feel extremely confident of the future. Hussan's attempt to turn the Scouts against me had proved that I had the unswerving loyalty of the whole Corps now – even that of the Nagirwals. He who controls the Scouts controls the Agency, and the feeling of complete power is a supreme emotion.

I received a wireless message from Peshawar on 24 November with some excitement.

To: BROWN
From: BACON   240900

You should leave Gilgit in aircraft which brings doctor 25th – stop – move temporary – stop – object is to give us full report.

Although we had both had a back-breaking day in the Lines, we worked like fiends throughout the night of 24th to 25th, putting the finishing touches to "Operation Jaler". We kept a kettle simmering on the hob and whenever we felt drowsy, we refreshed ourselves with steaming cups of strong black coffee. As the first grey light of dawn filtered through the drawn curtains, Jock clipped ten pages of closely written foolscap and charts together, and handed them to me.

I placed the scheme in my briefcase and locked it. We silently shook hands. Jock poured out some more coffee as I drew back the curtains and allowed the remnants of air to hiss out of the now flickering pressure lamp.

At about lunch-time a Harvard droned over Gilgit, circled and slowly cruised back down to the valley to a side-slip on to the landing ground. I went along to Agency House, collected the mail and other dispatches, which included the instruments of accession, and bade farewell to Mohammed Alam. I then cantered out to the aerodrome, collecting a large quantity of mail from the bazaar on the way. I made it quite clear to the letter-writers, that I would personally open and censor their letters.

It was with relief that I discovered that the pilot was the experienced and capable Ahmed.

A doctor had arrived. He had already decided that he was not going to like Gilgit. I think he lasted for a couple of months. I helped Ahmed to refuel with stocks of our valuable petrol. I then climbed into the cockpit, buckled on my parachute, and fixed the safety-belt. The engine roared into life. Ahmed taxied down to the apex of the strip at the Gilgit end. With open throttle, the little yellow plane was presently speeding across the rough surface of the ground. With yards to spare we became airborne and the cultivated terraces of the village of Dhanyor slipped past under the wings. Rising steadily to eleven thousand feet, Ahmed set course down the silvery thread of the river far below. I settled down to checking my reports and censoring mail – then a delicious sleep. One of the most difficult and dangerous flights in the world was no longer a novelty to me, and I knew I was in safe hands.

3. Peshawar

At about 4.00 pm we debouched from the narrow gorges of the Indus, and the old familiar landmarks of the Peshawar Vale came into view. Presently the little plane touched down to a perfect landing on the tarmac strip of the Peshawar airfield and taxied across to the distant hangars. A swarm of ground staff buzzed round like bees as we unbuckled our parachutes and alighted. After Ahmed had made his official report of arrival, he drove me round to Khyber House, the residence of the Political Agent of the Khyber Pass, and now the home of Colonel and Mrs Bacon. The Afridi *khassurdar* on sentry duty saluted smartly as we drove through the gates, flanked on either side by two ancient cannon of former days. A large rambling building surrounded by beautiful lawns and gardens, Khyber House is steeped in the tradition of Frontier history and might well be haunted by the shades of such famous Wardens of the Pass as Cavagnari, Roos-Keppel, and Warburton.

A little figure with a head of golden curls came rushing out from the verandah to greet me.

"Hullo, William. Come and see my stork. And you must see Missy and Takki too." Misgar and Mintaka, I should explain were the two little Kashgar terriers, with peke faces and curly tails, which the Mir of Hunza had presented to Mrs Bacon.

"Takki attacks the stork," Laura breathlessly continued, "and the stork pecks at him with his long beak. I'll make him do it now. Oh, and you must come to the stable and see Viceroy. He's very big but I ride him. There are two guinea-fowl as well. Missy and Takki chase them all round the garden."

And with that the little girl grabbed me by the hand and dragged me away.

"I had better report my arrival first," I said, "where's your Daddy and Mummy?"

"Oh, they're on the lawn. Tea is ready. Come on."

So off I went with this vivacious little lassie. Colonel and Mrs Bacon welcomed me in their usual kindly way. With infinite understanding, they did not shower questions upon me but accepted me as though I were one of the family and had just returned from an afternoon walk. Words completely fail me when I try to express my gratitude for the kindness and hospitality they showed me during my stay in Peshawar. All I can say is that I shall never forget it as long as I live for it was the friendly and sympathetic atmosphere of Khyber House which soothed and refreshed my nerves, keyed up as they were by weeks of tension, uncertainty, danger, and, above all, vital responsibility.

As we sat down to tea it seemed as though I were in a dream. This is the normal reaction on reaching civilization after months in the wilds. I have experienced it many times. Voices seem far away and quite unintelligible. You expect to wake up any moment and find you have dozed off on the roadside in some remote spot in Central Asia, whilst the ponies are resting. Then dream and reality merge and you realize that you are in fact in the land of the living. It is a very strange sensation which all must have experienced who have done much travelling at the back of beyond.

After tea from the old silver samovar with memories of many a cup on a crisp winter evening after shooting, the Colonel and I walked up and down the lawn whilst I gave him a full account of the course which events had taken in Gilgit since his departure. With his knowledge of conditions in the Agency, he quickly grasped the situation and made shrewd comments or chuckled as each incident was gradually unfolded. He was not surprised, but extremely interested as the only news which had as yet reached Peshawar regarding the revolt was a pack of distorted facts and lies which evidently Said had given to the pilot, Ahmed, when the latter flew Mohammed Alam in.

"By God, William, you must have had some fun," Colonel Bacon exclaimed as I finished the story. "I'll ring H E now. He's eagerly awaiting your arrival and no doubt will call us down to Government House immediately."

In due course the car drew up under the wide porch of Government House. An orderly opened the door of the car and we alighted to climb the red-carpeted flight of marble steps which led into the main hall. A lofty room, with panelled walls surrounded by heads of big game, a large fireplace in which a log fire was blazing, it somewhat resembled the traditional baronial hall except for the comfortable furniture and tasteful decoration in contrast to the Spartan living conditions of mediaeval times. We were duly ushered into the study and into the presence of Sir George Cunningham GCIE, KCSI, KSIE, OBE, probably the greatest living authority on the North West Frontier and on Pathans. Governor of the North West Frontier Province over the difficult years of 1937 to 1946, he had now returned at the special request of Qaid-i-Azam Mohammed Ali Jinnah, Governor-General of Pakistan, to continue as Warden of the most turbulent Marches of the world and to culminate a glorious career. Sir George was seated at his desk, poring over files, and although the hour was 8.00 pm, this was nothing out of the ordinary. As we entered he rose, and came forward to greet me with a firm springy step. Small and wiry, though now past the age for retirement, he is still as energetic as when he first came to the Frontier 23 years ago. A dour and quiet Scotsman, his personality is magnetic, and when he speaks the attention of all those present is immediately attracted, for they know that they will hear words of real wisdom. The capabilities of a Frontier administrator are judged by Pathans on his ability to handle *ajirgah* (Council of Elders), in the many and varied moods *ajirgah* can adopt. Sir George is a master at this, and that is saying a great deal when one considers his line of famous predecessors.

He greeted me warmly, and we sat down in large leather armchairs in front of the fire with his two liver and white spaniels at our feet. The soft lights, the cosy and friendly atmosphere, again made me feel as though it were all a dream; but I kept a firm grip of myself; this was no time for day-dreaming.

I handed over my report which Sir George read through. He was interrupted twice by telephone messages giving the latest developments in the Redshirt agitation. There was no secretary to answer the telephone – he believed in direct personal contact. After issuing clear, concise orders, he continued with my story. At length he looked up, asked some astute questions and made some shrewd comments from which I gathered that he had thoroughly summed up the course of events and the present position in the Gilgit Agency. He was particularly interested in Chitral. Evidently the Mehtar had just sent a long petition stating his claims to Kuh Ghizr and Yasin. Sir George allowed me to read the letter and asked for my written comments by the morning. This was not difficult since, as already described, Chitral had no claim whatsoever on the Gilgit Agency. I merely had to annotate the facts of history and the facts of the present situation to the best of my knowledge.

As we rose to go, Sir George added:

"Now look here, my lad, rest assured that you are not staying in Gilgit one minute longer than is necessary and neither is Mathieson. You may return to pack your kit and settle your private affairs. But you'll come back here again as soon as possible, and make no mistake about it. Disputed territory is no place for British Officers nowadays."

I accepted it fatalistically. How could I do otherwise?

Lady Cunningham, dressed for dinner, was in the hall.

"Hullo, William Brown. What's all this I hear about you? What have you been up to?"

She spoke in her blunt, straightforward manner which to a stranger seems gruff, but under which in reality there is a wealth of Irish kindness and sympathy. We chatted for a bit and then excused ourselves.

As we drove past the Club on the way home, Colonel Bacon suggested we might go in for one quiet drink before dinner. The bar was full of old friends who greeted me with a roar of welcome as we entered. Good natured banter flew back and forth.

"Welcome the rebel."

"Have you escaped from jail?"

And someone started singing The Wearing of the Green and presently the whole bar joined in. Drinks started piling in front of me, as, in response to popular demand, I gave a brief burlesque account of my adventures. It was a happy carefree gathering of folk bound together in a unique bond of comradeship, formed through a common life among the vicissitudes of the Frontier, a spirit so different from the close social circle of the cities. As I extracted from my wallet a wad of dirty crumpled notes to pay for a round, there was a shout of *"Lut mal"* (Looted property [Pushto]) from a friend at the far side of the bar. Everyone roared with laughter, even more when I played him for the bundle at dice and won. It was well past midnight when we staggered home.

"One quiet drink at the bar before dinner" I thought to myself, "and a report to write on Chitral yet."

The next few days proved very busy. I had to redraft the whole of my report so that it could be fully appreciated by those unaware of general conditions in Central Asia. I am afraid I had not paid much heed to this in the original, with the result that it could only be understood by Frontiersmen. I had to prepare maps to accompany the many copies which were required. I duly delivered the Instruments of Accession of Hunza and Nagir to Lt. Colonel A.J. Dring CIE, Chief Secretary to the Government of the North West Frontier Province and another well-known and popular figure on the Border, both in political life and as a great sportsman. When I called, he had just returned from hunting and was scraping the mud off his boots on the verandah – he was MFH of the Peshawar Vale Hounds, up till December 1948, when he was transferred to Bahawalpur State as Prime Minister.

I called on Khan Abdul Qayum Khan, the burly Frontier Premier and gave him the story of the revolt. An ardent supporter of justice being done in Kashmir, he was naturally extremely pleased that the will of the people had been enforced in the Gilgit Agency, and that Hindu rule had been overthrown. He listened with rapt attention and then offered me his heartfelt congratulations and thanks for all I had done. I found the Khan a man of strong personality, possessing progressive and liberal ideas. His moral integrity is above reproach – he is the only original Provincial Premier in West Pakistan who has weathered the storm with a clean conduct sheet, and he has always striven in an unbiased manner to give everyone a square deal. His hospitality and generosity is unbounding, as Colonel Bacon and I discovered when we were invited to a most sumptuous dinner in true Pathan style.

I visited Charles Duke, the Deputy High Commissioner for the United Kingdom in Peshawar. He is an old acquaintance as he had been Political Agent in South Waziristan when first I joined the South Waziristan Scouts in 1943. I gave him a revised copy of my report which, I understand, was eventually forwarded to Whitehall.

As I came out of Charles Duke's office which was then in a room in Dean's Hotel – it is now housed in a most palatial building – I ran into Douglas Brown of the *Daily Telegraph* who had just arrived in Peshawar. He had naturally been trying to contact me to get my story. We sat down on the lawn and over a pot of beer I gave him as much information as I could. An article for release to the public on events in Gilgit at that time naturally had to be handled with great care owing to the tense nature of inter-Dominion relations and the grave possibility of war. But Douglas Brown, in the very best traditions of the Press, allowed me to vet his draft telegram; and the article which eventually reached the headlines of the *Daily Telegraph* and *The Scotsman* was exactly in accordance with the draft I approved. I sometimes think that Douglas Brown must have thought that I did not play fair by him. Not long after, a fuller and more comprehensive article appeared in *The Times* from their Peshawar Correspondent and, strange to relate, the style of writing was mine. In fact there was every indication that I had written the article. What had actually happened was that a certain person, who had access to my official report, had repeated some of the contents verbatim to *The Times* Correspondent who in turn had copied and wired them verbatim to this newspaper.

On 28 November a long wireless message in code arrived from Jock. Colonel Bacon and I decoded it together in the study. As the words gradually began to make sense, I dropped into the depths of despair and frustration. It seemed that everything I had worked for in Gilgit had gone up in flames as soon as my back was turned.

To: BROWN
From: MATHIESON

Pass this to Chief Sec from PA (Political Agent Mohammed Alam) immediately – stop – Gilgit bazaar completely looted last night – stop – area cleared by Scouts after much difficulty – stop – curfew order imposed from today – stop – proved that where action against local population involved Scouts cannot be relied upon – stop – PA – therefore requests that six platoons Frontier Constabulary with automatic weapons be sent immediately otherwise administration difficult – stop – Sqdn Ldr Ahmed assures us Dakota can land Gilgit or Chilas if so please send FC by air otherwise by quickest overland route – stop – also send tear gas by first plane – stop – all quiet now.

I really felt like throwing in the towel, saying "to hell with Gilgit," and washing my hands of the whole business by not returning. It was the Colonel who brought me to my senses.

"There's no use crying over spilt milk. The bazaar has been looted and that's an end of it. You've had all the luck on your side up till now, and now that you're up against it, you can only make the best of a bad job."

So I passed the news to the Chief Secretary and then appreciated the situation in the light of the Colonel's words. Now that the bazaar had been completely looted, there seemed to be no further mischief which could be done. I knew full well that they would never dare massacre the Sikhs and Hindus. To send the Frontier Constabulary to Gilgit would only aggravate a situation which I knew would be fully under control now that steam had been let off in sacking the shops.

So I sent the following reply to Jock:

To: MATHIESON
From: BROWN

For PA from Brown – stop – Chief Sec consulted no hope of FC – stop – if necessary move platoons from Theliche and Jaglote to Gilgit handing over to local chighas (hue and cry detachments in Pushto).

After the dispatch of this message I heard nothing more of the incident until I returned to Gilgit and pieced together the full story.

As soon as possible, Lt. Colonel Iskander Mirza, CIE, OBE, Defence Secretary to the Pakistan Government, flew up to Peshawar from Karachi to hear the first-hand account of the revolt in Gilgit. He was an old friend of Colonel Bacon's: they had been at Sandhurst together. We went to meet him at the aerodrome and took him straight to Khyber House. Time was short, as he was leaving for Lahore after lunch, so we got down to business immediately on the lawn, bathed in the warm sunshine of a winter's day. Bubbling over with energy and enthusiasm for whatever task was on hand, I saw immediately that Iskander Mirza was a man who really got things done, regardless of the red tape and "normal channels" which usually cause an interminable delay in the launching of any Government project. He read my report with interest and from time to time gave exclamations of approval. When he had finished he turned to Colonel Bacon.

"Some story, Roger, isn't it? A damned good show! By Jove it is!"

I deemed that the time had now come, and that I was in the presence of the right man to give a preliminary idea of my plans for the future of the Gilgit Agency and of the Corps of Scouts. Pouring over a large-scale map of the area, which Iskander Mirza produced from his pocket, I explained in great detail the vital importance of holding the apex of country where the three Empires meet. Colonel Bacon confirmed what I said. The Defence Secretary became ardently enthusiastic and I knew I had won him over to my point of view. When I finished he said,

"The best thing, Roger, is for you to bring Brown down to the Prime Minister's Conference at Rawalpindi at the beginning of December. Liaquat Ali, the Pakistan Premier will be there, and I shall brief him regarding the situation in Gilgit beforehand. You two can then fill in the details and advise him as to the best course of action."

The Gilgit Agency had now become an obsession of Iskander Mirza's. He talked about nothing else up to and during lunch. As I later waved goodbye to the little Harvard taxiing away towards the strip, I knew it would be no fault of his if "Operation JALER" was not accepted. His last words had been,

"Why the hell, Roger, can't we keep this fellow Brown in Gilgit?"

"H.E. is adamant," Colonel Bacon replied.

I ruminated sadly.

4. The Sack of the Gilgit bazaar

It seems that as soon as the plane in which I was travelling to Peshawar was out of sight, the Scouts, the Police, and the bad-hats of the Gilgit Sub-division put their heads together and decided to loot the Hindu and Sikh property in the settlement.

Now before I proceed further with this shocking account, I would mention that I do not propose giving the names of the actual people who were the ringleaders and who took part in the nefarious operation. It will suffice to say that although every tribe was represented, not every man was involved by any means. Many downright refused to have anything to do with it. I took great pains to find out who these men were and I later let them know that I knew. I am also fully aware of those who took part in the looting and atrocities, both actively and as spectators. Let them never forget it.

The night of 27/28 November was chosen for the operation and at about 10.00 pm the balloon went up. The Scouts, the Police, and the locals began to strip the Hindu and Sikh shops and houses systematically. But what was intended to be an organized collection of loot to be distributed among the ringleaders, soon developed into a welter of chaos and confusion, which is the inevitable result of loosing a half-civilized mob in the face of booty. The bazaar area became so packed with humanity that one could scarcely move; the whole place was strewn with cloth, carpets, silks, cigarettes, and foodstuffs, being trampled underfoot and uselessly destroyed by the looters in efforts to find even richer spoil; free fights were in progress everywhere between the Scouts and the locals over sharing the ill-gotten gains.

It was not till 11.00 pm that Jock received a telephone message from the Subedar Major that the bazaar was being ravaged by the locals, and that the Scouts were doing their best to clear the area; they had failed so far, and that the situation was completely out of control. He informed Jock that he must on no account come down to the bazaar as his life would be in the greatest danger at the present juncture. Jock, little knowing the real state of affairs, urged the Subedar Major to continue his efforts to bring the situation under control and ordered him to make the Scouts fire high over the heads of the locals in the hope that they would disperse. There was immediately a burst of firing. In actual fact the Scouts fired high all right – into the air and in the opposite direction from the confusion. They then slung their rifles and rejoined the looting.

Jock went along to inform Mohammed Alam of what was happening. Mohammed Alam must have thought that another *coup d'état* was taking place and that he would soon be joining Ghansara Singh in captivity. For as soon as Jock appeared on the scene, the tough little Pathan covered him with his machine pistol which did not waver from Jock's heart until the position had been fully clarified and Mohammed Alam was sure that he was not on the proscribed list. Jock told me afterwards that he found it very difficult to concentrate on making a report whilst at the same time watching the pugnacious little man's forefinger curled tightly round the trigger of the Luger. They both agreed that they could achieve nothing by going down to the bazaar, and that it was merely running a useless risk. So they awaited situation reports from the Subedar Major. Despite repeated enquiries, he could not be contacted till 6.00 am.

Meanwhile the looters had become possessed with an utterly blind fury in which no one was aware of his actions. An attempt at arson lit up the scene like Dante's Inferno

The End Game (November 1947 to January 1948)   221

and spurred the madness to further outrages. Hindus and Sikhs, their womenfolk, and their children were rounded up in a caravanserai and forcibly lined up against the wall. The men pressed thousands of rupees on their assailants in an effort to prevent being molested. The money was accepted. Jewellery and ornaments were forcibly ripped from the women.

The crowds pouring in from the outlying villages to join in the fun found it quite impossible to enter the bazaar, let along loot it. So in a state of frustration they marched to the Hindu and Sikh temple at the corner of the Scout Lines and completely destroyed it in a wild orgy of idol breaking which would have delighted the heart of the great conqueror, Mahmoud of Ghazni.

A cold murky dawn knocked the spirit out of the pillagers and brought them back to sanity. The Scouts, suffering from the grim hangover of remorse after the wild intoxication of the night, cached their loot in various hides in the bazaar and skulked back to the Lines to avail themselves of much-needed first aid for the wounds received during the sharing of the spoils. The Subedar Major contacted Jock Mathieson on the telephone and told him that, after a tremendous struggle, the Scouts had at last brought the situation under control. The area had been cleared and it was now safe for Jock to come down, should he wish to do so.

Jock, accompanied by Mohammed Alam, lost no time in reaching the bazaar. The sight which met their eyes was a complete shambles of wanton devastation. The streets were knee deep in empty packing-cases, gunny bags, and nondescript litter. The doors to the shops were hanging open on their hinges showing a bare nothingness within, where previously cloth, carpets, silks, skins, and foodstuffs had been piled high to the roof. The entire area was deserted – after one of the most frightful nights in its entire history, the little bazaar now suffered in a strange sinister silence. It was this first scene of utter desolation and destruction which prompted the somewhat hasty message to the Chief Secretary, to the effect that the bazaar had been completely looted.

The results of a detailed investigation were more heartening. It appeared that only the Sikh and Hindu shops had been stripped. The Muslim shops had been left untouched. Now, as has already been described, the former had deposited the bulk of their goods and valuables with their fellow Muslim merchants; so in actual fact very little had been lost. This accounted for the conglomeration of old packing-material in the streets which the looters had scattered in all direction in their efforts to find real treasure. Jock organized a Scout search party immediately and, leading it personally, he soon unearthed the various secret caches. I would like to have seen the looks on the faces of the Scouts as their hidden spoils were discovered and they were made to carry them to the safety of the Treasury where they were later claimed by the real owners. It was estimated that about ninety-five per cent of the looted goods was eventually recovered. The arson amounted to a bonfire of packing cases – no damage whatsoever had been done to immovable property.

As to damage to humanity, there was no loss of life surprisingly enough – even among the minorities. There were many black eyes and broken heads among the Scouts, received in disputes over the share-out. The Sikhs and Hindus, though scared out of their wits, had not been subjected to any serious physical violence except for a few cuts and scratches.

As soon as Jock had recovered the loot, he removed the Sikhs and Hindus to the Lines where he set up the refugee camp as before. They were all naked, so he issued an appeal to the Scouts and locals to provide warm clothing and comforts. He was then treated to one of those strange phenomena of human nature. Within half an hour he had been presented with more than sufficient blankets, warm homespun suits, pullovers, socks, *chaplis*, women's and children's clothing, cooking utensils, in fact everything the wretched minorities required. More and more kept pouring in and when Jock, almost snowed under, suggested that he had got sufficient, the willing donors became most offended that their offerings were not required. The refugees were presently much better attired and equipped than they had been prior to the incident. Human nature is indeed strange!

Thus ended the sack of Gilgit. The situation was under control again.

The account I have just given was compiled from Jock Mathieson's report and from various other sources in Gilgit which I took great trouble to verify as reliable. I was extremely angry, yet not so much on account of the looting and atrocities, which to civilized standards must appear thoroughly shameful and outrageous. One must remember that the people concerned belonged to a race which, on account of its secluded mountain fastness, had progressed very little from time immemorial. Loot and women are the established right of the victor in barbaric warfare, and the vanquished know it. If viewed in the light of the terrible Punjab Massacres, which took place over this period, and in which those concerned were of vastly more enlightened races, I think we can justifiably say that the Gilgit incident was regrettable yet condonable.

I was angry however that the incident had taken place in my absence – immediately my back was turned, in fact. Yet at the same time human nature asserted itself. The Scouts and the local population of Gilgit had paid my power and personality a supreme compliment through not daring to undertake such an enterprise when I was present; and this is not self-glorification, for it is the unquestionable truth, that the bazaar would not have been sacked, the Hindus and Sikhs would not have been molested, their womenfolk dishonoured, had I not gone to Peshawar.

5. The Rawalpindi Conference

On the morning of 3 December, Colonel Bacon and I boarded a special Dakota and were presently airborne with the course set for Rawalpindi. The Peshawar Vale far below, fringed by purple mountains looked beautiful in the clear air of the early morning. Nowhere else in the world is the winter climate more pleasant than in the North West Frontier Province and the Punjab, with soft warm days and bracing nights with a touch of frost in the air. I amused myself by picking out on the natural map spread below the various places which brought back memories; shooting duck in the early morning on the Kabul River; encounters with outlaws and mad chases across country after absconders; Sunday picnics in quiet village gardens; the run of the season with the Peshawar Vale Hounds after a stout jackal; and all the other little incidents which help me to look back on my life and vow that I could not have wished it otherwise.

The Rawalpindi landing-ground, in the suburb of Chaklala, was a hive of activity. High-ranking military and civil officials jostled with policemen, plain-clothes men, the press, and various other hangers-on. Everyone seemed to be doing something, though what I do not know; nor do I think did they. A fleet of large cars was drawn up in front of the control tower. As we descended from the plane chaos turned to a sudden order and we were faced by a barrage of cameras, newspapermen, and a line of officials standing stiffly at attention. As soon as it was discovered that ours was not the Prime Minister of Pakistan's plane, which was also due in at this time, disorder started again. We chatted to Douglas Brown.

Presently the Prime Minister's plane touched down and drew up in front of the control tower. The door of the plane opened and Mr Liaquat Ali Khan stood for a minute at the top of the steps before descending to be introduced to those who had come to welcome him. A man past middle age, of small squat stature, he was dressed in a black *achkan* and snow-white jodhpurs. He wore thick horn-rimmed spectacles, and on his head was a black Kariculi fur hat. Iskander Mirza buttonholed us immediately and thereafter did not allow us out of his sight.

Introductions were completed quickly, and Colonel Bacon and I were whisked off in a large Buick to the Circuit House which was to be the scene of the Conference. The entrance was closely guarded and we were scrutinized by plain-clothes men before we were allowed to enter. I wonder if they noticed I had my loaded Colt tucked into the inside pocket of my double-breasted lounge suit. If they did, no mention was made of it. Everyone of importance in North and North West Pakistan was present in the large main hall. Khan Abdul Qayum and the Frontier contingent soon spotted us and we greeted one another warmly. The common bond of Border friendship united us in the way that hillmen stick by one another when down in the strangeness of the plains. We were introduced to the various Secretaries and Assistants who had accompanied the Pakistan Premier, to Khan Iftikhar Hussain Khan, Khan of Mamdot, Premier of the West Punjab, and to Sardar Mohammed Ibrahim, President of the Free Kashmir Government. I had a long and interesting talk with each and I was particularly struck by their patriotism for Pakistan. Pakistan and the Qaid-I-Azam were everything to them; I could detect no faction feeling or disagreement, and I became certain that if this state of complete unity continued, the prospects of the future prosperity of the Dominion were indeed bright.

Whilst Mr Liaquat Ali Khan conferred with his lieutenants on the proposed agenda, we were treated to an excellent breakfast. As soon as we had finished, business started and the first item for discussion was the Gilgit Agency.

Colonel Bacon, Colonel Iskander Mirza, and I were called into the ante-room. The Pakistan Premier was seated at a desk, poring over a large-scale map of Kashmir and Central Asia. He rose as we entered and greeted us warmly. I had been able to judge little of his character from the fleeting glimpse at the aerodrome, but as soon as he began to speak I realized that he had a brilliant personality. Astute and quick-witted, he had no time for trifles. He quickly grasped whatever point was at question, discussed it shrewdly, and thrashed it out to a decision. Nothing would side-track him. I could not help feeling that the Qaid-I-Azam was indeed lucky to have such competent and patriotic person as his right-hand man.

Mr Liaquat Ali Khan started by congratulating me and thanking me for all I had done in preserving peace in the Gilgit Agency. He then read my report, which, as I have already described, was not easily understandable, in some parts, to those who had not an intimate knowledge of Central Asia. So he asked Colonel Bacon to enlarge and, needless to say, he was shortly fully conversant with the peculiar conditions existing in that little-known corner of the world. The Prime Minister then looked at us keenly and started speaking slowly and deliberately.

"The Pakistan Government had given the Gilgit Agency a great deal of thought. We have fully appreciated its vital importance to the defence of the Subcontinent, and to world peace. We have decided that the responsibility has now fallen on us to defend the Agency against aggression. How are we going to do it? Brown, give me your ideas from a military point of view."

I took Operation JALER out of my briefcase.

"I have here a scheme, Sir, for the reorganization and strengthening of the Gilgit Corps of Scouts, which, if sanctioned, answers your question in a nutshell."

He glanced through the sheaf of papers.

"I shall study this in detail later. Meanwhile I shall pass it on to the General Staff for their comments," he said. "If we do decide to proceed with the scheme, what are the details of the authority you require so that you may proceed with the preliminary stages immediately you return to Gilgit?"

My heart leaped. From the tone of his voice, I knew that JALER was as good as sanctioned. I noticed that Iskander Mirza was ready with pencil and paper so I spoke slowly.

"I wish authority for the following:

1. to enlist 900 recruits in the Scouts;
2. to grant a limited number of Pakistan Commissions to deserving local Officers at present in the Scouts;
3. to base the Muslim element of the old 6th Kashmir Infantry on Bunji as a completely separate unit from the Scouts. All the Officers of the Kashmir State Forces should join this unit and none of them should be allowed to enter the Gilgit Agency without the Political Agent's permission."

"Give me this authority, give me the armament, clothing, equipment, and instructors as detailed in my plan, and I and Mathieson will do the job for you. I would also be grateful if you would give consideration to the disposal of Brigadier Ghansara Singh, Colonel Abdul Majid, and the two hundred odd Sikhs and Dogras from the 6th Kashmir Infantry who are all proving an embarrassment."

"Right," said the Premier. "That disposes of the military angle. Now Colonel Bacon will you give me your views on the political side of the question."

Colonel Bacon opined that the best way to administer the Agency was by pursuing the policy followed prior to 1 August as far as possible. He explained this in detail, laying great stress on the necessity for friendly relations and close co-operation with the Mirs of Hunza and Nagir and also that the status of the Scouts vis-à-vis the Political Agent should remain the same.

"All right," the Premier replied. "A directive will be issued to Mohammed Alam on those lines."

He then rolled up the map to signify that the conference was over. As we rose he looked at me rather ruefully.

"Sir George Cunningham insists that you and Mathieson must leave Gilgit as soon as possible. Under the circumstances the Pakistan Government cannot but agree. We would like nothing better than your staying on as Commandant of the Scouts. I assure you of this, but I am sure you will appreciate our point of view. Once again, thank you for all you've done, and good luck."

The Prime Minister was due to spend the rest of the morning in conference with the Provincial Premiers and other personalities, after which we were to be the guests of the Deputy Commissioner at a luncheon party. There seemed to be no point in Colonel Bacon and I hanging on at the Circuit House so we decided to drive in to Rawalpindi to do some shopping. As we emerged a bevy of the press swarmed forward for a story. The Colonel joked with them for a minute and made them laugh, which prevented their becoming offended at our inability to give anything away. Douglas Brown stood in the background with a quiet smile on his lips. He knew there was nothing forthcoming.

As we drove along I pondered over the friendly attitude of Liaquat Ali Khan towards Colonel Bacon and myself. He followed in the steps of his master, the great Qaid-i-Azam, by having only the interests of Pakistan at heart, and whether these interests were furthered by Pakistani or British Officers was quite immaterial. He showed no distinction between caste and creed but regarded all who had pledged their loyalty to Pakistan on an equal footing, and was ever ready to accept and act on the advice of British Officers as we had just witnessed. It was this policy which secured for Pakistan a flying start, as it led to the appointment of such illustrious Britishers as Sir George Cunningham, Sir Francis Mudie, General Sir Douglas Gracey, and Sir Ambrose Dundas. Despite this, I could not help contrasting Liaquat Ali Khan's attitude with that of another member of the Pakistan Government, an upstart I may say, who had reached a fairly high position through the rapid promotions occasioned by Partition. It was in Peshawar. I was pointing out that it was extremely unwise to allow the Gilgit Scouts to descend into the Vale of Kashmir and join up with the tribesmen. I opined that it was much sounder to use the Scouts for the defence of the Agency only – the task for which they had been enlisted and for which they were capable.

The worthy gentleman's rejoinder was: "All you bloody British are doing is to make every effort in your power to prevent Kashmir joining Pakistan."

We arrived at the Deputy Commissioner's bungalow at 1.00 pm. A goodly gathering was already present but the Premier was still in conference. Colonel Bacon and I fell into conversation with General Messervy, KBE, CB, DSO, Commander-in-Chief of the Pakistan Army and his Deputy (now C-in-C) Major-General Gracey, CB, CBE, MO. We discussed in particular the awkward task which lay ahead of the Commander who was in charge of the evacuation of the Frontier Post of Razmak. As the time wore on we became increasingly worried, as our plane was due to leave at 2.15 pm, and as yet there were no signs of the Prime Minister. At 2.00 pm we had perforce to excuse ourselves, and drove madly down the Chaklala road towards the aerodrome.

Just as we reached the edge of the strip, we saw our Dakota become airborne. We dashed up to the Control Tower and asked the wireless operator on duty to contact the plane and request the pilot to turn back. He seemed incapable of tuning in the set. A succession of atmospherics were issuing from the earphones. By the delighted look on the face of the operator and the way he was tapping on the floor with his feet, we presumed he thought he was listening to music. By the time we persuaded him he was not, the plane was out of range. We then asked him to contact Squadron Leader Jimmy Ellison in Peshawar, who we knew would send an Auster for us. Unfortunately Jimmy was away for his tea. So we gave it up as a bad job and returned to Rawalpindi to borrow a Government car from Iskander Mirza.

Iskander Mirza was on the point of leaving the Circuit House when we arrived.

"Your plan is accepted," he boomed at me, waving a piece of paper. "Here's the authority you require. Contact the Director of Military Operations, classify the armament, equipment etc. in order of priority, and he will arrange the supply. You'll hear about the disposal of Ghansara Singh and his merry men in due course. Now get on with it. Cheerio and good luck."

And with that he shook me by the hand and jumped into his car. Colonel Bacon had a word with him regarding a car to take us to Peshawar and he was told that one would be waiting at the Rest House.

As we drove there I felt exultant. I now had a free hand and the backing of the Pakistan Government to put all I had worked for into practice and to raise my own Corps d'Elite of Central Asia. It was a supreme moment. I felt like an ambassador returning to his country with some mission of vital importance accomplished, and certainly the news which I would release on the strength of the letter of authority would be acclaimed with the greatest enthusiasm throughout the Gilgit Agency.

"It will be just like the John Company days for you," the Colonel said with a smile, but he proceeded to give me some very sound advice on the course of action I should take on my return.

The Rest House was a hive of activity. A contingent of sinister looking individuals thronged the compound, whom we took to be leaders of the Free Forces of Kashmir.

They had long hair and beards and there was a wild fanatical look in their eyes. Their dress was nondescript – most of them wore jerkins, grey flannel trousers, and long jack-boots. They were talking in Pushto but strangely enough the Colonel and I could not recognize a single one of them. And between us we knew every important tribal leader from Gilgit to Quetta. For one fleeting moment we saw and recognized the legendary figure, whose name was on every lip at that time, whose identity was the subject of speculation in every club, lounge, and public meeting place. Colonel Tariq, the Supreme Commander of the Free Forces of Kashmir. He was wearing battle-dress, a side-cap, and had a large fawn blanket thrown round his shoulders. When he saw us, he covered his face with a corner of the blanket and quickly disappeared into the Rest House. We knew we could now answer the frequent topical question of "Who is Tariq?" But we did not, and it was most amusing to listen to the various theories put forward in Flashman's Hotel that night and later in the Peshawar Club. We said not a word.

The car had engine trouble. Whilst the Colonel was carrying out a diagnosis, I spoke to one or two of the *Ghazis*. They were inspired with every confidence of success.

"We shall take Kashmir, we shall then take Patiala, we shall then march on Delhi which is the historical capital and right of Muslims. The campaign at present? We are held up on the Uri front in complete deadlock. The fighting is raging in the south on the Jammu border. When we left today Akhnur was in flames – it will be in our hands shortly. We are gathering forces in the north at present in an effort to break the stalemate. The intention is to send a picked force up the Valley of the Kishenganga. They will then cross the difficult snow-covered mountains and drip into the Jhelum Valley near the Mahura Power Station. After destroying it, they will move downstream and catch those Indian pigs at Uri such a crack on the back that the way to Srinagar will be open to us again. How do we like the bombing and strafing by the Indian Air Force? It certainly puts us at a great disadvantage and gives us much trouble. We cannot retaliate as we have no anti-aircraft weapons. I don't know why the Pakistan Government does not help us. They could supply us with weapons and also use their aircraft to shoot down these sons of bitches. It is very strange. But we are doing our best on our own. The other day a party of the Suliman Khel was caught in the plains near Jammu by an Indian fighter plane which proceeded to dive-bomb them. The warriors stood up and loosed off such a volley of rifle fire, that the plane turned tail and fled. We think it must have crashed later as large clouds of black smoke were pouring out of the engines. We hope to have one fighter plane of our own which will be a match for those Indian dogs. You see, during the war the Mahsoud tribe all subscribed and bought a Spitfire to help the *Sarkar* (the British Government) against Hitler. The tribal leaders have recently sent a petition to Churchill Sahib saying that they would be grateful if he would return their plane now that the war is over and he has no further use for it. We are sure Churchill Sahib will agree. Then we'll knock the guts out of the Indian Air Force which pesters us all day long. The trouble in Kashmir is that we cannot hear aircraft approaching on account of the roaring mountain torrents in every valley and side valley. We have to employ special sentries who watch the sky all day long. Even when they see hostile aircraft approaching, they cannot give the alarm by whistle. So they immediately run round all our picquets shouting 'Mountbatten, Mountbatten!' Then we know to keep our heads down. *Puh makha de khun, Sahib.*"

"*Puh makha de khun,*" I replied as I wandered over to see how the Colonel was faring with the car.

"I'll bet these boys have seen some blood flowing," the Colonel chuckled, nodding in the direction of the *Ghazis.*

"I'll bet they have," I replied.

The car was all right now. But the hour was late and as the roads were far from safe at night at that time, we decided to camp in Pindi. So we staked a claim in a double room at Flashman's Hotel and made tracks to the bar for what we considered well-earned refreshment. We soon felt better and decided to go and call on General and Mrs Gracey (now General Sir Douglas and Lady Gracey). We were warmly welcomed and spent a most entertaining hour or so. The General, energetic, quickwitted, and with modern and sometimes delightfully unorthodox ideas on soldiering, had one fixed idea. This was the advancement of the Pakistan Army to the highest pitch of efficiency. A more loyal Commander-in-Chief Pakistan could not have found – indeed his attitude was typical of that of every British Officer who had elected to serve the Dominion. Mrs Gracey had spent a holiday in Chilas when her cousin had been Assistant Political Agent there. So we naturally found much in common to talk about. No mean artist, she showed me her sketch book of Chilasi views and personalities. I was carried away back over the passes to the grim and lawless, but so attractive Sub-agency.

On returning to the hotel, we went to the bar for a quiet drink before dinner. Douglas Brown joined us. Gradually more acquaintances, both Pakistani and British drifted our way. It wasn't long before a cheery party was in full swing. This developed into a wild carefree night. We must have broken up about three or four in the morning. I remember our singing Loch Lomond about midnight, transposing Kashmir in place of Scotland and Jhelum in place of Loch Lomond. This was greeted by roars of "*Zindabad*" which almost brought the roof down. After that I can recall little else till I woke in bed in the morning, fully dressed and feeling frightful.

"I hope we didn't manhandle anyone of importance last night," Colonel Bacon remarked as I blinked like an owl in the bright sunshine streaming through the window.

Being unequipped with the remedies for such a contingency, we hastened to the nearest chemist's shop for breakfast. After that we felt decidedly better.

General Gracey's car called for us at 10.30 am and took us out to Chaklala in time to catch the mail plane. It was a most disagreeable flight. The Dakota was packed with a heterogeneous collection of humanity. I was jammed in a bucket seat between a hamper of over-ripe vegetables and a woman with a brace of babies. Fortunately I soon fell asleep – so soundly that I might have been in a feather-bed.

As soon as I arrived in Peshawar, I was naturally madly keen to return to Gilgit. My flight however was delayed through a most alarming incident. I was sitting at the far end of the bar at the Club one evening with my great friends the Peshawar 'policemen' – a brotherhood which all will recognize who have been to these parts recently. Suddenly Jimmy Ellison shoved his head round the door.

"Anyone seen the Air Vice Marshal? Oh, hello, Willie. Can you spare me a moment? There's some important news."

I joined him on the lawn.

"B… pranged at Saidu on the Gilgit flight today," Jimmy began.

Now B…, a Pakistani chap of my own age, was a great friend of mine and Jimmy knew this. So he hastened to reassure me.

"He's badly battered and out for the count but by the grace of God he's still alive."

"Any details?" I asked.

"Yes. On the outward flight there was a fairly thick mist. He took the wrong turning at Bunji and instead of forking left up the Gilgit River he continued up the Indus. He had covered quite a distance before he realized he was off his course, and had naturally consumed a lot of petrol. He turned back and headed for Risalpur. Above Saidu in Swat the juice gave out. Seeing a suitable field, as the plane lost height, he decided to use it for a forced landing. The landing was perfect, but unfortunately a low bank about two feet high across the middle of the field had not been visible from the air. The plane struck the bank and the next minute the whole issue was upside down. No fire, thank God, but the kite is a write-off. There was no passenger, which was lucky.

They'll be bringing B.... in tomorrow in an ambulance. Now excuse me, Willie. I've got to pass on the report to the AVM."

I silently prayed to God that this would be the first and last prang on the flight, and I hoped that the other Pakistani pilots would not become demoralized. God did not answer my prayer, yet the Pakistani lads fearlessly continued the flights, not only straight flying, but later under circumstances in which the most outstanding acts of gallantry were performed. But that is another story.

A couple of days later I collected the official and personal mail for Gilgit, bade the Bacons farewell with deep gratitude for all they had done for me, and by 11.00 am was airborne in a beautiful clear blue sky. The pilot was a stranger but he handled the plane masterfully through the air pockets of the Indus gorges and I felt no qualms whatsoever. The country below presently became familiar and shortly after 1.00 pm we touched down on the little strip of six hundred yards rolled out among the rocks.

Jock, the bodyguard, and Said, looking as though he was going places, were waiting to welcome me.

"I think I should have done a 'Neville Chamberlain' stunt," I told Jock, "for in my pocket I have a piece of paper which contains everything that opens and shuts."

"Good work, Willie. I knew you'd pull it off," Jock exclaimed, his eyes lighting up.

"We'll not see it through, though," I replied and he knew exactly what I meant.

"Hullo, Said. Off to the North Pole?" I asked as this officer approached.

Said was embarrassed and stuttered, "No, I am going to Peshawar, Sir."

"And what are you going to do in Peshawar. Join the tribesmen and fight for your fatherland?"

Said became even more embarrassed.

"No Sir, I am proceeding to Jammu to join my family which is there. As soon as I have seen to their safety I shall return to Gilgit."

"Jammu is in the hands of the Indian Army, you know," I said.

"Yes, I know, but I shall manage to get through."

"I presume you have Mohammed Alam's permission."

"Yes," Said replied eagerly.

"Well," I said, "in view of certain instructions I have with me from the Pakistan Government, I think you should not go in the return plane today. We must discuss the matter further with Mohammed Alam in the light of the instructions."

Said demurred.

"You will not go in the plane today," I said with emphasis.

"All right, Sir," Said replied, walking over to the Rest House to arrange for the return of his kit to Gilgit, so I thought.

"Get Mohammed Alam on the phone, Jock."

There was a roar of aircraft engines. As the little yellow Harvard hurtled across the sandy surface of the landing ground, Jock rushed out of the telephone picquet. He looked around, asked some questions, and then ran across to me.

"That *banchoot* [an Urdu term of abuse – the translation is unrepeatable] Said has bolted," I said as the plane disappeared over the shoulder of Minawar. "I'll inform

Peshawar by wireless as soon as we get back. I wonder how much he paid the pilot, or they may have been relations."

We walked over to where the ponies were waiting and I was so pleased at seeing my own horseflesh again that I made a flying vault into Tadjik's saddle. He never moved a muscle. He was used to unexpected shocks.

6. The Last Phase

The task which lay ahead of us on my return to Gilgit from Peshawar was enormous. Why did we ever undertake it? Our days were numbered. I had only come back to Gilgit to pack my belongings. Any day a new Commandant would be arriving, who could have been left to shoulder the burden from the very initial stages. Yet undertake it we did. We threw our shoulders into the traces with a will, realizing full well that we would never see the fruits of our labours. At the time we thought little of it; there was work to be done and we would do it till we were checked. But looking back now, this period seems to absolve my conscience from the accusation that my activities in the Gilgit Agency were an ambitious effort to secure personal power and self-aggrandizement. In an area where one's sense of proportion is so inclined to become lost, I sometimes actually doubted that my motives were entirely disinterested; but this final phase put my mind at rest.

Conditions were general satisfactory. Mohammed Alam had now a staff consisting of a Punjabi Agency Surgeon, a Personal Assistant of his own tribe, a Treasury Clerk, and a Naib Tehsildar from Peshawar. An Assistant Political Agent was also on his way – an excellent choice in Khan Sahib Azad Khan, a trustworthy likable man, who had been Tehsildar up to the time of the change of power and so was fully conversant with the Agency. Under the direction of this staff, ably assisted by the local clerks, the political administration was working smoothly.

Thanks to Jock the work of modern training was proceeding apace among the Scouts and I noted with satisfaction that morale was high and discipline all that could be desired. News had come from Subedar Ghulam Murtaza that the Burzil Pass was now impassable, but I deemed it wiser to keep the listening post there, especially as he had also reported a concentration of Indian Army units in the Tragbal area. The fun would start in the spring. Except for one small picquet at Jaglote, to watch the activities of Mirza Hussan across the river, and the Haramosh detachment, I then withdrew all the outlying picquets to their respective headquarters in order that every man possible should take part in the intensive training.

With regard to Jaglote, there is one interesting story to recount. When flying back from Peshawar I had noticed that the Scouts had not occupied the Chowki according to my previous orders, but had thrown up a defensive camp at the edge of the grass farm some one mile away. As the picquet had just been relieved, I was lucky to be able to get a first-hand explanation from the NCO in charge of the relieved troops. Now he was a stolid old havildar whom I had known for years and who I knew was perfectly reliable and very much alive to the realities of life. When I asked him for an explanation as to why the garrison had not occupied the Chowki he looked worried.

"It is not a good place now, Sahib."

I pressed him a little further.

He became embarrassed but eventually explained rather shamefacedly.

"It is haunted, Sahib. Fairies live there now. My men have all seen them at night. I have seen them. We have also seen the fat Dogra Subedar moving about among the trees at night. He *was* killed, wasn't he, Sahib?"

I nodded my head.

"It is better we should not live there, Sahib; so that is why I built the camp further away."

"All right," I said dismissing him.

I made no enquiries.

I now set about the preliminary arrangements for implementing the authority which the Pakistan Government had vested in me. It was the middle of December. I reckoned that a fortnight was sufficient time to give the Pakistan Government to fly in and drop the essential items of clothing and equipment for she recruits. Similarly, a fortnight seemed sufficient time for Mohammed Alam to collect the necessary rations from the Districts for increased strength. So I made 2 January 1948 target date for the recruiting to start. Relying on the fact that these two operations would be carried out, all I had to do was to decide on the class composition of the "nine hundred" and inform the Mirs and Governors accordingly.

I apportioned the vacancies as follows, tentatively. On paper Hunza and Nagir were to provide 250 recruits each. In actual fact I would work it so that Hunza provided 300 and Nagir 200 by discarding 50 of the latter as physically unsound, which would not be difficult. On the other hand I could rely on the Mir of Hunza to provide 300 of the best fighting types available in Central Asia. Punial would give 100; Kuh Ghizr 100; Yasin 100; Gilgit Sub-division 50; and it was my intention to raise a platoon of 50 from Ishkoman for the first time in the history of the Scouts.

I had still not made up my mind about raising a Chilas platoon. Former attempts had proved disastrous, and there was too much at stake just now to court a regrettable incident. The Chilasis however answered the question for themselves by refusing to join up, and, as this was no occasion for press-ganging, in the guise of appeals to patriotism, I let the matter drop. I knew there would be no lack of good material from the other sources. Actually my eventual intention was to raise the strength of the Chilas Levy Corps and raise the standard of training and organization to a proper footing in the same way as Jock had done with the North Waziristan Khassadors. But this was a scheme which had to wait until the Scout reorganization was completed, and so we never had a chance to put it into action. It was a pity, as it was a scheme which would have been acclaimed by the Chilasis and would have done much towards the social development of the Sub-agency.

At the first opportunity, I contacted the Mirs and Governors on the telephone and announced my requirements of recruits. In every case I received overwhelming manifestations of loyalty and sincere promises of double the number of recruits required, should I so desire them. I told them that the dates for arrival in Gilgit of the various States and Districts would be announced later, and I was fully assured that tryst would be kept. To the Mir of Hunza I hinted that his allotment might be considerably increased.

"I'll send 400 young men, the flower of my country," he said.

And he kept his word.

It was now necessary to show the fruits of my down-country visit in an immediate practical way, as the New Year was still a fortnight away. Talk, plans, and promises cut little ice in Gilgit. Direct action is appreciated. So I decided that I would grant Subedar Major Mohammed Baber Khan a Pakistan Commission and promote him to the rank of Lieutenant.

I also let it be known that on Partition the Subedar Majors in every unit of the Frontier Corps on the North West Frontier had been promoted to commissioned rank. So the decision was popularly acclaimed by the rank and file who not only appreciated their efforts being recognized, but felt that the Gilgit Scouts were now being treated on the same footing as their counterparts down-country such as the famous Tochi Scouts and South Waziristan Scouts.

The ulterior and unofficial motive of the promotion was that it closed the door to Baber, against any possibility, however slight, of using his undeniable influence over the Nagir contingent, and the folk of the Sub-division, to create trouble. Henceforth, as a responsible officer holding a Pakistan Commission he was morally bound to support Mohammed Alam in every way. The result fulfilled my every expectation.

Now although I had the power to promote Baber myself, I did not wish to do so directly. With my departure so imminent, I wanted to do everything in my power to strengthen the hand of Mohammed Alam and this was the policy I pursued in every important matter affecting the Scouts in the future. So I wrote to him officially, and informed him that I proposed promoting the Subedar Major to Lieutenant under the powers vested in me. I asked him whether he had any objection, and, if not, would he please give me his permission. He agreed.

One afternoon we arranged a formal parade in the Lines to which the public were admitted. The Scouts were drawn up on three sides of a square, whilst Mohammed Alam and I stood on the fourth. The former made a short well-chosen speech, explaining the official reasons for the granting of a Pakistan Commission to Subedar Major Mohammed Baber Khan. Baber then came forward, saluted smartly, and the Political Agent affixed the badges of rank of Lieutenant on his shoulder lapels. I could sense great satisfaction among all as the parade broke up and we rode to Agency House for a sumptuous tea-party.

It had been a good day's work and I felt very satisfied as I sat by the fire that evening, toasting my toes. The reactions had not yet come in from the Agency but I had no fears. Blood is thicker than water. Baber's sister is married to the Mir of Hunza. Another sister is married to the Raja of Punial. A sister of the Raja of Gupis is married to his cousin, Sultan Mohammed of Nilt. Baber himself is married to the sister of the Mir of Hunza, and his brother is Raja of Yasin. With inter-relationship such as this it seemed unlikely that there would be any opposition. And there was not.

It took about a fortnight for the Scouts to recover from their astonishment at having one of their own folk raised to the dizzy height of Lieutenant. Then they began to

The End Game (November 1947 to January 1948) 233

put their minds together, excluding the Nagirwals, who of course were perfectly satisfied with their share of what the benign Government had to offer through their Commandant, but the others asked, "If one, why not another? Why should Nagir only get the sugared plum?" And the devilish trouble-makers of the Sub-division surreptitiously hinted at further Shiah domination.

This was just what I expected and wanted. I announced that owing to the imminent increase in the strength of the Scouts, it was necessary to promote one more officer to commissioned rank. A board would be convened consisting of myself as President, and Jock Mathieson and Haider as Members. All those who considered themselves fit for the appointment could appear and be interviewed by the Board.

About six candidates eventually appeared and we put them through their paces in turn.

Each candidate was first interviewed and asked various questions about his record of service and the reasons why he wished to take a commission. The answer to the latter question, in nearly every case, was a shameless admission of pure personal ambition – a straightforward admission which I could not help admiring, in contrast to the hypocritical ravings of being ready to lay down life for king and country, which one so often hears at Selection Boards.

Some simple questions were then asked on general knowledge and elementary tactics which were on the whole well answered. Each candidate was then given the task of preparing on paper a detailed scheme for the defence of the Agency with a Corps of 1500 Scouts, fully equipped and armed with modern materials. This, perhaps, was asking rather too much as the results proved, but the entire object of the Board was to give everybody a fair chance to display his talents so that there could be no grousing afterwards.

The final result, which my two Members unanimously gave me, was that Jemedar Shah Khan of Hunza was streets ahead of the other candidates in every way. Since I had taken this as a foregone conclusion before the Board sat, I accepted the decision without argument. Not only was Shah Khan competent in every way for a commission in the Gilgit Scouts but he would have made a first-class Officer in the old undivided Indian Army; and, further, the promotion of this blue-blooded Prince from Hunza was exactly what was required to level the balance of power and to remove the last lever available to trouble-makers for causing dissension and faction feeling.

With all due ceremony Shah Khan was promoted Second-Lieutenant amidst scenes of great enthusiasm, which were reiterated throughout the Agency. I then realized I had achieved complete unity among the Scouts at last.

I was most anxious to keep in touch with the situation in Chilas and also to start the Scouts down there on vigorous training courses such as were taking place in Gilgit. When Jock knew my wishes he immediately volunteered to go down there for ten days before Christmas. I persuaded the pilot of the plane which flew Azad Khan in to touch down on the little-used airstrip on the return flight and drop Jock.

I deemed it essential now that people's minds should be diverted into normal channels and there was no better way to do this than to restart polo, football, hockey and the various other festivities of everyday life. As the same old players rode with the same dash and spirit after the ball, as the band reached its wild crescendo again, as the *tambuks* were taken, as I sat with the Pakistani Officers in the Lines of an evening listening to the pipes and drums, I decided there was not much wrong in the Gilgit Agency.

Mohammed Alam, though not actually playing the various games himself, liked much to spectate, which enhanced his prestige and gave him closer contact with the people. I organized the weekly *chikor* shoots again and discovered that he was far from a bad shot. In fact we had one or two excellent days together and brought in some good bags, including two brace of hare from Minawar one Sunday.

So far as was consistent with the heavy work on hand, I arranged an entertainment of some sort at every opportunity; whenever possible I had bands playing. I realized my reward in the very satisfactory condition of the entire Agency. Yet I did not relax precautions in any way. I was constantly on the spot personally, day and night, so that not one false beat on the pulse of the countryside escaped my notice.

Jock returned on 20 December by road, "and a bloody sight safer too," as he remarked after describing his hairbreadth escape when landing at Chilas. His report was very satisfactory. As I expected, Muzaffar was doing a grand job of work, and had the Sub-agency completely under control. Jock's visit, however, had done much to reassure the people that they were not forgotten. The morale and discipline of the Scouts were high and he had put in the spade-work for various training courses which would start immediately. In consultation with the pilot, who had flown him down, he had carried out a survey of the airfield with a view to enlarging it to take Dakotas. They had agreed that this was feasible.

So I decided that after Christmas I would send Baber to Chilas for his first independent command as a commissioned officer. He could superintend the courses which would be under way by then, and also work out details for enlarging the strip. As soon as the recruits were in, I would arrange for the Sikh and Dogra prisoners of war to be escorted to Chilas where they could be used as labour on the airstrip in exchange for their board and lodging – their lives too for that matter.

After a trying morning in the office on the 21st, dealing with petty cases, I decided both Jock and I deserved an afternoon off; but an orderly appeared with a message.

To: COMMANDANT SCOUTS
From: DMO [Director of Military Operations] Rawalpindi

Investigating possibility of dropping equipment by air – stop – inform you results later – stop – repeat – stop further enlistments forthwith and continue with present forces till further orders. Sher Khan

I admit I was shaken. Without more ado, one immediate action was obvious.

"Come on, Jock," I shouted and we doubled along to Limbuwala's bungalow.

He was in the garden footling with some flowers. It required some self-control to appear calm. We passed the time of day for a few minutes, Limbuwala treating us to a violent tirade against the Tehsildar. The latter had evidently failed to supply a

The End Game (November 1947 to January 1948)

grain ration for Limbuwala's pony which, in spite, had just broken loose and eaten the chrysanthemums. I eventually managed to get a word in edgeways and told Limbuwala that I would be very grateful if he did not repeat to anyone the contents of the message which had just come from Rawalpindi.

"Never dream of doing such a thing, Major," replied Limbuwala. "Always ready to oblige. You trust me. Now as I was saying, the Tehsildar …"

We excused ourselves. We could do no more, though I hoped against hope he would keep his word. Actually he did, and I shall always be grateful to him. We then returned to the gun room in my bungalow, and, sitting on camp panniers, reviewed the situation. We had of course grasped the vital significance of the message immediately. The actual object behind the order was irrelevant for the moment. What was important was that if the contents of the message were released to the public, or if I failed to carry through the expansion scheme at the beginning of the New Year, the immediate reaction from the Agency would be that either the Pakistan Government was dishonouring the pledges given in their letter of authority to me, or that I had perpetrated a gigantic hoax. As can be appreciated, the situation was fraught with the gravest possibilities.

Some very quick thinking was necessary. Eventually I decided that this was a situation which could only be saved by unmitigated bluff. After more thought and discussion, whilst the floor became littered with cigarette-ends, we drafted the following message:

To: COLONEL BACON
From: BROWN

Received message from DMO to stop further enlistments forthwith – stop – please inform DMO that in accordance with PAR Premier's authority 500 already recruited and 400 en route – stop – two commissions given – stop – to stop further enlistments now disastrous with serious repercussions – stop – priority one equipment urgently required if impossible by air otherwise overland immediately – stop – ends – stop – what exactly is set up re Scouts scheme – stop – suggest Col Iskander Mirza be informed of matter.

We then encoded the message, typed out a fair copy on a message form, and destroyed the rough drafts. I carefully put the DMO's message in my money belt. I was determined that Operation JALER would go through at all costs, and I was prepared to face any opposition.

We took the message along to Limbuwala personally. He promised to dispatch it at the next contact. Whilst I engaged the old boy in a technical argument about a defect in his charging engine, Jock flicked through his file of copies of messages received. He extracted the one in question from the DMO and slipped it in his pocket.

With the festive season approaching we spent the rest of the evening planning a little celebration we were determined to have. Against our will and against the custom of *our* country, we decided that we would have to celebrate Christmas rather than the New Year for by 1 January we would be thoroughly tied up with the preliminaries of Operation JALER which would require clear heads and all the energy available. So we decided to take the day off on 25 December. I was confident we could risk letting our hair down once without regrettable consequences, provided we kept the matter a secret till the last moment.

The Commandant's bungalow was astir early on Christmas Day. It was a clear frosty morning, crisp and bracing, so that no man could lie in bed. We sang carols and the old Scottish psalms as we completed a hasty toilet and donned our shooting clothes. A word to Shawar Din and the orderlies were busy preparing guns and cartridges whilst the servants packed a couple of yakdans of provisions and drinks. Jock unearthed six bottles of beer, which he had found in the Chilas cellar on his recent trip.

After an excellent breakfast, we saddled up and headed for Dhanyor. It was indeed a glorious morning – one of those mornings when it really feels good to be alive and for a brief space we had cast aside responsibilities and were determined to enjoy ourselves in carefree abandon. As we passed the Scout Lines, I sent Jock in to rout Shah Khan out of bed, for no better companion could we choose for an expedition. The two appeared presently laughing and joking, Shah Khan dressed in plus-fours and sports jacket: the perfect subaltern. Our happiness was infectious and as we cantered along the road to the landing-ground the chatter and laughter from the bodyguard behind showed that they too had captured the holiday spirit.

On reaching the aerodrome we dismounted and led our ponies down the almost sheer cliff from the airstrip to the banks of the Hunza River. The good ship *Jacqueline* was already at the moorings and ferried us safely to the far side, ponies and all. We then remounted and scrambled up the ascent to Dhanyor Village, to the strains of the local band which had turned out to welcome us. Pausing for a second to offer a prayer for the soul of the departed Saint at Dhanyor's famous shrine, we then moved off to the first beat, whilst I issued orders to the beaters.

The first covey of *chikor* presently shot over our heads, like bats from hell, but I noticed with delight a little ball of fluttering feathers dropping behind each butt. It was a good omen. Then came a flock of swerving rock pigeon. I missed badly. As I was reloading I saw Jock claim a right and left. Then more *chikor* came swinging over the brow of their hill to leave five of their number behind. The guns were warm and the game carriers heavy by the time the beaters reached us and we moved on to the second beat.

We shot all morning and, at the end of an exciting third beat, moved over to a delightful walnut grove in the village for lunch. The Levy Jemedar laid the bag out on the grass whilst we poured some welcome and well-earned beer down our gullets. Twenty brace of *chikor*, four pigeons, and a woodcock was not at all a bad day's work for three guns.

I then paid off the beaters, cleaned the guns, saw to the comfort of the ponies and dogs whilst Jock and Shah Khan busied themselves with laying out the lunch. I returned to find a large white tablecloth laid out on the ground and piled high with our own special delicacies: Thermos flasks of Scotch Broth, piping hot; a cold goose bursting with stuffing and trimmings; innumerable roast *chikor*, chip potatoes sizzling on a frying pan; delicious curry puffs to whet the appetite and retain the thirst; a massive Christmas pudding decorated with sprigs of holly oak on which juniper berries had been tied; platters of home-made brown bread, butter, and cream cheese. I might add that every course on the menu at this sumptuous feast was "off the country," a point I used to pride myself in where housekeeping was concerned in Gilgit.

A tree-stump covered by an embroidered cloth served as the well-charged sideboard. As we took our places on cushions round the tablecloth, I remember complaining to an orderly that he had forgotten to bring champagne glasses.

"Oh well," replied Jock, "we'll just have to drink it from the tin mugs. We'll always feel we're roughing it as we should be under active service conditions."

This brought forth roars of laughter, seated as we were in the absolute lap of luxury. We then set to with a will, and some steady uninterrupted eating soon saw the boards empty. We then settled down to clearing the sideboard, "for" as Shah Khan remarked, "there's no point in taking home half empty bottles."

Now at the best of times a mixture of beer, gin, rum, champagne, and Burgundy is definitely dangerous but to us in our carefree mood it was decidedly fatal.

The Dhanyor folk, who are settlers from Hunza, had also been celebrating Christmas on local wine and were much in the same condition as we were. So the band struck up and we were entertained to a thoroughly abandoned display of dancing. The highlight of the programme was when an old man, well over sixty, with a long white beard and black *choga*, capered round the circle and after doing some fantastic evolutions, collapsed in the middle of the band in sheer exhaustion, scattering drums, clarinets and drum sticks in all directions. I then decided we had better wend our way home.

After negotiating with great difficulty the descent to the landing stage, eyes fixed on feet, we managed to get the ponies on board. It is amazing how docile a horse becomes when he realizes that those who are handling him are slightly under the weather. We did things with those savage stallions that day which would normally have resulted in violent death. The band then embarked and took up a position on the prow.

With the help of the bodyguard we then weaved an unsteady way up the gangplank. Jock, banging a tin plate, was bellowing "All aboard the *Jacqueline*. All aboard for the last trip round the Bass Rock today," whilst I ordered the skipper to cast off and head upstream into the dangerous uncharted upper reaches of the river above Dhanyor. The helmsman looked aghast, but did what he was told. We were presently tossing and pitching in swirling rapids but the sturdy little *Jacqueline* with her load of hilarious humanity and ponies held her course. I then gave the order to about turn and we shot downstream in the fast current whilst the wild music of the band reached a frantic crescendo. Eventually we drew into calm water of the landing stage on the Gilgit bank and disembarked. To this day I cannot imagine how that mad trip did not end in a regrettable incident. "The Deil is indeed gude to his ain."

News had reached Gilgit that the Sahib *log* (Sahib people in Urdu i.e. British Officers) were at play, for at the bridge there was a large deputation of locals, complete with band, and also the pipes and drums of the Scouts to fête us and wish us a Merry Christmas.

I made a tremendous effort to pull myself together as I had a grave suspicion that I was reeling in the saddle and the surrounding mountains seemed to be far from steady. We acknowledged the cheers and salutations and eased our way through the dense crowd. We scattered handfuls of largesse to the children and poor people, and in the resulting diversion we had no difficulty in crossing the bridge and passing through the bazaar with the pipes and drums skirling The Blue Bonnets in front of us.

Back home again, we surveyed the situation over tea, a massive iced Christmas cake, and mince pies. The situation seemed favourable for carrying the celebration on till the night, so I drew a bottle of John Haig from the cellar, which we had no difficulty in consuming before dinner. Then we soaked in hot baths for half an hour and donned dinner-jackets.

The dining-room had been tastefully arranged with Christmas decorations and the soft lighting from red candles in walnut candlesticks gave a congenial and festive atmosphere. A yule log was burning merrily in the fireplace as we entered and took our places for another excellent meal. Tomato soup was followed by ram *chikor* (ptarmigan) and pheasant served with the usual trimmings of vegetables and potatoes. Two excellent bottles of Chianti, which some American friends who had previously passed through Gilgit, had sent me up by plane, served to wash down the game in a pleasing fashion. Then came another Christmas pudding, soused in brandy, and all alight. Mince pies and cream rounded off the meal nicely. Solemn for a moment, we passed the Drambuie and rose to drink the toasts. Then we repaired to the comfort of the sitting-room to chat over our coffee, liqueurs, and pipes.

In a fit of devilment, I put the two empty Chianti bottles on the mantelpiece. Drawing back into the alcove, which gave a range of fifteen to twenty yards, we drew our already loaded Colts. As an orderly dropped a handkerchief we fired simultaneously. Both bottles shattered and the dregs of wine spurted over the yellow distempered wall. It was very satisfying.

We then decided to open the house and what was left in the cellar (we had no further use for it) to such as cared to attend from the Scouts. A telephone conversation between Jock and Shah Khan followed and presently the bungalow was filled to capacity with the lads. Hunza, Punial, and Kuh Ghizr were especially well represented and, in true bottle party style, they brought large quantities of local wine with them. The local band and the pipe band vied with one another simultaneously to bring down the rafters. The smoke-laden atmosphere was a heaving whirligig of humanity, brawling, dancing, performing feats of strength, or quietly passing into oblivion under the milling feet of the others.

In the wee small hours of the morning, I decided that the time had come to close Major Brown's Night Club. So I lined half a dozen empty bottles up on the mantelpiece, collected some pistols (all ammunition was safely in the care of the sober members of the bodyguard, though no one knew this except me) and managed to announce above the din that there would now be a shooting competition.

The effect was instantaneous. In five minutes everyone had excused themselves and gone home. There were far too many personal feuds among these lads to risk gun play at empty bottles on such an occasion when a purposely faulty aim under the excuse of drunkenness might settle a long-standing grudge once and for all. Life is very dear.

Boxing Day was the Governor-General of Pakistan's Birthday and a full Ceremonial Parade had been arranged in the Scout Lines to mark the auspicious occasion.

As I rode on to the parade-ground, to take over the parade from Jock, I must say I had certain qualms regarding the success of the venture in the light of the wild party which had been in progress until only a few hours ago. But as I rode round the ranks, carrying out my inspection, my fears were soon set at ease. The Scouts were as smart and steady as ever and not one bat of an eyelid or waver were apparent to show that anything out of the ordinary had happened during the night. I also noticed that a large crowd of enthusiastic spectators had turned out to see the parade.

In due course Sardar Mohammed Alam arrived, looking very distinguished on Ghansara Singh's huge charger, and wearing snow-white pyjamas, black *achkan*, and *puggri*. I drew the parade up to attention, saluted him with my sword and invited him to carry out an inspection. We circled the ranks together whilst the pipes and drums played a slow march. He then rode to his place under the flagstaff at the saluting base whilst I took my position at the head of the parade.

The remainder of the ceremonial procedure went through like clockwork, I am glad to say; the General Salute, the unfurling of the Pakistan flag, the Royal Salute, three hearty cheers for the Qaid-I-Azam; even the *feu-de-joie* was fired without a regrettable incident. This latter achievement must almost be a record in history of ceremonial in Gilgit. I then formed the parade up in column of threes and to the strains of the "Cock o' the North" we marched past the saluting base where Sardar Mohammed Alam, as Agent of the Government of Pakistan, took the salute.

I have seen the Gilgit Scouts do many marches past and I can truly say that on this occasion they lived up to their best traditions, which was most gratifying considering the difficulties we were working under. As the last file swung out of sight I turned to Mohammed Alam. He was almost speechless with admiration. And I admired him. This was the first time in his life that he had officiated at such a ceremony, and yet he had borne himself with a grace and dignity thoroughly befitting his position.

From the parade-ground we adjourned to the playing fields of the school where we were entertained with sports and gymnastic displays. It was most refreshing to see the boys so happy. The climax of the performance was a seven-a-side jousting tourney on donkeys, the armament being pillows. The audience was soon in fits of laughter at the antics of the youngsters on their stubborn mounts.

After that the others repaired to the mosque to offer midday prayers whilst Jock and I returned home to relax. It was a great relief to remove our tight-fitting patrol jacks which had corseted our somewhat weary bodies all morning.

Mohammed Alam threw a lunch party, and in the afternoon the old rivals, the Scouts and the Gilgit Sub-division played one another at polo. *Coup d'frat* or no *coup d'état*, such an encounter was bound to provide excitement and the big crowd which assembled at the Shahi Polo Ground certainly got their money's worth. It was a hard-fought game, in which twelve first-class players rode fearlessly, using every trick of the trade, legitimate and otherwise. We played level till the middle of the second chukka, when some teamwork between Shah Khan and myself resulted in two snap goals for the Scouts. We held this lead till the final bugle when the "Gilgit Roar" of applause echoed and re-echoed round the watchful mountains in the same way as in the good old days. Despite the fact that it was one of the coldest days of the year, with heavy snow falling, I was bathed in perspiration from head to foot.

In the evening the Scouts were entertained to a sumptuous feast at the expense of the Pakistan Government, and in high good fettle, they continued singing and dancing well into the night. As Jock and I rode home with Mohammed Alam about midnight, we agreed that it had been a most successful day in worthy honour of the great founder of Pakistan.

With the festivities finished, we got back in the traces again, for there was much work to be done.

The first and most important task was promotions in the Scouts, to fill the vacancies caused by the promotion of Baber and Shah Khan. The reader will appreciate by now just how difficult this task was. As my final report on the recommendations put it, the problem had to be solved in such a way that military efficiency and political equilibrium were maintained at the same time. This meant that:

1. those promoted had to be capable of leadership inaction against a modern army, as opposed to the previous role of the Scouts which was merely maintaining law and order within the Agency;
2. it was vital that the promotions were acceptable to the Mirs and, if possible, though not so important, to the Governors;
3. it was imperative that the promotions were acceptable to the Scouts themselves;
4. it was imperative that the promotions appeared to emanate from the Political Agent, on my recommendation, and not directly from me.

One false move in the consideration of these qualifications would obviously result in the gravest consequences.

For many hours of an evening I pondered over the problem and then suddenly the answer came whilst I was soaking my tired limbs in a hot bath after polo.

Subedar Azam Khan was the senior Subedar, and being thoroughly efficient in every way obviously held the right of becoming Subedar Major. But as already explained, he was now permanently lame, through a polo accident. The fact that he had been born on the wrong side of the blanket was another reason why he definitely could not become Subedar Major. On the other hand he would resign if he was passed over, and the Government would lose a first-class officer.

Muzaffar-ud-Din Shah, the Raja Orderly in Chilas, had been so closely connected with the Scouts in the course of his duties that he was thoroughly acquainted with administration, tactics, and strategy. He was loyal to the hilt, of high moral integrity, and always said what he thought – a rare qualification in Central Asia; furthermore having a faultless pedigree of blue blood, he commanded the full respect of every member of the Scouts and received implicit obedience to his orders in this feudal country. So the answer appeared to be to make Muzaffar Subedar Major and send Azam to Chilas to follow in the steps of his father and half-brother who had previously completed not unsuccessful tenures as Raja Orderlies.

Tough old Jemedar Safiullah Beg I would promote to Subedar – he thoroughly deserved it and was senior anyway. Being a zemindar, this would also appease any socialist elements.

To Jemedar, I would promote Havildar Sultan Ismail alias Janan, the blue-blooded lad from Nagir who had been Leader of my bodyguard.

The final vacancy of Jemedar I would fill with Havildar Firdos Ali Khan, son of the ex-Subedar Shah Rais Khan about whom we have already heard much.

And lastly came the question of what to do with Subedar Jamshed of Hunza. One of the old school, he obviously did not fit into the role which would be required of the New Gilgit Scouts. As soon as he came into Gilgit from Chilas, I would give him the chance of remaining in the Scouts as a Subedar in an administrative capacity, or retiring on pension in which case I would grant him the honorary rank of Lieutenant.

At the first opportunity I tested the water by casting a fly over Mohammed Alam with regard to the promotions. He sheered off as though pricked. He said that he considered it a matter which could be procrastinated indefinitely. What he thought, but did not say, was that he fully realized the complexities of the problem. He fully realized the dire consequences of one false move. He was not prepared to take the risk, even on my recommendation, for he felt that he was not yet strong enough to cope with an unfavourable reaction. What he did not realize was that my recommendations were based on several years of experience. Risks have to be taken sometimes; and supposing there had been a risk, then this was one of those occasions. For the only defence force this side of the snow-blocked passes was now tense with excitement, unable to concentrate on its work, and again becoming disunited in anticipation of the publication of new promotions.

I reconsidered the matter for a couple of days. What I really feared was that my relief might arrive before the promotions had been published. I would then have to leave behind me a legacy which would prove a bad one, for I knew full well that there was no one in Pakistan at that time, except Colonel Bacon and myself, who could plan these promotions without resultant trouble. I was desperately keen to hand over the Scouts with no matter pending which might lead to difficulties for my successor or for Mohammed Alam. I could, and would if necessary, disregard Mohammed Alam completely and make the promotions myself, but this only as a last resort, as it was entirely against my present policy of strengthening the hand of the Political Agent and boosting up his authority in the Agency. So I wrote my recommendations in an official letter and in the strongest terms possible I pointed out that procrastination would be fatal.

Even then Mohammed Alam was inclined to hesitate but, after a further persuasive and tactful talk with him, he agreed to consult the Mirs on the matter. This was precisely the correct procedure and exactly what I wanted. The Mirs naturally agreed with my proposals and Mohammed Alam in due course sanctioned them.

On 1 January 1948 the lists were published and I could tell immediately by the relaxed and happy atmosphere in the Lines that the Scouts were satisfied to a man. Although I had never doubted my judgment, it was a great relief to me, for a very awkward fence had been crossed without mishap.

30 December saw the arrival of an important message:

To: BROWN
From: BACON

Director Military Operations agrees to enlistment proceeding – stop – Aslam Khan expected to arrive in few days when both of you will be relieved – stop – arms etc will be sent by road as soon as possible.

Jock and I were naturally jubilant over the first part of the message, and I think we had reason to be. The second part made us very sad for it meant that we might not even be able to see the beginning of JALER. But we decided that under the circumstances there was no point in holding events back for Aslam Khan's arrival. We must proceed as though there was no question of transfers until I had actually signed the charge reports.

When Mohammed Alam read the latter part of the message, he too was really genuinely sorry. It seemed to knock the life out of him. He was a worried man; yet, as I pointed out to him, there was not the vaguest possibility of our remaining in Gilgit and he must face the fact by making the best of the situation. I later understood the real reason for his misgivings, for he had been in more recent contact with Major Mohammed Aslam Khan, whom I remembered as a most efficient company commander in the State Force detachment in Bunji years before, a pleasant personality with his head screwed on the right way, evidently, for he soon left the State Forces and took a regular commission in the Indian Army.

Two factors were restraining me from giving the signal which would bring two thousand candidates for recruitment to the Scouts, pouring in to the Gilgit township "frae a' the airts". Lack of uniform and equipment was one; lack of rations was the other.

In accordance with my policy, I had given Mohammed Alam the ration requirements so that he could arrange to have them brought in from the Political Districts. There was, however, a dispute going on about the price. The peasantry claimed that the grain and butter should be purchased on a *khushkharid* basis, that is to say at their price, which was exorbitantly high with the prospects of a thriving black market in Northern Chitral during the spring. The Political Agent, on the other hand, claimed that the commodities should be purchased on a *hukmikharid* basis, that is at a fair rate fixed by him, consistent with present market prices in the Gilgit bazaar. Mohammed Alam did not consider his hand strong enough yet to press his very just claim too hard, yet on the other hands he refused to give way to the demands of the peasants, whose ambition appeared to be to make as much money as possible out of the situation, rather than honour their obligations to Pakistan. And so the transaction was still at a deadlock at the New Year. I had no wish to interfere, as this would merely have undermined Mohammed Alam's authority. Rather I wished to bring indirect pressure to bear on him so that he would exert his position and dictate in no uncertain way his terms of business. If surplus grain and butter had been scarce it would have been a different matter; but I knew full well that every granary in Punial, Kuh Ghizr, and Yasin was well stocked and ready for the Northern Route opening.

I therefore fixed 5 January as a firm date for recruitment to start. We would ration the "young entry" from our reserve stocks, which I estimated would last a month. The prospect of having nine hundred enlisted men, without the means of feeding them, at the end of this period would surely force Mohammed Alam to use his power to make the *zemindars* sell on a *hukmikharid* basis. If it did not, then I would personally take a mule caravan to the Districts and collect the rations myself; but this only as a very last resort.

As for uniform, we had ample stocks of grey *muzri* cloth and leather in the stores. Each recruit would be given one grey suit of uniform and a pair of *chaplis* as a temporary measure until the battledresses I had indented for, arrived from down-country. The manufacture of these suits and *chaplis* I left to Jock and merely told him they were to be ready by 4 January – three days to prepare sufficient for nine hundred men! Needless to say, they were ready. He regimented every tailor and shoemaker in the settlement to help the Corps artisans; he arranged shifts so that the sewing-machines and cobbler's benches were never idle throughout twenty-four hours in the day, and he supervised the task personally, encouraging, reprimanding, and advising.

Shortly after the New Year we said goodbye to Haider for the last time. The strain of the days immediately preceding the arrival of Mohammed Alam had told on him severely. The reaction of relief when Pakistan eventually intervened caused him to become driftwood. He frankly admitted to me that he had no further interest in the Agency now that his ideals had been achieved in opposition to those of Mirza Hussan and his satellites. I allowed him to drift for a period; then I started working him lightly when I knew his balance of mind was more stable again. But he was uninterested. His heart was in his own country, Kashmir, and he was desperately keen to join up in the Free Forces to fight in the defence of his country against Hindu domination. So when he appealed to me at the New Year to be allowed to go to Peshawar and thence to Kashmir, I strongly recommended it to Mohammed Alam, who agreed. So he departed on the first available plane. I rode with him as far as the bridge.

As the time for parting came near, we were both filled with an intense sadness. We had come through such a lot together, through the dark days of uncertainty and danger in the true spirit of comradeship which recognizes neither caste nor creed, East nor West. We cut the final farewell short; I wished him God speed and the best of luck, and rode quietly back to Gilgit.

5 January opened with a clear, crisp, winter morning. Hopefully Operation JALER would pass from theory into practice today. I rode down to the Lines at about 10.30 am.

The football ground was surrounded on all sides by row upon row of recruits. There must have been about four hundred all told, and a glance told me that the Mir of Hunza had been as good as his word. For without a doubt the cream of the youth of the little mountain state had gathered to join the standard – fine upstanding lads with the fair complexions and proud bearing so characteristic of the Hunza folk. They were all scrupulously clean and had taken the trouble to deck themselves out in their best array for the occasion. White homespun *kois*, grey homespun choghas, and white *partugs* tucked into ibex skin *pabbus* were the order and the mass effect was most impressive. The pipes and drums played martial music in the centre and the whole atmosphere was one of quiet expectancy and cheerful enthusiasm.

As soon as everything was ready each candidate stripped to the waist and lined up in single file. I then walked round the ranks and by a quick preliminary inspection divided the lads up in my own mind into the three categories of probables, possibles, and impossibles. There were very few of the latter today, though one or two had to be discarded for one reason or another, to their disappointment.

I then carried out a much more detailed inspection paying particular attention to general physique, hair, ears, eyes, chests, teeth, straight and clean limbs, and feet. The batch was then divided up on the ground into probables and possibles with one or two more discards having to go, mostly for flat feet.

But when I took stock of the situation I found that the probables still numbered well over three hundred and fifty, which was highly disconcerting with the actual Hunza allocation being two hundred and fifty. It was a great temptation to enlist the lot of these fine lads for I knew full well that this was just the material required for the new Corps of Scouts. But an outburst of inter-tribal jealousy could not be risked, and galling though it was I knew the numbers would have to be cut down eventually. Age was another factor which had to be taken into consideration. Normally the best age to catch a recruit for the Scouts is 17 to 18 years. But under the present circumstances, with prospects of a short training period followed by possible action, it was obvious that a backbone of the steadiness of more mature years was required; so I extended the age limit up to about 25 years, and even more in certain cases.

The next procedure was to make those still in the running walk and run out in front of me to watch straightness of action and co-ordination of limbs. Even after this, the strength of the probables was far too high, so I very reluctantly had to weed out to the ranks of the possibles. I then stamped each probable on the chest with a special stamp to which no one had access except me, for I was well aware of the multiplicity of deceit and swindling which could take place as soon as they had passed out of my direct control. A clerk then registered their particulars, including identification marks, in a ledger, and they were now ready for the proper medical inspection. The possibles were still retained for they would have to fill the vacancies of those who failed in their medical.

After a short break over lunch-time, when the two bands kept spirits and interest up with a programme of war songs, we started work again at 2.00 pm. Then Humayun Beg came into his own for, from past experience of his medical knowledge, I had selected him as official M.O. to the Scouts. He worked continuously throughout the afternoon, carrying out inspection after inspection and I was much impressed by his quiet efficiency and cheerfulness under all circumstances; for as the day wore on he must have become desperately tired. Shah Khan and I helped him with weights and measurements. The squads gradually grew into platoons to which instructors were attached for keeping the control which was most necessary. Any lapse in this connection at this stage would have resulted in utter confusion.

At about 7.00 pm, after five hours' steady work Humayun passed out the last man with a friendly smack on the back. We broke off for five minutes to smoke a cigarette and then by the light of hurricane-lanterns I took final stock. We had enlisted 250 first-class men of genuine Hunza descent, and 50 tough little Wakkhis, that loyal tribe of refugees from Afghanistan which inhabits Gujhal in the northern territory of Hunza between Gulmit and Misgar. I was very pleased, for the figures fitted my calculation perfectly.

The recruits were marched off in perfect order and were presently tucking into a good hot meal – their first as members of the Gilgit Scouts. We saw them fed

The End Game (November 1947 to January 1948) 245

with as much as they could eat, for there's nothing like a full belly to give good first impressions and to prevent grousing, which is inclined to start when conditions are not just as perfect as one could desire. Each man was then issued with a blanket and barrack-rooms were allotted to platoons. The bare boards had been covered with straw, which was the best we could do with no beds available. However the recruits were quite cheerful about it and were soon making preparations for the night, as they were all very tired after the long trek in to Gilgit from the remotest regions of the mountain fastness of Hunza, and from the general excitement of the day.

On the following day there was no recruiting for there was much work to be done in organizing the intake of the previous day. The Quarter Master's store was the first port of call where the capable Fida Ali and his well-trained staff were ready to issue uniform, such as it was. As already explained we had pitifully little to offer – a suit of grey and a pair of *chaplis*. But we gave each man the little silvered ibex crest to wear on the front of his *koi* and other deficiencies were soon forgotten in the first flush of pride at possessing the badge denoting membership of the Gilgit Scouts.

Permanent sections and platoons were then formed, and the whole batch put under the command of Jemedar Sardar Mohammed Ayub, the polo stalwart from Hunza. And for the first time in his service this Gushpur really showed that there was more in him than wielding the wild cherry wand. For in the afternoon I ordered him to take his three hundred merry men over to Konidas and put them through their first drill parade. I happened to see them as they returned through the bazaar in the early evening. Marching in column of threes behind the pipes and drums, they were striding out like veterans with arms swinging and heads high. On being dismissed, they continued voluntary practice at turning and marching on the football ground for about half an hour. Then, laughing and joking cheerfully amongst themselves, they doubled away to wash and prepare for roll-call and cookhouse.

The Nagir candidates were on parade on the morning of the 7th. They too had come in large numbers and what they lacked in physique and cleanliness they certainly made up in enthusiasm. Discards had perforce to be many, not in order to cut down numbers, but because the bulk of the lads just did not make the grade I required. Three hundred of which one hundred were first-class, one hundred mediocre, and one hundred slightly better than useless eventually lined up for the medical inspection in the afternoon.

I knew that at least one hundred would fail so I took the precaution of supervising each inspection personally. This was not because I doubted the capabilities of Humayun Beg, but because the Nagirwals would undoubtedly accuse him of failing them through tribal rivalry, with his home the other side of the river. But with me present there could be no dispute which might lead to trouble. As I had forecast, exactly one hundred went out, mostly with weak eyesight though there were also many cases of enlarged spleens and general debility. Two hundred made the grade and were marched off at 8.00 pm to swell the ranks of the new Gilgit Scouts. Again Jock and I reached home after midnight.

The spirit of Durand was with us, I am sure, when the Punialis kept tryst on 9 January – those tough mountaineers who had rallied to his standard so loyally in 1889 to form the nucleus of the original Gilgit Scouts. They lived up to their traditions all right and I had no difficulty in selecting one hundred first class men.

The job was finished earlier that night, and while Jock remained in the Lines to see that all was shipshape, I returned to my bungalow to write some reports. He returned about 10.00 pm. Entering my study, he threw his greatcoat over a chair and warmed his hands at the stove, for it was a bitterly cold night. He then turned round and nodding at the maps spread out on my table remarked,

"What's the next move?"

"Skardu!" I replied.

I continued. "On 30 December Aslam was due to arrive in a few days. It is now 9 January. He may come yet, but what if they have decided to keep us here? Reports from Burzil show that there is no possibility of an Indian expedition this way from the Bandipur direction till spring. So my plan is this. As soon as the arms have arrived and the young entry is capable of taking an aim, we shall secure Skardu. I reckon that should be by the end of the month at the latest. We're not safe here till it's in the bag. I should say that everything depends on whether the garrison has been reinforced yet by Sikh and Dogra troops from Leh. I sent Baktawar Shah off this afternoon to get this information and to discover whether reinforcements are en route. If none have arrived, or are likely to arrive in the near future, the task is just too easy. If the answer is otherwise, then some strategy is required; for we cannot afford to reduce the place by siege. From my reckoning that would take at least three or four months and it would be fatal to have our ill-spared troops bottled up there for such a long period."

"We could move one force from the Burzil Pass over the Deosai Plains and lie up secretly in the vicinity of Skardu. In the meantime another could move up the Indus from Haramosh. A bit of synchronization and both these detachments could crack in on the Fort to add the finishing touches as soon as the balloon went up."

I pulled up a message pad.

To: COLONEL BACON
From: BROWN

Re reorganization of Scouts many important decisions pending owing Aslam's non arrival – stop – therefore grateful estimated date of arrival Aslam as if not soon must make decisions self – stop – if policy is non embroilment of self and Mathieson against Indian troops suggest immediate removal as action not distant and as officers must perforce be involved – stop – due non arrival equipment situation becoming critical – stop – almost up to strength but still no clothing etc to issue – stop – if airdrop impossible imperative repeat imperative sent overland immediately otherwise failure probable.

I showed the draft to Jock. He nodded agreement. We encoded it and arranged for its dispatch by wireless in the morning.

In the early afternoon of 11 January we were busy recruiting the Kuh Ghizr contingent when a couple of Harvards droned overhead, circled, and returned down the valley to land on the airstrip. Presently the landing-ground picquet reported that a Colonel Pasha and a Major Nadir Shah had arrived, who I guessed would be Major Aslam Khan and Jock's relief respectively.

It was quite impossible for either I or Jock to go and meet them for if we had left the scene of operations at that stage a muddle would have set in which would have taken days to sort out. So I sent out Shah Khan with a message of explanation which I knew Aslam, as a soldier, would appreciate. I also informed Mohammed Alam, as he had agreed to put them up until I eventually vacated the Commandant's bungalow. We then continued work at full speed and by evening had increased the strength even further with a hundred sturdy lads from Kuh Ghizr.

On the way home that evening, we looked in at Agency House to meet Aslam, and on Mohammed Alam's kind invitation stayed to dinner.

Aslam rose as we entered and greeted us warmly. A man of middle age, short, stocky and clean-shaven, he was dressed in a neat-fitting battledress. The other officer, Nadir Shah or, more properly, Mohammed Khan, I discovered was Aslam's younger brother.

We did justice to an excellent dinner of mutton pilau and *chikor* curry and then returned to the cosy warmth of the drawing-room. Throughout the conversation that night I studied Aslam. There was no doubt regarding his capabilities as a military officer and leader. But he was a professional soldier – the man to lead regular troops in straightforward warfare where the only consideration was to overcome the enemy. This made me anxious, for as can be well appreciated a Lawrence was required as Commandant of the Gilgit Scouts rather than a Montgomery.

My anxiety was further increased as the night wore on for I realized that the quiet retiring subaltern I had known of old, had now become impetuous, hot-headed and ambitious. I appreciated that he would brook no interference with his decisions, which would probably be sound from a strictly military point of view but would have consideration for no other factor.

And so I foresaw that before very long there would be a clash of wills between Aslam and Mohammed Alam: it would be no mean clash either as both were strong men and unlikely to give way. I could see that Mohammed Alam's thoughts were running on the same lines as mine; on several occasions that night he looked at me with a mixture of alarm and appeal in his eyes. I remained seemingly indifferent. To have taken sides now would only have made matters worse though I determined I would do my best to help him later when a convenient opportunity arose.

A very pleasant surprise awaited me in the morning, for after breakfast Shawar Din announced that envoys had arrived from His Highness The Mehtar of Chitral and requested audience. They were duly ushered in and to my pleasure I discovered that the ambassador was an old friend of mine from the days of my sojourn in the State, and a close relative of His Highness himself.

From the letters he presented, I gathered that this was a goodwill mission to maintain our personal friendship and to establish cordial relations between Chitral State and the Gilgit Agency. It was a great achievement for I knew that peace was at last assured on the Northern Border and that there would be no further trouble in Kuh Ghizr and Yasin. Yet it was ironical that the envoys should have arrived on the very day I was due to have no more controlling interest in Central Asian affairs.

I was invited out to the garden to decide whether His Highness' gift was acceptable. A Chitrali lad was holding a handsome Badakshani stallion, caparisoned over the head and neck with brightly coloured cloth as is the custom of the country when giving a horse as a present. Pulling the cloth back, I patted the animal on the neck to signify acceptance. He was short and stocky with the lines of speed and handiness. The marking appealed to me for there was a prominent white blaze on the forehead and face which extended over the nearside eye, whilst the legs had three white socks. I named him Madaglasht after a delightful pine tree glade in the mountains above Chitral where I had camped for a week in a little log cabin beside a rushing mountain torrent, when the summer heat of Drosh became too oppressive. I took a liking to the pony immediately, but it was a bittersweet liking for I knew there was scarcely time to call him my own.

His Highness had also sent two beautiful Chitrali *chogas:* the Chitrali style is much more useful from a practical point of view, as the *choghasare* cut as fitted coats in comparison to the loose flowing cloaks of Gilgit.

I wrote a letter of thanks to the Mehtar and also informed him that this was the eve of my permanent departure. I assured him, however, that there was every prospect of the most cordial relations between his State and the Agency under the new Political Agent. After rewarding the mission with quantities of cartridges, cloth, and money according to their status and informing them that they were my guests throughout their stay in Gilgit, I took the notables along and introduced them to Mohammed Alam.

I met Aslam at Agency House and we walked down to the Lines together so that I could hand over charge to him. This was not difficult. I had written out long and comprehensive handing-over notes of current events, advice, and recommendations. I did not attempt to ram them down his throat; I merely gave them to him for what they were worth. The accounts and confidential files were in order, the Regimental Treasure Chest correct, and the magazine complete to the last round of ammunition.

At 12 noon on 12 January 1948 in the little office which I had known for almost five years, I signed away everything I had worked for – an unfinished ambition. I felt no personal regret. I felt sorry for the Scouts, for the Agency, and for Pakistan since I was being removed from this vital corner of the world at a time when I was most needed, because I was proving an embarrassment to the British Government which after all was directly responsible for the impasse between the two Dominions over the entire Kashmir and Gilgit Agency question.

"It's all yours now, Aslam, and I wish you the very best of luck," I said, when the charge reports were complete.

"I know you really mean that," he replied.

Aslam departed to have a talk with the Pakistan Officers.

Only two jobs of work remained for me.

First of all I made out a list of those who I considered were deserving of recognition for the outstanding part they had played during the revolt and aftermath. With each name, I gave a short citation of the services rendered. After ante-dating this list, I sent one copy to Mohammed Alam and retained one copy for the Pakistan Government.

Secondly there was the question of Subedar Jamshed of Hunza to settle. Old Champagne Charlie was en route to Gilgit from Chilas but he had not arrived. So I had been unable to settle his case before I handed over charge. I therefore wrote an ante-dated letter to Mohammed Alam, recommending that as soon as Jamshed arrived he should be asked whether he wished to serve on as an administrative Subedar or to retire on pension with the Honorary rank of Lieutenant.

As I signed, sealed, and dispatched it, Jock came in. We were both naturally rather glum and sat for a minute in gloomy abstraction. And then the pipes and drums struck up outside. They were playing a lilting Punjabi tune called Krishna which went with a fine swing yet had an air of sadness about it. Of all the local tunes, except the Zakhmi Dil, I liked "Krishna" best and as I had insisted on it being played on many an eventful occasion, the skirl brought back a host of memories grave and gay.

A vast crowd had collected, for entertainment was promised with many first-class players in town. Zaffar Khan of Nagir, the number one player of the Agency now that the Raja of Punial had retired, was there mounted on a raking bay. Shah Khan, Mohammed Ayub, Akbar Hussain, heir apparent to Kuh Ghizr, Mashruf, Mir Ahmed and Amir Ahmed the heavenly twins from Gilgit, were all booted and spurred, each an absolute master. Zaffar Khan and I made out the sides together, balancing skill against skill to ensure an even game though there really was little necessity for this with the material at our disposal. By mutual agreement it was decided to play full out for one hour without stopping, as our ponies were in the pink of condition. And what a game followed in the very best traditions of Gilgit polo! For an hour we swung the ball from one end of the ground to the other, ponies galloping flat out, the crowd roaring with excitement as though it were a Jalsa final, and the band playing fit to burst. The end of the hour saw the score 8 all. Another quarter of an hour, at the same gruelling' pace, failed to find a decision. So we decided to call it a day – one of the best days we had had for a long time. As the final fanfare sounded and we slipped from our saddles exhausted, the entire dais and a large portion of the wall collapsed in a welter of dust, stones, and spectators.

We players looked at one another. Was it an omen? Was polo doomed by changing conditions?

That night the Scouts gave us a farewell party to which Mohammed Alam, Aslam, and the local notables were also invited.

We were due to leave for Peshawar by plane on the following day; so in the morning I sold up house, or rather disposed of the effects, for buyers knew full well that I could not possibly transport my heavy kit down country and must sell at any price. Large quantities of crockery, kitchen utensils, stores of food, furniture, curtains, and carpets went for a song; I did not grudge it at the time for I was past worrying about such mundane matters. But looking back on it now I realize that I must have lost well over half a year's pay on the deal.

Then came the breaking up of the stud, one of the saddest tasks I know. I seem to have had to do this so many times in my life and every time is worse than before. Tadjik and Samarkand I sold to Aslam at the price I paid for them. They were his right as my successor, and though he got a real bargain, I had no regrets for I had certainly had my money's worth from the splendid pair. Roshan I decked out in a new saddle and bridle, with an embroidered saddle-cloth, and returned to the Raja of Gupis with my grateful thanks. The newly arrived Madaglasht I presented to the Mir of Hunza with every hope that he would turn out a good 'un. All my spare saddlery and stable equipment I gave to my head *sais* who had looked after my stable so well over the years. It was indeed a heartbreaking business.

We were fortifying ourselves with a rum after this sad job of work when a plane droned overhead. We waited for the second – five minutes, ten minutes, there was no appearance.

Enquiries from the landing-ground revealed that only one plane could be spared that day in which one of us would proceed to Peshawar. The other would be flown out on the following day. It was decided that Jock would go first; and I would wait for the next plane.

It was depressing staying among the bare boards of my own bungalow so I accepted Mohammed Alam's kind invitation and moved into the guest room at Agency House. Throughout the afternoon there was an endless flow of visitors to bid me farewells so that by evening I was quite exhausted and very ready for a refreshing cup of tea in front of the drawing-room fire with Mohammed Alam. We chatted idly in the cosy atmosphere, though I could tell that he viewed my departure with much misgiving and was much disturbed about the future, in particular with regard to relations with Aslam.

I turned in early that night. It was touching to note that the old bodyguard were waiting on the verandah to protect me during the night as of yore, though it was of course an entirely voluntary gesture now that I had handed over charge. So I fell asleep knowing that I was still in good hands.

At about 1.00 pm on 14 January a plane arrived for me. It was the signal for a general convergence on Agency House of the Scouts, notables, shopkeepers, and most of the local population to bid me farewell. I first of all said goodbye to my private servants and rewarded them well for their faithful services over the years. Of them, the trusty Shawar Din was the only one who would follow in my wake when there was a spare plane. Many tears were spilt and this did little to help me as I too was rapidly approaching that condition.

I then faced the multitude which insisted on accompanying me as far as the aerodrome. I protested, but it was useless, and by now I was in no condition to resist.

So I bade farewell to Mohammed Alam at the gate of Agency House and wished him the very best of luck. He was a brave little man and one whom I shall always respect and remember. Then mounting Madaglasht I rode off down the hill behind the pipes and drums of the Scouts playing the Zakhmi Dil. The vast throng followed behind in a cloud of dust.

At the crossroads by the hospital a solitary figure was standing, dressed immaculately in a grey pin-stripe suit. It was old Limbuwala. I halted.

"So you're away too, Major," he said.

I grasped him by the hand.

"Goodbye, Limbuwala, and good luck. Thanks a lot for all you have done."

"Goodbye, Major, don't mention it. It was a pleasure. Always at your service," and tears started streaming down his face.

The bazaar was packed with people pressing forward to shake me by the hand and to implore me to return. After a great deal of difficulty we managed to break through to

The End Game (November 1947 to January 1948)   251

the bridge. At the far side of the bridge I realized I could bear it no longer. There was a lump in my throat fit to choke me, and I felt that I would break down with pent-up emotion at any moment. So I let it be known that apart from a few particular friends, I would take leave of the remainder on Konidas. Again there was a murmur of protest, but mustering what willpower I had left, I insisted. I must have shaken hundreds of hands. Each face as it came forward brought back vividly some memory or other. It was an ordeal I never wish to go through again.

Formalities at the landing ground were cut as short as possible. I occupied myself during the flight by writing a continuation of my previous report on events in the Gilgit Agency for the British and Pakistan Governments. In the latter copy I added a tactful paragraph to the effect that a clash of wills between Mohammed Alam and Aslam seemed imminent, which would result in an intolerable and dangerous situation. I suggested that the answer might be to prepare a directive for both of them, in accordance with the policy which Pakistan intended pursuing in the Gilgit Agency.

We came down low over Chilas and I dropped a weighted message of farewell to Baber and the garrison there. I wonder if he ever got it.

As we debouched from the Indus gorges I finished writing the report. A glance at the dual petrol gauge gave me a shock, and I was much relieved to see that the pilot was making tracks for Risalpur, rather than attempting to make Peshawar. We touched down about 3.30 pm and the ground staff were soon busy refuelling. I jumped down and proceeded to a safe distance to smoke a cigarette. I noticed that the staff and hangers-on gazed at me in awe-struck amazement as though I had just stepped out of another world – which in fact I had after all. I suppose I did present a rather strange spectacle with a bushy black beard reaching almost to my chest, a fur hat crowned with the heron's crest, heavy cord riding-breeches, a short coat lined with camel's hair and high jackboots, both manufactured in Tashkent from soft Russian leather. There must have been much speculation as to who I was and what I was doing.

As the plane became airborne again and slowly gained height over the Peshawar Vale, bathed in the last of the afternoon sun, a great feeling of peace came over me, which brought to mind the lines from *Recessional*:

"The tumult and the shouting dies."

The mingled days of triumphs and setbacks, dangers and security, depression and gaiety, over which always hung the cloud of uncertainty, seemed far away in the aeons of past history now that I was free from the ceaseless vigilance of heavy responsibility. In piloting the ship of the Gilgit Agency through the formidable shoals and reefs of Partition, I had acted in the way I considered just and right. The long trick was over and she had reached the open sea safely, to embark on her maiden voyage in other hands. Success had been achieved, without a doubt, and the object of making this vital corner of the world, where the three Empires meet, an integral part of Pakistan, attained. The course had been a hard one for me, but I had won through thanks to the devotion and courage of those officers and tribes who throughout the difficult days had maintained an unswerving loyalty to me.

Appendix I

Precis of Recent Events in the Gilgit Agency (1 August to 16 November 1947)

[Immediately after the arrival in Gilgit on 16 November 1947 of the Pakistan Government administrator Sardar Mohammad Alam, Major Brown compiled the following report on the events which had resulted in the collapse of the power of the Government of the State of Jammu & Kashmir in this region. This document, along with those reproduced here in Appendices II & III, is to be found in the India Office Records, British Library, File IVP & S/13/1860.]

1. On the 1st of August, 1947, charge of the Gilgit Agency was handed over to the Kashmir State under the orders of the Government of India. A high ranking Hindu Jammu & Kashmir State Army officer was appointed as Governor who attempted to model his administration on that of the previous British Political Agents.
2. It soon became apparent that the whole country, from the Rulers of the small States of Hunza and Nagir down to the humblest villager, loathed this new regime, regarding it as Hindu domination, an understandable loathing in the light of the fact that the population of the Gilgit Agency is 100 per cent Muslim. However, the people seemed to be prepared to endure this new regime provided the State of Jammu & Kashmir acceded to Pakistan, but as time passed it became increasingly obvious that the sentiments of the Maharaja lay with Hindustan, for the following reasons:
   a. A new motor road was in the course of preparation, connecting Srinagar, the Kashmir capital, with Hindustan via Pathankot;
   b. Mr Kak, the State Prime Minister, had been dismissed. He was, although a Hindu, in favour of the accession to Pakistan;
   c. General Scott and Mr Powell, British State employees, who were Chief of the General Staff and Inspector General of Police respectively, resigned or were asked to resign, it being believed generally that their resignations came about owing to their pro-Pakistan leanings.
3. The situation in Gilgit became tense and the people more ostentatious in their claims to join Pakistan. Pakistan slogans were shouted in the streets and chalked on the walls and buildings and a general unrest set in amongst the Corps of Gilgit Scouts, the local militia, both in Gilgit and Chilas, one of the outposts. Major W.A. Brown, Gilgit Scouts, who was in close touch with his second in command, Captain A.S. Mathieson in Chilas, warned the Governor that the situation was becoming serious and daily placed all the facts before him. The Governor, however, paid little attention to these warnings either through mistrust of Major Brown or through stubbornness, probably the former as subsequent events showed.
4. About the beginning of October, there was a disturbance in the Lines of the 6th Kashmir State Infantry stationed at Bunji some thirty miles S.E. of Gilgit, which resulted in a clash between the Muslims and Sikh elements each shouting their respective slogans and all resorting to fighting amongst themselves without arms. The Colonel managed to bring the situation under control but not before the news had reached the Kashmir

capital, whence orders were received from Capt. Hussan, the commander of the Muslim company, to be sent to Srinagar under arrest. The Governor, after consulting the Colonel, managed to get this order annulled on the grounds that such an order would aggravate an already serious situation. Major Brown was not informed of this incident but later found out about it through an untrustworthy and incompetent assistant to the Governor.

5. Major Brown and Captain Mathieson soon realized that an underground movement was at work, the members of which, and the actual power of which, could not be ascertained. It seemed that certain local people, under the guise of pro-Pakistan activities, were aspiring to political power, but the strength of the movement could not be gauged accurately nor could it be considered dangerous.

6. The news of the accession of Kashmir to Hindustan was received quietly in most parts of the Agency, though the atmosphere in the Lines of the Gilgit Scouts and in the Gilgit bazaar was tense. In Chilas, however, the situation appeared to be serious and Captain Mathieson, who was in command there, informed Major Brown at Gilgit that he was finding it difficult to restrain the Scouts, who, backed by the locals, wished to declare for Pakistan and raise the Star and Crescent. Major Brown ordered Captain Mathieson to do his best to restrain the Scouts and to maintain law and order.

7. On the 28th of October, reports were received that the Wali of Swat had moved into Tangir and was marching up the Indus River to Chilas. Other reports were received that His Highness the Mehtar of Chitral was collecting an army at Mastuj with the intention of taking over the two political districts of Kuh Ghizr and Yasin as a step to annexing all the territory up as far as Gilgit.

8. The Governor called Major Brown and asked him for his advice. Major Brown once again impressed on the Governor the seriousness of the situation and suggested that before taking any action the Governor should ascertain from the Kashmir Government what their policy was towards places like Tangir, a matter in which he (the Governor) displayed complete ignorance. The Governor appeared quite apathetic and tried to make it clear to Major Brown that he was capable of dealing with any situation. It was obvious, however, that the Governor was losing confidence in himself and that his powers of appreciation and judgement were wavering.

9. On the evening of the 28th of October, a further message was received from Chilas to the effect that pro-Pakistan fervour was reaching an uncontrollable pitch.

    On the 29th of October, the Governor declined to discuss the situation with Major Brown. Another report was received from Chilas that unless something was done quickly the Scouts, populace and the people of Darel and Tangir would declare a holy war. Major Brown discussed the matter with Subedar Major Baber Khan of the Gilgit Scouts, who was not helpful but said that he had been in touch with the Rulers of Hunza and Nagir whose advice was to refrain from violence and to remain calm. This advice was passed on to Chilas. The situation in Gilgit was still tense but quiet.

10. On the 30th of October, the Governor showed that he was quite incapable of coping with the situation and it was clear that unless something was done quickly, the result would be bloodshed and chaos.

11. Major Brown went to the Governor and asked him whether he had received any reply from the Kashmir Government as to what policy should be adopted and was told that no reply had been received. Major Brown then gave the Governor a verbal appreciation of the situation as follows:
    a. that since the population of Gilgit was predominately Muslim, the people objected strongly to the fact that the Maharajah had acceded to Hindustan;

b. that Gilgit was slowly being surrounded by the Rulers of Swat and Chitral States, who had already acceded to Pakistan and that an attack in the guise of liberation of Gilgit was imminent; that there were not sufficient troops on this side of the Indus River to stem such an attack and that in the circumstances it was unlikely that the Scouts would take up arms against their brother Muslims fighting in the cause of Pakistan;
c. that the Frontier Premier's speech of the previous evening, declaring on behalf of all Pathans that they pledged all their support to liberate the people of Kashmir, had a profound affect on the people of Gilgit;
d. that the use of Indian troops in Kashmir to suppress the will of the people had shocked Muslims throughout the World and no less so in Gilgit;
e. that World opinion on broadcasts of the previous evening had hinted at tyranny in Kashmir;
f. that the people of Gilgit had lost all faith in the Governor because he, as a bastion of Hindu rule, was in no position to stem attacks from Swat and Chitral in the name of Islam, or to protect the Agency from other outside aggression;
g. that unless the Governor took some action on his own initiative, Gilgit would be plunged into a blood bath like Kashmir;
h. that the will of the people should be ascertained and the question of a referendum be considered, failing which serious trouble would be sure to follow;
i. finally, that failure to take action would result in chaos, either in the form of an invasion from outside or through an internal upheaval, i.e. a holy war, in the confusion of which military discipline and oaths of allegiance would be forgotten and Muslims on one side and Sikhs and Hindus on the other would fight with one another with tragic results.

The Governor appeared to agree generally with the above appreciation and he said he would put three questions immediately to the Mirs and Rajas:

(1) Do you and your people wish to accede to Pakistan?
(2) Do you and your people wish to accede to Hindustan?
(3) Do you wish your country to become Yaghistan?

12. On the evening of the 30th of October, Major Brown approached the Governor and asked him what action had been taken and was told that the Mir of Hunza had declared that he and his people were quite prepared to carry on under the present regime, that the Mir of Nagir was out shooting, and assuming that his answer would be the same as the Mir of Hunza the Governor had not troubled to contact him; that before ascertaining the wishes of the people of the political districts, he would prefer to discuss the matter with the Raja of Gilgit who was in Gilgit the following day.

Major Brown, knowing the sentiments of the Hunza people, considered the reply incredible and contacted the Mir of Hunza on the telephone through the Subedar Major, who, speaking in the Hunza language, explained the whole situation to the Mir. The Mir in reply stated that neither had the Governor spoken to him on the subject nor had he ever expressed a desire to carry on under the present regime. The telephone line was tapped by the Governor who, although not understanding the Hunza language, must have realized the purport of the call.

13. On the 31st of October, Major Brown informed the Governor that he had advised and helped him to the best of his ability but since the Governor disregarded his advice, he could not be responsible in any way for subsequent events and he might be compelled to take steps on his own initiative to maintain law and order and to prevent bloodshed.

14. That same day the Gilgit wireless operator, Mr Limbuwala, showed Major Brown a message from the Mehtar of Chitral breaking off all relations with the Kashmir State and saying that neither his State nor Gilgit could accept the accession to Hindustan.

Appendix I   255

15. On the evening of the 31st of October, Major Brown was warned that an attempt on his life was contemplated by the local Sikhs at the instigation of the Governor. Major Brown left his house by the back entrance and made his way to the Scouts by a devious route. As he left his house, he noticed several armed Sikhs moving round the wall of his garden.
16. The situation in the bazaar was serious. Armed bands of Muslims and Sikhs were roaming about the bazaar and people were pouring in from the surrounding villages. The Mullahs had preached Holy War (Jehad) at the evening prayers, exhorting the people to kill the Governor and all Sikhs and Hindus.
17. On arrival at the Scouts Lines, Major Brown was told that an attempt had been made on the life of Subedar Major but had been forestalled. At about 6 pm the Subedar Major had been called to the Governor house but fortunately, as he was about to leave, he was warned that a band of Sikhs was lying in ambush for him.
18. At about 7 pm a report was received that some Sikhs were about to enter the Scouts Lines and blow up the magazine. Precautions were taken and several Sikhs were noticed retreating from various points round the perimeter wall. Subsequent searches proved the report to be correct and large quantities of primed guncotton and gelignite were found in possession of the Sikhs.
19. On the same day, the 31st of October, a message was received from Chilas that a declaration of a Holy War was about to be made by the Scouts and the local people unless an accession to Pakistan was made immediately.
20. Major Brown then appreciated the situation, which was very grave, and decided that it was his duty to prevent wanton destruction of life and property. He issued the following orders:
    a. one Platoon under the Subedar Major to proceed to the Governor's house and ask him to come to the Scouts Lines for protection: the Subedar Major had a letter to this effect;
    b. one Section to take over the Post and Telegraph office to ensure that telegrams likely to create panic were not sent;
    c. two Sections to be sent to the wireless operator's house to protect him and his set;
    d. one Platoon to be sent to the Bhup Singh Pari on the road to Bunji to prevent any movement towards Gilgit;
    e. one Section each to the Basin and Gilgit bridges;
    f. two Platoons to be sent from Chilas to hold the Partab Pul bridge over the Indus River and to occupy Jaglote;
    g. patrols to move about in the vicinity of the Gilgit bazaar to prevent looting and to reassure the people: sentries to be posted on the Hindu quarters;
    h. the remaining strength was to stand by as a mobile reserve and all permanent guards were doubled.
21. The repercussions to these orders will now be explained.
    Order (a). The Platoon visited the Governors House which seemed deserted. It was bright moonlight. The Platoon halted in the garden and the S.M. [Subedar Major] and another Scout officer entered the house, calling on the Governor to come forward. Receiving no reply, a systematic search of the house was begun. When he [the Scout officer] entered the Governor's bedroom, he [the Governor, Ghansara Singh] flashed a torch on the Scout and opened fire on them with a rifle. The Scouts retreated outside and the Governor taking up a position at a window fired a fusillade into killing one and wounding another. The Scouts then took up a tactical position around the house and firing from both sides continued. Being bright moonlight, there was no excuse for the Governor to think that he was being attacked by bandits.

By this time about a thousand locals armed with guns, swords and axes, had arrived in the vicinity of the Governors House and both the Scouts and the locals demanded an immediate rush on the house with the object of setting it on fire and murdering the Governor and the other occupants in revenge for the killing of the Scout sepoy. The Subedar Major, however, displaying considerable calmness and control, steadied the crowd and prevented an unfortunate incident. During a temporary lull in the firing, the S.M. moved forward and tried to persuade the Governor that the Scouts had come for his protection and that he should come out at once as the mob was after his blood. This announcement was answered by another fusillade followed by weird animal noises from which it appeared that the Governor was out of his senses. Later he took to firing through the roof and breaking up the interior of the bungalow. During a burst of fire by the Governor the Office Superintendent, who for some unaccountable reason was in the vicinity of the bungalow, was hit in the back and died instantly. A machine-gun was fired high to force the Governor into submission before further loss of life or destruction of property, but in vain. Major Brown therefore ordered a cease-fire and posted the Platoon round the bungalow to wait for first light. Through the S.M. he managed to move the local mob down to the Polo Ground, where a relative of the Raja of Gilgit, ex-Subedar Shah Rais Khan, a man of considerable influence, managed to pacify them. At first light the Governor surrendered and was taken to the Scouts Lines and put under protective custody, with full respect to his rank and position. His appearance suggested madness. The fact that he reached the lines safely reflects great credit on the S.M. and the Scouts.

Order (b). Carried out without incident. Telephone lines in both directions had to be cut but were repaired later when the situation came under control.

Order (c, d, e & h). Carried out without incident.

Order (f). Captain Mathieson was informed of the situation and agreed with Major Brown that the only way to prevent chaos was to abide by the will of the people. All non-Muslims were collected in the fort at Chilas, as the local population, irresponsible enough in normal times, were seething for a Holy War. With admirable foresight, Captain Mathieson sent messages to the various valleys of Chilas and Darel Tangir, exhorting the people to remain calm and not to do anything without a message from him. It says much for the courage and personality of this officer and that of the local Assistant, Muzaffaradin Shah, that the fanatical tribesmen of this part of tribal territory (Yaghistan) were held in check. Captain Mathieson, with a firm hand crushed the looting of the Chilas bazaar and then dispatched his men according to orders. He himself remained at his post at Chilas and did his best to maintain law and order. A declaration in favour of Pakistan was accepted as a fait accompli by Captain Mathieson, the alternative being a Holy War.

Order (g). It has been proved conclusively in the light of subsequent event that this order prevented the wholesale massacre of all non-Muslims in Gilgit.

22. On the 1st of November at first light, Major Brown, accompanied by his Adjutant, Lieut. Ghulam Haider, toured the affected area. It was obvious that Hindu rule in Gilgit had come to an end. At least two or three thousand people, armed with anything from modern sporting rifles to daggers were gathered on the Polo Ground shouting Pakistan slogans and demanding immediate accession and the murder of the Governor and non-Muslims. At least another thousand were patrolling the streets in the blood-thirsty excitement restrained only by the influence of the Scouts. The whole Corps of Scouts from the States' officers attached and the S.M. down to the latest joined recruit were pro-Pakistan and nobody in the world could have made them fire a round in defence of the Hindu regime. This fact, coupled with the knowledge that the Rulers of Hunza and Nagir and the political

Appendix I 257

districts were pro-Pakistan, convinced Major Brown that his theories were correct and the only solution was to abide by the will of the people and so avoid unnecessary bloodshed.

23. All non-Muslims were rounded up for their own protection and put into a refugee camp in the Scout Lines. The number of weapons and instruments of a dangerous nature found among them was remarkable and there were explosives sufficient to have caused considerable damage to life and property.

24. Major Brown then reinforced the Scouts at the Bhup Singh Pari, posted guards on all officer's houses and intensified patrolling in the Gilgit Area. One Platoon was sent from Gupis to Yasin to prevent any of the disgruntled elements there harming the Governor. He then called a conference of the Adjutant, S.M. and ex-Subedar Shah Rais Khan, who through his strong personality and his influence in Gilgit had done so much to restrain the locals from violence.

25. The results of the conference were extremely interesting. The suspicions of both British officers regarding an underground pro-Pakistan movement proved to be correct. Those attending the conference now made clear to Major Brown what had been afoot.

    The movement comprised: Captain Hussan (Kashmir State Forces), Captain Mohammed Said (attached Gilgit Scouts), Lieut. Ghulam Haider (attached Gilgit Scouts – this officer was working for Pakistan only and had no personal ambitions, as had the others), Subedar Major Mohammed Baber Khan (Gilgit Scouts), ex-Subedar Shah Rais Khan, plus 80 per cent of the Indian Officers of the Gilgit Scouts and 70 per cent of the other ranks.

26. The scheme of the underground movement was that the Muslim element of the 6th Kashmir Infantry in Bunji, the Scouts and the people of Gilgit Sub-division should declare a Jehad in favour of Pakistan and, having murdered all non-Muslims up to the Burzil Pass, should set up an independent State comprising the former Gilgit Agency and Astore, with all political power in their own hands, backed by the Scouts and the Muslim elements of the 6th Kashmir Infantry. Scouts not willing to serve should be dismissed, and others should be enlisted from the Gilgit Subdivision.

27. To oppose the wishes of this party on the 1st of November would have been suicidal. Major Brown therefore accepted the situation and helped to maintain law and order and advised all concerned to avoid any resort to violence.

28. Major Brown then persuaded the wireless operator to send a message to the Prime Minister of the North West Frontier Province at Peshawar that a coup d'état in favour of Pakistan had taken place in Gilgit and that a provisional Government had been set up. In reply Major Brown was informed that his message had been passed to higher authority and that in the meantime he should help to maintain law and order.

29. Meanwhile, there had been the following developments in Bunji. On the 31st of October, about 300 (75 per cent) of the Muslim State troops there left for Gilgit under one of their officers, Captain Hussan. This force met the Scouts detachment on the 1st of November at the Bhup Singh Pari and made it clear to them that they repudiated all allegiance to the Maharaja and intended killing all the Hindu and Sikh soldiers who had remained with the Battalion at Bunji. A message was then sent by this force in the name of Governor ordering all Hindu and Sikhs from Bunji to proceed to Gilgit to stamp out a revolution, the idea being to ambush them on the way. The plan, however, miscarried.

30. On the 1st of November the Commanding Officer from Bunji, Lt. Col. Abdul Majid, moved towards Gilgit, having locked the magazine and pocketed the key. The disposition of the Bunji Battalion on the 1st of November was:

    Colonel Abdul Majid and Captain Hussan with 300 Muslim troops on route to Gilgit;
    Captains Mohammed Khan, Baldev Singh, Sehdev Singh and Ranghunat Singh with Sikh and Hindu troops numbering about 300 on the left bank of Indus in Bunji with picquets at the Partab Pul Bridge and at Jaglote.

The keys of the magazine were in the Colonel's pocket. An interesting fact is that on the night of the 31st of October, as soon as the shooting started in Gilgit, a man named Naib Khan crossed the Gilgit bridge and made his way to Bunji by the left bank of the river with the obvious intention of warning the garrison that a revolution had taken place in Gilgit.

31. On the morning of the 2nd of November at 9 am the Pakistan Flag was raised on the tower in the Scout's Lines in Gilgit with all due ceremony and amidst great rejoicing. The ceremony was followed by prayers, dancing and festivities, but was cut short when it was realized that the crowd was getting out of hand.

32. To ensure continuity in the administration, the leaders of the underground movement formed themselves into a Provisional Government consisting of
President: ex-Subedar Shah Rais Khan,
C-in-C: Captain Hussan,
C.G.S.: Captain Mohammed Said,
Commissioner: Lieut. Ghulam Haider,
Chief of Police: Sub-Inspector Hamid.

It was agreed that all matters of importance should be referred to this Cabinet. This sounded all very well in theory but it was in fact useless in practice since the aim of each member was to gain power for himself. Major Brown pointed out the futility of attempting to form an Independent State of Gilgit and that the affiliation to Pakistan was the only way to ensure the future prosperity and safety of the country.

33. At this stage, a certain Mullah in a fanatical address urged the people to kill all non-Muslims in general and Major Brown in particular. But for the timely intervention of ex-Subedar Shah Rais Khan, a regrettable incident might have taken place. This Mullah was instructed in no uncertain terms that he had better refrain from such exhortations.

34. The 3rd passed without incident. Under the guidance of Major Brown the general administration started again, telephone lines were repaired, and the conditions seemed normal. In the evening Major Brown telephoned the Mirs of Hunza and Nagir and reassured them that all was well. They both expressed their wholehearted desire on behalf of these States to accede to Pakistan and requested that this information should be forwarded to higher authority by Major Brown. This was done. The Governors of Kuh Ghizr and Yasin sent similar messages.

35. On the 4th Gilgit seemed quite normal. Crowds ceased to collect in the streets, the bazaar was open and the people went about their normal work. A certain undercurrent was however apparent. Those who had in no way assisted in the coup d'état made it clear that they too wanted jobs in the Provisional Government, and the old bad feeling between Sunnis and Shias raised its head again. Intrigue and local party rivalry were at work.

In the afternoon the son of the Raja of Punial arrived with a written instruction of accession to Pakistan signed by the Raja.

36. At about 6 pm Major Brown received a message from Captain Mathieson which made it clear that messages had not been getting through and that Captain Mathieson was held up in Theliche for lack of information on the general situation. Major Brown accompanied by the Subedar Major left Gilgit at 7 pm, arriving at Jaglote at 11 pm to find it deserted, and at Theliche at 1 am on the 5th. An immediate exchange of information took place.

37. It seemed that the patrol left Chilas at 5 am on the 1st of November. It consisted of one Indian [local] Officer and 60 rifles with one machine-gun. Arriving in the vicinity of Jaglote during the night 2/3rd November communication was established with the local ex-Scouts of that area from whom the strength and habits of the Sikh and Hindu garrisons at Jaglote and Partab Pul were ascertained. The strength at Jaglote was one Hindu Subedar and 12 Sikh Sepoys, and 8 Sikh Sepoys at Partab Pul. The Indian Officer

in charge of the Scouts patrol appreciated the situation and made the following plan. At first light the ex-Scouts should seize the ferry boat at Jaglote and move it downstream. In the meantime half the patrol under a Havildar should be in position above Partab Pul whilst the other half under the Indian Officer and covered by the machine-gun should take up a position close to Jaglote Chowki. At first light the Sikh and Hindu garrisons should be called upon to surrender and both positions should be occupied.

The operation went according to the plan. Both garrisons refused to surrender and heavy fire was brought to bear on the Scouts. One Hindu Subedar and 7 other ranks were killed from Jaglote garrison as the Scouts moved in and captured the Chowki by force. Three other ranks escaped. They were later killed by the locals. The Scouts lost one killed and one wounded. The engagement lasted little over an hour. At Partab Pul, 6 other ranks of the garrison were killed or committed suicide by jumping into the river. Two managed to escape and took the news to Bunji. Scouts casualties were nil. Not long after the Scouts patrol occupied the bridge at Partab Pul, a large body of Sikhs appeared moving from the direction of Bunji. The patrol commander realizing what havoc would ensure should these Sikhs cross the river and enter Gilgit, set the bridge on fire, partially destroying it. This action undoubtable saved the situation.

38. On the 2nd of November at 6.30 am Captain Mathieson set off with a reserve patrol of 50 rifles and reached Theliche at 7 am on the 3rd. Major Brown had not issued orders to hold the Ramghat Bridge, as he had been informed by the C-in-C of the Provisional Government that Muslim troops from Bunji had already done this. However, when Captain Mathieson arrived at Theliche he found that Ramghat was not held, so he immediately sent two sections there via the Raikot bridge and the left bank of the Indus. Positions were occupied on the 4th when it was discovered that the bridge had been burnt and was impassable. It has not been discovered who destroyed the bridge, though it must have been done by locals. Captain Mathieson then fortified Theliche and made medium machine-gun positions to cover the track from Bunji to Ramghat on the far side of the river and awaited further orders.

39. On the morning of the 5th of November, Major Brown and Captain Mathieson carried out a reconnaissance and saw about 150 Sikhs on the far side of the river climbing on to the bridge between Ramghat and Shaitan Nalas. In order to prevent this and in order that the Sikhs should not escape, fire was brought to bear on them in the hope that they would double back. The range was however too long and the fire had no affect. An immediate message was sent to the C-in-C at Jaglote explaining the situation and requesting an extra Scouts platoon and an medium machine-gun The C-in-C declined to grant the request. Had he done so it is probable that the whole Sikh force would have been wiped out or forced into surrender by the end of the day.

40. Meanwhile the C-in-C was planning a frontal attack on Bunji from Jaglote with the Scouts and Muslim troops of the Bunji Battalion. These troops had moved up from the Bhup Singh Pari and the first Chilas patrol was also with him. Such an attack would have been disastrous. Fortunately it was not necessary as a message was received from Bunji that the Sikh and Hindu troops had during the night left Bunji and taken to the hills. Rafts were then collected and the C-in-C and his force crossed the Indus and occupied Bunji without resistance.

41. As soon as Major Brown heard the news, he had with Captain Mathieson and the Subedar Major moved up to Jaglote from Theliche, having received no reinforcements or supporting weapons. After encouraging the Scouts at Jaglote whose morale was fair, and ordering the disposal of the Sikh corpses, Major Brown and Captain Mathieson moved across to Bunji. In Bunji there was general confusion but the C-in-C acting on advice of Major Brown arranged perimeter protection for the night. Desultory sniping continued

260   Gilgit Rebellion

throughout the night from the Sikhs in positions in the hills above the camp. There were no casualties. Major Brown talked to all the Scouts present, encouraging them and reassuring them, with the result that morale very soon rose.

42. During the night the two British Officers pointed out to the C-in-C that it was essential to round up all the Sikhs and Hindus so that all the troops would be ready for action in the event of help being sent from Kashmir. Major Brown suggested that a 3" Mortar should be sent to Ramghat and an medium machine-gun to Theliche. Under covering fire from these two weapons, an attack could be made on the Sikhs on the Shaitan Nala ridge at first light and as they would be trapped, they would have to surrender. Also during the night a patrol should be sent to quietly get behind the Sikhs in position above Bunji so that they would be caught in the rear when frontally attacked at first light. Unfortunately the C-in-C did not act on this advice. Had he done so, it is probable that all the Sikhs and Hindus with their arms and ammunition and supporting weapons would have been captured that day. The result of the delay was that some of the Sikhs got through to Astore and over the Burzil Pass to Srinagar. Others destroyed their arms and took to the hills to die of exposure and starvation. Others ravaged local villages in attempts to get rations, and a small percentage surrendered but without arms and ammunition.

43. On the morning of the sixth, Major Brown, Captain Mathieson and the Subedar Major crossed to Jaglote and after arranging rations and amenities for the Scouts there proceeded to Gilgit. Along with their staff and a mounted escort they were given a triumphal welcome then they arrived at Gilgit late in the evening.

44. The situation in Gilgit was unsatisfactory. On the 5th Lieut. Ghulam Haider, seeing how intrigue and faction feelings were increasing had sent a wireless message to the Prime Minister of the North West Frontier Province, and to Lt.-Col. Bacon, Political Agent Khyber, requesting the latter to fly to Gilgit immediately.

45. Major Brown, ably assisted by Captain Mathieson, worked out schemes for the defence of the country in the event of an invasion from Kashmir or from the air. As many tactical positions as possible were occupied with the strength at their disposal. The ammunition from Bunji was dispersed in the various picquets in Gilgit, as was the patrol supply, to ensure reserves in the event of air bombardment. The morale of the Scouts was high and all were in good spirits. Daily meetings of the so- called Cabinet were held but for reasons already given it was with the greatest of difficulty that a decision could be reached on any point. The civil administration however, seemed able to prevent complete chaos and this was due to Lieut. Ghulam Haider who had been appointed Commissioner in the Provisional Government. He did his best in a job with which he was completely unfamiliar.

46. It soon became apparent that such a state of affairs could not last indefinitely. Major Brown and Captain Mathieson did their best to keep the peace between the various political aspirants but in spite of all efforts it seemed that a state of anarchy would be the outcome as the people began to doubt whether Pakistan was prepared to accept the accession of Gilgit. Eventually all agreed that unless a Pakistan representative arrived there was going to be trouble. The two British officers, realizing this danger only too well, sent a wireless message to Colonel Bacon at Peshawar on the 13th of November saying that they could not keep the peace for ever owing to excessive internal intrigue and that it was imperative that he or another representative should come to Gilgit immediately, as even a short visit would do much to reassure the people.

47. On the 14th of November Major Brown received a message from the Prime Minister [of the North West Frontier Province] at Peshawar that a representative was being sent at once with instructions. The message was received with immense relief and on the 16th Khan Sahib Mohammad Alam arrived to take over the duties of the Political Agent.

Appendix II

A Short Note on Current Events in Gilgit

[Soon after his relief from command of the Gilgit Scouts in January 1948, Major Brown compiled this short note, later amplified in the document printed here below as Appendix III.]

At a conference in Rawalpindi on the 3rd December 1947, at which the premier of Pakistan (Liaquat Ali Khan) presided, and at which the other members present were Colonel Iskander Mirza, Defence Secretary of the Pakistan Government, Colonel R.N. Bacon, P.A., Khyber, (ex P.A. Gilgit) and Major W.A. Brown, Commandant Gilgit Scouts, the following decisions were reached:

a. that the entire territory of the Gilgit Agency should be held by Pakistan at all costs against possible invasion by the Indian Army;
b. that in order to achieve this, the present strength of the Gilgit Corps of Scouts (i.e. 600) should be increased to 1500 (i.e. an additional 900);
c. that the Muslim element of the 6th Kashmir Infantry should be organized as a separate Azad Forces Unit, to be used as a possible striking force as and when the situation may demand, and should in no way be connected with the Gilgit Scouts;
d. that all ex-Kashmir Army officers in Gilgit should immediately join this Azad Forces Unit, and should assist in the formation of said striking force;
e. that certain deserving Local Officers of the Gilgit Scouts should be granted Pakistan Commissions.

On his return to Gilgit, Maj. W.A. Brown based and proceeded with his future programme in accordance with those orders. Pakistan Commissions were given to the two most deserving Local Officers and large-scale recruitment commenced.

Towards the end of December, the Political Agent Gilgit received a message from Norwef [North West Frontier] to the effect that Major W.A. Brown, Commandant Scouts, and Capt. A.S. Mathieson, 2i/c Scouts, would shortly be relieved by Major Aslam Khan and Captain Mohammed Khan, respectively.

On the 10th January, the two relieving officers arrived in Gilgit under nomenclature of Col. Pasha and Major Nadir Shah respectively.

Complete charge of the Gilgit Scouts and allied matters was duly handed over by Major W.A. Brown to Major Aslam, alias Colonel Pasha, on 12th January, with full information given and received.

Having taken over charge of Gilgit Scouts, Major Aslam, alias Colonel Pasha, then made it clear to all that he had come to Gilgit as a representative of the Azad Kashmir Government, and that he intended taking supreme command of all armed forces in the area. It is understood that he produced credentials to P.A. Gilgit which had been received by him from, and signed by, the Azad Kashmir Government.

262 Gilgit Rebellion

Colonel Pasha's immediate action after taking supreme command was as follows:

a. he declared that the Gilgit Scouts and the Muslim element of the 6th Kashmir Infantry would be amalgamated as one force;
b. he recalled all the remaining ex-Kashmir Army Officers from Bunji to Gilgit;
c. he gave certain of these officers command over the Gilgit Scouts under his amalgamation scheme;
d. he declared that this force would be entirely independent of the P.A. Gilgit;
e. he gave out preliminary warning orders for the removal of the entire Corps of Scouts from Gilgit Agency to Bunji;
f. he made it quite clear that the intended role of the Gilgit Scouts was of an offensive, and not defensive, nature, his plan being that one third of the entire force should capture and hold Skardu, whilst the remainder should advance on and capture Bandipur [about forty miles north west of Srinagar by the Wular Lake].

If the above is in accordance with the policy of the Pakistan Government, then the matter need not be discussed further, but, as shown in comparison with the decisions of the Rawalpindi conference, if it conflicts with the policy of the Pakistan Government, the matter is forwarded herewith for information, with the remarks that continuation of Colonel Pasha's present policy may have unfortunate repercussions. It is pointed out that the decisions reached at the Rawalpindi conference were done so after full consideration of the peculiar political as well as strategic conditions prevalent in the Gilgit Agency. Under the aforesaid conditions, the position of the Political Agent, Gilgit is being jeopardized to the extent of being almost untenable.

It may also be of interest to the Pakistan Government that on the 14th January, a British Air Force Officer, one Flight Lieutenant Lester, arrived in Gilgit from Risalpur, bringing with him a No. 19 wireless set, with which it is Colonel Pasha's intention to establish wireless contact between Gilgit and Risalpur, and Gilgit and the Azad Forces in Kashmir. It is not known if this was done with the concurrence of the Pakistan Government.

Appendix III

Precis of Events in Gilgit Since the Arrival of Sardar Mohammed Alam, Political Agent (16 November 1947 to 14 January 1948)

[Major Brown wrote this report in late January 1948 to amplify the narrative outlined in Appendix II above.]

On the 16th November, 1947, Sardar Mohammed Alam arrived in Gilgit bearing letters from the Pakistan Government to the effect that he had been appointed Political Agent of the Gilgit Agency. He was given an enthusiastic welcome by the local population and escorted in triumph to the Agency House. In a few well chosen words he exhorted the people to cast aside their faction feeling and to unite as one in the cause of Islam. This short speech was greeted with further bursts of enthusiasm before the crowd gradually dispersed.

On the 17th November at 9.30 am the Pakistan flag was hoisted on the flag pole at the Agency House whilst a Guard of Honour from the Gilgit Scouts paid full honours and the pipes and drums played the Royal Salute. Large crowds turned out to watch the ceremony and the intense approval of all was very noticeable. After a short speech by the Political Agent, Sardar Mohammed Alam, on the lines of the previous day, there was dancing and other festivities as is the custom of the country on joyous occasions, and the happy atmosphere in contrast to the tension of the past fortnight was very marked. During the afternoon Major W.A. Brown and Captain A.S. Mathieson gave Sardar Mohammed Alam a brief description of conditions in the Agency and of the events which led up to the coup d'état and aftermath. They also handed over to him the confidential files and papers which they had kept in safe custody during the time of the provisional Government.

On the 18th November the Political Agent accompanied by Major W.A. Brown and local notables inspected the Agency offices, hospital, Scout Lines, bazaar and other public institutions and the manner in which he was greeted at each left little doubt as to the sentiments of the people. He seemed somewhat astonished that the entire place was intact and that the bazaar was functioning normally with Muslims Sikhs and Hindus living in communal harmony whilst the various departments carried on the general administration as usual. In the afternoon the Mirs of Hunza and Nagir and the Governors of Punial, Kuh Ghizr, Ishkoman and Yasin arrived in Gilgit in response to a call made by Major W.A. Brown on the suggestion of Lt. Col. Bacon when Sardar Mohammed Alam's departure for Gilgit was announced. Captain Mirza Hussan also arrived from Bunji.

The latter lost no time in assembling the so called Cabinet of the Provisional Government who it seems were by this time prepared to forego their personal ambitions and accept the establishment of the Agency by Pakistan. It should be noted that Lieut. Ghulam Haider refused to attend this meeting. It is understood that Captain Mirza Hussan pointed out to the members of the Cabinet that their entire hopes of political supremacy had been thwarted by the arrival of Sardar Mohammed Alam and that to accept his power as Political Agent was their swan song. After further exhortations he managed with the able help of Captain Mohammed Said to sway the other rather reluctant members over to his side and the following nefarious plot was hatched.

On the following day the Provisional Government should announce the fact that it still held paramount power in Gilgit despite the arrival of Sardar Mohammed Alam, and that the latter should take no step or make any decision without the approval of the members of the Cabinet. It was also agreed that Lieut. Haider should be removed from his position of Commissioner and that Wilayat Ali of Nagir should be appointed in his place. Finally it was agreed that Major WA. Brown and Captain A.S. Mathieson should be removed from their appointments of Commandant Scouts and Assistant Commandant Scouts respectively and that to ensure that this was fulfilled the Gilgit Scouts should be informed immediately that on the following day the two officers concerned should not be paid their due respect and should be denied access to the Scout Lines. However, the loyalty of the Gilgit Scouts to their Commandant and Assistant Commandant ensured the complete miscarriage of this dastardly scheme and on the following day allegiance never wavered.

On the 18th November the Mirs of Hunza and Nagir and the Governors of Punial, Kuh Ghizr, Ishkoman and Yasin were introduced to Sardar Mohammed Alam by Major W.A Brown, and successful interviews were completed in the course of which both Mirs signed Instruments of Accession to Pakistan. The Governors expressed their sincerest loyalty to Pakistan on behalf of themselves and their people and the interviews concluded in an atmosphere of cordiality and good will.

In the afternoon the so-called Cabinet of the Provisional Government requested and was granted an interview with Sardar Mohammed Alam. The members lost no time in telling the Political Agent that the Provisional Government still held complete power in Gilgit and that he must not only consult it before making any decision but must also accept whatever recommendation was put up to him by it. Led by Captain Mirza Hussan and Captain Mohammed Said, with the other members rather reluctantly concurring, the recommendation was then put forward that Major W.A. Brown and Captain A.S. Mathieson should be removed from their appointments immediately, and the two spokesmen appointed in lieu. They strengthened their recommendation by saying that if it was not accepted they would instigate chaos in Gilgit. Sardar Mohammed Alam then made it quite clear to this bunch of trouble-makers that so long as he was in Gilgit his word was paramount and that under no circumstances would he be dictated to by the Provisional Government or any other unrecognized Government. He continued that he had not the slightest intention of even considering the removal of Major Brown and Captain A.S. Mathieson as both were officers for whom he held the highest respect and who, he considered, had devoted the utmost disinterested service in the welfare of the Gilgit Agency, and the cause of Pakistan. He sarcastically compared the two British Officers to the ambitious political aspirants with whom he was holding an interview. Sardar Mohammed Alam concluded by saying that if the Provisional Government wished to remain in power or contemplated instigating trouble in Gilgit the solution was very easy. He, along with the British Officers, would leave immediately and the Gilgit Agency would be left to its own fate. He pointed out, however, that in the event of this taking place it would not be long before faction feeling would reduce the country to internal strife whereupon interested parties outside would take the opportunity of annexing the whole area.

The members of the Provisional Government appeared to have overlooked this possibility as they then earnestly requested the Political Agent not to leave under any circumstance. It was obvious that the Political Agent had conducted the interview in such a way that he now held the whip hand and the Provisional Government departed realizing that it was powerless. The strong position adopted by Sardar Mohammed Alam showed that he was not a man to be trifled with and resolved an awkward problem once and for all and in such a way that repercussions were impossible.

It seems that in a last vain attempt to regain their position the members of the Provisional Government approached the Mir of Hunza with the request that he would put their case up to the Political Agent. From all accounts the Mir of Hunza declined to talk to them but sent out a message that they had better leave his garden immediately or he would order his bodyguard to throw them out. This was the last that was heard of the Provisional Government.

In the evening Sardar Mohammed Alam called Major WA. Brown and Capt. A.S. Mathieson and explained to them about the interview in the afternoon. Major W.A. Brown explained to Sardar Mohammed Alam that the most important task at the moment was to get the condition of the Scouts back to normal and to eradicate the unsteadying effects caused by their first operation. In order to do so it was essential that the ringleaders of all the trouble, Captain Hussan and Captain Mohhamed Said, and other Muslim officers of the 6th Kashmir Infantry should be sent across the Indus to Bunji and not be allowed to enter the Gilgit Agency without the Political Agent's permission. It was feared that the low morale and bad discipline of the Muslim element of the 6th Kashmir Infantry might prove a bad influence on the Scouts under the present difficult circumstances, so it was suggested that these troops should also be sent to Bunji under the same conditions as the officers.

It was also pointed out that the condition of the Sub-division was somewhat unstable and that to prevent a regrettable incident it was essential that a strong personality should be appointed Raja [of Gilgit], who would control the people and who could be held responsible in the event of an uprising of any sort. It was pointed out that the present Raja, Raja Jaffar Kahn, was useless, so it was suggested that he might be asked to retire honourably and ex-Subedar Shah Rais Khan, an individual who certainly held the necessary qualifications, be appointed in his place. The Political Agent agreed to give the suggestions due consideration.

On the 19th November Sardar Mohammed Alam held a conference at which Major W.A. Brown, Captain A.S. Mathieson, the Mirs of Hunza and Nagir, Captain Hussan, Captain Said and Subedar Major Mohammed Baber Khan were present. The Political Agent announced that he had decided to make Captain Hussan Military Governor of the Gilgit Wazarat, i.e. the country on the true left hand bank of the Indus from Bunji to Burzil Pass which was formerly under Kashmir and not part of the Gilgit Agency. Captain Mohammed Khan was appointed his second in Command and he was ordered to take the entire Muslim element of the 6th Kashmir Infantry with him for garrison duties. The Sikh and Dogra element including the officers was also made his responsibility, and it was stressed that these prisoners must on no account enter the Gilgit Agency. Captain Hussan seemed quite agreeable to this arrangement but pointed out that the position of Military Governor merited a rank higher than that of Captain and he requested the Political Agent that he might retain the rank of General which had been conferred on him by the ex-Provisional Government. Sardar Mohammed Alam told Captain Hussan that he might assume any rank he wished but that he would only draw the pay of a Captain. Captain Hussan then decided he would prefer to be an acting Lt. Col., to which the Political Agent agreed.

The conference ended in a private interview with Subedar Major Mohammed Baber Khan in which the Political Agent pointed out to him in front of the Mirs how foolishly he had been behaving in allying himself with Captain Hussan and that he must control his gullible nature and appreciate situations properly in discerning between right and wrong. He was admonished to return to his post as Subedar Major immediately and to refrain from meddling in other affairs. It should be noted here that it was decided at the conference that in future the designation of the 6th Kashmir Infantry would be the Gilgit Azad Forces.

On the 20th November Major W.A. Brown and Captain A.S. Mathieson spent the entire day in the Scout Lines and did their best to restore conditions to normal by the resumption of parades and general administrative duties. This they made their main aim and object during the next few weeks.

On the 21st an interesting incident took place which is worthy of note. At about 7 pm Major W.A. Brown inspected his daily situation reports and noted that the Sikh and Dogra officers from the Azad Forces had been sent to Theliche under an escort led by Subedar Sher Ali. Major W.A. Brown, knowing the Political Agents orders regarding these officers, immediately contacted Subedar Sher Ali at Theliche and asked for an explanation. Subedar Sher Ali explained that he had received orders that morning from Gilgit Headquarters that the Commandant's orders were that he should take over all the Sikh and Dogra officers from Captain Mohammed Khan in Bunji and escort them to Chilas where further orders would be received. Major WA. Brown ordered Subedar Sher Ali to take the prisoners back to Bunji immediately and leave them there. He then carried out an investigation as to how these orders have been passed.

It seems that in the morning Captain Mohammed Said and Captain Hussan had entered the Scout telephone exchange and the former had told the Signal Havildar that the Commandant had passed orders that a message should be sent to Subedar Sher Ali in Bunji that he should take over charge of the Sikh and Dogra Officers immediately and escort them to Chilas. From information received later it seems that the intention of these two officers was to send a further message in the name of the Commandant Scouts to Subedar Sher Ali as soon as he had reached Jallipur to the effect that the Sikh and Dogra Officers should be shot and their bodies thrown in the river. Both officers on being questioned denied that they had ever issued such orders until confronted by the evidence at the Political Agent's disposal, when they grudgingly admitted they had. Sardar Mohammed Alam then ordered Captain Mirza Hussan to leave for Bunji immediately and on no account to enter the Gilgit Agency again without his permission.

Not long after Captain Hussan had reached Bunji it became increasingly obvious that he was holding up the caravans of cloth, sugar and other imported commodities which were destined for Gilgit. The Political Agent sent repeated messages that the goods should be released immediately and forwarded to Gilgit, but no action was taken either through a policy of non-cooperation by Captain Hussan or because he wished to dispose of the commodities privately. Accordingly, on the 23rd November a strong Scout patrol under a Subedar was sent to Astore with orders to bring the caravan to Gilgit immediately. This patrol after a great deal of difficulty succeeded in its object and arrived back in Gilgit about the middle of December with large stocks of cloth and sugar.

On the 24th November Major WA. Brown, realizing that the danger of an attack by Indian troops was out of the question, owing to the heavy snowfall on the passes, closed all wings on their respective headquarters and started the task of re-equipping and reorganizing the strength which had been so long in the field. Morale seemed high and all ranks were in good spirits.

On the 26th November Major WA. Brown flew to Peshawar on orders from the Chief Secretary in order to report to the authorities regarding the recent events in Gilgit. Captain A.S. Mathieson officiated as Commandant Scouts.

At about 2 pm on the morning of the 28th November Captain Mathieson received a message from the Subedar Major that the Gilgit bazaar was being looted by the local population and asked what action should be taken. The Subedar Major further informed Captain Mathieson that he should on no account proceed to the scene of the looting until the crowd was under control as his life would be in serious danger and that he (the Subedar Major) would immediately double all officer's guards. Captain Mathieson ordered the Subedar Major to proceed to the bazaar forthwith and make every effort to get the situation in hand. He then went and reported to the Political Agent who decided that no useful purpose could be served by their presence in the bazaar and that to move down would only mean taking unnecessary risks. He therefore advised that the Subedar Major should be left in control. After about half an hour Captain Mathieson after a great deal of delay managed to contact the Subedar Major on the telephone and demanded a situation report. The Subedar Major reported that the strength of the looters was so large that he was making no headway and that the entire bazaar was being systematically looted. Abortive attempts at arson were also reported. Captain Mathieson then issued orders that the Scouts should be ordered to fire high over the crowds in the hope that the alarming effects of this might disperse the looters. After receipt of this order several volleys were fired as well as bursts from a machine-gun but it seems that this had little effect. Captain Mathieson wisely did not pass "shoot to kill" orders as it is extremely doubtful if the Scouts would have obeyed them under the circumstances and a refusal would have been disastrous.

At first light the Subedar Major reported to the Political Agent and Assistant Commandant and made the following report. At about 1 am he had received a report from the Police that the locals were looting the bazaar and that crowds were pouring in from the outlying villages to take part. He immediately turned out the *chigha* [hue and cry] party and proceeded to the bazaar. On arrival there he discovered that the bazaar was completely blocked by a crowd of at least three thousand Gilgitis and had already been completely looted. In his opinion the affair must have started at about 11 pm on the 27th November. He, therefore, called up the remaining available strength and attempted to clear the bazaar and prevent more people from entering it. This task, which should have been easy, proved, however, extremely difficult as it became obvious that the Scouts were not prepared to use violence of any sort against their fellow countrymen. The "high firing" too had no effect, as the locals were fully aware of the sentiments of the Scouts and knew that a "shoot to kill" order would never have been obeyed. As soon as the shops had been stripped the crowds began to disperse gradually and that was the position when the report was made.

On the strength of this report the Political Agent, after consultation with Captain Mathieson, sent a message to the Government of the North West Frontier Province to the effect that the Gilgit bazaar had been completely looted and requesting that six platoons of the Frontier Constabulary should be sent to Gilgit immediately by air as it had been proved that when action against locals was required the Scouts could not be trusted.

The Political Agent accompanied by Captain Mathieson then toured the affected area and supervised clearing operations. It then became apparent that the Muslim shops had been left untouched and only the Hindu and Sikh shops, about half a dozen at the most, had been looted and that the property of the Hindus and Sikhs in the residential area had also suffered. The temple, which had so far remained intact, had also been destroyed by those, it is said, who arrived on the scene too late to gain a share of the loot. An amendment was then sent to the previous message to the effect that only Sikh and Hindu shops had been looted but still stressing the need for Frontier Constabulary. The Political Agent then departed and left Captain Mathieson in charge of operations.

Captain Mathieson's first action was to re-establish the refugee camp in the Scout Lines where all Sikhs and Hindus were once again put under protective custody. Warm clothing and comforts were collected and distributed to those who had suffered and adequate ration arrangements were soon under way. Captain Mathieson then organized the Scouts into search parties and ordered a systematic search of Gilgit proper and the surrounding villages in an effort to recover looted property. This operation proved entirely successful and by midday, thanks to the personal leadership and resource of this officer, it was estimated that practically all the looted property had been recovered.

The Political Agent attempted to hold an investigation into the circumstances under which the bazaar had been looted. As anyone with a knowledge of the country will appreciate, the enquiry proved a failure since, as usual, nobody would come forward to give evidence. It was, however, clear that the whole affair was prearranged and the Police and Scouts were fully aware of what was going to happen and accordingly took no action until the Hindu and Sikh property had been looted. Whether the Police and Scouts actually took part in the looting is a matter for conjecture though under present conditions it seems likely that they did as the general chaos in the bazaar must have made control extremely difficult. At the investigation, influential quarters attempted to lay the blame on the Police on the grounds that the Scouts were not warned until the looting was well under way, but it was obvious that this was merely an unjust attempt to use the Police as scapegoats. It is also understood on good authority that the Political Agent was forewarned but he dismissed the warning as an idle rumour.

During the afternoon the majority of the Sikhs and Hindus embraced Islam and though this was in no way done under duress they obviously considered it the safest policy to pursue under the circumstances.

Meanwhile tension increased on the Chitral Border and repeated reports were received from Kuh Ghizr that the Mehtar of Chitral's army was about to march from Mastuj and invade the Northern Political Districts of the Gilgit Agency. The Political Agent kept the Government of the North West Frontier Province fully conversant with the situation.

During the recent disturbance Captain Hussan had not been idle in Bunji. Evidently he was not prepared to see his hopes shattered by the Political Agent's final decision and had once more started to instigate trouble. It is understood that he collected the entire Azad Force and told all ranks that they must swear on the Quran Sharif that they would obey him implicitly if be gave them the order to march and capture Gilgit and liquidate the Political Agent, the Commandant Scouts and the Assistant Commandant. The Azad Force unanimously refused.

On the 31st November Major Mohammed Aslam, alias Colonel Pasha of the Azad Kashmir Forces, arrived in Gilgit by air with the intention of organizing the Azad Forces in the area. He collected all officers of the Azad Force in Bunji and very rightly pointed out that their primary task was the capture and consolidation of Skardu in Baltistan as this position might well be a spring board for an attack on Gilgit. He then called for volunteers to lead the expedition but no one came forward. To a man the officers refused, each expressing some futile excuse. The officers concerned were: Captain Ihsan Ali, Captain Mirza Hussan, Captain Mohammed Said, and Captain Mohammed Khan.

Major Aslam did not attempt to conceal his disgust at this display of cowardice and proceeded to call in the V.C.Os of the Azad Force. It is understood that the V.C.Os expressed a complete lack of confidence in their present officers i.e. Captain Mirza Hussan and Captain Mohammed Khan, and appealed that these officers should be removed immediately. It was during this conference that the nefarious plot referred to in the previous paragraph came to light. Captain Hussan and Captain Mohammed Khan were then ordered to return to Bunji.

Meanwhile the Political Agent had sent Wilayat Ali of Nagir, a retired Tehsildar of Kashmir State, to Bunji with orders to check the Bunji and Astore Treasuries and report on their correctness or otherwise with the help of the Kashmiri Naib Tehsildar in Astore, who is reported to be honest. Wilayat Ali discovered that Captain Hussan had made several dishonest transactions and that there were definite discrepancies in the accounts of both treasuries. When confronted by this report. Captains Hussan and Mohammed Khan both admitted their guilt. The Political Agent therefore issued strict orders that in future no transaction would take place in either treasury unless the bill had been previously counter-signed by him.

Owing to the general unrest caused by recent events, faction feeling – the Shiah Sunni question – again made itself apparent but to such an extent this time that there was serious danger of a clash. Captain Mathieson therefore devoted his time in an effort to restore normal conditions and amongst other things re-started polo, the national game of the country. To an outsider this would seem a futile method of establishing the country, but those with experience of Gilgit will fully appreciate that a better course could not have been adopted. Captain Mathieson's efforts undoubtedly had the desired efforts and saved an awkward situation.

On the 8th December Major W.A. Brown arrived back in Gilgit by air with the following instructions from the Pakistan Government:

1. that the Gilgit Agency must be held at all costs against aggression by Indian troops;
2. that to facilitate this the strength of the Gilgit Scouts should be raised to 1500;
3. that to cope with the increased strength a limited number of Pakistan Commissions might be granted to deserving local Indian officers;
4. that the Muslim element of the 6th Kashmir Infantry should concentrate in Bunji and should on no account enter the Gilgit Agency;
5. that all officers of the Kashmir State Forces should join this force;
6. that the Sikh and Dogra element of the 6th Kashmir Infantry should be dispersed in groups throughout the Gilgit Agency.

On arrival at the Gilgit landing ground on the 8th December Major W.A. Brown was met by Captain Mohammed Said whose intention was to fly to Peshawar in the returning plane. It seems that the Political Agent had given him the necessary permission. Major Brown explained to Captain Said that he had brought certain important instructions from the Pakistan Government which affected him (Mohammed Said) and ordered him not to leave until he (Major Brown) had spoken to the Political Agent on the telephone. Major Brown then proceeded to the telephone which was some distance away and whilst talking the plane became airborne. On arrival back at the landing ground it was discovered that Captain Said had left contrary to orders. An immediate code message was wirelessed to Colonel Bacon at Peshawar for forwarding to the necessary authorities.

After consultation with the Political Agent it was decided that the first step which should be taken was the award of a Pakistan Commission to Subedar Major Mohammed Baber Khan on the grounds that the Subedar Majors of all the other Frontier Corps had been granted commissions on the change of power and that this would serve as a reward to the entire Gilgit Scouts for the part they had placed during the coup d'état as Baber Khan would be the first local officer of the Scouts to rise above the rank of Subedar Major. At a ceremonial parade on the 9th December the Political Agent after a short address to all ranks presented Mohammed Baber Khan with the insignia of a Lieutenant of the Pakistan Army. As later events showed, this move proved completely justifiable and popular throughout the Agency.

Major Brown and Captain Mathieson then started the immense task of raising the strength and reorganizing the Scouts according to the scheme which they had prepared and which had been accepted in principle by the Pakistan Government. The Mirs and Governors were approached and they promised to send the necessary numbers of recruits when required. Ration requirements were estimated and communicated to the Political Agent and after consultations the 1st January 1948 was fixed as target date for the start of enlistment.

Meanwhile reports were being repeatedly received that an attempt was going to be made to loot the Muslim shops in the bazaar on the grounds that prior to the previous looting the Hindus and Sikhs had lodged the bulk of their valuables with the Muslim shopkeepers. Major Brown and Captain Mathieson again urged the Political Agent to depose the present Raja of Gilgit and appoint ex-Subedar Shah Rais Khan in his place as this act would undoubtedly have stabilized the Sub-division once and for all. The Political Agent however did not agree on the grounds that his position was not strong enough to risk any repercussions caused by such action. He also refused to credit the possibility of further looting.

On the 11th December Captain Mathieson flew to Chilas as it was obvious that the Sub-agency and the Scout Detachment there were getting out of control owing to the continued absence of the Assistant Political Agent.

On the 13th December at about 10 pm Major W.A. Brown received information that the locals intended looting the Muslim shops in the Gilgit bazaar that night. He proceeded to the bazaar immediately and discovered a general exodus of all local shopkeepers in progress, along with their goods. On being questioned they admitted they were removing their wares to their homes but were unable to furnish any reasonable excuse for doing so. Major W.A. Brown then ordered them to return to their shops immediately along with their goods, and or no account to leave the bazaar. Pickets were then posted at various tactical positions in the area and intensive patrolling resumed. Major Brown himself remained in the bazaar till the early hours of the morning, and when conditions seemed normal went and reported the night's proceedings to the Political Agent.

On the night of the 14th December, the Political Agent on behalf of the Pakistan Government gave a dinner party to the entire Corps of Scouts. He himself attended the party in Gilgit which was followed by dancing, singing and other festivities, whilst similar entertainments took place in the outposts of Chilas and Gupis under the auspices of Captain Mathieson and the Post Commander respectively. This gesture was much appreciated by all ranks and was a befitting reward for the part the scouts had played during the recent coup d'état.

It should be added here that on the morning of the 14th December K.S. Asad Khan, former Tehsildar of Gilgit, arrived by plane to take over the duties of Assistant Political Agent. He was accorded this usual reception and, with his previous experience and knowledge, soon had the Agency Office administration back to normal.

Meanwhile reports from Bunji made it clear that the officers there were still intent on creating trouble. It is understood that Captain Mohammed Khan, with the connivance and able assistance of Captain Hussan, abducted the daughter of the Hindu postmaster and forcibly married her. It is said that the unit Mullah downrightly refused to perform the ceremony on the grounds that the marriage was illegal but later a local Mullah agreed to solemnize the proceedings. On the 20th December Captain Mathieson returned to Gilgit after successfully fulfilling his object in Chilas. Towards the end of the month it became obvious that it would be impossible to start recruiting on the 1st January as the Political authorities had taken no definite action regarding the collection of rations. Major W.A. Brown approached the Political Agent several times in this connection but, apart from vague promises, he received little satisfaction. It was at this stage that a marked difference in the attitude of Sardar Mohammed Alam became apparent. In contrast to his previous strong-headed policy his attitude now appeared to be that of apathetic disinterest. He seldom left his bungalow, he refused to take any step or make any decision on the grounds that he was not yet strong enough to counter repercussions, and he appeared to be generally losing his grip on the administration.

This lackadaisical outlook soon had very apparent effects. The Scouts became tense and upset owing to the Political Agent's refusal to approve certain important promotions recommended by the Commandant. Daily public meetings were held in the bazaar at which the administration was criticized and which invariably ended in large deputations invading the Agency House garden with futile requests. All officials with past experience of conditions in Gilgit advised the Political Agent to take definite steps to eradicate this lawlessness otherwise a state of anarchy would ensue, as it is well known to all that the Gilgit people must be ruled with a firm hand.

After a great deal of persuasion the Political Agent agreed to the Scout promotions which when published proved vary popular, and the condition of the Scouts became excellent with morale very high. Although the Political authorities had not yet collected the rations for the increased strength, Major W.A. Brown, realizing the urgency of the situation, decided to start recruiting with effect from the 7th January and to ration the new recruits from the reserve stock. It was thought that this action might bring home to the Political authorities the necessity for taking immediate action, and it did in fact have the desired effect.

By the 10th January some four hundred recruits had been enlisted from the states of Hunza and Nagir and, though conditions were adverse owing to a depleted staff and lack of proper medical arrangements, nevertheless the programme was being completed according to plan, thanks to the untiring efforts of Captain Mathieson, 2nd Lieut. Shah Khan, and the Compounder Humayun Beg. It might be mentioned that the daily working hours of this small staff were averaging about 18 hours. The physical standard and high sense of discipline of the recruits was remarkable and the latter did much to facilitate the squadding and organizing.

Orders had previously been received from the Government of the North West Frontier Province to the effect that Major W.A. Brown and Captain A.S. Mathieson would be relieved by Major Aslam and Captain Mohammed Khan during January, the reason being that the Government of Pakistan desired to avert any possibility of the British Officers fighting against Indian troops, and action seemed not far distant in which the two officers would have been morally bound to lead their men.

Major Aslam and Captain Mohammed Khan arrived on the 10th January by air and Major W.A. Brown and Captain A.S. Mathieson handed over their respective charges on the 12th January. Captain Mathieson flew to Peshawar on the 13th December and Major Brown on the 14th. Both officers were accorded a memorable and touching farewell from the Corps of Scouts and people of the Gilgit Agency.

Appendix IV

Glossary
[Compiled by Major Brown.]

Achkan: a skirted knee-length coat buttoning to a high neck. The national dress of Muslims in India and Pakistan.
Arak: as made in the Gilgit Agency, a beverage of crushed mulberries which has been allowed to ferment and then distilled.
Arz: request, Petition.
Azad: free.
Babu: an office clerk. Used down-country as a term of respect but on the Frontier to show contempt.
Badmash: scoundrel.
Badnam: slander.
Badshah: king
Banchoot: a term of abuse, the translation of which is unrepeatable.
Bandobast: arrangements.
Barampta: a reprisal.
Boz Kashi: a popular mounted game in Gilgit consisting of tearing the carcase of a goat to bits (from the Persian).
Buniah: a Hindu Shopkeeper or moneylender. The designation given to the ration contractor in Frontier Corps Units.
Caravanserai: a stage house on the ancient caravan routes.
Chabuk: a heavy leather lash attached to the short handle of wood or horn, and used as a whip by the horsemen of Central Asia.
Chaplis: stout leather sandals with nailed or rubber soles. The traditional footwear of the Pathans.
Charas: an intoxicating drug, prepared from hemp.
Chigha: a "hue and cry" party. Each Frontier Corps Post has a *chigha* party of one platoon "standing to" for 24 hours in the day and ready to move at five minute's notice.
Chillum: a hubble bubble pipe in which the smoke passes over water before reaching the smoker. The stem is straight (c.f. *Hookah*).
Chogha: the long, loose, homespun cloak which is the national dress of the people of the Gilgit Agency.
Chowki: a small outpost usually garrisoned by police.
Chowkidar: watchman, caretaker.
Compounder: an unqualified medical orderly in charge of a dispensary.
Dhoti: a garment consisting of a long sheet, worn round the waist in place of trousers, and usually tucked up through the legs. A mode of dress much favoured by Hindus, especially Bengalis.
Dogra: a martial race of hillmen living in the North of the Punjab. The ruling house of Kashmir was of Dogra origin, hence the term "Dogra regime".
Durbar: court or levee. It is also applied to the executive government of a state, eg the Kashmir Durbar.

Gah: mountain stream (Shina).
Gali: mountain pass (Shina).
Garm: hot.
Gasht: patrol.
Ghazi: holy warrior.
Ghi or *Ghee:* clarified butter.
Ghulawar: the tune played by local bands in the Gilgit Agency as warning for polo.
Goonda: gangster.
Gushpur: a nobleman of the Gilgit Agency. Blue blooded.
Harai: a mountain sheep or goat fold. (Shina).
Havildar: a rank in the Scouts and Army equivalent to that of sergeant.
Hindustan: the country of Hindus. A designation for the new Indian Union.
Hookah: see *Chillum*. The stem of the *hookah* is curved.
Id: the day of celebration in the Muslim Calender on which the fast of *Ramazan* is broken.
Inshallah: God Willing (Arabic).
Islam: the Mohammedan Religion.
Jalsah: the annual gathering of the clans in Gilgit.
Jehad: holy war waged against the Infidel.
Jemedar: an officer of the Indian Army who prior to partition held a commission granted by the Viceroy, and was thus known as a VCO (Viceroy's Commissioned Officer). In the Frontier Corps such officers are commissioned by HE The Governor of the North West Frontier Province or the Agent to the Governor General, Baluchistan, and prior to partition were known as IOs (Indian Officers). Those in the Gilgit Scouts were commissioned by the Resident in Kashmir, prior to partition.
A *Jemedar* is usually a platoon commander or holds a staff appointment such as
Jemedar Adjutant or Quarter Master *Jemedar*. See also *Subedar* and *Subedar* Major.
Jirgah: a tribal Council of Elders.
Jangly: uncivilized.
Kaffir: an infidel, unbeliever.
Kher Raghle: a Pathan greeting. Welcome.
Khuda Hafiz: may God protect you.
Khula: the conical (flat in the case of Pathans) cap round which the *puggri or safa* (turban) is wound. See also *puggri and safa*.
Kirpan: the traditional sword carried by Sikhs.
Koi: the traditional headgear of the folk of the Gilgit Agency, consisting of a tightly rolled up bag of homespun woollen cloth.
Kote: the fortified building in a fort or lines where the rifles are kept.
Kul: a water channel.
Lakh: one hundred thousand.
Lashkar: a gang of tribesmen on the warpath.
Lumbardar: a village headman.
Lunghi: a particular and most distinguished type of turban for which Peshawar City is famous. The colour is usually blue and white.
Lut Mal: looted property.
Mali: gardener.
Mulki Sahib: the designation given to the Assistant Political Agent, Chilas, by the locals.
Mullah: a Mohammedan priest.
Munshi: secretary, clerk, tutor.
Mufti: civilian clothing.

Muzri: a hardwearing grey cloth used as skirting in the Frontier Corps. It is also known as "Militia Cloth".
Nullah: valley.
Odrawar: stop! (Pushto).
Pabboos: soft knee-length boots made from ibex hide.
Pakistan: the Dominion of; means literally "the country of the pure."
Parri: an abutment of hillside jutting out into the valley.
Partugs: baggy trousers drawn in round the ankle (Pushto).
Pir: a saint, spiritual guide.
Puggri: an irregularly tied turban, one end of which, known as the *shamla*, drapes down over the back of the neck. When the *puggri* is tied neatly and regularly with the *shamla* tucked up, as on drill parades and ceremonial, it is known as a *safa*. Each tribe of the North West Frontier has a particular way of tying the *puggri* or *safa* which assists recognition.
Puh makha de khun: the Pathan farewell. ("May all be well ahead of you.")
Pul: bridge.
Quran Sharif: the Holy Scriptures of Islam.
Ramazan: the month of the year in the Muslim calendar when all Followers of the Prophet observe a strict fast from sunrise to sunset.
Rebab: a musical instrument rather like a mandolin.
Rupee: unit of currency valued at 1/6d in 1947.
SabAchcha: the customary "OK" or "All Well" report.
Safa: see *puggri*.
Sahib log: the Sahib people, ie the British.
Salaam Aleikum: the customary Muslim greeting. "May peace be upon you." The normal reply is *Wa Aleikum Salaam*, "and upon you peace", though the latter is not usually used in the Gilgit Agency, where the reply is a repetition of the original greeting.
Sangar: the stone breastwork thrown up for protection on a position occupied by a picquet.
Shabash: well done!
Shahi: royal.
Shikar: hunting, shooting, and fishing.
Shikari: a sportsman. Usually the term given to the person who acts as stalker and tracker on big game expeditions.
Sirkar, Sarkar: Government implying the Imperial Government.
Sitar: a musical instrument like a zither.
Sooer: pig.
Subedar: see *Jemedar* to which this rank is senior. A *Subedar* is usually a company commander or second-in-command in the Frontier Corps. In the Gilgit Scouts, before the 1948 expansion, *Subedars* were platoon commanders as the Corps was organized on a platoon basis.
Subedar Major: see *Jemedar*. *Subedar Major* is the highest rank of this grade of commissioned officer. The *Subedar Major* of a Corps of Scouts is the Commandant's right-hand-man, advisor, and go-between with the rank and file. He acts more or less in the same capacity as the Regimental Sergeant Major in a battalion of the British Army.
Tamasha: entertainment, festivity.
Taotis: strips of ibex or goat hide wound round the feet and legs, and kept in place by leather laces. Excellent footwear in the mountains both on rock and snow.
Tehsildar: a sub-collector of revenue.
Tikala: food, feast (Pushto).
Yarrik: the Central Asian system of conditioning horses.
Zulm: tyranny.